THE EVOLUTION OF
HITLER'S GERMANY

THE EVOLUTION
OF
HITLER'S GERMANY

The Ideology, The Personality, The Moment

BY

HORST VON MALTITZ

McGraw-Hill Book Company

New York   St. Louis   San Francisco   Düsseldorf
London   Sydney   Toronto   Mexico   Panama   Kuala Lumpur
Montreal   New Delhi   Rio de Janeiro   Singapore

This book was set in Century by University Graphics, Inc.
It was printed on antique paper and bound by Book
Press. The designer was Christine Aulicino. The editors
were Tom Quinn, Marie Longyear, Judith Duguid, and
Cheryl Love. Joseph Campanella and Bill Greenwood
supervised the production.

Cover design by Bob Aulicino.

07-067608-9

Library of Congress Cataloging in Publication Data
Von Maltitz, Horst, date
The evolution of Hitler's Germany: the ideology,
the personality, the moment.
Bibliography: p.
1. National socialism—History. 2. Hitler, Adolf,
1889–1945. 3. Germany—Politics and government—20th
century. 4. Germany—Race question. I. Title.
DD256.5.V67   943.086   73-3366
ISBN 0-07-067608-9

123456789BPBP79876543

To F. v. M.

Table of Contents

Acknowledgments

Acknowledgments for permission to use excerpts from copyrighted material include:

T. W. Adorno et al., *The Authoritarian Personality*. Copyright 1950, 1969 by T. W. Adorno. Used by permission of W. W. Norton & Company, Inc.

Hannah Arendt, *Eichmann in Jerusalem*. Copyright 1965 by Hannah Arendt. Used by permission of The Viking Press, Inc.

Erik H. Erikson, *Childhood and Society*. Copyright 1963 by Erik H. Erikson. Used by permission of W. W. Norton & Company, Inc.

Erich Fromm, *Escape From Freedom*. Copyright 1941 by Erich Fromm. Used by permission of Harper & Row, Publishers.

Erich Fromm, *Heart of Man*. Copyright 1964 by Erich Fromm. Used by permission of Harper & Row, Publishers.

Walter Z. Laqueur, *Out of the Ruins of Europe*. Copyright 1971 by Walter Z. Laqueur. Used by permission of The Library Press.

The New English Bible. Copyright 1970 by Oxford University Press, Inc. Used by permission of Oxford University Press.

Albert Speer, *Erinnerungen*. Copyright 1969 by Albert Speer. Used by permission of Propyläen Verlag.

Alfred Vagts, *A History of Militarism*. Copyright 1937 by Alfred Vagts. Used by permission of The Free Press.

Abbreviations

Only two abbreviations for documentation are used:

TMWC   The Reports of the *Trial of Major War Criminals* before the International Military Tribunal at Nuremberg (42 volumes)

TWC   The Reports of the *Trials of War Criminals* before Military Tribunals at Nuremberg (15 volumes)

THE EVOLUTION OF
HITLER'S GERMANY

For a long time now our entire European civilisation has been moving, with a tortured intensity that increases from decade to decade, as if toward a catastrophe: restlessly, violently, in headlong haste: like a mighty river yearning for its end, no longer pausing to think, fearful indeed of thought.

Friedrich Nietzsche,
Der Wille zur Macht, 1887

I

INTRODUCTION

This book grew out of the author's personal wish to find the answer to the questions: How was it possible? How could it happen? How could a people that, for many centuries, contributed a great deal to Western civilization, suddenly succumb to Hitler, to National Socialism, and engage with eagerness in a process of cultural self-destruction? How could large numbers of seemingly normal, orderly, law-abiding people engage in tortures and mass killings almost unrivaled in the history of the world?

These questions have been asked by many. They are all the more puzzling since, at least to any non-German, the National Socialist Movement had in it so much that seemed repulsive. The personalities of its leaders seemed to have so little that could arouse sympathy, so little good taste, tact, humanity or even simple understanding for others. The world and even many Germans were unable to see how such a Movement could ever take hold; and yet, within a few years, it proved to be popular and successful beyond anything previously experienced in German political and intellectual history. The enigma deepens when we remember that this seemingly crude, subintellectual Movement found its greatest support, not among an ignorant proletariat, but rather among the moderately well-educated lower middle class, as well as among university students and professors. It should be remembered, further, that Hitler was able to seize power legitimately and largely without violence. Indeed, he was, in effect, voted into power peacefully by more than seventeen million Germans.[1]

Our question "How was it possible?" has been asked more often than it has been answered, and no easy answer exists. Such answers as have been given have differed widely, in spite of the existing near-unanimity as to the events whose causes the answers were to explain. Some have seen National Socialism merely as one manifestation of that totalitarianism which appears to be specific to our century. Others have regarded it as an almost necessary outcome of German history and traditions which can be traced back for two hundred years or more, perhaps all the way to the Middle Ages. Still others have looked upon National Socialism as something into which a mere "lunatic fringe" led an unwary German people, or as a kind of unforeseeable "traffic accident" of history, or as a mere "aberration," an *Irrweg*

---

[1]Fritz Stern (ed.). *The Path to Dictatorship 1918–1930,* Appendix c.

(to use a largely untranslatable German term), a "deformation" of society, a kind of "mutation" in one member of Western civilization, or even an "honest mistake." The few psychologists or sociopsychologists who have considered the problem have, of course, their own answers. Some of them see the debacle as an outgrowth of a prevalent sadomasochistic structure of the German authoritarian character, or as a result of a pathological combination of narcissism, necrophilia, and incestuous symbiosis in Hitler, or as the consequence of a "loss of identity" after World War I. And there are additional answers.

The present study seeks the answer in a combination of a great many factors, some directly causative, some causative only in their interaction with others. The multitude of historical causes and the degree of their interplay have seldom reached the extent that confronts us in this situation. Many of the causative factors have, indeed, a very long history. We shall find quite quickly that National Socialism was far from being a mere incomprehensible accident of history or a mere temporary *Irrweg* or aberration, but rather that its ideology was the culmination of a long development of German intellectual history, even if it can be said to have been pushed into extremes by a violent, abnormal man. The ideology itself was, in fact, part and parcel of the nation's cultural heritage and traditions. (If we could speak of an aberration at all, we might have to go so far as to say that, viewed from the whole of Western civilization, the entire German nation, by the end of the nineteenth century, had begun to be an aberration, but this would add little to the discussion.)

All this, however, does not mean that National Socialism was a necessary or inevitable outcome of German history. Far from it. But it does mean that no one can understand the rise of National Socialism who does not recognize its extensive roots in German history — roots shared equally by its adherents and opponents. To a considerable extent, the evolution of National Socialism thus represents a confirmation of the general experience that total breaks in the continuity of the historical development of nations do not occur, but that even in far-reaching revolutions seemingly new ideological elements have a long intellectual past, and that old traditions remain alive and effective even in the shaping of revolutions.

What we shall do, then, is to try to lay bare those roots and to put some order into their tangle. We face, in fact, a very complicated subject, not only because of the inherent complexity of the whole mass of interacting ideas, doctrines, emotions, and motivations, but also because the various factors were, at the time, often dealt with by persons of little intellectual stature and objectivity, and were, at any rate, not recognized or treated as an ideological whole. Often noise outweighed intelligence. In our attempt to clarify the situation, we shall make an effort to identify the important ideological components of National Socialism and to put each of them into its own neat pigeonhole for individual consideration. (Briefly they are primarily the race theories, the Lebensraum doctrine, anti-Semitism, the Germanic cult, German Romanticism, nationalism, and militarism.) In doing so, we are not unmindful of the disapproval of something akin to this method by Geoffrey Barraclough—a very great authority on all things German —who has spoken critically of those "who embark on an erratic chase through German history . . . for delusions and aberrations which they mount and label in neat rows like butterflies."[2] Later, however, Barraclough said that "we shall fail to understand its [National Socialism's] success unless we are prepared to examine how far and in what ways it had roots in German history . . . ,"[3] and this, to an extent, is indeed what we shall try to do. At any rate, the roots of an ideology can hardly be discovered without laying them bare. Studying them individually should not be too risky as long as we remain aware that all the roots lead into a common trunk, in other words, that no single ideological component could, by itself, have generated National Socialism.

In any case, no better method seems available. Yet it clearly is not without its drawbacks. For one thing, trying to put each component of national socialist ideology into its own neat compartment will do a degree of violence to some of them because, in practice, they overlapped or were even interlocked. In fact, there was an interplay of the ideas not only among themselves, but also between them and personalities as well as political and economic processes. The individual treatment, the whole effort toward intellectual tidiness, involves a risk of oversimplification. Reality was much less tidy than this book. In some instances, the significance of a component can hardly be understood

[2] *The New York Review of Books,* Oct. 24, 1968, p. 14.
[3] *The New York Review of Books,* July 1, 1971, p. 41.

without a realization of its interaction with other factors. Also, dealing with each component individually will inevitably result in some measure of repetition, for there are historical facts, ideas, motivations, etc. which have relevance to more than one component. But in spite of all these disadvantages of schematization, it seems advisable to use it in order to understand a very complex situation.

At any rate, it was by no means the ideology alone that gave life to the Movement or made it succeed. Equally or perhaps more important was the personality of Adolf Hitler who very definitely was the protagonist of the whole drama. Without him, it is not likely that the Movement would ever have amounted to more than a small obscure band of noisy malcontents. This book, therefore, will devote a long chapter and much other time and space to Hitler, and it will attempt to show the ways in which the ideology was reflected in his thoughts and, indeed, was translated by him from theory into action, at least in part. A consideration of Hitler's personality will of necessity mean that we must examine his psychology, or perhaps psychopathology, his religiousness, and his sex life. Our discussion of his psychology will be tentative, fragmentary and unsystematic. The author makes no claim to expert knowledge in psychology.

Generally, a historiography of the ideas and personalities of that disturbed period in Germany—even more than most other history—can benefit greatly from whatever analyses by psychologists, sociopsychologists, and psychiatrists are available, and we shall devote a good deal of attention to them. So far, however, these analyses are few and rather meager, and, unlike the historians, each psychologist seems to go his independent way, in a strange total disregard of what his colleagues may have said before him on the same subject. Silent disagreements abound. Moreover, the amount of psychological conjecture on a minimum of established facts—or even a disregard of established facts—is frequently surprising.[4] Yet, in spite of all this, the psychologists have done work of great value and they have afforded much insight into complicated processes which, without them, might be misunderstood or remain obscure or go unnoticed. One minor purpose of this book will be to supply additional and—it is hoped—reliable

[4]Jacques Barzun ("History: The Muse and Her Doctors," in *American Historical Review*, Vol. 77, No. 1, Feb. 1972, p. 51) says quite aptly that "the greatest weakness of psycho-history as the unhyphened historian sees it: its handling of the evidence."

factual information to reinforce or put into question existing psychological theories and to point to material for others in the future. There is urgent need for a comprehensive psychiatric analysis of Hitler and of the German character structure prevalent in that period.

As stated before, there could have been no effective National Socialist Movement without the personality of Adolf Hitler. At the same time, it is not likely that Hitler would ever have gained national power, had he not been able to operate against a background of general political and economic conditions in the Weimar Republic which greatly favored the acceptance of his personality and of National Socialism by the German people who were in despair. It will, therefore, be important to discuss these conditions. We shall examine also the special help which National Socialism received from various sides, particularly the German communists, Moscow, the Western powers, and certain groups within Germany. All in all, the situation represented an extraordinary combination of factors in the causation of a historical disaster of unprecedented proportions.

What this book is *not* is a history of the events of the period (except that a description of the political and economic conditions during the Weimar Republic requires a limited discussion of certain events at that time). Generally, some knowledge, by the reader, of the history of the events is assumed. Essentially, then, this book is a history of the scattered *ideas* forming the national socialist ideology, the roots of their strength, and their development; and beyond that, the book contains a discussion of "the moment in history" when Hitler was able to translate the ideology into action. Part of that moment was the maturing of Hitler himself into the extraordinary personality he turned out to be, and the overwhelming impact of his personality on the great mass of the German people. The man and most of the ideology have since died, and we can do no more than to write of them in retrospect. Our judgment concerning them must inevitably be distorted, for we know what their ultimate effect was. We can no longer see them in the newness of their original impact. Much of what once was a holy creed to millions of Germans now seems merely grotesque, even to the present generation in Germany itself. In the most charitable view, some of National Socialism's fundamental ideas now seem to have a stale, unhealthy odor of the late nineteenth century about them, as indeed does Hitler himself. It is as if, at that time, they crawled out of an old unaired attic, but with surprising and terrifying vigor and determination.

Yet the very vigor and determination of the national socialist adherents confirm the old experience that no one can be more forceful and implacable than an ideological crusader—and it is indeed as such that the faithful regarded themselves, unable to comprehend moral corruption and human degradation. Essentially, there was no possibility of compromise for them in their commitment to their ideological position; and like other ideologists, they were entirely prepared to do and to endure violence for the sake of that position. But in the process, in the twelve years the Third Reich lasted, the leaders and millions of followers soiled the German name with very great crimes. Those twelve years, the life span of Hitler's promised Thousand-Year-Reich, were enough in frightful intensity to come close to the destruction of the past thousand years of German civilization. At any rate, much of the damage done—physical, spiritual, and cultural, as well as damage to honor and to esteem—is beyond all repair.

It is well to remember the balance of death of National Socialism. A total of approximately 43 million people died, that is, about 20 million Russians, 6.5 million Germans, 6.28 million Poles, 6 million Jews, 1.7 million Jugoslavians, 800,000 French, 500,000 Gypsies, 405,000 Americans, 400,000 British, plus smaller numbers of Rumanians, Czechs, Italians, Greeks, etc.[5] The Jews lost about 27 percent of their worldwide human substance, but a far greater percentage of it in Europe—perhaps 80 or 90 percent.

Finally, the author is conscious that this book does an injustice to a great many Germans of that period. It focuses on the lowest point in German history and civilization, and, therefore, says little that is good about the German people. In the context of the subject matter, the book had to remain largely silent on all the remarkable qualities and talents of the Germans, their creativity in many fields, their in-

---

[5] Some of these figures are mere rough approximations, and it is particularly the round figure of 20 million Russians that introduces uncertainty into the total. In connection with the various figures, see Reinhard Henkys, *Die nationalsozialistischen Gewaltverbrechen,* pp. 167–176; Walther Hofer, *Der Nationalsozialismus: Dokumente,* pp. 261–263; Karl Dietrich Bracher, *Die deutsche Diktatur,* p. 505; *Der Spiegel,* Feb. 9, 1970, p. 88; *The New York Times Almanac 1971,* p. 706.

telligence, their high intellectual daring, their personal warmth and capacity for love, and even their humor. None of this really emerges from this book in any just proportion to the mass of adverse, critical material that it presents. Nor is there much mention of those many Germans who viewed the events of the Hitler years with mounting embarrassment, horror, and loathing. All this the author regrets, but it is, indeed, in remembrance of those unnamed Germans that he wrote this book.

One considerable difficulty in the writing of this book was the nearly unbelievable abundance of available records and literature bearing on the subject matter, that is, primary as well as secondary source material. It is, in fact, physically impossible to read more than a fraction of it, and it is probably fair to say that a person who wants to read it all could do nothing but steady reading from his childhood to his grave twenty-four hours a day. No doubt, there has never been a period in history which was as thoroughly recorded, chronicled, protocolled, and written about as the Hitler years. (And this work extended even to the ugliest aspects, such as the weekly reports of the *Einsatzgruppen*—mobile killing units—in the Soviet Union concerning the number of persons killed, and the medical experiments on inmates of concentration camps.) One task in the preparation of this book was, therefore, a constant effort to restrict the selection of the source material to the most essential and valuable. There will be readers who will say that this or that book should also have been referred to; and the answer may well be that these readers are right, but that, in fact, 100 or 200 other books should have been mentioned in addition. There are limits to what can be done in a book of reasonable length.

But the abundance of source material is, of course, of great value. For what other historical period do we, for example, possess a verbatim (or nearly verbatim) transcript of the ruler's informal conversations during and after lunch and dinner, as we have it in *Hitlers Tischgespräche* (1941/1942)? It is a most valuable source book from which we shall quote hundreds of statements. Unusual and valuable, also, is the voluminous stenographic transcript of Hitler's daily "situation conferences" *(Lagebesprechungen)* with his generals during the war. We have, further, a four-volume collection of most of Hitler's speeches and proclamations (1932–1945) by Max Domarus. And there are many others.

All translations from the German quoted in this book are by the author (who spent his first twenty-three years in Germany, the rest in the United States). There are a few exceptions to this rule in cases when the author was unable to obtain access to the original German texts and had to rely on someone else's translation. These exceptions will be apparent from the text or from footnotes.

II

THE
COMPONENTS OF
NATIONAL SOCIALIST
IDEOLOGY
AND THEIR
EVOLUTION

Chapter 1

Some General Considerations

In the following discussion of individual components of national socialist ideology, certain basic facts must be borne in mind. The *first* is that, by and large, this ideology was not "consciously created" by the National Socialist Movement or any movement preceding it. In this respect the history of the ideology differs sharply from that of communism. No creative scholarly writings, no "sacred books," such as those of Karl Marx or Lenin on communism, constructed or developed a coherent ideological foundation for national socialism. Its ideology, in fact, did not contain a single idea of any substance which had not been derived from, and had not long been part of, the German intellectual or cultural heritage (what the Germans call the *Gedankengut* of the nation).

The existing national socialist writings cannot really be compared with the fundamental works of Marx and Lenin. No systematic, complete exposition of national socialist ideology was ever prepared during the Hitler era. If someone had asked an average high or low party official what the components of the ideology were, that official would in all probability have been hard put to give a coherent answer. Anyone wanting to ascertain the ideological components would have had to look into a great many different publications. Among them would have been the published speeches of Hitler, Himmler, and other party officials, the party newspaper *Der Völkische Beobachter*, manuals for the SA *(Sturm Abteilung)*, the SS *(Schutzstaffel)*, and the Hitler Youth organization, various monographs on some aspects of national socialist thought including works by historians, certain novels, and so forth.

Two books which seemingly made some effort to be full expositions of the ideology were *Mein Kampf* by Hitler and *Der Mythos des*

20. Jahrhunderts by the so-called party theoretician or ideologist Alfred Rosenberg. Both did offer at least scraps of all sorts of ideas which were part of the ideology; and Hitler, in fact, was conscious of his own effort to present in his book a whole *Weltanschauung*. But neither book can be called a systematic exposition of the ideology, nor is either in any sense creative. Both were more in the nature of verbose propagandistic diatribes, imprecise, often naïve, and even romantic. Above all, both books confined themselves to dredging up essentially old ideas, frequently vulgarized and reduced to simple terms but presented in a mantle of doctrinaire fanaticism. The truth is that the ideology of National Socialism, in its important components, had its beginnings, and essentially was fully developed, decades before anyone conceived of National Socialism.

It is significant, in this connection, that even the party elite, at least unofficially, did not think much of Hitler's and Rosenberg's books, if indeed they had bothered to read them at all. Hitler himself, in private, made highly derogatory remarks about Rosenberg's *Mythos*. He said that he, like many of the national socialist leadership, had "read only a small part of it"[1] and that it represented "regression into medieval notions."[2] None of the twenty-one defendants at the Nuremberg Trial of Major War Criminals had read the book.[3] And as far as *Mein Kampf* is concerned, Albert Speer, for example, reported that he could not bring himself to read it.[4] This is undoubtedly true of most other Germans in spite of their dutiful purchases of vast numbers of copies of the book.

There is no doubt that the evolution of the ideology (and its acceptance by millions of Germans) was far from being a sudden disaster which unexpectedly struck the German people out of a clear sky. National socialism was not a lone isolated phenomenon without antecedents in the history of the German mind. There was a rather consistent path in that history that led down to Hitler, and — if we may, for the time being, disregard his pathological extremes — it is clear that he was very much a product of that history. By and large, he did no

---

[1] *Hitlers Tischgespräche* (hereafter cited as *Hitler's Table Talks*) (edited by P. E. Schramm), pp. 269–270.
[2] Albert Speer, *Erinnerungen*, p. 110.
[3] G. M. Gilbert, *Nuremberg Diary*, pp. 349–350.
[4] Speer, op. cit., p. 136.

real intellectual violence to the majority of the Germans of his time. To a considerable extent, he merely expressed—even if far more intensely or fanatically—what they had been thinking or feeling for many decades, in some respects more than a hundred years. But he was the one who *took action* on these thoughts and feelings, and it was this action which indeed gave a new dimension to the thoughts and feelings.

It should be added, however, that the ideology included components in which Hitler himself had no faith at all, particularly the cult of the Germanic and some aspects of German romanticism. But they were so deeply ingrained in German feelings and attitudes and had become so definite a part of the cultural heritage that Hitler had to accept them. They remained part of the whole ideological package which was loose and amorphous in any event. But to an extent the ideology, thus, led a life independent from the leader of the Movement who was normally very much in control of it.

The *second* basic fact which must be borne in mind in our discussion of national socialist ideology is that the Hitler Movement represented largely a revolution of the lower or, perhaps better, of the lowest middle class, the petty bourgeoisie, the *Kleinbürgertum*. This was true in spite of Hitler's cynical private view that "There is no population group that is more stupid in political things than this so-called bourgeoisie."[5] Previously, up to the end of World War I in 1918, imperialist Germany had been governed by the nobility and the upper bourgeoisie. In the Weimar Republic that followed, a socialist proletarian regime took power for a brief period, from the end of 1918 to June 1920. Proving rather ineffective, this was replaced by a succession of governments of the Center and moderate Right (composed largely of the middle class, not the lower middle class), which led an uneasy existence until Hitler's seizure of power in 1933. In other words, it was Hitler who for the first time propelled the petty bourgeoisie into a position of importance or power. Initially, the industrial proletariat and the middle and upper middle classes had little to do with his Movement. The Movement received its main support and much of its leadership from groups such as very small business men, farmers, minor employees, minor public officials, tradesmen, and the

[5] *Hitler's Table Talks*, p. 348.

like. Some of them or their parents had moved up from the labor class, and there was danger, in times of economic crises, that they would slide back into that class. Frequently dispossessed by war, inflation, and the Depression, and socially *déclassé*, they harbored much social resentment and had accumulated a great deal of hostility, born of frustration, humiliation, insecurity, and anxiety. They were apt to overcompensate for all this by political radicalism and ethnic intolerance. In any case, after the abdication of the princes, the nobility, and the proletariat, the time of the small bourgeois had come.

The fact that what took place was a revolution of the petty bourgeoisie is indicated fairly clearly, though not completely, by the surprising contrast between the election returns of 1928 and 1932 (shortly before Hitler's seizure of power). In 1928, the various centrally oriented liberal parties still received almost 28 percent of the votes, and the National Socialists obtained only 2.6 percent. In 1932, on the other hand, the liberal parties of the center had dropped to 5 percent of the votes, and the National Socialists had increased their share to 37.3 percent.[6] It was reasonably clear that the masses of the petty bourgeoisie (and some others) had become radicalized. It could be said also that what took place was a revolution of the center and not of the right or left.

From the point of view of our consideration of national socialist ideology, it is important to note that the general background of these people of the petty bourgeoisie was frequently provincial and that, above all, their education was limited. They were wholly unsophisticated. But, unlike the proletariat, they were not aware of their educational and other limitations and tended to consider themselves "just as good as anybody else." Their faces were apt to express obsequiousness when dealing with their superiors, but a peculiar kind of impudence and cunning, also bravura, when dealing with others.

To some extent, but not completely, Hitler himself exemplified this type of person of the petty bourgeoisie. His father, of peasant origin, had worked his way up to become a minor customs officer in

[6]See M. Rainer Lepsius, *Extremer Nationalismus*, pp. 6, 8. For a detailed discussion of the election results and lower-middle-class support of Hitler see H. A. Winkler, "Extremismus der Mitte?" in *Vierteljahrshefte für Zeitgeschichte*, Vol. XX, 1972, pp. 176–181, 188.

a small Austrian town on the German border. His mother had been a peasant girl and a domestic servant before her marriage. Hitler's own formal education was limited. He was what in the United States today would be called a "high school drop-out"; he missed the last three years of school. (But he evidently supplemented this formal education by very extensive, though unsystematic, reading.) In his social origin and the extent of his formal education, he was a fairly typical petty bourgeois. But he differed from the normal, hard-working, reasonably respectable member of that group in that, sometime after dropping out of school, he became an unemployed drifter in Vienna and lived there in public lodging houses for men. (He was "rescued" from this kind of life by the outbreak of World War I for which he volunteered.) Nevertheless, his group membership in the petty bourgeoisie remained sufficiently definite in manners, speech, and ideas to make it easy for the group to identify with him. Ideologically, at any rate, there was little difference between them. Only his general resentment against the world and his accumulated hostility presumably exceeded in quantity and quality what anyone else could offer.

Not only the great bulk of supporters and minor leaders of the National Socialist Movement lacked real education and sophistication, but this was true also of many members of the higher echelon, even though a few of them had their origin, not in the petty bourgeoisie, but in the middle class. We have already mentioned Hitler's limited formal education. The average level of education in the whole top group of the national socialist elite was not very different. Albert Speer (who, like Goebbels, was an exception) summarized the matter:

> . . . the party politicians of [Hitler's] entourage, on the average, had received no higher education. No more than ten of the fifty Reichleaders and district leaders had finished a university [college] education; some had bogged down in their studies, and most of them had not progressed beyond junior high school *(Mittelschule)*. Hardly any one of them could show a significant accomplishment in his own field, and almost all of them demonstrated an astonishing lack of intellectual interest. Their educational standard did not in any way come up to what one had a right to expect from the leading elite of a nation with a traditionally high intellectual level. Basically, Hitler preferred to see

in his intimate entourage assistants of the same social origin as his own; among them, he probably felt most comfortable.[7]

On the whole, as Karl Dietrich Bracher says, the elite was "characterized by provincial and low social origin, moderate school education, military service, and professional difficulties."[8] Geographically, their origin was frequently Bavarian, rural or small town. A good many of them differed from the rank and file of their supporters in that they had hardly led a respectable bourgeois life, had held no real jobs, had spent adventurous years in the Army in World War I and, thereafter, in paramilitary organizations *(Freikorps)*. They had not been able to fit themselves into civilian life, but longed for the old routine of commanding and obeying; they had not established a family but preferred rough male companionship, adored strong leaders, were in some instances actively homosexual, or, in others, came close to it, and tended to take a romantic view of some acts of brutality. In appearance, many of them were heavyset, undistinguished men with crude, sometimes brutal faces. On the whole, the elite had little interest in fine points of national socialist ideology and took the whole ideology for granted as their cultural heritage. Hermann Göring, in fact, went so far as to say in Nuremberg that he had "joined the party because it was revolutionary, not because of that ideological stuff."[9] For some of the elite and for even more of the lower party members, if not for a great many Germans in general, ideological considerations at that time took second place to simple brutal rules of hostility and destructiveness, such as "beat the daylights out of them" or "lick 'em." At least in the early days of the party, politics was a kind of brawl; compromise did not exist. And some of that attitude remained alive to the end and even carried over into international relations.

Other members of the petty bourgeoisie approached the ideology with considerable earnestness and even idealism, but in their case the ideology was nevertheless, to an extent, aptly characterized as *Stammtischphilosophie*, a contemptuous description sometimes used

---

[7]Speer, *Erinnerungen,* pp. 135–136.

[8]Bracher, *Die deutsche Diktatur,* p. 301. For a detailed analysis of the elite, see pp. 298–312 and 256 of that book; less reliable is Daniel Lerner, *The Nazi Elite.*

[9]Reported by the Nuremberg prison psychiatrist Dr. Douglas M. Kelley, *22 Cells in Nuremberg,* p. 64.

for it by the German intelligentsia of the big cities. A *Stammtisch* was a reserved table in a restaurant or bar at which a group of men of the lower middle class would gather for weekly meetings to drink beer or wine and enjoy male companionship in a more or less alcoholic haze.

The fact that Hitler and other leaders had only a limited formal education disturbed few of their followers. In their eyes, this was not an imperfection, but possibly an advantage, because the intellectuals seldom had their hearts in the right place.

The ideology was, in any event, a loose and amorphous system of ideas, values, sentiments, and attitudes much of which, over the decades, had been developed or put together by mediocre men for mediocre people. It was, on the whole, a *simple* ideology—sometimes vulgarized and reduced to simple terms from something more complex —and it was addressed primarily to people of limited education and sophistication, to untrained minds. It embodied all kinds of appeals to the vanity of the socially insignificant person and also some appeals to his lower instincts and drives. But it is important not to read complications into the ideology, even if its historical evolution does at times involve circuitous routes of German thought processes. (It is dubious to suggest, as Albert Speer in his memoirs likes to do, that national socialism represented a kind of dictatorship of modern technology over the German people. That would have required the use of much more ability than the mediocre leadership in general possessed.) The only exception to the general simplicity of the ideology was perhaps its anti-Semitic component which, upon analysis today, appears quite complex; but this was something of which the national socialist movement itself was hardly conscious. Its postulate was simply that the Jews had to be suppressed because they were evil and dangerous. On the whole, the ideology, in its final form, was a great deal simpler than that of democracy, in theory as well as in practical application; and it was probably simpler also than the ideology of Marxism or communism. In fact, sometimes it is hard to see any ideology at all behind all the brawls, stinkbombs, pogroms, insults, and sentimental slobbering. But it was there.

The ideology of the Weimar Republic had still been the intelligent conscious work of the German bourgeois intellectual elite, which was morally directed and was oriented largely toward the West. The lowering of the ideological standards to those of National Socialism stood in direct relation to the change in the German social structure by which the petty bourgeoisie was propelled into the political and social sunlight from its stuffy, unaired quarters, from its hand-embroidered sofa cushions and lace covers on the upright piano. This social group was proclaimed to consist of "Germanic heroes," and, to its own surprise, it was told to become the governing class. But the group had hardly any of the necessary intellectual and ethical qualifications to lead and administer a highly developed country, and it quickly became intoxicated with its own importance and power. These simpleminded, intellectually primitive people found no guidance in traditional behavior patterns of a ruling class, and it did not take them long to go berserk. But even they did not generally realize the savageness of their top leaders; and, if they had, most of them would not have approved it.

Our emphasis, so far, on the fact that the National Socialist Movement represented a revolution of the petty bourgeoisie, should not by any means be taken as suggesting that no other layers of German society participated in the Movement and promoted the aims of its ideology, at least after National Socialism had established itself. A later chapter will discuss the very great contributions which other groups made to Hitler's success. Their participation is not surprising, because much of national socialist ideology had for long decades been part of their own cultural heritage, even if less vulgarized and less fanatically presented than in National Socialism. Such ideological components as racial superiority, anti-Semitism, the cult of the Germanic, German romanticism, nationalism, and militarism had considerable appeal not only to the petty bourgeoisie but, selectively and in varying degree, also to the middle and upper classes, and to a lesser extent, even the labor class. Hitler's early political successes abroad, his early spectacular bloodless acquisitions of new territory, his accomplishments in overcoming the economic depression, did not fail to make a profound impression on most Germans of *all* classes, to flatter their nationalistic feelings and to make them close their eyes to the brutalities of the regime and to its dubious future. Only the really cosmopolitan intelligentsia remained resistant to such temptations. But that intelligentsia did not include the bulk of the university professors and students. The latter two, in fact, played a considerable part in the early promotion of the Movement. The university students, coming from diverse population groups and displaying much conviction, noise, and violence, demanded the abolition of parliamentary democracy and a national socialist government. Later, most of them died silently in the War, but the published letters which they had sent home do not indicate that they ever regretted their earlier judgment.[10]

The ideology, as stated before, was quite unoriginal in its individual components, but the Movement did two things that lent some measure of originality to the whole undertaking. It produced a kind of aggregation of the various ideological components—not very systematically, not in one or two books, not precisely defined, but still with sufficient definition here and there to enable the people to recognize the individual components as belonging to a whole fairly consistent ideological structure. Even a mere aggregation of old elements can, to an extent, result in something new. The training program of the SS is of some interest in this context because it did seem to reflect a fairly systematic grouping of some important ideological components:[11]

Racial biology
Care of the race
Contempt for inferior people
The Germanic age
The *Führer* principle
Unconditional obedience
Fight for the sake of fight, etc.

The lack of definition, the vagueness and murkiness that remained, were, in fact, implicit in the romantic coloration of the whole ideology; and, indeed, a lack of precision, an intellectual haziness and dreaminess, seemed to appeal to the German mind. A poorly defined ideology, moreover, had its practical uses; and the lack of precision may not have been wholly unintentional. It left desirable leeway for new interpretations when propagandistic maneuvers required this.

Definition was replaced by the religious fervor in which National Socialism clothed its ideas and by the dedication with which these ideas were pursued. There is little doubt that, to Hitler and millions of his followers, at least some components of the ideology took on aspects of a religion—not a gentle religion but one that called for fanaticism.

[10]See *Kriegsbriefe gefallener Studenten 1939–1945*, Tübingen, 1952.
[11]See *Anatomie des SS-Staates*, Vol. I, pp. 276–277, which, however, does not seem to see anything particularly "systematic" in this.

". . . I am acting in accordance with the will of the Almighty Creator [said Hitler]. . . . I am fighting for the work of the Lord."[12] Millions were obsessed with this religion and were willing to live and die for it. Clearly, this added a new quality to the old ideological components. The old ideas—many from the nineteenth century—which seemingly had been dragged out of grandmother's trunk in the attic, came very much to life. And at any rate, the National Socialists were really the first advocates of these ideas who had the courage of their ideological convictions. They did not merely believe in anti-Semitism, as the Germans had for a hundred years, but they actually deported their Jews (and later killed them, though few Germans were aware of that). They did not merely have the long-standing German contempt for the "inferior" Slavic race, but they proceeded to subdue the Czechs, Poles, and Russians and to kill millions of them. The ideology became a fighting gospel.

Thirdly, a general factor in our consideration of the ideology must be what Erich Fromm calls "the authoritarian character" which is typical for many Germans. The essence of that character, Fromm says, is "the simultaneous presence of sadistic and masochistic drives."[13] Sadism he describes as "aiming at unrestricted power over another person more or less mixed with destructiveness; masochism, as aiming at dissolving oneself in an overwhelmingly strong power and participating in its strength and glory." The presence of such drives in the average German of the Hitler period (and earlier periods) is obvious: he wallowed in his power over the Jews and other "inferior" races, and he wallowed also in dissolving himself in the strength of national socialist power and participating in its glory. The sado-masochistic drives will be referred to more in detail in our discussion of some individual components of the ideology. Fromm says that sadomasochistic persons "are not necessarily neurotic" and that the sadomasochistic character is "typical" for "great parts of the lower middle class in Germany and other European countries."[14] But surely this character structure must have been far more dominant in Germany than elsewhere in Europe (and there remains unanswered the more basic question why this should have been so).

[12]*Mein Kampf*, p. 70.
[13]Fromm, *Escape from Freedom*, p. 221.
[14]Ibid., p. 163.

What is important, in the context of our present discussion, is that the sadomasochistic person is not necessarily conscious of the driving forces which dominate him and that he rationalizes them as originating in other, much more "respectable" motivations. "A person can be entirely dominated by his sadistic strivings and consciously believe that he is motivated only by his sense of duty." [15] This kind of unconscious rationalization is discussed also by another sociopsychologist, T. W. Adorno, who says with respect, for example, to anti-Semitism that "if the conflict within the individual has been decided against the Jews, the decision itself is almost without exception rationalized moralistically" [16] (and to the same author, in fact, "the whole complex of the Jew is a kind of red-light district of legitimatized psychotic distortions" [17]).

It seems possible, then, that important components of national socialist ideology were nothing but rationalizations of sadomasochistic drives and other drives of the authoritarian personality. And if such ideological components amount to no more than cover-ups for the rather unappetizing basic motivations, the importance of exploring the history of the ideas might seem to be diminished. Unsolved problems of the relationship between psychoanalysis and history raise their heads. At least one recent student of the history of German ideology, George L. Mosse, objected to what he called the "psychological view," and took the position that this view can do no more than "provide clues in individual cases—or in all cases from the point of view that all of men's actions are open to psychological explanation." [18]

At any rate, all this is an area of doubt and uncertainty. There is, for example, the fact that in other European countries, for instance Switzerland and Holland, the authoritarian personality seemed also strongly represented, but that these countries remained democratic and that, in fact, the authoritarian personality there supported democracy and fought totalitarianism. At the very least, this would seem to call for a search for motivations in Germany, in addition to sadomasochistic drives, for example, environmental factors and historical reasons why one set of rationalizations, and not another, was used to

[15] Ibid., p. 163.
[16] Adorno (and others), *The Authoritarian Personality*, p. 630.
[17] Ibid., p. 617.
[18] Mosse, *The Crisis of German Ideology*, pp. 300–301.

cover up the drives. How and where, moreover, did the ideas for the rationalizations originate? How were they put into use? Even Adorno admits that

> . . . we [psychologists] may be able to say something about the readiness of an individual to break into violence, but we are pretty much in the dark as to the remaining necessary conditions under which an actual outbreak would occur. . . . Outbreaks into action [by prejudiced persons] must be considered the results of both the internal potential and a set of eliciting factors in the environment. [19]

Another sociopsychologist, Bruno Bettelheim, speaks of the necessity for a "nucleus of reality" in connection with the rationalizations, and he says that the "means" of rationalization must be

> . . . satisfactory to the individual's controlling institutions and to the group to which he belongs. Reality is not tested out of context, nor are rationalizations developed independent of the prevailing frame of reference. . . .
>
> If ethnic intolerance is rooted in the intolerant individual's personality, then we must ask ourselves what in this society shapes personality in such a way that ethnic intolerance seems a frequent, if not a favorite, outlet for hostility. [20]

The matter will be discussed again later, particularly in relation to the causes of anti-Semitism.

There may also be a possibility that the national socialist ideology existed in its essentials before the authoritarian character was born and that the character was, in fact, molded in part by the ideology. This would not have been inconsistent with the individual's use of the ideology to rationalize his drives. The two could have supplemented each other, and the relationship may have been reciprocal.

At any rate, in our consideration of the ideology we shall, at all times, have to bear in mind the probability that, no matter how slow and complex the evolution of an ideological component may have been,

---

[19] Adorno, op. cit., p. 972.
[20] Bettelheim and Janowitz, *Dynamics of Prejudice*, pp. 156, 162-163.

it did, at a particular point in history, serve some individuals or groups, in whole or in part, as a rationalization of sadomasochistic drives. What will follow, then, is a discussion of the individual ideological components, their origins and surrounding circumstances, their acceptance by the German people, and their ultimate historical consequences. In sum, it is the story of the political and social emergence of the long-repressed and disdained petty bourgeoisie with all its intellectual and psychological faults and shortcomings, under the leadership of a (probably) psychopathic member of this group. It is the story of how he and they became intoxicated with their own power, filled with narcissism; gave way to their sadomasochistic drives backed by an immature, sometimes savage ideology; became totally corrupt and went berserk as success followed success; and finally were subdued only by stronger physical force from outside, but not before a total of about 43 million people had been killed.

Chapter 2

The Race Theories

A. The Origins

The race theories no doubt were the very core, the central component, of the national socialist ideology. In fact, other components (such as the Lebensraum doctrine, anti-Semitism, and the Germanic cult) functioned to an extent as mere satellites of the race theories. It is, therefore, a curious fact that the race theories had their origins, not in Germany, but in other European countries and that the authors of the basic writings on these theories, who were most influential in Germany, were French and British. It is significant, in this connection, that the German word *Rasse*, meaning "race," originated as a mere Germanized spelling of the French word *race* and was not taken into the German language until the second half of the eighteenth century.[1]

Chronologically, the first writer who developed a race theory of substance was the French Count Joseph Arthur de Gobineau (1816–1882). In 1853, he published his four-volume *Essai sur l'inégalité des races humaines*, which presented a complete theory of race as the deciding factor in the rise and fall of civilizations. Pure races rose to power, bastardized races went down to defeat. The "Aryans" were the most valuable race, but even they were in the process of inevitable degeneration because of their mixture with other races. Among the Aryans, the Germanic race was the best because it had remained purest, and it was still destined to carry out a few great tasks. It was Gobineau's conviction that the concept of race must be given complete

[1]Grimm, *Deutsches Wörterbuch*, Leipzig, 1893, Vol. VIII, p. 143.

primacy, not only over the individual but also over the nation.[2] He did not, however, intend to promote anti-Semitism.

Gobineau's doctrines did not find acceptance, either in France or in Germany, at the time when he first developed them. His pessimistic emphasis on the inevitable decay of race and civilization was not in line with the faith in eternal progress which was fashionable in those days (and it certainly furnished no support for the subsequent teachings of National Socialism concerning the coming Thousand-Year-Reich). Gobineau was attracted more by the decline than by the rise of civilizations. It was about forty years before he received recognition, and then mostly in Germany and not in France. The development of the more optimistic Darwinistic doctrine of the survival of the fittest was needed to permit placing Gobineau's theories into the framework of an acceptable ideology. Charles Darwin (1809–1882) had published his *Origin of Species* in 1859, and it received immediate, overwhelming acceptance. His *Descent of Man* followed in 1871. Darwin himself related his theory of evolution, his principles of natural selection and struggle for life, primarily to animals and plants; but he did discuss them also in relation to man, thus anticipating what was later to be called "social Darwinism." Significantly, he said:

> . . . as man suffers from the same physical evils as the lower animals, he has no right to expect an immunity from the evils consequent on the struggle for existence.
> . . . .
> With savages, the weak in body or mind are soon eliminated; and those that survive commonly exhibit a vigorous state of health. We civilised men, on the other hand, do our utmost to check the process of elimination; we build asylums for the imbecile, the maimed, and the sick; we institute poor-laws; and our medical men exert their utmost skill to save the life of everyone to the last moment. . . . Thus the weak members of civilised societies propagate their kind. No one who has attended to the breeding of domestic animals will doubt that this must be highly injurious to the race of man. It is surprising how soon a want of care, or care wrongly directed, leads to the de-

[2]Gobineau, *Essai sur l'inégalité des races humaines*, Vol. 1, Chap. IV.

generation of a domestic race; but excepting in the case of man himself, hardly anyone is so ignorant as to allow his worst animals to breed.[3]

No one would have been greatly surprised if some of these statements had appeared in speeches by Hitler and Himmler seventy years later. But the conclusions they drew from the analogy between breeding animals and men were totally different from Darwin's, because he had said:

> The aid which we feel impelled to give to the helpless is mainly an incidental result of the instinct of sympathy. . . . Nor could we check our sympathy even at the urging of hard reason, without deterioration in the noblest part of our nature. . . . We must therefore bear the undoubtedly bad effects of the weak surviving and propagating their kind; . . .[4]

The so-called social Darwinism, which developed after Darwin, applied his doctrines of the fight for life and survival of the fittest to political and social relationships. It gradually shed his "instinct of sympathy" and it overlooked his warnings against a "deterioration in the noblest part of our nature." Social Darwinism found many interpreters in Germany, and the conclusions which they drew from Darwin's original, socially innocuous teachings became increasingly radical and extreme.[5] Those living beings whom Darwin himself had characterized merely as "biologically fitter" came to be regarded as "superior," "more valuable," in a metaphysical sense, and Gobineau's theory of the superior Germanic race could easily be blended into this pseudo-Darwinism. The importance of this seemingly small modification in a biological theory can hardly be overestimated. It was to have a profound effect on the history of Europe and the world because, without this modification, the much later claims that the Germans were a master race destined to rule and that certain other races were

[3]Darwin, *The Descent of Man*, Modern Library edition, New York, pp. 608, 501.
[4]Ibid., pp. 501–502.

[5]Among such interpreters were Ernst Haeckel, Wilhelm Schallmeyer, Alexander Tille, A. Plötz, Friedrich Lenz, and Ludwig Woltmann, whose books, while widely read and influential in those days, make tedious reading today.

subhuman *(Untermenschen)*, destined to perish, could never have been made.

Nations or ethnical groups came to be regarded as "biological organisms," so that it was logical to argue, under Darwinistic principles, that a stronger nation had a natural right to dominate or even exterminate weaker nations in the general struggle for survival. The principle of natural selection was made the basis for all higher development among nations as among individual men and animals.[6] Civilization, moreover, was regarded with suspicion as something that artificially interfered with nature's way of selection and with the law that the best survive; for civilization, with its humanitarian principles, protected the weak and unfit instead of letting them perish and promoting the growth and survival of the biologically most valuable elements. The best thing to do, therefore, was to put a stop to this dubious kind of civilization and, in its place, to help nature along in selecting the fittest and letting the others die. What later became known as "racial hygiene" had its origin here.

The maintenance of the species, the nation's eternal fight for life, was pushed into the center of the theory. War truly became the father of all things; it was inevitable, and the preparation for it required strengthening of the German racial community to the utmost by biological and all other means. This included not only the maintenance of the pure German race, but also the elimination of all biologically worthless or damaging elements, for example, the Jews. The original Darwinism (and even some subsequent interpretations) had had no specifically anti-Semitic or racist tendencies, but these gradually developed and became increasingly pronounced. The concept of race, and particularly the mythical Nordic race, finally became the focal point of the entire theory. Social Darwinism and pure racial theories merged. "By the end of the nineteenth century, racial thought had transformed the struggle for the survival of the fittest into a racial imperative."[7]

[6]See Hans Günter Zmarzlik, "Der Sozialdarwinismus in Deutschland als geschichtliches Problem," in *Vierteljahrshefte für Zeitgeschichte*, Vol. XI, Heft 3, July 1963, pp. 246–273. See also Daniel Gasman, *The Scientific Origins of National Socialism. Social Darwinism in Ernst Haeckel and the Monist League*, who shows quite convincingly the rather close intellectual ancestry of the social Darwinist Ernst Haeckel (1834–1919) for National Socialism and even Hitler himself.

[7]George L. Mosse, *The Crisis of German Ideology*, p. 106.

But it was another Englishman, Houston Stewart Chamberlain (1855–1927), who was to be the greatest impetus in the popularization of the race theories in Germany and particularly in imbuing the Germans with the idea that it was the "Germanic" race that was superior to the others and destined to rule them. Chamberlain, "one of the strangest Englishmen who ever lived,"[8] was born in Portsmouth, England, the son of an English admiral. As a young man he was irresistibly drawn toward Germany, where he finally made his home and became a citizen. At the outbreak of World War I, he broke with Great Britain. He was profoundly influenced by Richard Wagner's racial views and by Germanic myths, and ultimately he married Wagner's daughter, Eva. He settled in Wagner's "holy ground," Bayreuth.

There was no doubt that Chamberlain was a man of vast intelligence and knowledge in many fields. He wrote in German, a language which, according to Hitler, Chamberlain once described to him as "the most valuable and beautiful for thinkers."[9] By far the most important of Chamberlain's books was *Die Grundlagen des XIX. Jahrhunderts* (The Foundations of the Nineteenth Century), published in 1900. In spite of its 1,246 pages, the book, in twenty-eight editions, became an enormous success throughout Germany. Over the next thirty-five years, it had a profound effect on millions of Germans, including Kaiser Wilhelm II.

The book credits the Germanic people with nearly all great cultural achievements. It considers the Jews as incapable of anything creative, although Chamberlain recognized them as a "pure race," just as pure, in fact, as the Germanic people. These were the only two pure races; all the others, particularly the Mediterranean races, represented a "chaos of peoples" *(Völkerchaos)*. He sometimes went so far as to concede that the Jews were not inferior to the Germans, but merely different.[10] The whole tenor of the book, however, was strongly anti-Semitic. At any rate, Chamberlain's conclusion was that the Germans were now superior to all other races and that this gave them the right to be the world's masters.[11]

[8]William L. Shirer, *The Rise and Fall of the Third Reich*, p. 103.
[9]*Hitler's Table Talks*, p. 396.
[10]*Grundlagen*, p. 384.
[11]Ibid., pp. 596–597, 820.

Naturally, the Germans liked to hear this, and they particularly liked to hear it from an Englishman who was presumably less biased than a German might have been. The book, moreover, had precisely the quality that appealed most to the more or less educated German middle class: it seemed to combine the results of scientific research with a good dose of romanticism. It spoke to the mind as well as to the German soul.

In truth, the book, or at least much of it, was a pseudoscientific, partly tendentious enormity. It went so far as to contend that Jesus was an Aryan. But to National Socialists, it became a kind of Bible, [12] and fundamentally Chamberlain had probably given to them the first seemingly authoritative and complete exposition of some of their basic theories. Above all, it told them that they were the superior creators of culture, the master race destined to rule. As Karl Dietrich Bracher states it: ". . . Chamberlain had created a fusion of the racial mysticism of Wagner, Gobineau, and of the new anti-Semites; he was copied by Alfred Rosenberg, [13] and Hitler and Himmler drew the consequences." [14] Bracher quotes in this connection the pertinent observation made by Alexis de Tocqueville in a critical letter to Gobineau: "Alone in Europe, the Germans possess the particular talent of becoming impassioned with what they take as abstract truths, without considering their practical consequences. . . ." [15]

Hitler himself was deeply influenced by Chamberlain, and there is little doubt that the *Grundlagen* was a book Hitler had actually read. Chamberlain is one of the few authors to whom Hitler referred in *Mein Kampf* [16] by name, and he mentioned him twice also in his *Table*

[12] It was called this *(Evangelium)* in the party newspaper *Völkischer Beobachter* of Sept. 5, 1925.

[13] Rosenberg was the so-called "ideologist" of national socialism and author of *Der Mythus des 20. Jahrhunderts.* (Even this title shows some analogy to that of Chamberlain's book.) In 1927, Rosenberg published a pamphlet, *Houston Stewart Chamberlain als Verkünder und Begründer einer deutschen Zukunft* (H.S.C. as Proclaimer and Founder of a German Future). Much information about Rosenberg is contained in Robert Cecil, *The Myth of the Master Race: Alfred Rosenberg and Nazi Ideology.*

[14] Bracher, *Die Deutsche Diktatur,* p. 31.

[15] English translation taken from Alexis de Tocqueville, *The European Revolution and Correspondence with Gobineau,* New York, 1959, p. 294.

[16] P. 296.

Talks. [17] In 1925, Hitler visited the aged, ill Chamberlain in Bayreuth. Chamberlain was deeply impressed with Hitler and, after this dramatic encounter, wrote to him: "My faith in the Germans had never wavered for a moment, but my hope, I must admit, had sunk to a low ebb. At one stroke, you have transformed the state of my soul. Germany's vitality is attested by the fact that, in the hour of her greatest distress, she brought forth a Hitler. . . ." [18]

The great impact which Chamberlain had on Alfred Rosenberg, the "ideologist" of National Socialism, was probably much less fateful, even though Rosenberg incorporated Chamberlain's ideas into his *Mythus des 20. Jahrhunderts.* Rosenberg's book never became popular. Far more important is the fact that Chamberlain had had a *direct* profound impact on countless millions of Germans, whether National Socialists or not—and this long before anyone thought of National Socialism.

It is perhaps ironic that it should have been one Frenchman (Gobineau) and two Englishmen (Darwin and Chamberlain) who were the most important intellectual ancestors of the racial theories of National Socialism. But there were also many influential German writers, of lesser stature, who spread radical race theories between about 1850 and 1945, such as Ludwig Schemann, Julius Langbehn, Friedrich List, Aldolph Wagner, and the composer Richard Wagner about whom more will be said later.

Moreover, the same theories (and others) were intensively propagated by a rather important organization, the Pan-German Association *(Alldeutscher Verband)*, which was generally considered "respectable" in Germany. Its membership consisted of numerous university professors, high school teachers, members of the free professions, and the nobility, as well as other segments of the middle and upper classes. Founded in 1891, The Pan-German Association, in the course of the years, became strongly racist, anti-Semitic, and nationalistic. It was closely allied with the Gobineau Society of Ludwig Schemann. The Pan-German Association spread racial doctrines far and wide, particularly through its numerous members who were in

[17] Pp. 155 and 396.
[18] The entire letter is quoted in *Houston Stewart Chamberlain der Seher des Dritten Reiches* by Georg Schott, 1934, 1941, pp. 11-13.

the teaching professions. Their effect on German youth during the pre-Hitler period was very strong.

The philosophy of the Association is typified by the following quotation from the association journal, *Alldeutsche Blätter*, of 1913:

> The racial-biological ideology tells us that there are races that lead and races that follow. Political history is nothing but the history of struggles among the leading races. Conquests, above all, are always the work of the leading races. Such men can conquer, may conquer, and shall conquer. And they shall be masters — for their own benefit and for the benefit of others. That is true of our age just as it was true of the classical age. For not destruction but higher development is the result of the invasion by a high-minded noble race. This race serves the Lord of the army legions, and what it does is the work of the Saviour. [19]

That statement, word for word, might have been found in *Mein Kampf* or in Hitler's speeches, but it was made while he, as a young man, was still leading a dubious existence in a men's lodging house in Vienna. No wonder then that some historians have spoken of National Socialism as "a child of the Pan-Germans," [20] and that the Association has been called "the amniotic fluid from which grew arrogance, terror, and crime, about a generation later." [21] Hannah Arendt goes so far as to contend that "Nazism . . . owe[s] more to Pan-Germanism . . . than to any other ideology or political movement," [22] and it is true that the early Hitler described himself as "Pan-German in my convictions." [23] But much of the ideology of Pan-Germanism, in turn, had been derived from the earlier race theories. It was an intermediate way station.

Ultimately, the Pan-German Association broke with the ascending National Socialists, and it was disbanded under the Hitler regime.

[19] Quoted in Hermann Huss and Andreas Schröder (eds.), *Antisemitismus*, p. 27.
[20] See Mosse, *Crisis*, p. 225.
[21] E. L. Ehrlich in *Judenfeindschaft in Deutschland*, p. 234. See also Eva G. Reichmann, *Flucht in den Hass*, pp. 181–182; Peter G. J. Pulzer, *The Rise of Political Anti-Semitism*, pp. 281–282; Wanda Kampmann, *Deutsche und Juden*, pp. 320–321; Friedrich Meinecke, *Die deutsche Katastrophe*, p. 50.
[22] Arendt, *The Origins of Totalitarianism*, p. 222.
[23] In his Munich trial in 1924, quoted in Werner Maser, *Adolf Hitler*, p. 176.

But it had done much to formulate what became national socialist ideology and to lay the foundation for its popular acceptance.

By 1914, at the outbreak of World War I, when Hitler joined the Germany Army as a modest private, the theories of social Darwinism and the racial doctrines of Gobineau, Chamberlain, and others had come to occupy a great deal of space in the ideological arsenal of the German middle and upper classes. Chamberlain, in particular, had taught them to feel contempt for most foreign nations. By 1914 and thereafter, quite definitely fixed stereotypes regarding the merits of foreign nations had developed among the vast majority of German children and adults, even those of some education. They were likely to regard the French as clever but degenerate, inefficient and not very clean; the Russians and Poles as dirty barbarians; the Italians as lazy, unclean and undependable, even though rather likable; the Americans as lacking culture, being soulless *(seelenlos)* and uncouth, though proficient in purely technical things; the British as decadent and hypocritical, although rather handsome and entitled to credit for the manner in which they had built up a colonial empire. The list of such contemptuous prejudices could be extended almost ad infinitum. Whatever good qualities could be found in other nations were often attributed to German immigrants. Exceptions in the general picture of contempt for the rest of the world were only the Scandinavian countries and Holland (the "Nordics"), as well as Switzerland (the latter, however, Hitler called "merely a miscarried offspring of our people"[24]), and as to all these, there was a feeling that they should really be part of Germany. They belonged to the German race and *Kultur.*

The sociopsychologist T. W. Adorno has analyzed such ethnocentric attitudes:

A primary characteristic of ethnocentric ideology is the *generality* of outgroup rejection. It is as if the ethnocentric individual feels threatened by most of the groups to which he does not have a sense of belonging; if he cannot identify, he must oppose. . . .

The ethnocentric "need for an outgroup" prevents . . . identification with humanity as a whole. . . . The inability to identify with humanity takes the political form of nationalism. . . . It

[24] *Hitler's Table Talks*, p. 162.

takes other forms, all based on ideas concerning the intrinsic evil (aggressiveness, laziness, power-seeking, etc.) of human nature. . . .[25]

The psychiatrist Erich Fromm sees the origin of these attitudes in narcissistic pride, which he calls "a very effective form of satisfaction," consisting in "the inflated image of . . . [a group] as the most admirable group in the world, and of being superior to another racial group that is singled out as inferior."[26]

It is clear that this vast German narcissism, this inability and unwillingness to identify with the world, which Hitler thoroughly shared,[27] could only be helpful to him when he decided to lead the Germans into the conquest of Europe.

The hatred and contempt for other races has, of course, additional psychological and sociopsychological aspects. Thus, the psychiatrist Bruno Bettelheim points out that "the concept of 'race' has to the unsophisticated person a wealth of emotional connotations which relate it far more closely to mythical (magical) thinking than to reason."[28] To many, moreover, the hatred of one or more other races is nothing but a cathartic outlet for the discharge of that general hostility which, according to Bettelheim, is continuously accumulating in the anxious and the insecure and for which there is no other easy outlet.[29] The race theories evidently provide not only targets against whom the hostility can be vented but, above all, rationalizations of the socially offensive hostility itself. "Race [Adorno says] is a socially harmful idea," and "the greatest dangers of the race concept lie in its hereditarian psychological implications and in its misapplication to cultures.[30] Such psychological considerations, however, were unknown to the Germans of the Hitler period and of the fifty years preceding it, and if they had been told of them, most Germans would probably have smiled in disbelief. To them, the theory that their race was superior to all others was an entirely central, historically grown dogma, which

[25] Adorno, *The Authoritarian Personality,* pp. 147–148.
[26] Fromm, *The Heart of Man,* p. 79.
[27] See f.i., *Hitler's Table Talks,* pp. 144, 175, 220; also *Hitlers Zweites Buch,* p. 128.
[28] Bettelheim and Janowitz, *Dynamics of Prejudice,* pp. 142–143.
[29] Ibid., pp. 171–173.
[30] Adorno, op. cit., pp. 102–103.

could not have been shaken by any such theories. It must be remembered also that those were the decades when the whole Western world was still deeply impressed with Darwin's relatively new discoveries of races, species, and natural selection. It was also the period when the new natural sciences, in any event, commanded enormous respect.

B. The Race Theories in the Ideology and Their Practical Application

The whole bundle of race theories which, as we have seen, had become part of the German cultural heritage long before Hitler appeared on the scene, was accepted by him *in toto*. He expressed these ideas over and over again in a thousand speeches, conversations, and writings, and he never deviated from them to any significant extent. The fundamentals of these theories were, for example, clearly reflected in two confidential speeches which Hitler addressed to groups of officer candidates on May 30, 1942, and June 22, 1944. Both speeches were long and carefully prepared and quite evidently stated the "basic truths" closest to Hitler's heart, which he wanted young army officers to understand most clearly. He said in the 1942 speech:

A profoundly serious statement of a great military philosopher[31] says that struggle and, therefore, war is the father of all things. Anyone who looks at nature as it really is will find that statement confirmed as to all living beings. . . . The entire universe seems to be dominated only by this one thought, that an eternal selection takes place in which the stronger one in the end stays alive and maintains the right to live, and the weaker one falls. One man may say that nature thus is cruel and pitiless, but another man will understand that, in being so, nature follows only an immutable logical law. . . . That law will continue in force. Anyone who believes that, because of his suffering, his feelings or his attitude, he can rebel against this law, will do away not with the law but only with himself.

History proves that peoples became weak. They did not eliminate the law, but they themselves disappeared without trace.

[31] Presumably Heraclitus.

Other peoples remained strong. They, too, had to make their sacrifices; but in the end, as a whole, they were given life. . . .

This fight . . . consequently leads to a continuous and eternal selection, to the selection of the better and tougher ones. In this fight we see, therefore, an element of the building process of everything that lives and is alive. We recognize this in primitive nature. . . .

This is the world order [*Weltordnung*] of force and strength. There is no world order of weakness and surrender, but only a fate of surrender. This fate means disappearance and extinction. . . .[32]

Similarly, in *Mein Kampf*, Hitler had said many years earlier: "What [nature] wants, is the victory of the stronger one and the destruction of the weaker one or his unconditional subjection."[33]

Other, less formal statements of pseudo-Darwinistic content were made by Hitler on many other occasions, and the most significant ones were perhaps those made in the relaxed atmosphere of the table conversations at mealtime at the Führer headquarters:

I am working toward a condition in which everyone knows: he lives and dies for the maintenance of the species![34]

If I want to believe in one divine command, it can only be: Preserve the species![35]

I am an ardent champion of the belief that in the struggle between nations the better average will always prevail. The whole system of the laws of nature would be set aside if the inferior were able to subdue the stronger.[36]

Hitler, on rare occasions, was even willing to draw corresponding conclusions from Germany's approaching defeat in the war. In March, 1945, he told Albert Speer quite logically that "the [German] people have shown themselves to be the weaker ones . . . the future belongs exclusively to the stronger Eastern people [*Ostvolk*]" and "the ones

[32]Speech of May 30, 1942, reprinted in the appendix to *Hitler's Table Talks*, pp. 493–504. The speech of June 22, 1944, was very similar but by no means identical.
[33]p. 372.
[34]*Hitler's Table Talks*, p. 155.
[35]Ibid., p. 153.
[36]Ibid., p. 442 (indirect speech transposed).

who will be left over after this fight will be inferior, anyway, because the valuable ones have been killed."[37] (It never seems to have occurred to Hitler that he himself might have been the "weaker one," as compared, for example, with Stalin or Churchill; and he proved wrong also in his assumption concerning the nation to which the future "exclusively" belonged.)

By the time Hitler was attending school in Austria (1895–1905), the race theories had come to represent established dogma of the German (and Austrian) middle and upper classes. (They remained dogma, in fact, at least until the collapse of the Third Reich.) Hitler thus had no particular difficulty in persuading the great mass of Germans that these doctrines furnished a sound basis for domestic and foreign policy. Nearly everyone believed in them in any event. It would be wrong to say, as some have, that these were ideas which national socialism "manipulated . . . to fit its need of the moment"[38] or that they were used merely as a "technique of domination."[39] Of course, the theory of the inevitable domination of the inferior races by the superior German race did serve to furnish the Germans with an ideal doctrinal justification for political conquest; and there were some cynical National Socialists (such as Goebbels and Göring) who probably saw the situation solely in that light. Even Hitler himself was clearly an opportunist and was certainly not above using beliefs to buttress his realpolitik. This has led some to the erroneous view that the ideology was nothing but utilitarian or opportunistic.

Hitler's *Mein Kampf*, which sets forth nearly his entire ideology and program, never mentioned Darwin's name,[40] but it abounds in unmistakable social-Darwinistic pronouncements. The same is true of the 359 pages of transcripts of *Hitler's Table Talks*. It is possible that Hitler never read Darwin and that he read no more than some popular science version of social-Darwinism. In any event, the fact is that Hitler saw in these doctrines adequate justification for (or rationalization of the right to) the extermination of all Jews and the subjugation

[37]Speer, *Erinnerungen*, p. 446. An almost identical remark was reported by General Heinz Guderian; see Walther Hofer, *Der Nationalsozialismus — Dokumente 1933–1945*, p. 260. See also Bracher, *Die deutsche Diktatur*, p. 442.

[38]Kurt Sontheimer in Fritz Stern (ed.), *The Path to Dictatorship*, p. 34.

[39]Franz Neumann, *Behemoth*, p. 467.

[40]See in this connection Werner Maser, *Hitlers Mein Kampf*, footnote on p. 92.

of other nations. Before Hitler (with the exception of the German-colonial war against the Hereros in 1904–1907, discussed later), social-Darwinism and concomitant race theories had been written about extensively and had been accepted by the vast majority of the German people, but nobody had really drawn the final consequences from these thoughts and put them into action.

The simple, straightforward, and completely radical manner in which Hitler's followers applied social-Darwinistic principles to the extermination of the Jews is reflected in the so-called *Wannsee-Protokoll*, that is, the minutes of a meeting, on January 20, 1942, of high national socialist officials (such as Heydrich and Eichmann) and representatives of various German ministries and other government departments. The meeting dealt with definite plans for the Final Solution, the extermination of the European Jews. Some of Heydrich's statements in his conference memorandum, dealing with the preparatory steps, follow:

> In large labor gangs, with the sexes separated, those Jews who are capable of working will be brought into these areas [the East], employed in road building, in the course of which a large proportion will be eliminated by natural diminution. The ultimately remaining members, being undoubtedly the strongest elements, will have to be treated accordingly [*entsprechend behandelt*], since they, representing a *natural selection*, would, if released, constitute a germination cell for Jewish reconstruction. (See historical experiences.) (Italics added.) [41]

Social-Darwinism, and more specifically racial breeding, again underlies a speech by Himmler on December 14, 1943:

> It is quite obvious that there will always be some racially very good types in this mixture of peoples [Slavs]. Here, I believe, it is our

[41] German text in Hofer, op. cit., p. 304–305. In national socialist terminology, the words "treated accordingly" *(entsprechend behandelt)* meant simply "killed." National socialists seemed to feel reluctance, in countless thousands of official and unofficial papers, to speak of killing, exterminating, etc., and they developed a considerable vocabulary of circumlocution. The same phenomenon became noticeable in the U.S.—Vietnamese War when army officers spoke of "wasting" civilians, and the Central Intelligence Agency substituted "eliminate with extreme prejudice" for "kill."

task to take their children for ourselves . . . and even if we have to kidnap or steal them. . . . Either we shall gain that good blood, which we can use, or gentlemen — you may call it cruel, but nature is cruel — we shall destroy that blood. . . ."[42]

The general narcissistic attitude of contempt of the Germans for other nations, which we have discussed before, explains, in some measure, the brutal treatment received by Polish and Russian civilians and prisoners of war at the hands of the occupying Germans.[43] The contemptuous attitude (and more) is reflected in the following quotations from statements by Hitler, Himmler, and Göring:

Hitler:

The Poles, in direct contrast to our German workmen, are born especially for hard labor. . . . as to the Poles, there can be no question of improvement for them. On the contrary, it is necessary to keep the standard of life low in Poland. . . . All representatives of the Polish intelligentsia are to be exterminated. . . . It will . . . be proper for the Poles to remain Roman Catholics. . . . The task of the priests is to keep the Poles quiet, stupid and dull-witted. . . .[44]

Himmler:

For the non-German population in the East, there shall be no school beyond a four-year elementary school. The purpose of that elementary school is to be nothing but simple counting to 500 at most, writings one's name, teaching that it is God's commandment to be obedient to the Germans and to be honest, hard working and well-behaved. I do not think that a reading ability is necessary.[45]

[42]German text in Hans Buchheim, Martin Broszat, Hans-Adolph Jacobsen, and Helmut Krausnick, *Anatomie des SS-Staates*, Vol. I, pp. 301–302.

[43]See, generally, Alexander Dallin, *German Rule in Russia 1941–1945;* Martin Broszat, *Nationalsozialistische Polenpolitik 1939–1945;* Reinhard Henkys, *Die National-sozialistischen Gewaltverbrechen.*

[44]Martin Bormann's notes on a meeting of Hitler with high officials on Oct. 2, 1941, Nuremberg Proceedings (British), Part VI, pp. 219–221, quoted by Alan Bullock, *Hitler,* p. 693.

[45]Himmler's "Memorandum concerning the Treatment of Aliens in the East," of May 1940. *Vierteljahrshefte für Zeitgeschichte*, Vol. V, 1957, p. 197.

Himmler:

What happens to the Russians or Czechs is totally immaterial to me. What these nations can offer in the nature of good blood of our kind we shall take by kidnapping their children, if necessary, and raising them with us. Whether the other nations live in prosperity or starve to death interests me only to the extent to which we need them as slaves for our *Kultur;* I have no other interest in that. Whether 10,000 Russian women keel over from exhaustion while digging an antitank ditch interests me only to the extent that the antitank ditch is finished for Germany. We shall never be cruel and heartless when it is not necessary; that is clear. We Germans, who are the only ones in the world who have a decent attitude toward animals, will also show a decent attitude toward these *human animals*, but it would be a crime against our own blood to worry about them. . . . (Italics added.) [46]

Hitler:

To struggle against the [Russian] hovels, chase away the fleas, provide German teachers, bring out newspapers — very little of that for us! . . . Let them know just enough to understand our highway signs so that they won't get themselves run over by our vehicles.

For them the word "liberty" means the right to wash on feast days. . . . [47]

Göring's remarks to the Italian Foreign Minister, Count Galeazzo Ciano, in November 1941:

This year, between 20 and 30 million persons will die in Russia of hunger. Perhaps it is well that it should be so, for certain nations must be decimated. [48]

---

[46] Himmler's speech to SS-officers in Posen on Oct. 4, 1943, *Trials of Major War Criminals (TMWC),* Vol. XXIX, pp. 122–123, Doc. 1919-PS.

[47] Quoted from Bullock, op. cit., p. 656, who cites it as *Table Talk.* This particular *Table Talk* (Oct. 17, 1941) is not contained in Picker (ed.), *Hitler's Tischgespräche,* usually cited here.

[48] *Ciano's Diplomatic Papers,* pp. 464–465, London, 1948. For similar statements by lower German officials see Dallin, op. cit., pp. 163, 167. See also *Goebbels Diaries,* p. 88, Feb. 15, 1942; also A. Hillgruber, "Die 'Endlösung' und das deutsche Ostimperium . . .", in *Vierteljahrshefte für Zeitgeschichte,* Vol. XX, 1972, pp. 140–141.

The extremes in German brutality against Polish and Russian civilians and prisoners of war, as well as the Final Solution itself, represented the ultimate logical conclusion which a radical mind could draw from a fusion of social Darwinism and Gobineau's and Chamberlain's race theories. Drawing this conclusion was really Hitler's and Himmler's "contribution" to these theories.

But acting on this conclusion presented a good many practical difficulties. Above all, the translation of mere theory into action required the help of a great many people, as well as the acquiescence of many others. Most of these people had certain inhibitions against committing excessive brutalities, not to speak of mass murder. They had to be presented with plausible reasoning to overcome these inhibitions. The process that took place has been well analyzed above all by Hans Buchheim and Helmut Krausnick in *Anatomie des SS-Staates.* [49] A full understanding of this analysis is indispensable to anyone who asks how the Germans could have committed these acts. The ultimate reasoning of national socialist ideology was this: If it is true, as history teaches us, that nations and whole cultures perish when they disregard the "natural laws" of survival of the fittest or best, of racial purity and superiority, etc., then it is indeed necessary and urgent to take decisive action to prevent this from happening to Germany; and it would be wrong to be timid in the choice of means. These natural laws or laws of history, unlike what we might here call "man-made" laws, operate necessarily and logically beyond good or evil, right or wrong. In a nation's fight for life, for the survival of the species, all ethical and legal considerations are consequently out of place and must be regarded as "suspended." As Buchheim says of true national socialist thinking, ". . . logically, the alternative of right or wrong can have only secondary importance; for in first place there is the question what the laws of history demand at any given time." [50] In fact, right or wrong might have no importance at all.

As time went on, the scope of the natural laws or laws of history appeared to become increasingly wide. It embraced not only the really important actions, such as the need to kill millions of people, but also

[49] Vol. I, pp. 332–346, 300–302, 295–297; Vol. II, pp. 285–286, 297–298. This remarkable book seems to consist largely of expert opinions previously submitted by the authors to German courts in proceedings against former National Socialists.

[50] *Anatomie des SS-Staates,* Vol. I, p. 332.

a thousand minor things, ranging from the extraction of tooth gold from live Jewish prisoners for the gold supply of the German Federal Bank[51] to simple crimes against human dignity, such as the whipping of Polish civilians as punishment. It was all beyond right or wrong. Moreover, these laws were entirely unchangeable. Someone born into an inferior race could never improve himself; a subhuman necessarily had to remain subhuman. Only the Nordic race, at least in Europe, was able to become still better, still more superior than it already was, provided it avoided racial contamination.

Under this philosophy, the individual German was to be no more than a willing tool in the application of these supreme laws; and if in applying them, he violated the man-made criminal law, he was immune from prosecution or moral blame. As Buchheim has pointed out, such a person "need not, therefore, have lost his inborn feeling for [man-made] law; he can also still be quite able to hear the voice of his conscience."[52] But all this must yield to the natural laws. Such a person could even see a "moral accomplishment" in his suppression of old ethical values and human feelings for the sake of the higher laws. He could be proud of "overcoming a private weakness in favor of the general welfare."

Looking at such attitudes from a psychological point of view, Adorno points out that "the fascist-minded personality, it seems, can manage his life only by splitting his own ego into several agencies, some of which fall in line with the official doctrine, whilst others, heirs to the old superego, protect him from mental unbalance and allow him to maintain himself as an individual."[53] Elsewhere Adorno says that "hatred [in psychological totalitarianism] is reproduced and enhanced in an almost automized, compulsive manner which is both utterly detached from the reality of the object and completely alien to the ego."[54]

The result of this process is that on one level the professional mass killers functioned as perfectly normal people. Many of them came from, and maintained, decent middle-class families and would never have done any such thing as stealing from, or killing, someone of their

[51] See Nuremberg Doc. No. 4317 of July 20, 1943; also Henkys, op. cit., p. 122.
[52] *Anatomie des SS-Staates,* Vol. I, p. 333.
[53] Adorno, *The Authoritarian Personality,* p. 735.
[54] Ibid., p. 633.

own ethnical community. Undoubtedly, they retained complete awareness of right or wrong in relation to ordinary crimes under the manmade German Criminal Code. On the level of the laws of nature, on the other hand, they regarded themselves as clearly innocent in killing and not as acting from criminal motives. On that level, they did not know that they were doing wrong—in itself a terrifying phenomenon of a totalitarian system. Albert Speer says in his memoirs that "the whole structure of the system was designed not to let conflicts of conscience even arise."[55] A *Herrenmensch* (a member of the master race) was not necessarily subject to ordinary morals. To him, something evil could even be a more noble expression of something good.

One example of this type of "normal" personality of a mass killer on one level was Adolf Eichmann. Hannah Arendt reports that, at his trial in Jerusalem, half a dozen psychiatrists certified him as normal— "more normal than I am . . . after having examined him," one of them said, while another found that "his whole psychological outlook, his attitude toward his wife and children, mother and father, . . . 'was not only normal but most desirable.'"[56] He encountered no conflict of conscience because, on the level of the laws of nature, he was doing what his conscience—the conscience of any indoctrinated national socialist—prescribed.

The "split-level" functioning of the national socialist personality became apparent particularly in 1947 during the Nuremberg trial of twenty-two commanders and subunit commanders of the *Einsatzgruppen* (special task groups),[57] and it is worthwhile to spend a little time on a closer analysis of some of these men. The *Einsatzgruppen* were units consisting of altogether about 3,000 men, mostly SS members, augmented by local auxiliaries, which were attached to and closely cooperated with the German Army. They advanced with the Army into the Soviet Union in 1941 and 1942. Under a carefully prepared plan of surprise and utter ruthlessness, these units, directly behind the front lines, ferreted out and killed whatever Jews, Communist officials, gypsies, and miscellaneous "undersirables" they could find. The total number killed is uncertain, but the best estimate is probably that of Raul Hilberg, who believes that at least 900,000 Jews

[55] Speer, *Erinnerungen*, p. 46.

[56] Arendt, *Eichmann in Jerusalem*, pp. 25–26.

[57] *Trials of War Criminals (TWC)*, Vol. IV (*United States v. Otto Ohlendorf et al.*, the so-called *Einsatzgruppen-trial*).

were murdered by these units.[58] (Hilberg deals only with Jewish victims, but the number of non-Jews was small, perhaps no more than 30,000.) The results achieved by the *Einsatzgruppen* thus were a considerable contribution to the Final Solution.

The Nuremberg Military Tribunal convicted twenty-two leaders and subleaders of these units.[59] An analysis of the background of these twenty-two mass killers reveals facts, which, if it were not for the split-level operation of the national socialist personality, would be very surprising. Nine of these men were graduates of law schools, and most of these had practiced law or had been "government lawyers." Among the others were a doctor of philosophy (who had been a university professor and dean), a Lutheran minister, an opera singer, an economist, a high school teacher, an importer, and an architect. Only three of the twenty-two lacked a university education and might be regarded as "professional partymen." Certainly, the great majority of the twenty-two were not desperados, gangster types, sex maniacs, or even professional soldiers. They were not frustrated types but had, on the whole, been successful in their respective prior pursuits. To all outward appearances, they were, by and large, respectable middle-class citizens. They probably would not have committed a "normal crime."

But they all had one thing in common: they had spent years, some of them many years, in national socialist organizations and had no doubt been heavily indoctrinated with the "laws of nature" about the need to eliminate a "subhuman" race like the Jews. (There is not even much indication in the trial record that they found this duty particularly distasteful.) When facing trial, of course, they did not base their defense on this ideology; before three American judges, this would obviously have been unwise. On the whole, they fell back on the old defense that they had merely obeyed an order of the Führer to whom, as the defendant Otto Ohlendorf put it, he had "surrendered [his] moral conscience."[60]

[58]Hilberg, *The Destruction of the European Jews*, p. 256. The decision of the Nuremberg Court repeatedly referred to "one million" killed, but failed to indicate the method of computation. See, f.i., *TWC*, Vol. IV, p. 429.

[59]For the opinion and judgment of the Court, see *TWC*, Vol. IV, pp. 411–589.

[60]*TWC*, Vol. IV, pp. 247, 305. Of course, in the case of many National Socialists, the matter of obedience to an order of a superior and their oath to the Führer played an important part, regardless of their ideological motivation. This will be discussed later.

Ohlendorf had previously been, successively, a practicing lawyer, political scientist, and section chief of two scientific institutes. He had been a member of the Party and the SS for about fifteen years. As commander of an *Einsatzgruppe*, he ordered and supervised the killing of from 70,000 to 90,000 men, women, and children.[61] What is significant about him is not only that his previous civilian pursuit had been eminently respectable but also that in 1943, when his job with the *Einsatzgruppe* came to an end, he had no difficulty in resuming an equally respectable civilian career. He became a *Ministerialdirektor* and *Staatssekretär* in the Ministry of Economy.[62]

Another interesting member of the *Einsatzgruppen* was Ernst Biberstein. He was commander of a subunit and as such killed far fewer people than Ohlendorf—only about 2,000 or 3,000. He had been a member of the Party since 1926 and of the SS since 1936.[63] Prior to his *Einsatzgruppen* post, he had been a Protestant minister for eleven years and a theological expert for the government for five years. But then he joined the Security Police and Gestapo. He did give some indication of his ideological indoctrination at the trial. When he was asked why, as a former minister, he did not offer religious comfort to those about to be killed in his presence, he said that he could not cast "pearls before swine"[64] (mostly Jews). Evidently, his acceptance of the national socialist theory of the subhuman races and of the necessity to eliminate them was so complete that, in this situation, it outweighed not only all considerations of man-made law but also his theological indoctrination and every vestige of Christian compassion. He, like Ohlendorf, was sentenced to death at Nuremberg, but his sentence was commuted to life, and, surprisingly, he was released not long thereafter.[65]

Typical, also, was an answer which Rudolf Höss, the commander of the Auschwitz extermination camp, gave to the American prison psychologist G. M. Gilbert. When asked whether he had been convinced of the guilt of the murdered Jews, Höss said that "there was

[61] Ohlendorf testimony, *TWC*, Vol. IV, pp. 255–256.
[62] Ohlendorf affidavit of Mar. 4, 1947, Doc. NO-2409.
[63] Biberstein depositions of June 29, 1947, Doc. NO-4997.
[64] Biberstein's testimony is in *TWC*, Vol. IV, pp. 209–211, 542–545.
[65] Henkys, op. cit., p. 253; Hilberg, op. cit., p. 704. In this as in many other cases of convicted national socialists the commutation of sentences and their early total release remain a puzzle.

something unrealistic about such questions" and that "he never gave much thought to it." [66] From Höss's point of view, the question was indeed unrealistic, because the law of nature that called for the extermination of the Jews was fundamentally not predicated on their being guilty of anything. Being Jewish was enough for the applicability of the law. Höss and Gilbert were thus operating on different levels. Incidentally, throughout his remarkable book, *Kommandant in Auschwitz*, Höss repeats that he, too, had a heart and felt great pity for the Jewish children and their mothers. (The strange fact is that this was probably true.) Höss says that he overcame such inhibitions by telling himself that they "came close to being treason against the Führer." [67]

And, indeed, pity of this sort, any humanitarian instincts, were what the regime was most careful to guard against among its servants, presumably as an essential device to prevent the two levels from merging. A motto of the SS guards in the concentration and extermination camps was "Pity is Weakness!" [68] Himmler, more than anyone else, repeated over and over the theme of the absolute need to overcome humanitarian instincts, and in doing so, he sometimes mentioned the difficulties which this imposed on the executioners:

> I can tell you, it is ugly and awful for a German man to be forced to watch . . . [a mass execution]. This it is, and if it were not ugly and awful for us, then we would not be German men and would not be Germanic [*Germanen*] anymore. As ugly as this is, it has been necessary — and will in many cases continue to be — to carry this out. . . . It will always have to be true that such an execution is most difficult for our men. And yet, it must also be true that they will never be soft, but will grit their teeth and do it.
>
> It is in many cases a great deal easier for a company of soldiers to go into battle than it is . . . to suppress a disobedient population of culturally low level in some territory and to carry out executions, to transport people to other territories, to send crying and sobbing women away. . . . What is often much more difficult — believe me — is this quiet duty to act, this quiet activity, *this guard duty for the ideology* [*Weltanschauung*], this being

[66] G. M. Gilbert, *Nuremberg Diary*, pp. 259-260.

[67] Höss, *Kommandant in Auschwitz*, Stuttgart, 1958, p. 129.

[68] *Der Auschwitz-Prozess — Eine Dokumentation*, Vienna, 1965, Vol. I, p. 466.

forced to be consistent, to make no compromises—that is often much, much more difficult. (Italics added.) [69]

At the same time, Himmler expressed a great deal of pride in the ability of his men to suppress their humane instincts:

Most of you [SS leaders] will know what it means when 100 corpses [of executed persons] lie there, when 500 lie there or when 1,000 lie there. To have remained unrelenting and—apart from exceptions of human weakness—to have remained decent, that has steeled us. This is a glorious page in the book of our history which has never been written and is never to be written. . . ." [70]

Another high SS official, Reinhard Heydrich, said this as early as 1935:

To maintain our nation [*Volk*] we have to be harsh toward our enemy, even at the risk of hurting some enemy. . . . If we, as National Socialists, do not fulfill our task in history because we were too objective and too humane, we shall nevertheless not be credited with mitigating circumstances. We will simply be told: they did not fulfill their task in history. [71]

Of course, there were occasions when even hardened national socialists showed some awareness of the dichotomy between the two levels on which they operated, and when the conventional level of man-made laws and of ethics encroached upon the new level of the laws of nature and history. Thus, Hans Frank, the so-called "butcher of the Poles"—a rather insecure and ambivalent personality, in any event—confessed to the American prison psychologist Dr. G. M. Gilbert that he had felt sometimes as though he were "two people":

"Me, myself, Frank here—and the other Frank, the Nazi leader. And sometimes I wonder how that man Frank could have done

[69] Himmler's speech to SS officers of Sept. 7, 1940, *TMWC*, Vol. XXIX, pp. 104–105, Doc. 1918-PS. See also *Mein Kampf*, pp. 195–196.

[70] Speech by Himmler to SS leaders in Posen on Oct. 4, 1943, *TMWC*, Vol. XXIX, p. 145, Doc. 1919-PS.

[71] Heydrich, *Wandlungen unseres Kampfes*, quoted in Buchheim et al., *Anatomie des SS-Staates*, Vol. I, p. 333.

those things. This Frank looks at the other Frank and says, Hmm, what a louse you are Frank!—How could you do such things?—You certainly let your emotions run away with you, didn't you? . . . Just as if I were two different people. . . ."[72]

Dr. Gilbert's comment on this in his Diary was: "Very fascinating in a schizoid sort of way."

The Auschwitz commander Rudolf Höss reported humanitarian doubts and reactions of pity not only by himself but also by various SS men in the camp who confidentially asked him "again and again: 'Is it necessary that we exterminate hundreds of thousands of women and children?'"[73] But most or all of them seem to have succeeded in overcoming their doubts and in avoiding a significant merger of the two levels.

All in all, the picture that emerges of the average mass killer in the middle and lower echelons is that of a man from the respectable middle classes, reasonably well educated, quite decent, moral, and law-abiding in his personal life, a good family man, but thoroughly indoctrinated with national socialist ideology, able upon command to suspend all considerations of normal law and ethics, systematically hardened against any feelings of pity for the "inferior races," and totally loyal and dedicated to the regime. It was primarily in the racial sphere that his basic values had been revalued or perverted and that a fictional world of new values had been created for him, in part to hide the perversion. He could spend the day killing thousands of helpless people and (as a character witness in a German court trial testified) could still be "a man with a sense for everything good and beautiful" who in the evening reads to his family from Adalbert Stifter's *Indian Summer,*[74] or he could be an SS officer "who, after a hard day's work at the gas chambers, relaxes by playing the violin."[75] He was a *gut bürgerlicher* (respectable middle class) killer. The retention of normal decency by this average mass killer is perhaps the most frightening aspect of this construction of a personality by a totalitarian regime. This may essentially be what Hannah Arendt meant by "the banality

[72] Gilbert, op. cit., p. 116.
[73] Höss, op. cit., p. 127.
[74] Reported in Gerald Reitlinger, *Die Endlösung*, p. 244.
[75] Ralf Dahrendorf, *Gesellschaft und Demokratie in Deutschland*, p. 394.

of evil" which she saw in Eichmann.[76] In a limited sense, not only the murdered masses but even the murderers themselves became the victims of totalitarian society.

It should be remembered, in this connection, that no voices from outside of Germany, which might have reawakened a normal awareness of right and wrong, were able effectively to penetrate through the wall of censorship around Germany. Apart from some news broadcasts by the British Broadcasting Company, which hardly dealt with such problems in any event, the average person had no access to evaluations of the events by anyone other than German propaganda organizations. A very tight censorship, supported by terror, may be one of the most pernicious aspects of totalitarian regimes.

One regrettable result of the whole situation was that much later, when some of the mass killers were finally tried in the German courts long after the war, they were given astonishingly low sentences,[77] on the basis of the entirely conventional judicial reasoning that by then the defendants had for some years led a very respectable life, had become decent successful businessmen and were good family men. The courts, it seems, never understood that these estimable qualities had always coexisted with the worst, and that conventional standards of law and morality lose their meaning in a totalitarian society.

The national socialist creation of a kind of fictional world of perverted values, based on "laws of nature," did not, of course, exclude the possibility that additional nonideological inducements stimulated the participation of many individual Germans in the mistreatment and killing of their victims. In some cases, there may have been no more than a thin ideological coating superimposed on all kinds of other motivations. Higher pay, liquor rations, and frequent leave periods were offered to members of execution details. Also, inertia, primitive lust for power, or fear of superiors played a part. And finally, there were certainly sexual aspects involved in the torturing and killing. A high national socialist official in occupied Soviet territory complained to an SS leader that his "men got themselves sexually excited during these executions."[78] Unspeakable cruelties, sexual in nature,

[76]Arendt, *Eichmann in Jerusalem*, pp. 252, 287-288. Bettelheim, in *Die Kontroverse*, Munich, 1964, pp. 93-94, 97, seems to interpret the phrase differently.

[77]See the enumeration in Henkys, op. cit., pp. 346-350.

[78]Nuremberg Doc. NO. 4317 of July 20, 1943.

were reported by a witness in the German Auschwitz trial, so frightful that it is hard even to read about them. [79]

But the national socialist regime did not really want such "excesses," as they were called, and while the regime was willing to close its eyes to a great many of them, it did make an effort to suppress them. What was desired was motivation by "pure ideology," even "idealism," an awareness of the laws of nature, and the historical necessity to do away with the inferior races. But the ideology of National Socialism was, of course, no less responsible for the excesses than it was for authorized killings. It had deliberately created a general climate of contempt, hatred, and violence against millions of "inferior" people whom countless publications, speeches, and orders denounced day in and day out as animals, bacteria, vermin, or the like. It was a climate in which the lowest forms of sexual and other base instincts found it easy to prosper. Not everyone, moreover, could be expected to have a clear understanding of the extent to which it was proper to suspend his awareness of right or wrong and the extent to which that awareness still had to remain in operation.

Considering the enormous, overriding importance which the concepts of the master race, inferior races, and subhumans had in national socialist ideology, it is astonishing how little systematic, not to speak of scientific, effort was made to define what these terms were to mean and who was to be covered by them. (But Hitler did not hesitate to proclaim that "National Socialism is a sober doctrine— based on realities—of the most exact scientific knowledge and of its thoughtful formulation." [80]) Millions of people died because they were stamped inferior or subhuman without any serious attempt to determine what they really were. The only important exception to this general state of vagueness were the Jews. There were definite laws defining Jews, half-Jews, and quarter-Jews, and the selection for extermination presented no fundamental problem. (It is true, however, that even these laws ran into certain temporary difficulties in connection with the massacres of minor population groups in Lithuania and the Crimea. [81])

[79] Hermann Langbein (ed.), *Der Auschwitz-Prozess—Eine Dokumentation*, Vol. I, p. 466. See also Henkys, op. cit., p. 219, and Arendt, *Origins*, p. 454, fn. 159.

[80] Speech of Sept. 6, 1938, in Max Domarus, *Hitler Reden und Proklamationen 1932–1945*, p. 893.

[81] See Hilberg, *The Destruction of the European Jews*, p. 241.

Generally, the concept of race, as used in the practical application of national socialist ideology, lacked nearly every scientific meaning. It could hardly even be called "pseudoscientific." To quite some extent, it related back to myths of the distant Germanic past and to sentimental popular fiction. The life or death of millions of people depended on nebulous ideas conceived in this fashion. All this is in line with Adorno's findings in his investigations in the United States that ". . . the prejudiced individual is prepared to reject groups with which he has never had contact. . . ."[82]

It should be emphasized, however, that the very vagueness of the race concepts enabled the regime to use them as a political tool in the manipulation of the German people and in leading them into aggressive action against other races. Whoever was to be the next political victim could officially be declared to be racially inferior, first the Czechs, then the Poles, then the Russians. The highly efficient propaganda machine saw to it that the average German, as a member of the master race, felt called upon to assert himself against the "racially inferior," whether they were mere undesirable local groups or ethnic minorities or whole nations. And in case some Germans doubted the objectionable character of any particular racial group, it was usually possible to contend that in back of that group there stood "international Jewry," the worst enemy of all. Thus, while the racial theories were a genuine component of national socialist ideological thinking, their practical application could often become a matter of political expediency, and they lent themselves well to this purpose.

The concept of the master race itself, in spite of its vast practical importance, was likewise never defined in any scientific sense but rested largely on sentiment, conviction, convention, narcissism, and the like. And naturally, that concept would hardly have withstood any sober scholarly examination. (One thing, incidentally, that does not, at any time, seem to have occurred to Hitler, Himmler, and any of the other national socialist leaders is that a genuine master race — if there be such — would be politically astute enough not to speak of itself as a master race.) As a practical matter, any "Aryan" German and Austrian seemed to be regarded as included in the master race, and in this connection little attention was paid to the fact that, as a

[82] Adorno, *The Authoritarian Personality*, p. 149.

race, the Germans and even more so the Austrians could surely not be considered pure, but were greatly "contaminated"—to use a national socialist term—by an admixture of Slavs and Celts. [83] Hitler himself, as a matter of fact, seems to have been opposed to the concept of a *German* race. In a decree of August 9, 1941, he prohibited the further use of this term because it would lead to the "sacrifice of the racial idea as such in favor of a mere nationality principle." [84] But the concept of the master race, as distinguished from the German race, was never abandoned. It was entirely basic to national socialist ideology. Presumably, the Germans (plus Austrians) could be a master race, even if they did not constitute a pure Germanic race. It is entirely possible, however, that if the Swedes or the Dutch or other "Nordics" had volunteered their cooperation, Hitler would have welcomed them into the master race with open arms.

"We are a master race which must remember that the lowest German worker is racially and biologically a thousand times more valuable than the population here," [85] said Erich Koch, Reich-Commissioner for the Ukraine, in a speech in Kiev on March 5, 1943. And according to Hitler "[in the Eastern territories] a new type of man will . . . come forth, real masters whom, of course, we cannot put to use in the West: viceroys." [86] The viceroy idea was probably derived by Hitler from the British rule over India, which never ceased fascinating him because he regarded India as an example of a country where a population of 300 million was successfully being ruled and exploited by 60,000 members of the British master race. [87] The entire German policy in occupied Poland and the Soviet Union was determined from the point of view of the relationship of the master race to potentially rebellious slaves; and it resulted in a regime of unpre-

---

[83] Hitler in private indicated some awareness of German racial contamination. Thus, in his *Table Talks* (p. 256) he said that "Our strength vis-à-vis, for example, the United States, which has only a slightly larger population [sic], is that our Germanic racial nucleus is considerably larger, because it comprises four-fifths Germanic people" (indirect speech transposed). The figure four-fifths was, no doubt, arbitrarily selected. Incidentally, in earlier years Hitler appears to have held a much more favorable opinion of the relative American "racial value." See *Hitlers Zweites Buch*, pp. 124–125.

[84] *Verfügungen, Anordnungen, Bekanntgaben*, cited by Hannah Arendt, *Origins*, p. 412, fn. 68.

[85] Nuremberg Doc. 1130-PS.

[86] *Hitler's Table Talks*, p. 137.

[87] Ibid., particularly, p. 239; also pp. 143, 190, 218–219.

cedented cruelty, terror, and neglect. Millions were starved to death or executed for minor infractions; millions of others were deported to Germany as slave labor under wretched conditions.[88] In the early days of the Russian war, the Germans, including the German Army, permitted from three to four million Soviet prisoners of war to die from starvation, lack of shelter, and disease.[89] Of this disaster, Himmler, in 1943, had no more than this to say: "Tens of thousands, hundreds of thousands of prisoners [actually far more] died from exhaustion, from hunger — something that in the final analysis, in terms of generations, is not to be regretted [*schade*], but which is regrettable [*bedauerlich*] today because of the loss of the labor force."[90]

The policy of utter ruthlessness of the occupation regime naturally resulted in deep hostility, even on the part of those groups of the native population who might otherwise have had some inclination to cooperate or to acquiesce in it, at least for the duration of the war. No one is willing to be stamped subhuman under the terror regime of a self-proclaimed master race. The native hostility immeasurably increased the difficulties of the occupation regime. Moreover, the mistreatment of the Soviet prisoners of war, which soon became known in the Soviet Army, greatly increased the determination of its soldiers never to surrender under any circumstances. More farsighted National Socialists, such as Alfred Rosenberg and even Joseph Goebbels, recognized these disadvantages and dangers, but their objections were useless. To Hitler, Himmler, and countless other national socialist leaders, the importance of asserting themselves as the master race and other ideological racial considerations had unquestioned priority. It was one of many instances in national socialist rule in which ideology took precedence over political and military expediency.

To Hitler, politics meant almost nothing but the domination of others, and this included a conscious effort to let the others know that they were being dominated. This was part of his sadomasochistic character structure, which we shall discuss later. At least, this was

---

[88]Broszat, *Nationalsozialistische Polenpolitik*, pp. 46-49, 93-111; Bullock, *Hitler*, pp. 695-696; Henkys, op. cit., pp. 74-85; Dallin, *German Rule in Russia, 1941-1945*, pp. 428-453.

[89]Dallin, op. cit., p. 427.

[90]*TMWC*, Vol. XXIX, Doc. 1919-PS, p. 112.

the attitude as between the master race and races which, in its view, were subhuman, like the Poles and Russians. German policy in occupied France, Holland, Belgium, Denmark and Norway was very different.

The master race concept was deeply embarrassing to millions of educated Germans, whether they were living within Germany or abroad. The claim of being a master race seemed particularly grotesque when it came, as it did, from numerous national socialist leaders with limited education and from a low social level, sons of small provincial public officials, minor school teachers, shopkeepers, and the like. Even in appearance, they frequently did not meet the purely physical criteria that they themselves had established for their master race. Many of them were not blue-eyed and blond. The fact that Hitler himself was far from showing Nordic physical characteristics presented its problems. The periodical *Die Sonne* found it necessary to assure its readers that he *was* blue-eyed and blond.[91] Anyone who has traveled in Germany is well aware that, while there are a good many "Nordic" types among the population, millions of others are far removed from that ideal and, on the contrary, are small, stocky, obese men and women, many with heavy necks and crude facial features. The master race claim is seriously discredited by a glance at the picture of monstrous female German guards at the Bergen-Belsen concentration camp, reproduced in Wolfgang Scheffler, *Judenverfolgung im Dritten Reich.*[92]

Himmler, the master enslaver and executioner, himself by no means a Nordic type, made countless references in speeches and writings to the value of Nordic or Germanic blood. Thus, on September 7, 1940, in a speech to a group of SS officers he said: "[I want to] create an [SS] Order which will disseminate this idea of the Nordic blood, so that we will draw all Nordic blood in the world to us, make it a part of us, so that Nordic blood, Germanic blood will never again . . . fight against us to any significant extent. We must take it for ourselves—and the others may not have any. . . ."[93] In France, Himmler wanted to undertake "fishing expeditions" for this "blood" once a year, and Hitler seemed to agree.[94] "Germanic blood," and

[91] Mosse, *Crisis,* p. 106.
[92] Opposite p. 97.
[93] *TMWC,* Vol. XXIX, Doc. 1918-PS, p. 109.
[94] *Hitler's Table Talks,* p. 253.

all it stood for, was indeed a precious commodity in national socialist ideology. The criteria for determining the presence of this blood were purely physical. Anyone with blue eyes and blond hair seemed to have it, unless, of course, he was a Jew. In the occupied Soviet Union, Himmler once attended the execution of a group of a hundred people. In that group, he noticed a blue-eyed blond young man, and this indication of Germanic blood, about to be lost, seems to have disturbed him. There was this dialogue:[95]

> Are you a Jew?
> Yes.
> Are both of your parents Jews?
> Yes.
> Do you have any ancestors who were not Jews?
> No.
> Then I can't help you.

The process of determining the proper blood was carried to great lengths. Hitler even declared Jesus to have been an Aryan,[96] and in this, indeed, he merely repeated what Chamberlain had previously proclaimed.[97] Some have called all this "the cult of the blood." And there were Germans in those days—even people of more than average intelligence—who naïvely transferred the abstract racial blood concept to the sphere of the purely physiological function of human blood. Thus, during the war, the High Command of the Armed Forces (OKW) issued the following order: "For reasons of racial hygiene, it is undesirable to use prisoners of war as blood donors for members of the German folk community, because we cannot be sure that no men of mixed Jewish blood among the prisoners would be used for blood donations."[98]

[95]Report by SS leader Erich von dem Bach-Zelewski in *Aufbau* (New York) of Aug. 23, 1946, p. 2.

[96]*Hitler's Table Talks*, p. 154.

[97]*Grundlagen*, pp. 254–256. An important German social Darwinist, Ernst Haeckel, had proclaimed Jesus to have been only half-Jewish, because his father allegedly was a Roman officer who had seduced Mary. (D. Gasman, *The Scientific Origins of National Socialism*, p. 157). No one seems to have argued that Jesus might have been only half-Jewish under the doctrine of immaculate conception.

[98]*OKW Befehlssammlung* No. 15 of Aug. 10, 1942, in Bundesarchiv/Militärarchiv, Freiburg, File III W 170.

The national socialist concept of "racial hygiene" represented a further logical step since, as we have seen, the purity of the German race was considered essential to the preservation of the species and its development. National Socialism began, but never finished, a giant program of organizing a new biologically determined European community by exterminating racially inferior elements and groups regarded as dangerous, by Germanizing or Nordicizing *(Aufnordung)* inferior but salvageable races, by sterilizing other groups, resettling undesirable elements in remote areas, and similar methods. All these actions were not really punitive in nature, and they were not war actions; but they were rather part of the entire European-wide scheme of racial hygiene.

It was a kind of cattle breeding program on an enormous scale. For the improvement of the race, Himmler wanted the SS men to be the breeding bulls: "It must be a matter of course that the most copious breeding should be by this [SS] Order, by this racial elite of the Germanic people. In 20 to 30 years we must really be able to furnish the whole of Europe with its leading class."[99] And Hitler said: "I am firmly determined to station racially valuable military units, such as formations of the *Waffen-SS*, in all areas where the present population is [racially] bad, so as to have them take care of a freshening-up of the blood [*Auffrischung des Blutes*]."[100]

Hitler's own sex life, as we shall see later, seems to have been quite abnormal; and perhaps as a result of this, he appeared to have a naïve belief that, as in the case of bulls and cows, the mere temporary placing of men in the same locality with women would quickly and inevitably result in sexual intercourse and children.[101] He advocated "the conscious breeding of a new human being" and, looking at young German children, he exclaimed enthusiastically that they all looked "as if they had emerged from a single egg." "*We* regulate the relations between the sexes; *we* form the child," he said.[102]

But as far as the main "breeding ground" for the Germanic blood was concerned, this was to be in the occupied Eastern territories

[99] Himmler's speech to SS leaders on Oct. 4, 1943, *TMWC*, Vol. XXIX, p. 171, Doc. 1919-PS.
[100] *Hitler's Table Talks*, p. 334.
[101] See also *Hitler's Table Talks*, pp. 288, 463.
[102] Domarus, *Hitler Reden*, pp. 717, 724, 762.

which were to be annexed for German settlers. Thus, Himmler said: "What is unalterable is that we shall fill that area [the East] with settlers, that we shall establish a nursery garden of Germanic blood there in the East."[103] Hitler was particularly anxious not to enrich other nations with precious Germanic blood: "Above all, we have to see to it that Germans don't intermarry with Poles and thereby introduce new Germanic blood into the Polish leadership level. . . . Incidentally, we have to be just as careful with the Czechs as with the Poles. . . ."[104]

On the other hand, in matters of racial selection, Hitler had great admiration for the British: "England has wonderful human selection in its upper classes. But the lower classes are trash [*Dreck*] . . . . But in the English upper class—even in the tough, wiry, although unattractive, English women of that class—we can see the selection of a thousand years."[105]

Compared with his extremely high regard for the breeding of purely physical racial characteristics, Hitler paid little attention to a possible "breeding" of the human mind. He seemed to think that the development of good minds was not so much a matter of breeding as of the survival of the fittest: "The hard struggle for life, above all, . . . will by itself take care of the selection of those [gifted] minds. Many will break and perish, and thus will not prove destined for the highest, and only a few will ultimately appear chosen."[106] In later years, Hitler acquired, at any rate, a great deal of contempt for the "German professor":

A dwarf with nothing but learning fears strength. Instead of telling himself that a healthy body must be the basis of his learning, he rejects strength. Nature adapts itself to habits, and if the world were put in charge of the German professors for a few hundred years, only cretins would be wandering around here after a million years: giant heads on minute bodies.[107]

[103] Himmler's speech of Aug. 3, 1944, quoted by Bracher, *Die deutsche Diktatur*, p. 448.
[104] *Hitler's Table Talks*, p. 256.
[105] Ibid., p. 244.
[106] *Mein Kampf*, p. 497.
[107] *Hitler's Table Talks*, p. 179.

For a few years the national socialist regime made Europe, and particularly "the East," into an enormous laboratory of racial policies; and all ideas of changing the racial composition were pursued with deadly seriousness—"deadly" often in an entirely literal sense. Much of the frantic police and administrative activity in Germany and in the occupied areas was dominated by these considerations. Large population groups were moved around, resettled, given land, deprived of land, given food, put on starvation rations, placed in ghettos, decimated or totally exterminated, merely because someone felt that considerations of racial policy required this. There was not the slightest scientific investigation of the need for, or advisability of, all these radical measures, which not only affected or destroyed the lives of millions of people, but hampered the German war effort, cost vast amounts of money and ruined German relations with the people of the occupied territories. There was simply an unshakable belief in the existence of an immutable law of nature that called for these actions. It was accepted as a fundamental law of the exact sciences, like the law of gravity. Nothing could be more wrong, therefore, than to say, as the historian Friedrich Meinecke did, that in Hitler's case the "glorification and enthronement of his own race . . . was in the nature . . . of an immensely effective instrument of power which can be dropped when a still more effective instrument is found or when it no longer seems opportune to use it."[108] It was much more than that. It was a central, firmly held tenet of national socialist ideology, never to be abandoned, though it was, to be sure, at the same time an "immensely effective instrument of power."

Generally speaking, there was no room in national socialist ideology for the recognition that human civilization could fundamentally change that immutable law of nature and that thinking, morally directed human beings, unlike animals, might succeed in overcoming the crude natural process of selection and survival. Hitler's belief in this law does not, for example, seem to have been affected by the fact that Houston Stewart Chamberlain, one of the important ancestors of his ideology, was ill his entire adult life and that his survival, enabling him to write his books, was due to the medical achievements

[108]Meinecke, *Die deutsche Katastrophe*, p. 91.

of civilization and was incompatible with principles of the survival of the fittest. The same could be said of Darwin himself, who was also ill most of his life; but Hitler, who never mentioned Darwin's name, was probably unaware of this fact. In *Mein Kampf*, Hitler characterized as "typically Jewish in its effrontery . . . and stupid" the contention that "man simply overcomes nature,"[109] and elsewhere he described as "mortally dangerous" the alleged claim of the Jews that they can "play a trick on nature, to make a hard inexorable struggle for existence unnecessary."[110] In his speech to army officer candidates of June 22, 1944, he said that "a creature on this Earth, like man, cannot escape from a [natural] law which applies also to all other creatures. . . ."[111] To a considerable extent, these views were an essential part of Hitler's masochism. This will be discussed in detail later.

But certain doubts did, at times, occur to him as to the wastefulness of war, which he normally regarded as a process of natural human selection. Near the end of the war, for example, he told General Guderian, as mentioned before, that "Those remaining alive after the battle are the inferior ones . . . because the good ones have been killed."[112] And much earlier, in his *Second Book* (unpublished during his lifetime), he went so far as to say that "the nature of war implies . . . a racial selection within a people, which favors the destruction of the best elements" and that wars lead "to the slow bleeding to death of the best and most valuable elements of a people," but he reserved to himself the decision: "one may only sometimes let men die so that a people may live."[113] He was, however, under sad illusions as to the number of German men (and women and children) whom he would ultimately let die. As late as January 28, 1942, he said that "If this war costs us a quarter of a million dead and 100,000 cripples, they will be given back to us by the excess of births over deaths. . . ."[114] Actually, it has been estimated that in the end approximately 2.15 million

[109] *Mein Kampf*, p. 314; see also p. 267.

[110] Ibid., p. 149.

[111] Quoted in Buchheim et al., *Anatomie des SS-Staates*, Vol. I, p. 299. These statements by Hitler closely followed pronouncements by the social Darwinist Ernst Haeckel. See D. Gasman, *The Scientific Origins of National Socialism*, pp. 34, 163.

[112] Quoted in Hofer, *Der Nationalsozialismus*, p. 260.

[113] *Hitlers Zweites Buch*, pp. 49, 52.

[114] *Hitler's Table Talks*, p. 172.

of the German Armed Forces were killed and that a total of about 6 million soldiers and civilians died.[115]

At any rate, the wastefulness of war gave Hitler concern solely with respect to *German* lives. Those of other nations presented no problem to him. Here, in the conflict between Germans and other nations, "natural selection" had full swing. Hitler, on the whole, took a strangely primitive view of modern war: ideologically, it seems to have been to him something like a fight between medieval knights in which the stronger, better fighter is bound to win. He might have changed his ideas had he lived to experience nuclear bombs, which do no natural selecting.

It is possible that the frequent efforts by national socialists to liken their enemies to animals represented an attempt, conscious or unconscious, to counter any possible suggestion that civilization might have overcome that much-touted unchangeable law of nature when it came to humans. Hitler spoke of Russian soldiers as "beasts,"[116] and he called the Jews a "pack of rats"[117] and "wild animals."[118] Himmler said that Poles and Russians were "human animals" *(Menschentiere)*[119] and "unrestrained beasts."[120] On one occasion, he used this picturesque language: "Don't bedbugs, rats, and other vermin have to fulfill a purpose in life, too? And yet, don't human beings have the right to defend themselves against this vermin . . .?"[121] Goebbels called the Russians a "conglomeration of animals."[122] (Even the Rumanian peasants, allies of the Germans, were described as "miserable piece[s] of cattle."[123]) And if some of these humans were not animals, then they were subhumans *(Untermenschen)*, and these, in fact, were sometimes described as even lower than animals. The SS Main Office had this to say about them:

The subhuman—that creation of nature, which biologically is

[115] Ibid., footnote by Schramm.
[116] Proclamation to the soldiers of Oct. 2, 1941, Domarus, op. cit., p. 1756.
[117] *Mein Kampf*, p. 331.
[118] Quoted in Buchheim et al., op. cit., Vol. II, p. 325.
[119] *TMWC*, Vol. XXIX, Doc. 1919-PS, p. 122.
[120] Ibid., p. 121.
[121] Himmler as quoted by SS leader Erich von dem Bach-Zelewski, *Aufbau* (New York), Aug. 23, 1946, p. 2.
[122] *Diaries*, p. 206.
[123] *Hitler's Table Talks*, p. 183.

seemingly quite identical with the human, with hands, feet, and a kind of brain, with eyes and a mouth—is nevertheless a totally different and horrible creature, is merely an attempt at being man—but mentally and emotionally *on a far lower level than any animal.* In the inner life of that person there is a cruel chaos of wild uninhibited passions: a nameless urge to destroy, the most primitive lust, undisguised baseness. . . .

But the subhuman lived, too. . . . He associated with his own kind. The beast called the beast . . . .

And this underworld of subhumans found its leader: the eternal Jew![124] (Italics added.)

Even the Germans themselves were sometimes equated with animals, but then mostly animals of a more impressive kind than rats and vermin. If Hermann Rauschning can be believed, Hitler strongly proposed this for German youth:

I want violent, imperious, fearless, cruel young people. . . . The free, magnificent beast of prey must once again flash from their eyes. . . . I want youth strong and beautiful. . ., and athletic youth. . . . In this way I shall blot out thousands of years of human domestication, I shall have the pure, noble stuff of nature. . . .[125]

But, more than anything else, the equating of man and animal may have been a propagandistic device, a tool of persuasion, and, in any case, it represented an effort to justify the ruthless treatment of the enemy.

[124] The full text is quoted in Hofer, op. cit., pp. 280-281.

[125] Rauschning, *Gespräche mit Hitler,* p. 237. Rauschning is cited here with some hesitation because his quotations of Hitler's statements often contain obvious embellishments, and, in reliability as source material, they cannot compare with *Hitler's Table Talks.*

Chapter 3

The Lebensraum Doctrine

A. The Origins and Hitler's Reasoning

In simple terms, the Lebensraum doctrine meant that the Germans needed more living space in order to develop or merely to survive. For decades even before Hitler, the doctrine had, however, acquired considerable emotional content. Erik H. Erikson says quite correctly that "the non-German does not realize that in Germany these words carried a conviction far beyond that of ordinary logic."[1] The origins of the doctrine are not as easily or definitely traceable as those of the race theories, although the Lebensraum doctrine is a good deal younger.

Suggestions of Lebensraum ideas, it is true, are already contained in the writings of the German poet and patriot Ernst Moritz Arndt (1769-1860); but the term "Lebensraum" itself, in its later geopolitical meaning, was perhaps first used in 1901 in a book then published under this title by the German geographer and geopolitician Friedrich Ratzel. (A selection from Ratzel's writings was republished in 1940 by the German geopolitician Karl Haushofer with the statement that Ratzel's teachings had been made popular by Hitler's speeches.[2]) At any rate, by the time of World War I, there existed an abundance of variants of Lebensraum theories, which could support the imperialistic German war aims of that period. But perhaps the most important ancestor of what was to become Hitler's doctrine was the British geopolitician Sir Halford John MacKinder (1861-1947), who propounded the concept of a "Eurasian heartland," which he saw as central to

[1]Erikson, *Childhood and Society*, p. 345.

[2]Ratzel, *Erdenmacht und Volkerschicksal*, Introduction by K. Haushofer, 1940, p. X.

63

world domination.[3] He had much influence on the above-mentioned
Karl Haushofer, who, in turn, was a friend of Hitler's loyal vassal Rudolf Hess. In fact, Haushofer dedicated his book *Weltpolitik von heute*
(1934) to Hess. It is likely, at any rate, that Hitler was briefed in the
theory by Haushofer himself (then professor of geopolitics at the
University of Munich), who at times visited Hitler and Hess at the
fortress-prison in Landsberg[4] where Hitler wrote parts of *Mein
Kampf.*

Hitler himself imbued the Lebensraum doctrine with considerable
pseudosocial-Darwinistic flavoring. He stated it most concisely in his
so-called *Second Book* (1928):

Uncounted are the species of all living beings on earth; unlimited
in each one is his drive to survive and the urge to procreate, but
limited is the space in which this whole process of life unrolls. . . .
It is this limitation of the Lebensraum which forces us into the
fight for life but, on the other hand, the fight for life is the basis
for higher development.[5]

Much later, he stated his doctrine a little more in detail in his
Table Talks:

Each people appears on earth with the task to procreate and
each people is restricted in doing so by the limitations of the
Lebensraum. Here is the eternal conflict: If the population is to
grow — which is what Nature orders and what Providence wants
— then the Lebensraum must grow with the population. If the
Lebensraum is not enlarged, then some day there must be disproportion between the population figure that continues to grow
and the Lebensraum that remains static. That is Nature's intention: it is its way to force man to fight, like any other creature
on earth. It is the fight for food, the fight for the basis of life. . . .[6]

Also in the *Table Talks* Hitler said:

According to an eternal law of Nature, the right to the land
belongs to the one who conquers the land because the old bound-

[3]Mackinder, *Democratic Ideals and Reality,* 1904.
[4]Werner Maser, *Hitlers Mein Kampf,* p. 152.
[5]*Hitlers Zweites Buch,* p. 47.
[6]*Hitler's Table Talks,* p. 497.

aries did not yield sufficient space for the growth of the population. The fact that we have children who want to live justifies our claim to the newly gained space in the East [*Ostraum*].[7]

Thus, as usual, Hitler had found a "law of Nature" which could justify, indeed demand, invasions and wars, and it became of fundamental importance. (Years earlier, in *Mein Kampf,* he had still spoken of a mere "moral right [of the Germans] to conquer foreign soil."[8]) The correlation of the doctrine to social-Darwinistic and racial principles was clear, and sometimes Hitler tried to make it even clearer. Thus, in the so-called "Hossbach-Memorandum" (the minutes of a secret meeting between Hitler and five top generals and officials on November 10, 1937) he was reported to have explained that

. . . the German population consists of 85 million people who, in terms of numbers and their self-contained settlement area in Europe, represent a racial nucleus which is firmly integrated within itself to an extent not found in any other country, and which implies . . . the right to a larger Lebensraum—more so than in the case of other nations. The fact that politically nothing had so far been accomplished in relation to the Lebensraum corresponding to the German racial nucleus is the result of a historical development of several hundred years, and a continuation of this condition would be the greatest danger to the preservation of the German *Volkstum* on its present high level. . . . the German people, with their strong racial nucleus, will find the most favorable conditions [for gaining more Lebensraum] within the continent of Europe.[9]

Apart from the natural-law aspects of the Lebensraum theory, Hitler did cite two rational reasons for the need of more land. One was that the agricultural possibilities of the small German land area were so poor that the steadily increasing population would ultimately be exposed to starvation.[10] In this, he closed his eyes to the fact that

[7]Ibid., p. 172.

[8]*Mein Kampf*, p. 1 (italics added). See also pp. 146–147.

[9](Indirect speech transposed.) The full text of the "Hossbach-Memorandum" is in Hofer, *Der Nationalsozialismus: Dokumente,* pp. 193–196. Colonel Hossbach's transcript sounds rather awkward and may not be wholly accurate.

[10]*Mein Kampf*, p. 728; *Hitlers Zweites Buch* p. 120; "Hossbach-Memorandum" in Hofer, op. cit., p. 194.

at least in peacetime industrial goods can be freely traded for food and that many countries do so. His second reason had to do with military strategy and had more validity, assuming Germany had to fear an attack. He pointed out that, in war, geographically small countries are more likely than large countries to be overrun by their enemies, so that a large land mass offers security.[11] This was certainly true in the case of the Soviet Union in World War II and may be even more true under conditions of nuclear warfare than it was in Hitler's time. The military expert Sir B. H. Liddell Hart has said that "Space [of the Soviet Union] spelt first his [Hitler's] frustration, and then his defeat."[12]

All in all, it is thus apparent that the Lebensraum doctrine was a mélange of several ideas of various sorts: a law of nature, racial and social-Darwinistic thoughts, the need of space and food for an expanding population, and strategic military considerations. Yet, in Hitler's statements about it, one can vaguely sense a deliberate effort to expound a rational ideological basis for aggressive warfare and territorial acquisitions. There may be doubt whether he himself was wholly convinced. It is possible, at any rate, that psychologically much of the Lebensraum doctrine represented a rationalization of general destructive drives, not only on the part of Hitler but also of many other Germans.

From the very start, Hitler did not believe that Germany should reacquire colonies outside of Europe,[13] but he felt strongly, and said in *Mein Kampf*, that new land should be obtained within Europe itself, particularly at the expense of the Soviet Union:

> Of course, such a territorial policy cannot find fulfillment in the Cameroons [a former Germany colony in Africa] but now almost nowhere except in Europe. . . .
> And thus we National Socialists deliberately put an end to the direction of our prewar [World War I] foreign policy. We begin where we broke off six centuries ago. We put a stop to the eternal movement of the Germanic people to Europe's South and

[11]*Mein Kampf*, pp. 150, 728.
[12]Liddell Hart, *History of the Second World War*, p. 141.
[13]The question of Hitler's colonial aims *outside* of Europe is treated in overwhelming detail in Klaus Hildebrand, *Vom Reich zum Weltreich*, 1969.

West and we turn our eyes to the land in the East. . . . In speaking of new territory in Europe, we can, above all, have in mind only Russia and its subjugated border states.[14]

(No one outside Germany seems to have paid any attention to this perfectly frank early statement of Hitler's territorial aims in *Mein Kampf,* until it was too late.)

B. German Territorial Aims in the Two World Wars

In his *Table Talks,* Hitler claimed that his territorial policy was "without historical parallel,"[15] but actually this was far from true. Quite similar, even if less determined, German war aims rose to the surface during World War I, and for an understanding of the historical evolution of National Socialism, it is valuable to compare the German territorial aims of the two wars. In World War I, the German government sought to sever the Ukraine from Russia and to bring it under its own domination;[16] it planned to establish a military, political, and economic affiliation of Lithuania and parts of Latvia (Courland) with Germany ("since we need more land to feed our people"[17]); it intended to acquire a "border strip" and perhaps an additional "security strip" in Poland;[18] it planned to place the occupied Crimea under German influence;[19] and the Kaiser even wanted to "keep all options open" in Transcaucasia which could be "a bridge to central Asia and a threat to the British position in India."[20] (He made the flat pronouncement that peace "between the Slavs and the Germanic peoples is entirely impossible."[21]) A memorandum regarding a confidential discussion between Chancellor Theobald von Bethmann-Hollweg and his adviser on August 21, 1914, said: "In the evening, long discussion

[14]*Mein Kampf,* pp. 152, 742. See pp. 148–154 generally; also p. 741. See, further, *Hitlers Zweites Buch,* p. 163.

[15]*Hitler's Table Talks,* p. 230.

[16]Fritz Fischer, *Griff nach der Weltmacht,* pp. 426–427. See also Andreas Hillgruber, *Deutschlands Rolle in der Vorgeschichte der beiden Weltkriege,* pp. 62–67; Hans W. Gatzke, *Germany's Drive to the West;* and Fritz Fischer, *Krieg der Illusionen.*

[17]Fischer, *Griff,* pp. 396, 398, 421, 526–527, 233, 239.

[18]Ibid., pp. 230, 239.

[19]Ibid., p. 483.

[20]Ibid., p. 493.

[21]Ibid., p. 511.

about Poland and the possibility of a loose affiliation [*Angliederung*] of other countries with Germany—a central European system of tariff differentials, Greater Germany with Belgium, Holland, Poland as close protectorates, and Austria as a less close protectorate."[22] It should be remembered also that in November, 1918, German troops held a line in Russia extending from Finland to the Crimea. "A German eastern empire was thus once a reality, even if only for a short time."[23]

In the West, Hitler's territorial policy was also not without antecedents in World War I. As to France, Chancellor von Bethmann-Hollweg had then proposed the annexation of Belfort, a coastal strip from Dunkirk to Boulogne, and other areas.[24] From Belgium, he had wanted Liège, Verviers, and perhaps Antwerp; all of Belgium, moreover, was to become a German "tributary state" and "economically a German province."[25] "Deserving noncommissioned officers and enlisted men" were to become settlers in the areas to be annexed from both France and Belgium.[26]

In fact, in the enthusiastic mood of August 1914, some individual German professors demanded German world leadership. Professor Karl Lamprecht (a Pan-German) said the following in a newspaper article of August 28, 1914: "Subjectively it is recognized and objectively it has been proved that we are capable of the highest achievement in this world and that we are regarded as at least one who has been called to rule the world."[27]

All the plans for territorial acquisitions in World War I were essentially quite similar or analogous to the corresponding plans in World War II, which will now be discussed. The difference between the plans was, of course, that Hitler's and Himmler's aims reached out even farther into the territory of their enemies. Another difference was in the ideological motivation. The German aims of World War I were essentially based on nothing but the then traditional realpolitik or sheer imperialism, whereas those of World War II were ostensibly founded in racial, social-Darwinistic, and Lebensraum

[22]Quoted in Fischer, *Krieg*, p. 761.

[23]Hillgruber, op. cit., pp. 62–66. See also A. Bullock, *Hitler*, pp. 317–318, dealing with the ambitions of General Erich Ludendorff in the East in World War I.

[24]Fischer, *Griff*, p. 93.

[25]Ibid., p. 93, 100, 219.

[26]Ibid., p. 99.

[27]Quoted in Fischer, *Krieg*, p. 748.

theories. Curiously enough, however, the net result was very much the same. Psychologically, quite similar emotional processes seem to have been at work in Germany in both wars, although under the mantle of different rationalizations. It is worth noting, in this connection, that a good many of the far-reaching plans for territorial acquisitions in World War I have been uncovered only recently and can hardly have been known to Hitler and his associates. In both wars, the amount of irrational wishful thinking and of dreaming was astonishing.

As far as the East was concerned, there was almost no limit to national socialist ideas for the expansion of the German Lebensraum. While the extent of the desired space was never precisely delineated, there can be no doubt that large pieces of Poland would have been included as an impoverished, oppressed colony. Poland, according to Hitler's order to Hans Frank, was to be "booty country" which was "to be ruthlessly impoverished [and which], in its economic, social, cultural, and political structure, was, figuratively speaking, to be converted into a rubble heap."[28] Thousands of members of the Polish elite were actually executed,[29] and thousands more would probably have been killed later, for no purpose other than to deprive the country of all leadership. As for the Soviet Union, Hitler privately seems to have suggested a German-Soviet border along a line from Archangel on the White Sea in the North to Astrakhan on the Caspian Sea in the South.[30] The Crimea was to be settled by Tyroleans who "merely have to sail down a German river, the Danube, and there they are."[31] (Earlier, Himmler had had different plans for the Tyroleans. He told an assembly of generals on March 13, 1940, that the Tyroleans were to be settled in Burgundy which would first have to be conquered by the army.[32]) Generally, Himmler wanted to go farther in the East than Hitler: he saw the Ural Mountains as the Lebensraum frontier.[33] But Hitler put it this way: "What India meant to Britain, the East will mean to us."[34] At any rate, a vast area of Soviet Russia — perhaps all

[28] *TMWC*, Vol. XXIX, p. 369.
[29] Martin Broszat, *Nationalsozialistische Polenpolitik*, pp. 162–163.
[30] *Hitler's Table Talks*, p. 458, fn. 2.
[31] Ibid., pp. 429–430.
[32] *Vierteljahrshefte für Zeitgeschichte*, Heft 1, January 1970, p. 108.
[33] *TMWC*, Vol. XXIX, Doc. 1919-PS, pp. 151, 172.
[34] *Hitler's Table Talks*, p. 143.

of its European territory—would have become a German colony, and much of the native population would have been forced into Siberia.[35] "Some day [Hitler said] we certainly want to have that entire previously Russian country settled by Germans."[36] "The aim of my policy in the East—at long range—is to open up a settlement area for about 100 million Germanic people in that territory."[37]

Many other areas in Europe were also to become part of the Lebensraum.[38] The Czechoslovakian provinces of Bohemia and Moravia would, for example, have been included. Hitler said of them in a proclamation of March 16, 1939, that "for a millenium [they] belonged to the Lebensraum of the German people."[39] Holland and Norway were to become a part of the greater German empire[40] and so was Belgium, which "150 years ago was still a province of ours."[41] With respect to Holland and Belgium, any German claim to Lebensraum as such made really no sense at all. Both were the most densely populated countries in Europe and, if anything, they needed more land themselves.

As for France, Hitler's territorial ideas were astonishingly far-reaching. It seems that he wanted all of the Channel coast,[42] indeed, all of "Northern France," described by him as "old German land of which we were robbed, and the return of which we have every right to demand."[43] He explained that his French headquarters between Soisson and Laon was located "exactly on the future German western border"[44] (about 50 miles northwest of Paris). He wanted military or naval bases on France's Atlantic coast, and he demanded even all of Burgundy, where, he said, "a big piece of German history had taken place" and which, "therefore, was age-old German soil stolen by the

[35] According to the so-called *"Generalplan Ost"* of 1941. See Grebing, *Der Nationalsozialismus*, p. 117; also A. Hillgruber, "Die 'Endlösung' und das deutsche Ostimperium . . .", in *Vierteljahrshefte für Zeitgeschichte*, Vol. XX, 1972, pp. 141-142.

[36] *Hitler's Table Talks*, p. 469.

[37] Ibid., p. 330 (indirect speech transposed).

[38] The subject of Hitler's war aims was discussed also by H. R. Trevor-Roper in "Hitler's Kriegsziele," in *Vierteljahrshefte für Zeitgeschichte*, Heft 2, 1960, pp. 121-133, but he puts the entire emphasis on Hitler's plans for the *East* only.

[39] Domarus, *Hitlers Reden*, p. 1098.

[40] *Hitler's Table Talks*, pp. 254-255, 183, 409, 418, 358.

[41] Ibid., p. 360; also p. 409.

[42] Ibid., pp. 336, 338.

[43] Ibid., p. 313.

[44] Albert Speer, *Erinnerungen*, p. 366.

French when we were weak."[45] Hitler did seem to feel a little awkward about the extent of his proposed territorial claims against France, because at one point he said, "nobody can take it amiss [*mir verdenken*] if, with respect to France, I take the position: if I've got it, I've got it! For if anyone gives away what he has, he commits a sin, because he gives away what he, as the stronger one, has laboriously conquered on this Earth."[46] It will be noted that in this statement Hitler had to take refuge in straight pseudo-Darwinism mixed, however, with the pseudoreligious concept of a "sin" committed by the violation of a law of nature.

Himmler once even spoke of stationing troops "far in the South of Africa,"[47] but he probably meant North Africa.

The final goal no doubt was mastery of the world, but this was mentioned seldom and then only in secrecy (even though it is true that Hitler had naïvely said in *Mein Kampf* that "A country which, in the age of the poisoning of the races, dedicates itself to taking care [*Pflege*] of its best racial elements, must someday become the master of the world"[48]). Goebbels, in his diary, reported these statements by Hitler:

> The Führer gave expression to his unshakable conviction that the Reich will be the master of all Europe. We shall yet have to engage in many fights, but these will undoubtedly lead to the most wonderful victories. From there on, the way to world domination is practically certain. Whoever dominates Europe will thereby assume the leadership of the world.
>
> In this connection, we naturally cannot accept questions of right or wrong, even as a basis of discussion.[49]

Himmler, too, wanted to "found a Germanic world empire."[50] His SS men had a popular marching song with the lines

> Today we own Germany,
> Tomorrow it will be the whole wide world.

[45]*Hitler's Table Talks*, p. 296 (indirect speech transposed); see also Bracher, *Die deutsche Diktatur*, p. 441.

[46]*Hitler's Table Talks*, p. 320 (indirect speech transposed).

[47]*TMWC*, Vol. XXIX, Doc. 1918-PS, p. 106.

[48]*Mein Kampf*, p. 782. See also A. Hillgruber, "Die 'Endlösung' und das deutsche Ostimperium . . .", in *Vierteljahrshefte für Zeitgeschichte*, Vol. XX, 1972, pp. 135–136.

[49]*The Goebbels Diaries* 1942–1943 (English translation), p. 359.

[50]*TMWC*, Vol. XXIX, Doc. 1919-PS, p. 137.

It would have been an empire, partly "colonial," extending from the Arctic to the Italian frontier or even to North Africa, and from the Atlantic Ocean deep into European Russia, perhaps to the Ural Mountains. It was a gigantic dream by little men and probably the biggest exercise in wishful thinking the world has ever witnessed. Surely, it represented a case of megalomania and narcissism quite unprecedented in dimension. In principle, the war aims clearly had not changed a great deal between the two wars. Unfortunately, however, in World War II the plans did not by any means remain mere dream and delusion. A great part of the program temporarily became reality at the expense of tens of millions of lives, before a stop could be put to it.

While the war was still in progress, the Allies were not even aware of the fate that awaited them, had they failed to win the conflict. In the light of the German war aims and other aims in World War II, it is entirely impossible to understand such "America Firsters" as, for example, Colonel Charles A. Lindbergh, who still contend that the United States should not have participated in the war at all. The only possible assumption can be that they have never learned what the German war aims really were. At a minimum, a defeat of the Soviet Union would have meant the death of millions of surviving Russian Jews, and perhaps of Jews elsewhere. It would have meant the establishment of a German empire—partly colonial—in Poland, Russia, and even in large parts of Europe under a merciless regime, with the death of untold members of the native populations and suffering for nearly all. It would have meant the establishment of a German political and military complex of enormous strength and reserves, rivaling or exceeding that of the United States, all under an utterly irresponsible pugnacious regime which never hesitated to attack unless it faced quite insurmountable military and logistical difficulties. And it should be borne in mind that the men of that regime were—as will be outlined later—psychologically of a kind who "cannot stop," but whose general hostility is such that they must seek successive outlets for it in further and further aggression under any rationalization of pretexts.

Chapter 4

Anti-Semitism

A. The Rise of German Anti-Semitism

Anti-Semitism was the most virulent of all the components of the national socialist ideology. It was the one that was most loudly proclaimed, most insistently pursued, most sincerely believed in, as well as the one that in the end brought about the death of about 27 percent of the entire Jewish world population. The only other ideological components to which a still higher death toll was attributable—if such attributions can be made at all—was the combination of the race theories and the Lebensraum doctrine which, directly or indirectly, caused the death of about 25 million Poles and Russians. Yet the murder of about 6 million Jews no doubt represented in its way the most intense discharge of interethnic hostility in history. In the late Hitler years, being a Jew was ipso facto a death sentence (indeed, every Jewish baby was born guilty), whereas the majority of Russians and Poles were killed in "normal" warfare. Unlike the Jews, they at least were not under an unconditional death sentence for being ethnically or racially what they were. (But it is true that even some millions of defenseless Russians and Poles were killed either intentionally or negligently, for example between 3 and 4 million Soviet prisoners of war in German custody. [1])

At the same time, anti-Semitism was a far more complex component of the ideology than any of the other components, in its origins, causation, and its psychological aspects. It will, therefore, require more extensive investigation and analysis.

[1]Alexander Dallin, *German Rule in Russia 1941-1945*, p. 427. Reinhard Henkys, *Die Nationalsozialistischen Gewaltverbrechen*, pp. 17, 167, 173.

Anti-Semitism was, of course, related to some of the other ideological components here discussed. Obviously, it was closely related
to or even a part of the racial theories in general. It was related also
to the Germanic cult, if only because "the Jew" was considered to be
the "counterperson" to the ideal of the Germanic hero. And finally,
anti-Semitism was related to German Romanticism because, as we
shall see, here again, the Jew was, if not a counterperson, then at least
a hated misfit in the general romantic utopia. He was essentially a
creature of the city and not of the idealized soil; he was not really
suitable as a member of an ethnical German *Volk* community; he was
Western or even internationally oriented.

Anti-Semitism, to be sure, is far from being a German invention.
Its history reaches back into antiquity, and it seems to have occurred
in the Western world whenever and wherever Jews lived in the
diaspora with other nations, although there have been great variations in the degree of intensity of feeling. None of the large or small
European countries has been without anti-Semitism, and it is perhaps
significant that "pogrom" is a Russian word which has been taken into
various languages. The causes of all this anti-Semitism have been
manifold and have varied in the course of the centuries and from country to country. In any case, anti-Semitism has been remarkably persistent for about 2,000 years; and the astonishing fact is that the Jews
have survived as a group at all. Freud said that "what held them together was an idealistic factor, their common possession of definite
intellectual and emotional assets" and that the monotheistic idea

> was guarded by them as their most precious possession and now,
> on its part, kept the people alive by granting to it the pride of
> being the chosen people. It was the religion of the original God
> the Father to which the hope for reward, distinction and, finally,
> world domination was tied. This last wishful phantasy, long ago
> abandoned by the Jewish people, still lives on among its enemies
> who believe in the conspiracy of "the Elders of Zion."[2]

Another thing that is noteworthy about the whole astounding
Jewish phenomenon is that the German Jews themselves never under-

[2]Sigmund Freud, *Der Mann Moses und die monotheistische Religion* in *Gesammelte Werke*, Vol. 16, pp. 231, 191.

took more than superficial investigations into the causes of anti-Semitism and practically no systematic research into the question how it might be overcome or avoided. ". . . It must be admitted that the Jew . . . has consistently refused to solve . . . [the problem of anti-Semitism]."[3] With respect to the Jews in Germany, we lack unfortunately such highly useful studies as T. W. Adorno (et al.), *The Authoritarian Personality* (1950, 1969) and B. Bettelheim and M. Janowitz, *Dynamics of Prejudice* (1950), which deal with American anti-Semitism and were both supported by the Americal Jewish Committee. On the whole, the great mass of German Jews seem to have been inclined to accept anti-Semitism as a fact of life or as a law of their God, and this weird paralysis of their judgment and initiative may, in part, have been induced by the macabre prophecy of the Old Testament (Deuteronomy 28):

> Just as the LORD took delight in you, prospering and increasing you, so now it will be his delight to destroy and exterminate you, and you will be uprooted from the land which you are entering to occupy. The LORD will scatter you among all peoples from one end of the earth to the other . . . . Among those nations you will find no peace, no rest for the sole of your foot . . . . Your life will hang continually in suspense, fear will beset you night and day, and you will find no security all your life long. Every morning you will say "Would God it were evening!", and every evening, "Would God it were morning!", for the fear that lives in your heart and the sights that you see.[4]

Most German Jews seem to have felt that "to remain a Jew in the Christian world one must pay a price, and that price unfortunately is antisemitism."[5] "We elevated and hypostatized our history of suffering into a destined role imposed upon us, as the servant of the Lord, for the sanctification of His name. Ours is a definite mission and our suffering is a part of it."[6]

In Germany, anti-Semitism may date back a thousand years, and

[3]Koppel S. Pinson (ed.), *Essays on Antisemitism*, p. 39.

[4]Translation as rendered in *The New English Bible*, Oxford University Press, Cambridge University Press, 1970.

[5]Pinson, op. cit., p. 39.

[6]Ibid., p. 45.

its savage emergence during the Hitler years certainly cannot be viewed as a sudden accident of German history. The Germans were not suddenly seized by some new demonic, diabolic powers during those twelve years. On the contrary, the hatred of the Jews by the National Socialists had ample precedent. Anti-Semitism was, for example, already virulent in Luther's day, and he himself was a savage anti-Semite. In 1542 he published his pamphlet *Against the Jews and Their Lies (Gegen die Juden und ihre Lügen)*. The title itself is significant, but it does not begin to describe the depth of abuse and hatred which this pamphlet of a man of the church contains. Here are a few brief quotations:

> . . . the Jews, being foreigners, should truly and certainly own nothing, and what they do own must certainly be ours . . . . when a Jew, through his usury, steals and robs ten tons of gold, he [thinks he] is better than God himself.
>
> . . . they [the Jews] are a heavy burden on us, like a plague, pestilence. and sheer misfortune in our country. . . .
>
> Anyone who now likes to shelter, feed, and honor those poisonous snakes and young devils, that is, the worst enemies of Christ, our Lord, and who wishes to let himself be oppressed, robbed, pillaged, ravished, spat at, cursed, and to undergo everything evil, he need only be commended to the care of the Jews. If that is not enough, he . . . should crawl into the Jew's behind and worship this sanctuary. . . .[7]

Luther advocated burning down synagogues and Jewish schools, destroying the houses of the Jews, and expelling them from Germany.[8] In a subsequent pamphlet, he became even more abusive, saying that perhaps Judas's "guts tore open and . . . his bladder burst" and that the Jews "ate and drank" the "Judas piss . . . together with the other sacred treasures. . . ."[9] The national socialist pervert Julius Streicher could hardly surpass this in his own anti-Jewish ravings 400 years later, and it is significant that these long-forgotten writings

---

[7]Martin Luther, *Von den Juden und ihren Lügen* (1543) in *Luthers Kampfschriften gegen das Judentum*, Berlin 1936, pp. 162, 199, 210. For a discussion of Luther's views of the Jews see Wanda Kampmann, *Deutsche und Juden*, pp. 41–48.

[8]Ibid., pp. 201, 202, 208.

[9]Martin Luther, *Vom Schemhamphoras* (1543), in ibid., p. 89.

by Luther were republished in Germany in 1936 during the Hitler years.

For purposes of the present study, it may otherwise be sufficient to discuss the condition of German anti-Semitism during the period from about 1870 to the end of the Hitler period in 1945. [10] It was during the early decades of that period that anti-Semitism received particularly strong impetus. In 1873, following grave German business scandals in which various Jews were implicated, a sensational pamphlet was published by a passionate anti-Semite, Wilhelm Marr, under the significant title *Der Sieg des Judenthums über das Germanenthum* ("The Victory of Judaism over the Germanic World"). It fell on fertile soil and was followed by similar publications. Actions by Jews in the business scandals seemed to reflect the image held by Germans, since time immemorial, of the Jews, as represented, for example, by Veitel Itzig in the immensely popular novel by Gustav Freytag, *Soll und Haben* ("Debit and Credit," 1855): greedy, grasping, tricky, ruthless, ugly, rootless, and without soul. In the German mind, this image was to adhere to the Jews all the way into the gas chambers of the concentration camps.

These business scandals, however, were probably no more than surface motivation for the rise of the ingrained, deep-seated anti-Semitism of that time; but at any rate, by about 1880 anti-Semitism had spread with fury over all of Germany. A "League of Anti-Semites" came into existence; Jews were insulted and boycotted, though comparatively little serious violence seems to have occurred. A great many books and articles were published, attacking every aspect of Jewish life. In 1881, Eugen Dühring, an early classic of racial anti-Semitism, published his influential *The Jewish Problem as a Problem of Race, Ethics and Culture*. To him, the Jew was "one of the lowest and most abortive creations of nature."

Another strong and articulate anti-Semite was Adolf Stöcker,

---

[10]See, in this connection, Helga Grebing, *Der Nationalsozialismus* pp. 7–19; Ernst Ludwig Ehrlich, *Judenfeindschaft*, in K. Thieme (ed.), *Judenfeindschaft in Deutschland;* Josef Müller, *Die Entwicklung des Rassenantisemitismus in den letzten Jahrzehnten des 19. Jahrhunderts;* Paul W. Massing *Rehearsal for Destruction;* Mosse, *Crisis. . . ,* pp. 126–145; K. D. Bracher, *Die deutsche Diktatur,* pp, 35–48; Hannah Arendt, *The Origins of Totalitarianism,* pp. 28–50; Kurt Wawrzinek, *Die Entstehung der deutschen Antisemitenparteien;* Peter G. J. Pulzer, *The Rise of Political Antisemitism in Germany and Austria;* Kampmann, op. cit.; Hermann Huss and Andreas Schröder (eds.), *Antisemitismus—Zur Pathologie der burgerlichen Gesellschaft.*

the official preacher at the imperial court. He lent the respectability and prestige of his position to the cause. A petition was even submitted to Bismarck, demanding that Jews be excluded from schools, universities, etc. In 1886, an "anti-Semitic congress" was held and resulted in a union of various anti-Jewish organizations under the name "German Anti-Semitic Association" *(Deutscher anti-semitischer Verein)*. Even the eminent historian Heinrich von Treitschke gave the sanction of his great name to the anti-Jewish agitation and, in doing so, probably did more than most others to infuse intellectual respectability into the anti-Semitism of that era. In 1887, Theodor Fritsch published *The Anti-Semitic Catechism;* this work went through 40 editions and was finally republished in 1936 during the national socialist regime, which honored Fritsch as the "old maestro."[11]

It was in this period, too, that Gobineau's anti-Semitic *Essai sur l'inégalité des races humaines*, which had been published in France as far back as 1853, finally received recognition in Germany. "Gobineau societies" sprang up. Chamberlain's *Foundation of the 19th Century* was published a little later, in 1900. One of his accomplishments was that, as Wanda Kampmann has said, his teachings "permitted the educated bourgeoisie to remain faithful to their youthful idealism, to proclaim their continued membership in the Christian church, and to be anti-Semitic."[12] It was to prove of the greatest importance.

Of the numerous smaller anti-Semitic writers of that period, one is of some special interest in the present context, because he is more in the nature of a genuine, direct forerunner of National Socialism than most others. This is Hermann Ahlwardt, a turbulent demagogue for some years and a highly controversial member of the German parliament. He was the author of *Der Verzweiflungskampf der arischen Völker mit dem Judentum* (The war of desperation between the Aryan peoples and Judaism) published in 1890. He actually suggested the hanging of Jews, and, at any rate, he proposed all kinds of restrictions on them. They were to be declared aliens in Germany. Ultimately, he wanted them deported from Europe, but their money was to be kept by the German state—all curiously similar to the

[11] Mosse, *Crisis*, p. 112.
[12] Kampmann, op. cit., p. 319.

national socialist party program and specifically the so-called "Madagascar Plan," which the national socialist regime was to consider fifty years later.

Some of Ahlwardt's statements might have been taken verbatim from remarks by Hitler. Thus, he contended that: "The people [*Volk*] which rids itself of its Jews first and most radically and thus frees the way for the natural development of its culture, will be summoned to be the bearers of culture and, consequently, also to be the ruler of the world."[13] Compare this with the following statement by Hitler: "A state that in this age of race poisoning dedicates itself to the cultivation of its best racial elements must some day become the ruler of the world."[14] Ahlwardt went so far as to say in a speech in the German parliament in 1895 that the Jews were "beasts of prey" which had to be "exterminated": "One always hears: you must be humane toward the Jews. The humanitarianism of our century, this humaneness for beasts of prey is our curse. . . . You had better exterminate those beasts of prey."[15]

There is no indication that Hitler ever read Ahlwardt's book, which was published when he was one year old. But, at any rate, Ahlwardt, who was adored by large masses of Germans of his time, reflected in great measure the opinions of millions; and many other writers shared these opinions in varying degrees. There was, moreover, no dearth of similar writers and politicians in Austria-Hungary where Hitler spent his formative years. The lines of German anti-Semitic agitation were closely followed or imitated in that country, but the hostility against the Jews was even more intense, owing perhaps to their proportionately larger number. In 1895, even the Pope sent his blessing to the local anti-Semitic political leaders (which he later retracted).

One person who stood in the center of a mystic racial anti-Semitic movement in Austria before World War I was a renegade monk, Adolf Lanz, who called himself Dr. Jorg Lanz von Liebenfels and was the publisher of *Ostara, Zeitschrift für Blonde* (Magazine for Blond People), a widely read periodical of racial mysticism. It seems likely that

[13] Ahlwardt, *Der Verzweiflungskampf*, p. 239.
[14] *Mein Kampf*, p. 782.
[15] *Reichstag, Stenographische Berichte*, Mar. 6, 1895, p. 1297, quoted in Massing, op. cit., pp. 300–305.

Hitler had some contact with Lanz and did read *Ostara*. It has, in fact, been contended that Lanz was the man who "gave Hitler his ideas."[16]

But above all, Hitler, in his early days in Vienna, was deeply influenced by two strongly anti-Semitic Austrian politicians, Georg Ritter von Schönerer and Karl Lueger, the latter the mayor of Vienna for whom Hitler had the highest admiration. He discussed both men at some length in *Mein Kampf*.[17] Later, when he came to power, he seems to have made a conscious effort to fuse the views and tactics of these two men into his own political opinions and strategy.[18] But, on the whole, both men had done no more than present the anti-Semitic clichés then current in Germany and Austria-Hungary.

Of course, the anti-Semitic fury of the late nineteenth century was by no means confined to Germany and Austria-Hungary. It was widespread, for example, in Russia, Rumania, and France. (Hannah Arendt has called Rumania "the most anti-Semitic country in prewar Europe."[19]) In Russia, murderous anti-Jewish riots, rapes, and burning of houses took place in 1881 in about 170 towns and villages. In France, there was a strong anti-Jewish movement in the 1880s, led by Edouard Drumont; and above all, there was the Dreyfus case, which lasted from 1894 to 1906.[20] It was this case that served as a kind of catharsis for the whole French nation and may have helped to discourage more serious anti-Jewish actions in France in the decades thereafter.

What followed was a period of temporary decline of anti-Semitic movements, though not of anti-Semitism, a relative, but deceptive, quiet on the anti-Jewish front from about 1900 to the end of World War I in 1918. On the surface, these movements seemed to have had no real success or at least no *visible* success. Legally, the Jewish Emancipation Act of 1869 remained in force, and Emancipation proceeded apace; the Zionist movement was promoted. After the Dreyfus affair and other anti-Jewish excesses, there even was some embarrassment among the anti-Semites in France and in a few other countries. But all this was far from signifying that anti-Semitism in Ger-

[16] Wilfried Daim, *Der Mann, der Hitler die Ideen gab* (1958).

[17] Pp. 74, 95, 107-110, 132-133; see also Alan Bullock, *Hitler*, pp. 44-46; Konrad Heiden, *Der Fuehrer*, pp. 63-64.

[18] See Max Klesse, *Vom alten zum neuen Israel*, p. 248.

[19] Arendt, *Eichmann in Jerusalem*, p. 190.

[20] For a detailed discussion of this affair, see Arendt, *Origins*, pp. 89-129.

many had disappeared or even that it had become less intense. What happened was merely that Germany was entering a period of aggressive imperialism and industrial expansion. The middle class, which had always been the main source of anti-Semitism, could share in the glory and greatness of Kaiser and Reich; it reveled in claims to African colonies, the build-up of the navy, the Kaiser's aggressive speeches, and his threats of war. In fact, during that period, specifically in 1904–1905, a now forgotten but very real genocidal war was carried on by Germany against the Herero tribe in South West Africa. (This will be discussed in a separate chapter later.) And, finally, there was World War I. The discharge of German interethnic hostility [21] was directed toward other nations, the British, French, Russians, Chinese, and Hereros.

The imperialism of Wihelm II's Reich, as Massing has said, [22] rendered anti-Semitism innocuous and yet preserved it. The decline of the openly anti-Semitic organizations and, generally, anti-Jewish propaganda after 1900 is thoroughly deceptive. These organizations had, in fact, done their work. In thirty years of intense propaganda, they had disseminated anti-Semitism throughout Germany and had created a firm ideological understructure on which Hitler later could build. By about 1900, anti-Semitism had become a domesticated, indigenous, and accepted doctrine to the vast majority of the German people. It had ceased to be a live issue, and there no longer was a need for the anti-Semitic agitation of the late nineteenth century. ". . . if intolerance is institutionalized or generally accepted much of the motive for discussing it disappears." [23] But the absence of anti-Semitic agitation, in turn, added to the respectability of the doctrine. Ehrlich contends that "the 'tame' anti-Semitism is the nourishing soil for the crimes against the Jews." [24]

Adorno has said that

In all probability, the presentation of extreme and anti-Semitic statements as if they were no longer disreputable but rather something which can be sensibly discussed, . . . may stimulate imitation even in cases where the individual's "own" reactions

[21] To use Erich Fromm's terminology in *Escape from Freedom.*
[22] P. W. Massing, op. cit., p. 206.
[23] Bruno Bettelheim and Morris Janowitz, *Dynamics of Prejudice,* p. 9.
[24] E. L. Ehrlich, op. cit., p. 247.

would be less violent. This consideration may throw some light upon the phenomenon of the whole German people tolerating the most extreme anti-Semitic measures. . . .[25]

Germany's defeat in World War I put a disastrous and traumatic end to the imperialistic ambitions of the Reich. All the interethnic hostility which the Germans, until 1918, had been able to discharge against neighboring countries could suddenly find no outlet other than in anti-Semitism. The result was a far more intense and vicious expression of the latent anti-Semitism than ever before, fed strongly by the so-called *Dolchstosslegende* (stab-in-the-back legend). This was the theory that the defeat in the war was due solely to betrayal by the Communist-Jewish Left. Hitler started his career not long thereafter, in 1919, as an obscure agitator on an intensely anti-Semitic platform; and he had no great difficulty in attracting millions of fellow anti-Semites to his movement by his very practical and outspoken approach to the cause. "The arsenal was fully assembled in 1918. It was merely a question of waiting for an order to fire."[26] Here again, as in the case of the other components of national socialist ideology, Hitler found what he needed, ready at hand. He, of course, vastly expanded the existing anti-Semitism, systematized it, even codified it in statutes, and translated theory into action. That was his contribution, and it did give anti-Semitism a new dimension.

To be sure, Hitler's followers originally wanted perhaps no more than to give noisy expression to traditional hatred, but he himself already had vague thoughts of exterminating at least certain numbers of Jews by gassing. In *Mein Kampf*, written in the 1920s, he said:

If at the beginning of the War and during the War twelve or fifteen thousand of these Hebraic corrupters of the people had been held under poison gas in the same manner as hundreds of thousands of our very best German workers from all levels and occupations had to endure it in the War, then the sacrifice of millions at the front would not have been in vain. On the contrary, the elimination of twelve thousand scoundrels at the right time might have saved the lives of a million decent Germans who would have been valuable for the future.[27]

[25]T. W. Adorno et al., *The Authoritarian Personality*, p. 607.
[26]Pulzer, op. cit., p. 300.
[27]*Mein Kampf*, p. 772.

Perhaps the most damaging effect of the quiescent state of anti-Semitism from about 1900 to 1918 was the misunderstanding of the real situation created by it among the Jews. They thought they were living in a "golden age of security"[28] (and, in fact, they essentially continued in this belief almost until Hitler seized political power in 1933). Since no one had brutally attacked them for about twenty years, they were under the illusion that anti-Semitism was vanishing. They could not imagine that a rather primitive and seemingly pathological man could ever succeed in ejecting them from the German nation, not to speak of killing them. It was a fatal misunderstanding and miscalculation; but millions of educated Germans, it is true, were almost equally wrong. We shall have further opportunities in this study to consider Jewish miscalculations.

B. The German-Jewish Symbiosis

For centuries, a uniquely special relationship had existed between Germans and Jews. Erich Kahler, in his brilliant little book *The Jews among the Nations* (1967), describes that relationship as a "psychic and mental interpenetration," a "peculiar affinity," an "interpenetration of dispositions and destinies, which in both peoples, through accordances and discordances, touched the nerve of existence."[29] Other writers have found a similar relationship. Eva Reichmann speaks of a "mysterious attraction [between Germans and Jews], burdened with the weight of ambivalence . . ."[30] and of a "peculiar mixture of Jewish and German cultural elements."[31] Robert Weltsch said "it was fate—and today this seems an irony of history—that the German cultural world of the classics, of Enlightenment and tolerance, of Romanticism, philosophy and music, was the first and real partner of the Jews on this road [to the free European spirit]."[32] Henkys says that God "tied His people and our [German] people to each other in a unique way; the Jewish and German minds and cultures entered into

[28] See Arendt, *Origins*, pp. 50–53.

[29] Kahler, *The Jews among the Nations*, pp. 99, 102, 119. It is in these meanings that the word "symbiosis" is used here. Adolf Leschnitzer, *The Magic Background of Modern Anti-semitism*, uses it in a much broader, rather uncertain meaning, perhaps as the equivalent of "coexistence."

[30] Reichmann, *Flucht in den Hass*, pp. 292–293.

[31] Ibid., p. 145.

[32] In *Juden im Deutschen Kulturbereich*, 1962, p. XIX.

a union which even the German genocide against Judaism was probably unable to dissolve."[33] (This may have been true of the old generation of German Jews.) Or, as Ernst Feder put it, in speaking of outstanding Jews in Germany:

> Completely integrated into German culture, these personalities remained Jews, and as German ways [*Wesen*] impressed themselves on their character and mind, so their Jewish qualities colored their non-Jewish surroundings. What took place might be described as a reciprocal assimilation that benefited both parties and resulted in a cultural flowering as it had not existed since the last century of Jewish history in Spain and Portugal.[34]

The famous German rabbi Leo Baeck said that only three times in Jewish history did the encounter of Jews with another culture lead to creative production: the first time in the Hellenistic period of antiquity; the second, in the Spanish-Arabic period of the Middle Ages; and the third, at the encounter with German culture.[35] The Jewish philosopher Julius Guttmann has said that "Germany is the birthplace of modern Judaism,"[36] and according to Robert Weltsch, for a German Jew, even a Zionist, "Europe inevitably meant German-ness."[37]

The very special relationship existing between the Jews and the German language is perhaps the strangest and also one of the most significant phenomena of the entire German-Jewish "interpenetration"—and this on an almost worldwide scale. The universal language of lower-class Jews is not Hebrew, but Yiddish, which is essentially German as spoken in the Middle Ages[38] (plus some Hebrew and Aramaic words and words taken from local languages). Any German, with a little effort, can understand Yiddish—in fact, usually a great deal better than sophisticated upper-class non-German Jews. For centuries, Yiddish has been the language of the Jews of Poland and

---

[33] Henkys, *Die nationalsozialistischen Gewaltverbrechen*, p. 20.

[34] In Weltsch, (ed.), *Deutsches Judentum*, p. 120.

[35] Ibid., p. 7.

[36] Ibid., p. 8.

[37] Quoted in Mosse, *Germans and Jews*, p. 78.

[38] *Mittelhochdeutsch*. For a discussion of Yiddish, see Yudel Mark, "The Yiddish Language: Its Cultural Impact," in *American Jewish Historical Quarterly*, December 1969, p. 201.

Russia—that great human reservoir from which Jewish life throughout the world used to renew itself. The culture of Eastern Jewry,
moreover, was strongly oriented toward Germany.

The writings and thoughts of the representatives of German
intellectual life were widely spread among the Jews of the East.
The ideal of many young Jews was to sit at the feet of German
professors, to learn their language, and to enjoy Germany's
freedom and culture. . . . Even those who could not travel felt
attracted by Germany. . . . A foreign language became home to
us [Jews]; we forgot that we were not living in our own country. . . . And when my heart longed for the spirit of the people,
I was driven toward Germany—I might almost say, to the mother
country of my language. [39]

And as the German-Jewish philosopher Theodor Lessing once said:

. . . wherever Jews live, we found that they preserve the trea-
sure of the German spirit, more faithfully often than the assimi-
lable Germans themselves. What, after all, is Eastern Jewry,
what is its much misunderstood Yiddish? It is childish German,
born in tears, from the distant Middle Ages. [40]

Jewish religious and intellectual leaders throughout the world
were strongly influenced by German civilization, which, indeed, operated as a kind of "intellectual melting pot" for them. "The most important forms of Jewish life and thought of our time found their characteristic shapes in Germany, the religious liberalism and the modern
orthodoxy, the reform movement as well as Jewish nationalism." [41]

It is significant that Theodor Herzl, a Hungarian Jew, the spiritual father of the State of Israel, wrote his book *Der Judenstaat* in
German. German was the language of the early Zionist congresses.
The Jewish novelist Franz Kafka, born and raised in Prague, wrote
in beautiful German. Martin Buber, the well-known Jewish philosopher, was raised in Poland but embraced German civilization as his
own and published his countless writings in German. In fact, he was

[39] S. Adler-Rudel and H. G. Adler, quoted in Klesse, op. cit., pp. 178–179.
[40] Lessing, *Deutschland und seine Juden*, p. 10.
[41] Weltsch (ed.), *Deutsches Judentum*, p. 17.

apt to write the romantic nebulous kind of language that is so uniquely German. Wilhelm Michel, the German literary scholar, said of Buber that "no one speaks the German language as he does unless he has profoundly and earnestly surrendered to the destiny of the people from whom this language stems."[42] All this seems highly significant if, as Wilhelm von Humboldt has said, the mind of a people and the formation of its language are so intimately connected that it should be possible to deduce the one from the other. Here, it seems, the minds of *two* peoples could be deduced from *one* language.

And there were, indeed, a good many resemblances between Germans and Jews or rather between certain groups of each of them. The Jewish-German poet Heinrich Heine, more than a century ago, went very far in noting such resemblances:

> The intimate elective affinity . . . [between Jews and Germans] is, in fact, striking. This elective affinity did not originate in history although the Bible, the great Jewish family chronicle, served as the book of education for the whole Germanic world, and both Jews and Germans, from the early days on, were implacable enemies of the Romans and were natural allies. This affinity has a deeper root. Both peoples are basically so similar that the former Palestine might be regarded as an oriental Germany, just as today's Germany could be considered the home of the Holy Word, the mother soil of prophetdom, the citadel of the pure spirit.[43]

Most of this no doubt amounted to vast exaggerations of a poet who was then in love with Germany, and, at any rate, Heine did not really explain what the "deeper root" of the affinity was, which he saw.

Somewhat more sober views as to the resemblances between Jews and Germans were stated more recently by Friedrich Sieburg, a well-known German journalist and popular essayist. He describes both peoples as

> . . . admired and hated . . . both equally unable to make themselves liked, equally ambivalent between servility and arrogance,

---

[42] Ibid., p. 36.

[43] In *Shakespeares Madchen und Frauen (Jessika), Heinrich Heines Werke*, Verlag "Das Bergland-Buch," Salzburg, no date, pp. 1130–1131.

equally indispensable as well as troublesome to the world, equally aggressive, equally inclined to self-pity, equally vilified without distinction and admired for the wild boldness of their thinking; musical, talented for speculative thinking, but hopelessly different in one point: in their attitude toward violence. How deeply and inextricably they were interwoven with our life! Today, it is surely too late, even though by no means useless, to say that Jewish activities in Germany can be condemned only if sixty years of the German Reich are also condemned. . . . It was a people's enigmatic fate which gave us this companion as long as we were great and mighty, and which brought us down when we sought to destroy him. This association, which was a fertile symbiosis, is now gone forever. It was unparalleled. . . . [44]

Much of this is undoubtedly true. Sieburg might have added that there was also a good deal of resemblance between the methods of thinking of the talmudic scholars and some German philosophers. In both peoples, though more so among the Jews, there was for centuries great dedication to learning and education. Also, both Jews and Germans showed similar eagerness to develop comprehensive ideological conceptions of the world and of all aspects of man's place in it *(Weltanschauung)*. In both, the span between the best and the worst qualities was very wide. Both have usually had an abundance of enemies. In both, the capacity for discontent, self-pity and wailing is very large.

Kahler believes that the Germans and Jews are both transnational peoples and that this "unites them . . . above all."[45] The Jews have undoubtedly been transnational for 2,000 years, and they were transnational 200 years ago when they first began their unhappy love affair with the Germans. At that time, the Germans, divided as they were into about 300 principalities, could also be called transnational, though in a narrower political sense. But for the last 100 years or more, the Germans have slowly shed all transnationality (except as forced upon them by the division after World War II); and they have, indeed, belatedly become quite national. Kahler's theory can, therefore, be regarded as applicable only to a period long past, but even then it may be quite significant in relation to the early development of the special German-Jewish relationship.

[44]Sieburg, *Die Lust am Untergang*, Hamburg, 1954, pp. 34-35.
[45]Kahler, op. cit., pp. 111-112.

There is no doubt that for a period of about one hundred years before National Socialism seized power, the German Jews benefited immensely from their symbiosis with German civilization; and the benefit to the Germans was also very great. The symbiosis seemed to bring to the surface the very best the Jews had to offer (and also a good deal of the worst). There was, during that period, a flowering of Jewish creativeness in Germany as never before in history—in the natural sciences, medicine, philosophy, psychiatry, literature, film, music, the arts, the law, and many other fields. The very comprehensive book *Juden im deutschen Kulturbereich* (Jews within the German Cultural Sphere) [46] lists in its index the names of about 2,100 Jews who, before 1933, had been prominent in Germany in practically every field of human endeavor. Germany made it possible for these Jews to develop and unfold their enormous talents, and conversely Germany benefited immensely from them. They greatly enhanced its reputation throughout the world. Freud, Einstein, and, in a different sense, Karl Marx changed modern civilization.

It can hardly be accidental that today, although German literature and music are again flourishing, there is a sad decline in the natural sciences, medicine, psychiatry, and other fields. Anyone who has had many dealings with today's lawyers in Germany knows how much lower their standards are than those of their former Jewish colleagues. The German film industry has never recovered at all. Other examples could be added. Hans Kohn says that "the expulsion of the Jews from Vienna has had a devastating effect upon its cultural life." [47]

The prominent German historian Theodor Mommsen stated long ago that "Providence has understood . . . why a few percent of Israel had to be mixed with the Germanic metal to shape it." [48] And Friedrich Nietzsche said: "What a blessing a Jew is among Germans!" [49] But the history of the Jews in Germany shows that even useful gifts by a minority to the majority of a people will sometimes not be received in good grace and can indeed result in disastrous consequences to the minority.

[46] Edited by Siegmund Kaznelson.
[47] Kohn, *The Mind of Germany*, p. 251.
[48] Quoted by Klesse, op. cit., p. 192.
[49] Quoted by Kahler, op. cit., p. 110.

Conversely, it may be that the Jews need life within gentile nations, interpenetration, cross-fertilization with non-Jews, for their own maximum cultural productivity. Ehrlich says:

> It was not until their Jewish neighbors had been expelled or murdered that the other Germans fully realized, if they did, that this German Jewry, within about 100 years, had succeeded in creating and representing a type of Jewish person, nonexistent in any other country in modern times, whose power of mind radiated far into European and American Jewry.[50]

The closed Jewish ghettos had at all times been unproductive, and not much of great cultural value seems to have come out of Israel since the founding of that state. But it may well be that much more time is required before any such judgment can be made as regards Israel.

In one respect the German Jews never showed affinity to the Germans, and that was the interest of the Germans in developing the body, in the physical side of life. The above-mentioned book *Juden im deutschen Kulturbereich*[51] does list a good many Jews who were active in sports and achieved some degree of success, but on the whole there is little doubt that the vast majority of German Jews were "antiphysical," were weak in body, and were not eager to display physical courage. "Physical heroism [Kahler says] has no prominent role in their tradition"[52] (but this now seems to be different in Israel). The German Jews were dedicated primarily to things of the mind, and by and large, they detested what Kahler calls "this latent quality in the German, this potential of becoming arrested and immured in his own body, this emphasis on brute force."[53] They detested the crude and clumsy simpleton, the *"reine Tor"* or, to use a Hebrew word, the "goi."

Actually, the strong Jewish tendency toward physical weakness and timidity in those days in Germany stands in strange and seemingly inexplicable contrast to the physical accomplishments and courage of the agricultural settlers in today's Israel and particularly to

[50] E. L. Ehrlich in Thieme (ed.), *Judenfeindschaft in Deutschland*, p. 238.
[51] Pp. 926–936.
[52] Kahler, op. cit., p. 117.
[53] See Kahler, op. cit., pp. 116–118.

the fighting qualities shown by the Israelis in the war against the Arab countries. It is possible that the German Jews merely adopted an attitude, a pretension of physical helplessness, which, they *thought*, might please and placate the Germans. Perhaps it was an effort "to stay in their place." But if so, the Jews showed poor judgment. Their seeming aversion to the "physical Germans" resulted in counter-aversion, and at any rate, the Germans generally had contempt for the weak and timid *Jüdlein*. Possibly, going a step further, there is some limited truth in the ideas, which George Steiner discusses, that "the temptations [German Jewry] offered to bestiality were too subtle, too intimate to be resisted" and that there must have been "some hidden complicity between torturer and victim."[54] Similarly, Hochheimer says that "it seems that, at least in part, there was a sado-masochistic involvement of murderer and victim."[55] And Adorno points out that "the expression of weakness or masochism . . . provide[s] psychologically adequate stimuli for destructiveness."[56] But this is getting ahead of our later discussion of the causes of German anti-Semitism.

It would not be correct to describe the entire Jewish-German relationship as being of the "love-hate" variety. Unfortunately, no public-opinion surveys of that period exist, and we can rely only on impressions. The Jews probably "loved" all those Germans who were sensitive, gentle, and intellectual; and they "hated" all those who were merely "physical." As far as the Germans were concerned, in spite of the undoubtedly existing symbiosis, no more than a rather small, sophisticated group could be said to have much liking for well-assimilated Jews, and even that German group was apt to have an intense dislike for certain "Jewish qualities" and, in any event, for all unassimilated Eastern Jews. But there is no doubt that many deep individual German-Jewish friendships did develop. The great majority of Germans, on the other hand, probably hated *all* Jews in varying degrees. Whatever "love affair" the Jews carried on with the Germans was, thus, largely one-sided; to an overwhelming extent it ran from the Jews to the Germans. The Jews, however, seldom realized this,

[54]George Steiner, *Language and Silence*, New York, 1967, p. 111.

[55]Wolfgang Hochheimer in Huss and Schröder (eds.), *Antisemitismus—Zur Pathologie der bürgerlichen Gesellschaft*, p. 110.

[56]Adorno, *The Authoritarian Personality*, p. 608.

and not unnaturally they preferred to close their eyes to it. At any rate, George Steiner is hardly right in saying, in the context of the German-Jewish problem, that "all men kill the Jew they love."[57] The ones who did the killing, or knew of it, never had any love for the Jews. Also, those who ordered or carried out the killing did so, not so much because of hate or perversion of love, but because, as we have seen, it had been hammered into their heads that "natural laws," the "laws of history," "historical necessity," and the like required it.

It is a fact, moreover, that a great many Jews labored under severe misapprehensions as to the real nature of the average German. They created in their minds an idealized image of the German as a person imbued with humanism, classicism, and idealism—an image which may have been true of the Germans of the first half of the nineteenth century, but the truth of which had slowly and gradually evaporated during the decades thereafter until this image could be said to apply to only a very small group indeed. But the average Jew obtained much of his knowledge of the Germans from books, and his personal acquaintance with the average German was rather superficial. The fact is that many Jews thus liked an idealized image of the German (and, conversely, that many Germans disliked a caricature of the Jew). This is part of the whole complex of Jewish misunderstandings and miscalculations in the German-Jewish relationship.

In view of the extremely close association between German culture and Jews, the impact of the sudden forced separation was, of course, tremendous. Strong cultural bonds, which had existed for centuries, had to be cut almost overnight, with results that often were tragic. The sadness of the German Jews and their tragedy is reflected in a kind of farewell editorial addressed to the German people by a Jewish-German Zionist newspaper in 1933, shortly before Judaism in Germany came to an end:

We want the German people to know: a historical union of centuries cannot be dissolved so simply. Our loyalty to Jewish folkdom has never meant that we gave back or could give back something that the German mind gave us. We were educated in it and we know what we owe to it. National Jewry learned from

[57]Steiner, op. cit., p. 111.

German writings—alongside its Jewish sources and treasures—
what character and freedom means. . . .

Thousands of German Jews, brought up in German education, are now forced to leave this country. . . . Years and decades
will pass, and we know that generations will remain faithful to
what they received from the German mind.[58]

No less touching was what the German-Jewish philosopher Theodor
Lessing wrote in 1933, shortly before his assassination by national
socialists:

And so, we are German and shall remain German. And so, we are
Jews and shall remain Jews. And yet, we are something totally
different and far more than only Jewish and only German!

Bearers of world conscience, vessels of divine spirit, thanks
to which humanity exists, and humanness, as well as sense and
values and victory—beyond all hells of nature and life.[59]

Anyone who has met emigré German Jews in their second diaspora, the one from Germany, knows the degree of their "German-
ness," their homesickness for Germany, their admiration of German
civilization, their difficulties in adjusting to the mind of another country. Strangely enough, these difficulties seem to have been much
greater among German-Jewish exiles than among non-Jewish German
emigrants.

C. The Causes of German Anti-Semitism

a. SOME PRELIMINARY CONSIDERATIONS

The German-Jewish symbiosis was an astonishing historical phenomenon; and in the light of it, the savage fury of German anti-
Semitism during and before the Hitler years may seem particularly
incomprehensible. In actual fact, however, our analysis of some of
the causes of German anti-Semitism will show that the very close-
ness of the German-Jewish relationship was one of the motivating
factors. The present investigation will be confined to the more im-

---

[58]*Jüdische Rundschau* of Apr. 13, 1933, quoted in Weltsch (ed.), *Deutsches
Judentum*, p. 367.

[59]Lessing, *Deutschland und seine Juden*, p. 31.

portant causes which were operative or virulent in the decades before as well as during the Hitler period. Freud has said:

> A phenomenon of the intensity and durability of the hatred of the Jews by the nations must, of course, have more than only one cause. It is possible to guess quite a number of causes, some manifestly derived from reality that need no interpretation, and others deepseated, stemming from secret sources, which one would like to acknowledge as the specific motives. [60]

National socialism, at any rate, invented none of the causes, but, as usual, intensified and aggravated what it found, gave brutal expression to old resentments and grievances and, finally, put mere thoughts into action.

The first thing that strikes anyone studying the German-Jewish relationship during the decades from about 1900 to 1940 is how little the Jews themselves seemed to know of the operative causes of anti-Semitism, under what delusions they lived, and how little they did to eliminate any of these causes, even insofar as this might have been in their power. Some Jews, in fact, did not even understand that there was any causal connection between Jewish nature and peculiarities, and anti-Semitism. Arnold Zweig, for example, made the extreme statement that "the nature and character [*Wesen*] of the Jews should be left completely out of consideration in connection with the emergence of anti-Semitism." [61] And even as careful and brilliant an analyst of the situation as Eva Reichmann [62] still said in 1956 that "to look for the causes of the catastrophe of the German Jews in the actual Jewish Problem would be to look for them in a place where they cannot be found" and that "the German anti-Semitism of those interwar years was a phenomenon attendant on the national socialist successes." Miss Reichmann believes that "in reality anti-Semitism is hatred of Christianity," a theory she derived, among others, from Freud. [63] She sees in the Germany of that period "an increasing indifference to the fact

[60]Freud, *Der Mann Moses und die monotheistische Religion*, in *Gesammelte Werke*, Vol. 16, pp. 196–197.

[61]Zweig, *Caliban oder Politik und Leidenschaft*, 1927, p. 30.

[62]Reichmann, *Flucht in den Hass*, pp. 119, 287–288, 239, 286. Helmut Krausnick, in Hans Buchheim, Martin Brozsat, Hans-Adolf Jacobsen, and Helmut Krausnick (eds.), *Anatomie des SS Staates*, Vol. II, p. 284, accepts some of Miss Reichmann's views.

[63]Freud, op. cit., Vol. 16, p. 198.

whether a fellow-citizen was Jewish or not." Another brilliant analyst of the situation, E. L. Ehrlich, made the strange statement in 1963 that "[anti-Semitism] . . . cannot be fought by concrete experience with the Jews; their actual existence plays hardly any part at all in relation to anti-Semitism."[64] Finally, Franz Neumann went so far as to state the opinion in 1942 that "the German people are the least Anti-Semitic of all."[65]

It is difficult to agree with these views, and they reflect the unfortunate but fundamental fact that "the basic image of the Jews in the minds of the non-Jews was different from the image which the emancipated Jews conceived of their own position in [German] society."[66] On the whole, the average German Jew in the pre-Hitler era, while aware of some anti-Semitism, was far from realizing the depth, extent, and nature of the resentment and hostility surrounding him; and he probably did not want to know it. Moreover, had he known it, he would not have fully understood the causes. To a considerable extent, this Jewish state of mind was natural and understandable. The Jews saw themselves as law-abiding citizens who were making a valuable contribution to German society. They naturally tended to close their eyes to the existence of less valuable and less acceptable members of their group and to undesirable qualities of any members.

It is only normal that anyone who likes his own group and is convinced of its merits will find it difficult to understand why other groups should hate it. But, as Miss Reichmann says in her "Conclusions," looking to the future, the Jews "must draw certain conclusions [from their status as a minority group] . . . , even if they are hardly still aware of their membership in the group. They must learn to look at themselves not only with their own eyes but also with the eyes of the world around them."[67]

Some writers, however, Jewish and gentile, have been quite realistic in their appraisal of the role played by the Jews themselves in the causation of anti-Semitism. Kahler says that "We [the Jews] should not, as it is too often done, represent ourselves as the mere victims, and it is unworthy of our traditions and unjustified by our

[64]Ehrlich, op. cit., p. 244.
[65]Neumann, *Behemoth*, p. 121.
[66]Robert Weltsch in *Deutsches Judentum*, p. 19.
[67]Reichmann, op. cit., p. 290.

history to represent Judaism in terms of passion and passivity only."[68] Hannah Arendt goes so far as to speak of the "absurd assertion of a kind of collective innocence of the Jewish people."[69] It was not until quite recently, however, that two prominent Jewish intellectuals, Walter Z. Laqueur and Max Beloff, ventured forth into a discussion of *specific* causes of anti-Semitism based on Jewish actions or attitudes.[70] (The details will be considered here later.) Laqueur attributes the past "neglect" of this subject to the fact that "it is so delicate." It is, of course, delicate, but the German Jews might have done themselves a great deal of good, if they had publicly discussed the subject forty years earlier. The difficulties, however, which even the most perceptive Jews seem to encounter in the situation are indicated by Beloff's concluding sentence. After an extraordinary and very useful discussion of specific causes of anti-Semitism, he reverts, strangely enough, to traditional Jewish thought patterns: "Why this particular burden [of having to deal with anti-Semitism] should have befallen the Jews is something which individuals can attribute to the will of God or the legacy of history, as their own particular faith (or lack of it) dictates." There are better explanations than that, and, indeed, Beloff's article itself does much to uncover them.

But no matter whether the Jews themselves contributed to the causes of anti-Semitism or not, it is clear that the degree of fanatic hatred which Hitler and other National Socialists developed toward the Jews defies any possible efforts to discover a rational causation. This is the point at which psychopathology may have to take over. But there remains the fact that the great majority of Germans showed themselves highly receptive to Hitler's anti-Semitic ravings and were willing to follow him a long way down the road of terror, even if they "did not wish anti-Jewish actions, the radicalism of which would have been comparable to those actually taken by the government."[71] It should not be forgotten that Hitler, on an intensely anti-Semitic party

[68]Kahler, op. cit., p. 96. See also Mosse, *Crisis*, p. 301.

[69]Arendt, *Eichmann*, p. 297.

[70]Laqueur, "The Tucholsky Complaint," in *Encounter*, October 1969; Beloff, "Rootless Cosmopolitans," in *Encounter*, November 1969. It should be noted here that Adorno's brilliant *The Authoritarian Personality* deliberately "excluded an investigation into the role played by the 'object'—that is to say, the Jews—in the formation of prejudice." Adorno, however, does not "deny that the object plays a role. . . ." (p. 607).

[71]Reichmann, op. cit., p. 282.

program, was democratically voted into power by about 44 percent of the German electorate and that he received even far more votes in subsequent referenda. An examination of the reasons for this receptivity of the Germans to anti-Semitism is *one* of the purposes of the following discussion of the individual real or possible causes of German anti-Semitism.

From a largely psychological and sociopsychological point of view, anti-Semitic attitudes have been explored in brilliant analyses and investigations in T. W. Adorno (and six collaborators), *The Authoritarian Personality* (a very inadequate title), B. Bettelheim and M. Janowitz, *Dynamics of Prejudice,* and Erich Fromm, *Escape from Freedom.* All these studies were undertaken *after* the Jewish catastrophe in Germany, and they used various *American* sample groups for testing. But since the chief authors of these three studies were émigré Germans, it can hardly be assumed that their conclusions, at least in a general way, were not peripherally intended to deal also with the German anti-Semitism of the pre-Hitler and Hitler years; and, indeed, on a good many occasions the authors refer expressly to that German anti-Semitism. Adorno, as mentioned before, explains that his sample "excluded an investigation into the role played by the 'object'—that is to say, the Jews—in the formation of prejudice," although he does not "deny that the object plays a role."[72] He then goes on to say:

> . . . we start with the general assumption that the—largely unconscious—hostility resulting from frustration and repression and socially diverted from its true object, *needs* a substitute object through which it may obtain a realistic aspect and thus dodge, as it were, more radical manifestations of a blocking of the subject's relationship to reality, e.g. psychosis. This "object" of unconscious destructiveness, far from being a superficial "scapegoat," must have certain characteristics in order to fulfill its role. It must be tangible enough; and yet not *too* tangible, lest it be exploded by its own realism. It must have a sufficient historical background and appear as an indisputable element of tradition. It must be defined in rigid and well-known stereotypes. Finally, the object must possess features, or at least be capable

[72]Adorno, op. cit., p. 607.

of being perceived and interpreted in terms of features, which harmonize with the destructive tendencies of the prejudiced subject. Some of these features, such as "clannishness" aid rationalization; others, such as the expression of weakness or masochism, provide psychologically adequate stimuli for destructiveness. There can hardly be any doubt that all these requirements are fulfilled by the phenomenon of the Jew. This is not to say that Jews *must* draw hatred upon themselves, or that there is an absolute historical necessity which makes them, rather than others, the ideal target of social aggressiveness. Suffice it to say that they *can* perform this function in the psychological households of many people. [73]

If the conflict within the individual has been decided *against* the Jews, the decision itself is almost without exception rationalized moralistically. [74]

But Adorno is careful to acknowledge that his

findings are strictly limited to the psychological aspects of the more general problem of prejudice. Historical factors or economic forces operating in our society to promote or diminish ethnic prejudice are clerely beyond the scope of our investigation. . . . Outbreaks into action must be considered the results of both the internal potential and a set of eliciting factors in the environment. [75]

To an extent, Adorno (and other sociopsychologists) thus merely begs the question; and what we shall have to discuss are some of these "historical factors," "economic forces," and other "eliciting factors in the [German] environment" which promoted anti-Semitism and the final German "outbreak into action." In doing so, we shall also enter what Adorno drastically describes as a "red-light district of legitimatized psychotic distortions." [76] We shall have to discuss, further, what

[73] Ibid., pp. 607–608.
[74] Ibid., p. 630.
[75] Ibid., p. 972. (As heretofore mentioned, Mosse, *The Crisis of German Ideology*, pp. 300–301, objects to what he calls the "psychological view," but he does not mention Adorno, and it does not seem likely that he would object to the latter's views with the limitations stated by Adorno himself.)
[76] Ibid., p. 617.

Bruno Bettelheim calls the "nucleus of reality" that remains a necessity for the rationalizations, and the "means [of rationalization] which are satisfactory to the individual's controlling institutions and to the group to which he belongs."[77]

Erich Fromm approaches the matter more from the point of view of the subject (the Germans) than the object (the Jews). Fromm sees National Socialism as an expression of the "authoritarian character" which he regards as typical for "great parts of the lower middle class in Germany and other European countries"—a character the essence of which is "the simultaneous presence of sadistic and masochistic drives." The sadistic drives aim "at unrestricted power over another person," for example, the Jews. But these drives are frequently not consciously realized and are rationalized as originating in quite different motivations.[78]

It is thus important, in the following consideration of specific causes of German anti-Semitism, to bear in mind at all points that what the Germans may have regarded as legitimate causes of anti-Semitism may at least partly have been rationalizations of sadistic drives of their character structure, supported by various elements of the factual situation. According to Fromm, persons with dominant sadomasochistic drives "are not necessarily neurotic."[79] According to Adorno, speaking of ethnic prejudices, "two subvarieties of the ethnically prejudiced must be distinguished: the conventional and the psychopathic."[80] Hitler himself and many of his executioners were probably psychopathic, but millions of other Germans presumably were merely conventional in their ethnic prejudices.

b. THE RELIGIOUS MOTIVATION

In considering the effect which Christian religious beliefs might have had in the causation of German anti-Semitism, it will be well to distinguish, to the extent possible, between the conscious and the unconscious level.

On the Conscious Level. During the decades before Hitler and during the Hitler period itself, religiousness played only a minor part

---

[77] Bettelheim and Janowitz, *Dynamics of Prejudice*, p. 156.
[78] Fromm, *Escape*, pp. 221, 163.
[79] Ibid., p. 163.
[80] Adorno, op. cit., p. 972.

in Germany. In fact, the Christian churches faced a degree of indifference which they are only beginning to face in the United States today. To those increasingly few Germans who were devout Christian believers, anti-Semitism might have been a kind of natural reaction. True enough, Judaism is the womb of Christianity, but the central Christian figure not only was not recognized by the Jews but was killed by them. They put Christ on the cross (even if in cooperation with the Romans); they were "the killers of the Lord," and, moreover, they never repented. Clearly, this was strong motivation for hatred by devout Christians. And for centuries this probably was a powerful element, though not the only element, in anti-Semitism throughout the Christian world. The crucifix was a symbol of Jewish crime and eternal guilt. (Adorno has said that "Psychologically, the idea of eternal Jewish guilt can be understood as a projection of the prejudiced person's own repressed guilt feelings. . . ."[81])

Moreover, the Jewish denial of the divine nature of their fellow Jew Jesus and of his being the long awaited Messiah and Saviour hit the very foundation of the Christian faith. It could raise troublesome, annoying doubts in the minds of those who tried to be believers — doubts which could at least be partially removed by hostility against the Jews. There may also be elements of normal hostility between son and father in the Christian-Jewish religious situation:

> Christianity as the religion of the "Son" contains an implicit antagonism against the religion of the "Father" and its surviving witnesses, the Jews. . . . Christians resent bitterly the openly negative attitude of the Jews toward the religion of the Son, since they feel within themselves traces of this negative attitude based upon the paradoxical, irrational attitude of their creed.[82]

As regards the Jewish claim of being the chosen people, it is difficult to say with any degree of certainty to what extent, if at all, it contributed to German anti-Semitism. Among the German intelligentsia, the claim probably caused merely amusement. On the lower German social levels, this Jewish contention may have created no more than mild annoyance. But no public opinion polls are available,

---

[81] Adorno, op. cit., p. 633.

[82] Ibid., p. 728. To a similar effect, Max Horkheimer and Theodor W. Adorno, *Elemente des Antisemitismus* in *Dialektik der Aufklärung*, p. 188.

and we should probably not close our eyes to the possibility of much greater resentment. The claim of having been chosen by God as His people was, after all, a manifestation of supreme arrogance; and this — in German eyes—all the more, when the claim was asserted as it was by a tiny weak minority that was still struggling for full social recognition and should, if anything, have shown humility. It may have been particularly annoying that the claim was supported by the Word of God, the Bible (even if of Jewish authorship), which had told the Jews expressly "I will adopt you as my people, and I will become your God" (Exodus 6:7) and ". . . out of all peoples you shall become my special possession; for the whole earth is mine. You shall be my kingdom of priests, my holy nation" (Exodus 19:5).[83] The Bible did seem to indicate a very special relationship between God and the Jews, a kind of exclusive partnership contract, a covenant binding on both.[84]

It was true enough that all this had been said in the Old Testament and had been reported with pro-Jewish bias in the first place. It might not apply at this late date. (Indeed, if if still did apply, then all Jews should have been an object of Christian veneration.) But certainly, to anyone at all religious, an element of doubt could remain. If the Jews were, in fact, God's chosen people, could that be the reason for their survival through the persecutions of thousands of years? Were they actually selected for a divine mission? Would they ultimately emerge as victors in history? (A religion of Jewish provenance had, after all, already conquered Western civilization.) These were painful, even intolerable thoughts, and they could only result in increased resentment of the Jews. That such thoughts did occur at least to some Germans is shown, curiously enough, by the fact that they were stated by Hitler, in his pathetic fashion, in *Mein Kampf:*

Just once more — and it was the last time — anxious, depressing thoughts came to me in deep mental anguish.

As I explored the activities of the Jewish people over long periods of human history, the worrying question suddenly occurred to me whether inscrutable Destiny, for reasons unknown to us miserable humans, might not after all desire the final vic-

[83]Translations as rendered in *The New English Bible*, Oxford University Press, Cambridge University Press, 1970.

[84]See the interesting discussion of this point in Kahler, op. cit., pp. 13-15.

tory of that small people, in eternally unchangeable determination.

Was it possible that the Earth had been promised as a reward to that people which forever lives only for this Earth?[85]

It is not impossible that it was, in part, this jealousy of the Jews and the pressing desire to eliminate it which induced Hitler's wish to exterminate Jewry in its entirety. But this is by no means equivalent to saying that the anti-Semitism of all or even many Germans was similarly motivated. Hitler, while hostile to the churches, was, as we shall see, an intensely religious person, far more religious than most Germans. The kind of jealousy of the Jews expressed by Hitler in the above quotation from *Mein Kampf* could have occurred only to someone deeply and naïvely religious; and this is not what most Germans were.

The argument might be carried further, as is done by Huss,[86] by saying that, in the view of the National Socialists, the annoying fact of the "chosen people" had to be eliminated so as to make room for the Thousand Year Reich of the Germanic people whom nature had destined to be the rulers. Naturally, the claim of the "chosen people" tended to devalue that biological myth. But this argument again presupposes a far deeper religiousness than the Germans and particularly the National Socialists possessed. The argument might, however, still have some validity in relation to Hitler himself.

(It might here be mentioned in passing that the SS officials who were concerned with the extermination of the Jews in the camps in Poland, sometimes referred to Jews jocularly as "chosen people" in a double meaning, namely, as meaning Jews as such, as well as Jews chosen for execution.[87])

Kahler goes so far as to contend that "the adherence to the revelation of a spiritual, universal God, their very possession of such a revelation . . . made the Jews . . . an 'odium generis humani,' an abomination to mankind."[88] Hitler might have agreed with him, but there were probably few other Germans, even deeply religious Germans, who would have gone that far.

[85]*Mein Kampf*, p. 69.
[86]Huss and Schröder (eds.), *Antisemitismus*, pp. 31–32.
[87]See, for instance, Raul Hilberg, *The Destruction of the European Jews*, p. 313.
[88]Kahler, *The Jews among the Nations*, p. 97.

At any rate, the number of Germans to whom any of these religious considerations could have been important on a conscious level was undoubtedly small. Hitler himself (no matter what his own religious motivation may have been) recognized this and deliberately did not rely on religion in his anti-Jewish teachings. He said expressly, in fact, that basing anti-Semitism on religion rather than race was a "mistake."[89]

It might be mentioned that our view of the relative unimportance of conscious religious motivation of German anti-Semitism is supported by the results of a survey of anti-Jewish (and anti-Negro) attitudes of about 150 discharged American soldiers, which B. Bettelheim and M. Janowitz published in 1950.[90] They reported that "throughout the interviews when reasons for the dislike of Jews were mentioned, references to religion were almost totally absent."[91] In fact, curiously enough, they reported that: "in studying the association between religious attitudes and anti-Semitism it was found that stability of religious conviction was *significantly* associated with tolerance toward Jews. Such association was *not* encountered in the case of the Negro. . . ."[92] But the opposite was found true in Adorno's investigations: ". . . it appears that those who reject religion have less ethnocentrism than those who seem to accept it. . . . values of tolerance, brotherhood, and equality . . . are more firmly held by people who do not affiliate with any religious group."[93]

Among the conclusions which Bettelheim and Janowitz drew from their investigations were the following, all of them no doubt being intended to hold true on the "*conscious* religious level":

> In modern times when religious appeals have been introduced as a basis for the persecution of Jews, they have nearly always fallen flat. Religious fear, or such inner conflicts as are based on it, is just no longer important enough to motivate large

[89] *Mein Kampf,* pp. 130–131. See also Hitler's early "expert opinion" on the Jews, quoted in Werner Maser, *Adolf Hitler,* pp. 173–174.

[90] Bettelheim and Janowitz, op. cit. It may, of course, be risky to equate the anti-Semitic attitudes of a group of American men in 1950 with those of the German people some twenty years earlier.

[91] Ibid., p. 166.

[92] Ibid., p. 155. See also Massing, *Rehearsal for Destruction,* p. 75.

[93] Adorno, op. cit., pp. 213, 219. He admits, however that his "data on religion [are] scarce." (p. 727).

masses. Again and again ritual murder stories have been circulated, but have never been widely believed, or at least not in urban centers. The only places where they were lent some credence were in Eastern Europe, where economic, political, and religious organization was still very similar to that of the Middle Ages. . . . Religious conversion which protected Spanish Jews was ultimately of little help to Jews in Germany. . . . The racial issue raised in National Socialist Germany seems but a return to the Middle Ages with racialism taking the place of religion. . . .[94]

Even in regard to the Middle Ages, the religious motivation of anti-Semitism may have been widely exaggerated. It seems more likely that Kahler is right when he says that "the Jews have always been felt by the gentiles to be something more and something other than the representatives of a mere creed. . . ."[95] It is probable that "group hostility" (discussed below) was a powerful causative factor also in the Middle Ages, even though membership in the Jewish religious community no doubt placed someone much more definitely in the hated outgroup at that time than it does today.

The German Jews themselves, during the fifty or sixty years before Hitler, still strangely overvalued the (conscious) religious factor. Many thousands of them had themselves baptized, in the naïve and touching belief that this would help to integrate them into the German community and to avert anti-Semitism. In the end, it availed them nothing. National Socialism, and even the Germans in general, never saw the slightest difference between a Christian Jew and a Jewish Jew. Race decided. An early anti-Semitic writer, Theodor Fritsch, said that "the certificate of baptism cannot invalidate the document, written in blood, which nature has engraved upon each individual for his racial membership."[96] But in general, the Jews failed to sense this attitude. The German-Jewish poet Heinrich Heine was far ahead of the Jews of a much later period. More than a hundred years ago he asked the question, "is religion, after all, only a pretext, and do men hate each other in order to hate each other, just as they love each other in order to love each other?"[97]

[94] Bettelheim and Janowitz, op. cit., p. 166.
[95] Kahler, op. cit., p. 2; see also Heinrich Heine, *Werke*, op. cit., pp. 1132–1133.
[96] Quoted in Josef Müller, *Die Entwicklung des Rassenantisemitismus*, p. 39.
[97] Heine, op. cit., p. 1131.

On the Unconscious Level. While it thus appears that conscious religious motivation of anti-Semitism was of relatively little importance, the picture may be rather different on the deeper *unconscious* level. Two thousand years of religious hostility cannot be wiped out in a few decades, and they must have left a hidden residue of profound unconscious antagonism. The son-against-father relationship between the two religions (heretofore mentioned) was bound to continue on a deeper level. Adorno says that the fight against the Jews seems to be modeled after the fight between the Redeemer and the Christian Devil; that the hatred toward Jewish bankers and moneylenders has its biblical archtype in the story of Jesus driving the usurers from the Temple; that Judas betrays not only Jesus but also the ingroup to which he has been admitted,[98] presumably the counterpart of the German *Volk* community. It is possible, in fact, that the resemblance between the German word *Jude,* meaning "Jew," and the traitor's name, *Judas,* established an ineradicable connection in the German unconscious between Jews and hateful treason.

All this and other potentially anti-Jewish elements of the religious heritage were kept fairly close to the surface by more or less compulsory religious instruction which German children received in the public schools. "They were still taught a drama of Christian salvation in which the Jew is always the villain."[99] Most of these children, upon entering adulthood, *consciously* abandoned this heritage, but *unconsciously* much of it was probably carried over into their adult life; and the childish ill will against the Jews continued, fed by perhaps long-forgotten religious springs. This must have been true especially in the case of Hitler himself who, as a child, was exposed to extensive religious instruction, attended countless church services, received communion, sang in the choir, and was an altar boy. Consciously, as an adult, Hitler became strongly hostile to all churches, but unconsciously no doubt his childhood impressions continued to carry over.[100] At any rate, he remained a deeply religious person to the end—and this on a conscious level[101]—no matter how antagonistic

[98] Adorno, op. cit., pp. 728–729.

[99] Pinson (ed.), *Essays on Antisemitism,* p. 50.

[100] But he himself thought that he had "liberated" himself. Domarus, *Hitlers Reden,* p. 745.

[101] ". . . deep down, I am a religious person all the same. . . ." (Speech of June 26, 1944, quoted in Speer, *Erinnerungen,* p. 570.) Also, speech of Nov. 8, 1943, Domarus, op. cit., p. 2057.

he was to the churches. (All this will be discussed in detail in the section on Hitler's religiousness.)

Other devices which served to keep the unconscious religiously motivated anti-Semitism fairly close to the surface in Germany as elsewhere were the cross and the crucifix, symbolic reminders of Jewish "crime." The Christian religion had possibly been declining in Germany to the point where it was no more than a mere shell, but its content was "preserved and 'consumed' in a haphazard way as a cultural 'good' like patriotism or traditional art." [102] Its basic ideas, including hostility against the Jews, had become a conventional formula which regulated various aspects of one's life.

It may not go too far, in fact, to suggest, as Horkheimer and Adorno do, that " . . . the fanatical faith of which the Führer and his followers boast, is none other than the dogged faith which in former times made the doubters hold on; only its content has become lost. Of this content, there still is alive solely the hatred against those who do not share the faith." [103]

Freud went further than anyone else in looking for motivation of anti-Semitism in the unconscious, and he went beyond the mere religious sphere. In a monograph written just before his death in 1939, during the Hitler period, he said:

> The deeper motives of the hatred of the Jews are rooted in times long past; they work out of the unconscious of the peoples, and I am prepared to be told at first that these motives are not plausible. I venture to contend that the jealousy of the people who claimed to be the first-born preferred child of God the Father has still not been overcome by the others—as though they had faith in the truth of that claim. Moreover, among the customs by which the Jews segregated themselves, circumcision made an unpleasant, sinister impression, which can probably be explained by the fact that it is a reminder of the dreaded castration and thus touches a bit of the primeval age which we would like to forget. And finally the latest motive in this series: one should remember that all those nations who now excel in the hatred of the Jews did not become Christians until late in history, often driven to it by bloody force. One might say that they were "badly baptized"; under a thin coating of Christianity they have re-

[102] Adorno, op. cit., p. 729.
[103] Horkheimer and Adorno, op. cit., p. 185.

mained what their ancestors were who paid homage to a barbaric polytheism. They have not overcome their resentment of the new religion that was forced upon them, but they have shifted this resentment to the source from which Christianity came to them. The fact that the Gospels tell a story which takes place among Jews and, in actual fact, deals only with Jews has facilitated this shift. Their hatred of the Jews is basically hatred of Christianity, and it is not surprising that in the national socialist revolution this intimate relationship between the two monotheistic religions is expressed so plainly by the hostile treatment of both.[104]

As Freud himself suggests, the plausibility of some of this reasoning seems indeed questionable, but another psychiatrist, while not going nearly so far, also raises the specter of primeval castration fear. Erik H. Erikson asks:[105]

Does the Jew remind the Western world of those sinister blood rites . . . in which the father-god demands a token of the boy's sexual member, a tax on his masculinity, as a sign of the covenant? Psychoanalysts offer the explanation that the Jew thus arouses "castration fear" in peoples who have not accepted circumcision as a hygienic measure.

At any rate, the widespread abandonment of a conscious religious motivation of anti-Semitism and the overt change to a racial-biological anti-Semitism could only be disadvantageous to the Jews. Baptism, in theory at least, could be an answer to the purely religious complaints. There was no answer at all to the racial accusation. It made the Jews collectively guilty simply because they were *Rasse-Juden*, and there was no possibility of exculpation. This aspect of incorrigibility under pseudo-Darwinistic laws of nature was, in fact, to become a point of central importance in the minds of fanatic National Socialists. In the end, it came to mean that there was no solution other than the Final Solution, that is, the extermination of the group that was unable to change or improve.

[104] Freud, *Der Mann Moses*, Vol. 16, pp. 197-198.
[105] Erikson, *Childhood and Society*, p. 354.

c. GROUP HOSTILITY

A fundamental cause of German anti-Semitism was the factor of group hostility or "outgroup" hostility, no matter whether the Jewish outgroup-character was based on religion or race or other causes. Small as the German-Jewish group was (when compared with the American-Jewish group) — only about 550,000 in a population of approximately 65 million — it was, for the most part, a very definite, distinctive group. It seemed to be a highly disturbing factor among people who, while themselves not "racially pure", were at least ethnically rather homogeneous and, at any rate, contained no other minority groups that were particularly noticeable. Erik H. Erikson, with his usual emphasis on "identity," says that "Jewry is a singular example of an old entity which clings to its identity — be it racial, ethnic, religious, or cultural — in such a way that it is felt to be a danger to emerging identities;"[106] and National Socialism presumably was what Erikson would call an emerging identity. In any case, the Jews were "a solid combination of a religious and tribal community and were, therefore, subject not only to religious intolerance but also to other antagonistic instincts."[107] Actually, the religious intolerance seemed insignificant compared with the "other antagonistic instincts," which, as usual, had been aroused by the mere fact that the Jews were "different," that they did not completely conform. It would be exaggerated to say that the German-Jewish community was a "state within a state", but it did lead a "peculiar life of its own."[108]

According to Toynbee, the Jews once were part of the so-called millet-system of the Ottoman Empire, which was

. . . a systematically organized version of a communal structure of society which had grown up spontaneously in the Syriac world after the Syriac peoples had been inextricably intermingled with one another by the malice of an Assyrian militarism that . . . had shattered the survivors abroad in order to make sure that they could never find a chance of retrieving their political fortunes.

Under that "millet-system" various coexisting communities were

[106]Ibid.
[107]Weltsch (ed.), *Deutsches Judentum*, p. 114.
[108]Ibid., p. 12.

differentiated, not territorially, but primarily as religious and occupational groups. In the subsequent diaspora, the Jews, one of these millet-groups, were forced to collide with the Western countries, the "essential feature of . . . [whose] political ideology had been its insistence on taking as its principle of political association the physical accident of geographical propinquity". [109] Toynbee seems to attach much importance to this collision of incompatible systems as a basic cause of anti-Semitism. Jewry, he said, was "a fossilized relic of a civilization that was extinct in every other way" and in Western Christendom "a millet looked like an offensive anomaly." [110]

Group hostility may indeed have been a motivating cause in anti-Semitism throughout the centuries, and in this sense it might be regarded as a "normal" source of anti-Jewish feeling in the diaspora. Freud has called group hostility a phenomenon of possibly "elemental" character:

> . . . Closely related tribes repel one another; the South Germans do not like the North Germans; Englishmen say evil things about the Scots; Spaniards have contempt for the Portuguese. We are no longer surprised that larger differences result in aversions which are difficult to overcome: that of the Frenchman against the Teuton, of the Aryan against the Semite, of the White against the Colored. . . .
>
> In the aversion and repulsion, which manifest themselves unconcealed against closely connected strangers, we can recognize the expression of a self-love, of a narcissism which strives toward its own self-assertion and acts as if the appearance of a deviation from its individual characteristics implied a criticism of the same and a demand to modify them. We do not know why so great a sensitivity should have directed itself especially at the details of the differentiation; but it is unmistakable that in this whole human behavior there manifests itself a readiness to hate, an aggressiveness, the origin of which is unknown and to which we might ascribe elemental character. [111]

Similarly, Huss speaks of "group tensions . . . which exist inextricably in the structure of human life in society. . ." and he regards

[109] Arnold Toynbee, *A Study of History*, Vol. VIII, pp. 184-185, 275, 534.
[110] Ibid., pp. 274-275.
[111] Freud, *Massenpsychologie und Ich-Analyse* in *Gesammelte Werke*, London, 1940, Vol. XIII, p. 111.

this as "normal."[112] Bettelheim says that "hostility against outgroups is probably as old as society," but he adds, "the particular form in which hostility occurs is particular to the society in which it appears."[113] He regards "interethnic hostility as a symptom of the individual's effort to maintain balance in his psychic economy by discharging tension through the channel of ethnic intolerance."[114]

What makes a group a hated group within a society, such as the German? Freud believed that small differences may be quite enough and may, in fact, be more important than fundamental distinctions:

> Quite unpardonable, however, are . . . other qualities of the Jews. In the first place, that in some respects they are different from their "host people." Not basically different, for they are not Asiatics of an alien race, as their enemies contend, but rather they are, for the most part, composed of remnants of the Mediterranean peoples and are heirs to Mediterranean culture. Yet, they are different, frequently in some indefinable way different especially from the Nordic peoples; and the intolerance of the masses, strangely enough, manifests itself more strongly against small differences than against fundamental distinctions. . . .[115]

Eva Reichmann perhaps puts it best when she says that the smallness of the deviation

> . . . gives [to the Jews] exactly that degree of resemblance and nearness which causes the remaining differences . . . to be perceived as particularly irritating.[116]

Actually, the difference between the Jews and Germans may not even have been so small as Freud assumed. Contrary to what he said, not only enemies of the Jews but also some of their Jewish friends regarded them as "Asiatics." Walther Rathenau, a prominent Jew who was later to become German Foreign Minister, called the Jews an "Asiatic horde."[117] Martin Buber once said that "Here we [the Jews] are a wedge which Asia has driven into Europe's structure, an

---

[112]Huss and Schröder (eds.), *Antisemitismus*, p. 40.
[113]Bettelheim and Janowitz, op. cit., p. 163.
[114]Ibid., p. 95.
[115]Freud, *Der Mann Moses*, Vol. 16, p. 197.
[116]Reichmann, *Flucht in den Hass*, p. 40.
[117]In an essay published in 1897, quoted by Kampmann, *Deutsche und Juden*, p. 440.

element of fermentation and disturbance of the peace."[118] (Hitler, hardly an authority, took the same view: " . . . in the final analysis, the Jew is actually an Asiatic, not a European."[119]) On another occasion, however, Buber stated that the Jews say to the Germans "we are different . . . different but not alien" (*anders, aber nicht fremd*).[120]

Rathenau took a different view: "Within German life an aloof human tribe of alien kind. . . . In close cohesion among themselves, in strict isolation toward the outside; there they live in a semi-voluntary ghetto, no living part of the people but an alien organism in its body."[121]

At any rate, even if the Jews were merely different, not alien, this was quite enough to arouse hostility. Freud, as stated above, has pointed out, that *small* differences are particularly objectionable. Kahler says of today's Jews in other countries that they are "the quintessence of political and social abnormality," that there is a "quasi-biological and intellectual obstinacy" about them and their way of life, that they are an "abnormality in the body politic" of the nation, and that they act as a "constant challenge to the peoples of the world."[122] To some extent, all this was true of the German Jews of the pre-Hitler era. On the most obvious level, the Jews differed from the Germans in physical appearance, and many of them seemed to look unpleasant to the Germans. Rathenau describes the Jews of his period as "decked out in a fashion that was showy and to their own taste, of hot-blooded, impulsive behavior."[123] Pulzer quotes an anti-Jewish pamphlet of 1886 which objected to "the unseemliness, the offensiveness and the noise, as if they [the Jews] were entirely amongst themselves. . . ."[124] Jewish voices frequently appeared loud to the Germans, and their voice quality sometimes disagreeable. The Germans had a standard description for *any* loud group: "Noisy like a Jewish school." Jewish temperament, on occasion, seemed more exuberant than called for,

[118] Quoted in Weltsch (ed.), op. cit., p. 33.

[119] *Hitler's Table Talks*, p. 378.

[120] Weltsch (ed.), loc. cit. Max Beloff in *Encounter*, November 1969, p. 40, calls the present Jewish distinctiveness "a mutation from an originally religious distinctiveness which nowadays takes on new and secular forms."

[121] Rathenau quoted in Kampmann, op. cit., p. 440.

[122] Kahler, *Jews among the Nations*, pp. 31, 32, 38, 11.

[123] Rathenau, in Kampmann, loc. cit.

[124] Pulzer, *The Rise of Political Anti-Semitism*, p. 26.

and there was not always enough tact and reticence. Kahler calls it "lack of human balance . . . misjudgment of the right place and due distance."[125] As usual, of course, the conspicuous Jews drew far more attention and disapproval than justified by their numbers; and the quiet, well-mannered, "conforming" Jews remained unnoticed. The thousands of quiet, dedicated Jewish physicians, dentists, and scholars were disregarded. It did not seem to occur to the Germans that they, too, had their own, not inconsiderable, share of unattractive people.

The image of the objectionable German Jew became entirely stereotyped, and as Bettelheim says of a much later period in the United States, "whoever fitted the stereotyped picture of the Jew was accepted as such and used to support the validity of the stereotype, . . . whoever eluded the pattern was either not recognized as a Jew, or declared a rare exception."[126] At the very least, the Jews failed to come up to the standards of the idealized blond Germanic hero-type; and all in all, they did not fit well into the utopian "German folk community." It should be remembered, in this connection, as Pulzer has emphasized, that German "folkdom" *(Volkstum)* was "central to German-Jewish antagonisms." The idea of *Volkstum*, as he says, was, of course, one of "self-admiration"[127] or narcissism.

The Jewish religion also made its own, if minor, contribution to the difference between Jews and Germans. Even those Germans to whom the Christian religion meant little had to be aware of the historic fact that the Jews, on the whole, had been obdurate and had tenaciously resisted conforming to the general faith. The concept of the "chosen people" in itself was naturally one of extreme differentiation between the Jews and the rest of the world. The German anti-Semitic movement did not, of course, let this pass unnoticed.[128] Also, under pseudo-Darwinistic theories, a foreign element like the Jews meant a biological weakening of the homogeneous organic body of the German people.

To the average German, moreover, the Jews were a mysterious, enigmatic, inscrutable group—really essentially alien, not merely different as Martin Buber had claimed. They were reported to follow

[125]Kahler, op. cit., p. 87.
[126]Bettelheim and Janowitz, op. cit., p. 34.
[127]Pulzer, op. cit., pp. 312-313.
[128]See, for instance, Müller, *Die Entwicklung des Rassenantisemitismus*, p. 68.

secret oriental rituals which no German properly understood; they slaughtered animals by some undisclosed allegedly cruel methods; they had their own holidays when they fasted, instead of eating opulent meals like the Germans on *their* holidays; they sat in oriental-looking synagogues with hats on their heads, separated from their women; their rabbis (in itself an ugly-sounding word to a German) wore temple curls and long caftans; most Jews did not care much for liquor. Even beer, the German drink favored in many regions, did not seem to appeal to them much. They were clannish and cooperated with each other, and this, too, could be a source of apprehension to the Germans, particularly in business. To be sure, much of this could possibly apply only to the relatively small group of orthodox Jews in Germany. But most Germans knew little or nothing of differences within the Jewish group and cared less.

The strong element of incomprehensibility about the Jews and the inability to understand them, in turn, caused a feeling of fear in some Germans, particularly in light of the fact that, as we shall see later, much of the press and of the intellectual life was dominated by Jews. Adorno, speaking from a psychological point of view, believes that the "infantile fear of the strange is only subsequently 'filled up' with the imagery of a specific group, stereotyped and handy for this purpose. The Jews are favorite stand-ins for the child's 'bad man'." [129]

And then there was what Erikson calls "the historical Jewish identity of invincible spiritual and intellectual superiority over a physically superior outer world." [130] The Jews, of course, were careful never openly to assert this feeling of superiority, but the Germans may well have perceived it and found it odious.

It is interesting to note, in this connection, in what manner a sensitive German Jew, the well-known novelist Jakob Wassermann, perceived German anti-Semitism of the pre-Hitler period, exaggerated as his report may be:

For the first time I encountered [in the German soldiers of World War I] that torpid, rigid, almost speechless hatred which had penetrated into the masses and which the word "anti-Semitism"

---

[129] Adorno, *The Authoritarian Personality,* p. 609.
[130] Erikson, *Identity, Youth and Crisis,* p. 324.

does not really describe, indicating neither the nature nor the source nor the depth nor the aim. This hatred shows elements of superstition as well as voluntary delusion; of fear of evil spirits as well as a priestly rigidity; the malice of the disadvantaged and defrauded, as also ignorance, lies, and lack of conscience as well as calculated defense, apelike spite, and religious fanaticism. Lust and curiosity are in it, and thirst for blood, fear of being tempted and seduced, desire for the mysterious, and low self-estimation. In this mixture and depth of background, it is a particularly German phenomenon. It is a German hatred.[131]

This was indeed quite a catalog of elements of German anti-Semitism, and a good many of them, at least in this intensity, may have existed only in the mind of this gifted fiction writer. Yet Wassermann's description does tend to suggest the depth of the abyss between Jews and Germans that existed long before Hitler's ascent. His statements may be significant also as indicating strong counterhatred on the part of the Jews. At any rate, as far as the Germans were concerned, deep psychological rejection and fear of the strange and unfamiliar in the Jews had developed and grown to strong hatred long prior to Hitler's appearance on the political scene. He himself, as anyone reading *Mein Kampf* will readily see, perceived of the Jews primarily as a mysterious, strange, and highly dangerous group. This important focus of antagonism and violence against the Jews could have been avoided by them only if they had stopped being Jewish, because what made them Jews, made them also into an odious, alien group. And the Jews were no doubt quite unable to shed their Jewishness—at least not within less than two or three generations—but, above all, they were surely quite unwilling to do so. They could, by and large, look back on a proud history of thousands of fruitful, productive years during which they had maintained their identity and ethnic cohesion with unparalleled determination and at enormous sacrifice.

The problem, moreover, was greatly compounded by the arrival of large numbers of Polish and Russian Jews in Germany before World War I and in the 1920s. These so-called *Ostjuden* were a shabby and dirty-looking group to whom the odor of the Eastern ghettos still

[131]Jakob Wasserman, *Mein Weg als Deutscher und Jude* (1921), quoted in Klesse, *Vom alten zum neuen Israel*, pp. 215-216.

seemed to cling. The historian Heinrich von Treitschke remarked as far back as 1880 or so that the Eastern Jews should have been trained to use soap and comb before being granted German citizenship.[132] They spoke Yiddish, or a German adaptation of it, which sounded distinctly unpleasant to the Germans and no less so to the assimilated, highly refined German Jews, who, themselves, as Adorno says,[133] discriminated heavily against the immigrants from the East. It was easy for rabid anti-Semites to hold up Yiddish as an "insult" to its German parent language.[134] These Eastern Jews, roaming the streets of Berlin in search of a little business, were an unpleasant sight. Hundreds of years of ghetto life had taught them tough and yet obsequious manners in dealing with generally hostile gentiles. They did not seem to know or care whether they made themselves unpopular. And few Germans realized or were willing to admit that people who were confined to ghettos and treated as outcasts for hundreds of years must necessarily develop attitudes which were far from reflecting their true qualities or any real racial characteristics.

What was, in the final analysis, worst about the Eastern Jews was that their encounter with the Germans tended to drag down the image of all Jews in the German mind, even of those numerous highly cultured, assimilated Jews whose families had lived in Germany for centuries. (Some Jews had arrived at the site of Cologne with the Roman soldiers in A.D. 50 before any Germans occupied the site.) The influx of Eastern Jews had far more damaging effects on gentile-Jewish relations in Germany than in the United States, where the population, at least in the big cities, is generally accustomed to the immigration of large alien groups of the lowest social levels and is willing to wait for their assimilation. The Germans were totally unaccustomed to immigration. By and large, the German view had been, ever since the 1880s or earlier, that all Jews were bad and that any belief in "exceptional Jews" could only be dangerous.[135]

As long as the Jews remained Jewish, they were, on the whole, unassimilable in Germany. As far back as 1886, an anti-Semitic periodical, *Antisemitische Correspondenz*, rejected as an outrageous

[132] See Kampmann, op. cit., p. 353.
[133] Adorno, op. cit., p. 624.
[134] See Klesse, op. cit., p. 176.
[135] See, for instance, Müller, op. cit., p. 62.

demand the idea "of accepting the scum of the earth into our national community and of letting our good blood be mixed with its satanic poison."[136] The German refusal to permit large-scale assimilation of the Jews may, in fact, reflect a profound difference between Germany and other countries. (It is worth noting, however, that Adorno found that "despite their demand for total assimilation, most [American] anti-Semites seem to feel that the 'basic Jewishness' is permanent."[137]) At any rate, any effort at a genuine incorporation of the Jews into the "German folk community" resembled a surgical transplant of another person's organ which the receiving body forcibly rejects. The Jewish philosopher Theodor Lessing calls it "ejecting [the Jews] from the nations of Europe like a foreign body, it being immaterial whether the foreign body which disturbs the life process is a glass splinter or a diamond."[138] Rathenau, too, called the Jews "a foreign organism in the German people's body."[139] The entire German-Jewish "symbiosis," discussed earlier, may have had aspects of an overcompensatory effort to avoid that bodily rejection; and the symbiosis involved only a thin upper layer of intellectual Germans. It seems, in any case, that only the most sophisticated in any group of people find it interesting and profitable to explore an alien group and to learn from it.

Moreover, group hostility of the type of the German anti-Semitism, directed as it was against a weak outgroup, seems to be psychologically self-inducing. Freud said that ". . . the sense of community of the masses requires for its completion the hostility against an outside minority, and the numerical weakness of the excluded group represents a challenge to suppress it."[140] Erich Fromm applies this particularly to the authoritarian German who loves power: "The very sight of a powerless person makes him want to attack, dominate, humiliate him." He is "the more aroused the more helpless his object has become."[141] In part, this reaction may be sexual.

Speaking of the United States in 1960, Bettelheim suggests that

---

[136] Quoted in Müller, op. cit., p. 77.
[137] Adorno, op. cit., p. 99.
[138] Lessing, *Deutschland und seine Juden*, p. 16.
[139] Quoted in Kampmann, op. cit., p. 440.
[140] Freud, *Der Mann Moses*, Vol. 16, p. 197.
[141] Fromm, *Escape*, p. 168; see also p. 225.

moderation in feeling about Jews, while "of a rather tenuous nature, . . . will perhaps be maintained so long as another outgroup [the Negroes] provides objects for the displacement and persecution [*sic*] of instinctual [hostile] tendencies. . . ."[142] In fact, intense American propaganda has provided an additional outgroup, loosely identified as Communists. To a very minor degree, communists were also an outgroup in Germany, but not sufficiently to attract much of a discharge of general hostility. In fact, National Socialism usually identified communists as "Jewish-bolshevists," thus channeling also this portion of the hostility toward the Jews.[143]

Group hostility against a minority feeds on itself on one respect. It creates a community of interest within a society that may otherwise be divided. Anti-Semitism had for decades been a common meeting ground for many levels of German society, a kind of unifying factor, and this was intensified under Hitler. Almost everybody could agree on cursing the Jews. In the nineteenth and early twentieth century the great bulk of anti-Semitic support came from the middle class and students. They remained the most important segments under Hitler, but he did broaden the anti-Semitic base considerably. On the whole, however, he had to do no more than articulate the general determination to reject the Jews and translate the prevailing ideas and feelings into action. Of course, the Final Solution, at which he arrived much later, went far beyond the vague purposes of the existing group hostility.

d. RACE HATRED AGAINST THE JEWS

German hatred of the Jews as a race was a very prominent part of the entire syndrome of race theories of National Socialism, heretofore discussed. We saw that under these theories, as finally developed, there was a law of nature that gave to racially stronger and superior nations, and particularly to Germans, a natural right or even a kind of biological duty to suppress or exterminate weaker or inferior groups—a procedure sometimes called "racial hygiene." The Jews were the most inferior of all groups; they were subhuman, animallike, mere bacilli, vermin. Their suppression was biologically essential

---

[142]Bettelheim and Janowitz, op. cit., pp. 159–160.
[143]Hitler called bolshevism "this Jewish disease" (*Mein Kampf,* p. 277).

to prevent damage to the Germans and other people, to avoid racial contamination.

What was then called race hatred might today be largely comprised within the concept of "group hostility" (or interethnic hostility), which is the subject of the preceding section. It may even be logically inappropriate to attempt to discuss race hatred separately from group hostility. It is possible, for example, that the race theories were largely rationalizations of existing elemental group hostility. One reason for such a process of rationalization may be that pure group hostility has a certain aura of irrational viciousness about it and is ethically hard to defend. Race hatred against the Jews, on the other hand, was able to make some claim to "legitimacy." Within national socialist ideology, it was in line with pseudo-Darwinistic doctrine and, thus, could be given the appearance of a sound basis in the natural sciences.

Moreover, race hatred offered the advantage that, while mere group hostility can be avoided by leaving the group, difficult as this may sometimes be, race hatred is largely inescapable. The national socialist regime was extremely thorough in seeing to it that once the stigma of membership in the hated race attached, it remained attached in perpetuity. It followed from grandfather to father to son to grandson, and so forth. There was a whole system of *Ahnenpass* (ancestor passport or identification) to which every German was subject.

Of course, it may well be doubtful whether there is a Jewish race in a strict ethnological sense. It was a fact, however, that the Jews in Germany constituted a group within which, whether as a result of inbreeding or for other reasons, large numbers of a similar type occurred—a type which showed easily recognizable characteristics in physical appearances, voice quality, mentality, behavior, and temperament. In any event, whether the Jews were a race or not, the important consideration in the present context is that the Germans quite definitely *looked* upon them as a race different from their own.

Adorno, who seems to be opposed to regarding "race" as separate from "group" in a sociopsychological sense, speaks of "race" as a "socially harmful idea,"[144] and there are, indeed, few who would

---

[144] Adorno, op. cit., p. 102.

question this, particularly in the light of the whole disastrous German experience. But the race concept is still very much alive even today, and at any rate, in a historical review of national socialist ideology, we cannot dispense with it. [145] There is no question that this concept was entirely basic in that ideology and that it determined a thousand practical actions. The hostility against the Jewish group as a race seemed just as real then as the antagonism of large numbers of Americans against the Negro race today. Within the scope of mere group hostility, it would indeed be difficult to comprehend the intensity of the German anti-Jewish feeling and action, the depth of the emotional commitment. Some inexplicable dark residue of something other than mere group hostility remains. But of all the causative factors of anti-Semitism, the matter of sheer race hatred is the most elusive. In the absence of far more research on the problem of the causes of race hatred, no answers of any consequence can be given here.

Much of the German hatred of the Jews seemed to have been caused by sheer irrational physical revulsion, perhaps not unlike that of one dog against another. There was among some Germans a kind of instinctive physical abhorrence of Jews. In 1922, when Hitler was still largely unknown, Hans F. K. Günther, who was later to be appointed a kind of official national socialist race expert, published a book about the German race with an elaborate Supplement entitled "Racial Science of the Jewish People." In it, in rather sober, scientific language, he described the Jews as short of stature, squat, short legged, and frequently with ample fat deposits. Jewish women were characterized as often particularly fat. Many Jews were said to be narrow chested and bowlegged; their calves lacked all muscle. Their heads were short, their noses hooked and pointed downward, their lips mostly thick and bunched-up *(wulstig)*. The lower lip protruded—in some cases so far that the lip structure resembled that of a camel. The eyelids often were heavy as if thick. This was said to give the Jews a furtive look. The ears of some stuck out conspicuously. The odor of their skin was mostly "sweetish." Their bodies were covered with a strong growth of hair. The texture of their hair was kinky or

---

[145]Bettelheim (op. cit., p. 32) proceeds on the surprisingly narrow "basic hypothesis . . . that intolerance is a function of deprivation and anxiety. . . ." This seems negated by much of the history of anti-Semitism in Germany, and even Bettelheim does not strictly adhere to his hypothesis.

kinky-woolly (negroid). Their eyes glowed strangely or had a moist glow. Jewish gestures were soft.

All in all, it was not an appetizing description of a people, and it was topped off with the presumably devastating criticism that the total appearance of the Jews was "unsoldierlike."[146] It need hardly be mentioned, in this connection, that to the Germans the stereotyped wretched body of the Jew was merely a reflection of his equally wretched mind and soul. The Jew simply offered no redeeming qualities whatsoever.

There was perhaps nothing more significant in relation to German race hatred of the Jews than the widely held theory that Jewish men contaminated German women by sexual intercourse.[147] Merely the intercourse itself, even without pregnancy, was considered to result in irreversible racial contamination of the woman. Hitler himself (admittedly an abnormal case) spoke of "the black haired Jew-boy [who] for hours lies in wait, satanic joy in his face, for the unsuspecting girl whom he soils with his blood and thus ravishes from her people,"[148] and he accused "those black-haired parasites of the people [who] systematically sully our inexperienced young blond girls and thus destroy something that cannot be replaced on this Earth."[149] A marching song of the SA included the following lines:

Whet the long knives on the pavement!
Let the knives slide into the Jewish body!
*(Wetzt die langen Messer auf dem Bürgersteig!
Lasst die Messer flutschen in den Judenleib!)*[150]

A book for children (10 to 14), *Der Giftpilz* (The Poisonous Mushroom), contained a story entitled "Inge at the Jewish Doctor's Office," from which the following is quoted:

Inge has been waiting for an hour. Once more she opens a book and tries to read. Then the door suddenly opens. Inge looks up.

[146]Hans F. K. Günther, *Rassenkunde des deutschen Volkes*, 1922, pp. 374–377.
[147]See, in this connection, the Law for the Protection of German Blood and Honor of Sept. 15, 1935 (*Reichsgesetzblatt* I, 1146).
[148]*Mein Kampf*, p. 357.
[149]Ibid., p. 630.
[150]Quoted in Grebing, *Der Nationalsozialismus*, p. 69. See also Mosse, *Crisis*, p. 305.

The Jew appears. Inge utters a cry. Overcome by fear, she drops the book. She jumps to her feet in terror. Her eyes are fixed on the Jewish doctor's face. It is the face of the Devil. In the middle of this diabolical face is a huge hooked nose. Two criminal eyes gleam behind the spectacles. "At last I have you, little German girl!" And the Jew flings himself on her. His fat fingers lay hold on her. . . .[151]

Attitudes such as those reflected in the foregoing quotations do seem to go far beyond mere normal group hostility. Sex, of course, played a part in them. It is possible that the authors projected their own repressed sex urges toward the Jews and hated them for these urges. But even then these attitudes do point toward race hatred.

It may be worth noting, in this connection, that Hitler once said in a very early letter (1919) that "anti-Semitism based on pure *emotion* will find its final expression in the form of pogroms. *Rational* anti-Semitism must lead to systematic legal opposition to, and removal of, the privileges of the Jews." (Italics added.) [152] It is possible that he had a vague understanding of a distinction between what we would today call "group hostility" and race hatred.

The above-mentioned German image of the fat kinky-haired Jew with thick lips, hooked nose, fat fingers, etc., contrasted strongly with the utopian vision which the Germans had of their own people: blond, tall, erect, blue-eyed, narrow-faced, with thin lips and nose, noble and kind of countenance.

As far as the fear of contamination by Jews is concerned, it may be worth noting that Adorno found this present even in the United States. He reports "the fear that Jews may, if permitted intimate or intensive contact with Gentiles, have a corrupting or degenerating influence . . . moral, political, intellectual, sensual, and so on . . . in the same way as one may be organically infected by a disease." [153]

Race hatred, moreover, could feed on itself. To the underprivileged, the loafer, the good-for-nothing, it meant that he could still feel superior to someone, the Jew, merely because of his qualification as a

---

[151]Ernst Himmer, *Der Giftpilz*, 1938, quoted in Leon Poliakov, *The Weapon of Anti-Semitism*, in Baumont (ed.), *The Third Reich*, op. cit., p. 840.

[152]Quoted in Joachim C. Fest, *Das Gesicht des Dritten Reiches*, p. 32.

[153]Adorno, op. cit., p. 98.

non-Jew. In this respect, he could feel perfectly equal to the rich, the successful, the elite. Race hatred was a great equalizer for everybody except the Jews, and this was an incidental attraction to a good many Germans.

There is little doubt that the race hatred did not all run in one direction and that a good many Jews found many Germans racially as repulsive as the Germans found them. But the Jews were a very small, weak minority in the midst of a large, pugnacious nation; and whatever hostility they may have felt could not safely be expressed. It is possible, however, that the Jewish tendency toward destruction of typically German traditional values (which will be discussed later in detail) was an indirect means of expressing Jewish hatred of the Germans.

The Jews themselves were actually no strangers to the practice of racial discrimination against others. In fact, such discrimination began in biblical days. According to the Old Testament, Ezra 6:10, the priest Ezra discovered upon his return from Babylon to Jerusalem that a group of Jews, who had returned earlier, had "not kept themselves apart from the foreign population [in Jerusalem] . . ." and had "taken women of these nations as wives for themselves and their sons, so that the *holy race* has become mixed with the foreign population . . ." (9:1, 2). [154] Ezra became greatly upset and quoted to the assembled Jews God's command "do not give your daughters in marriage to their sons, and do not marry your sons to their daughters, and never seek their welfare or prosperity. Thus you will be strong and enjoy the good things of the land, and pass it on to your children as an everlasting possession" (9:12). The Jews then proposed "to dismiss all these women and their brood" (10:3). [155] A formal inquiry "into all the marriages with foreign women" (10:17) discovered a great many, and all the men "dismissed them [the wives], together with their children" (10:44). A German-Jewish writer, Fritz Kahn, writing in 1922, called this "a magnificent act of deliberate racial breeding, unique in the history of nations" [156]—a statement which he presum-

[154]Italics added. All translations as rendered in *The New English Bible—Old Testament,* Oxford University Press, Cambridge University Press, 1970.
[155]The *Apocrypha* (I Esdras 8:93) says "expel all our wives of alien race with their children."
[156]Kahn, *Die Juden als Rasse und Kulturvolk,* p. 146.

ably would not have made if he had been able to look into the future. We should add, however, that while the national socialist regime was ordinarily vastly more radical in racial matters than the priest Ezra, it never did require the dissolution of existing marriages between gentiles and Jews or the "dismissal" of Jewish wives and their children. [157]

Jewish conservative opposition to intermarriage with non-Jews has continued through more than 2,000 years to this day, [158] and, indeed, without it the Jews could hardly have survived as a people in the diaspora.

It is interesting to note incidentally that no significant group hostility or race hatred arose in one close, if temporary, encounter by the Germans with another ethnic group after World War I. This encounter occurred when White Russian refugees fled to Germany, mostly to Berlin, to escape from the new Red Russian regime. These refugees established themselves in Berlin for varying periods of time, had their own newspaper, folk music and dance groups, restaurants, and so on. They lived on the German economy which was then far from being stable or prosperous. This was an ethnically quite alien group of Slavs, but the Germans, with rare exceptions, received them with open arms, admired their distinctive culture and their warm Russian personalities. It was an ethnic or race relationship which is difficult to understand in the light of the strong German hostility against the Russians twenty-three years later, which the Russians certainly did not provoke. It was a relationship, also, which was worlds apart from that between Germans and Jews. But at least that encounter with the Russians showed that the Germans, under some circumstances, were quite able to tolerate a different ethnic group in their country and even to be helpful to it, at least temporarily.

e. ENVY OF THE JEWS AND THEIR COMPETITION

Hannah Arendt says that it "is a 'truism' that has not been made truer by repetition that antisemitism is only a form of envy." [159] Clearly it would be wrong to say that German anti-Semitism was *only* a form of envy—it was much more—but there is no doubt that

---

[157] For details, see Raul Hilberg, *The Destruction of the European Jews*, pp. 114-115.

[158] See, f.i., *The New York Times*, Mar. 19 and Nov. 8, 1970.

[159] Arendt, *Origins*, p. 241.

envy of Jewish wealth and resentment of their quick social progress as well as their superior intelligence were a significant causative factor in the rise of anti-Semitism in pre-Hitler Germany.

To some extent, this causation of anti-Semitism must be understood in a historical setting, reaching back hundreds of years. In the Middle Ages and for centuries thereafter, the Jews, on the whole, were excluded from owning land, from joining manufacturing companies, artisan guilds, and the army. All that was left to them was moneylending and pawnbroking (prohibited to Christians by clerical laws) and being middlemen in financial transactions and trading. For centuries, their moneylending put the stamp of usury on them, in itself a hateful stigma, and to this day they have been unable wholly to free themselves of a reputation for "sharp" business practices. At any rate, as Heine said, "they were forced to become rich and then were hated because of their wealth."[160]

The moneylending developed into banking and the pawnbroking into trade in secondhand and, later, new goods, including clothes, gold, and diamonds. All this led to trade in mixed merchandise; and finally large Jewish-owned department stores sprang up in many German cities.

In the case of the Jews, trade was not only their business but also their fate. It is fairly easy to see where German-Jewish antagonism could arise. The small German farmer had to get loans from Jewish moneylenders or bankers to tide him over to the next harvest; and if he could not pay back the loan, his farm might be foreclosed. He had to sell his products to Jewish grain and cattle dealers, and, of course, he felt that the prices they paid were too low. The small German store owners were threatened by the competition of the Jewish department stores; they had to obtain their financing from Jewish bankers, or their goods were bought on credit from Jewish wholesale merchants. Everybody seemed to be in debt to a Jew, and, in fact, a great many of the injustices of the entire capitalist system could be blamed on the Jews. The average German, moreover, always felt strongly that a mere middleman, like a moneylender, banker, trader, wholesaler—who himself "produced" nothing—never did "an honest day's work." Such middlemen were regarded essentially as parasites, swindlers,

[160]Heine, *Shakespeares Mädchen und Frauen,* in *Werke,* p. 1133.

and frauds, bloodsuckers on the clean body of the German economy, and the acquisition of wealth by them was deeply resented. High finance, supposedly Jewish, was regarded as the most sinister agency of the whole evil system, and this all the more so since it was world-wide in scope.

The German-Jewish relationship was not much better in the free professions, although here the difficulties did not begin to arise until the latter part of the nineteenth century. Upon Emancipation around 1869, the young Jews started to stream into the German law schools, medical schools, and dental colleges. Here was their chance to throw off, once and for all, the distasteful restrictions which had tied the Jews for centuries to finance and trade. Talmudic training and learning over the centuries had kept their wits sharp and agile and had accustomed them to abstract reasoning. Highly intelligent, quick-witted, and well educated as they were, they possessed ideal qualifications to be good lawyers and doctors, and many of them were indeed superior to their German colleagues. Emotionally, moreover, as their heritage in the diaspora and in the tradition of their Bible, they readily identified themselves with those who suffered or needed help. It did not take the German public long to discover all this, and no matter how anti-Semitic the German farmers, storekeepers and others might have been, many of them found it useful to be represented by a Jewish lawyer and to be treated by a Jewish doctor or dentist. The result could only be an intense competitive struggle with their gentile counterparts and considerable anti-Semitism. This competition was not relieved until national socialist legislation removed all Jews from the free professions.

The industrial proletariat had its own special reasons for envying and hating the Jews. Fundamentally the trouble was that the German Jews had never been proletariat themselves. While the Jews became industrial proletariat in Russia, Poland, and, temporarily, in the United States, they succeeded in avoiding that fate in Germany and Austria. "To the true proletarian, the Jew is primarily the bourgeois . . . an agent of the economic sphere of the middleman, . . . the executor of capitalist tendencies, . . . who 'presents the bill.'"[161] That, as a historic fact, official restrictions on their occupations had prevented

[161] Adorno, op. cit., p. 638.

the Jews from joining the labor classes was something that the modern proletariat did not know or to which it would have been indifferent. All that the proletariat could see was that here was a group which seemingly without much effort and, at any rate, without "productive" or "honest" work had moved and continued to move from a very low social status directly into the petty bourgeoisie or even into the prosperous middle classes. It could happen that in one generation the son of a Polish immigrant Jew would become an affluent dentist, and there was no limit to how far the son of that dentist might advance. All this would not be at all unusual in the United States, among Jews as well as non-Jews, but it must be borne in mind that Germany was a country in which social upward mobility was generally very slow, partly for economic and partly for traditional reasons and lack of initiative. The defiance of all these reasons by the Jewish group was a cause of envy and resentment on the part of the proletariat and others.

All this, however, does not mean that the German socialist labor party, as an organization, ever became really anti-Semitic. In fact, the party, in theory and practice, was opposed to anti-Semitism; and in this respect it never wavered. Indeed, it could hardly have done anything else because many of its founders and leaders were Jews. [162] This meant that the anti-Semitism of the proletariat was largely inarticulate. But it was, nevertheless, entirely real, and when National Socialism began to develop, numerous defections took place from the socialist party to the National Socialists. It remains true, however, that National Socialism at all times drew its main strength from the lower middle class rather than the proletariat. [163]

The social upward mobility of the Jews caused hostile reactions also in the petty bourgeoisie or lower middle class *(Kleinbürgertum)* as well as in the middle class *(Mittelbürgertum)*. On both of these levels, the quick advance of the Jews into these classes was resented. In the case of members of the lowest middle class, which itself had only recently advanced from the labor class, there was apprehension, moreover, that the new Jewish competition on the same social level

[162] See Massing, *Rehearsal for Destruction*, pp. 155, 190–206. For the whole complex question of anti-Semitism in the German (and European) labor movement, see Edmund Silberner, *Sozialisten zur Judenfrage*, 1962.

[163] See Massing, op. cit., p. 75; Pulzer, *The Rise of Political Anti-semitism*, p. 279.

could force a retreat to the lower level; and this was true particularly during periods of economic crises. What took place, in other words, was to an extent a traditional European class struggle. But this was compounded by the very definite feeling on the part of the Germans that the unwelcome "alien" Jews, who were disliked or hated for a good many reasons, should not be where they were in the first place.

From a sociopsychological point of view, Adorno believes that the "petty bourgeoisie" blames the Jew for the total economic process because "for the equilibrium of their ego . . . they must find some 'guilt' responsible for their precarious social situation: otherwise the just order of the world would be disturbed." He says that "in all probability, they primarily seek this guilt within themselves and regard themselves, preconsciously, as 'failures'" and that "the Jews relieve them superficially of this guilt feeling."[164]

In every case, whether it concerned the German labor class or petty bourgeoisie, the middle class or the intelligentsia, the Jews increased the competitive struggle—not infrequently to a dangerous degree. At a minimum, the Jews made life more difficult for the Germans. They increased the dog-eat-dog aspect of modern life. Anyone with a reasonably assured place in the social system naturally looked with distaste on those who could rise to the same or even a higher place, seemingly without much effort and sometimes by "sharp practices" or by elbowing others out of the way. Bettelheim, moreover, has found a direct relationship between downward social mobility and intolerance, and upward mobility and tolerance.[165] Pulzer calls attention to the early inhibition of social mobility in Germany (by the guilds, etc.) and to the large-scale survival of "precapitalist" classes. He regards this as highly important to the student of anti-Semitism.[166]

Much of all this was the result of superior Jewish intelligence and other superior abilities. It may well be that the Jews are outstanding evidence for the correctness of the theory that there are genetic differences in the intelligence of the human races. It is also possible that the astonishing Jewish intelligence and drive were the result of various other factors (which, at the same time, favored some lack of

[164]Adorno, op. cit., p. 756.
[165]Bettelheim and Janowitz, *Dynamics of Prejudice*, p. 61.
[166]Pulzer, op. cit., p. 24.

creativity in the visual arts, musical composition, and literature). Freud says that the monotheistic religion "forced upon the [Jewish] people an advance into spirituality which, meaningful enough in itself, opened the way, moreover, to high esteem for intellectual labor and to further suppression of instinctual drives."[167] Hundreds of years of Talmudic and other intellectual training in the isolation of the ghettos had resulted in a very high faculty for abstract thinking. These abilities were to become useful in a thousand ways outside the ghettos. The young Jews, moreover, were traditionally eager to learn and were thrilled by new thoughts. There had been, in addition, a desperate need for the Jews through the centuries to maintain themselves against adversity by accomplishing more than the non-Jews, overcompensation for a feeling of social inferiority, and other factors. Also, centuries of life under adverse conditions in the diaspora had made the Jews adaptable, tenacious, tough, and frugal. They believed in sobriety and the value of strong family bonds. Their standard of life was generally modest, at least until they reached considerable affluence.

The result of the high Jewish intelligence became apparent, not only in the very large number of well-known Jewish scientists, philosophers, lawyers, physicians, and publishers, in Germany but also in the extraordinarily large number of Nobel prizes that Jews received. Of the 183 Nobel prizes granted up to 1936, 9 percent were granted to Jews in Germany and Austria, although they represented only about 1 percent of the population. (11 percent of the prizes were given to Jews throughout the world.)[168] In developing their intelligence, the Jews were assisted by the education which they were able to obtain at the German public schools at little or no expense. Moreover, almost all Jews, except recent Eastern immigrants, graduated from the highest level of these schools *(Gymnasium)*, whereas only a comparatively small percentage of the Germans did so. Many Jews, but relatively few Germans, went on to the universities. Over a short span of time and to a surprising extent, the Jews had become a successful, affluent segment of the middle class, and even more than their German counterparts, they reaped all the material and educational advantages of that class.

---

[167] Freud, *Der Mann Moses,* p. 231. See also Erikson, *Childhood and Society,* p. 355.
[168] Wolfgang Scheffler, *Judenverfolgung im Dritten Reich,* p. 14.

Equipped with higher intelligence and, on the average, a better education, the Jews had, by and large, found it fairly easy to get ahead of the Germans in the competitive struggle. Their superiority in business, in seeing opportunities, in striking good bargains, in getting the better of non-Jews, was generally recognized, and it was, of course, much resented. It is surprising that this kind of superiority should have been so much in evidence in the German-Jewish relationship and not, for example, in American-Jewish relations. It may be that the Germans, while certainly not stupid, were generally slow, overly direct, and simply untalented in business matters. It should be remembered that for centuries business activities had traditionally been looked down upon by the Germans, who liked to contrast the "Germanic hero" with the "Western merchant" or "shopkeeper." The money-conscious Jewish trader, merchant, shopkeeper, and financier was necessarily the "counterperson" to the idealized "Germanic hero," and this was particularly disturbing when that contemptible counterperson seemed better able to make a success of his life in the German environment than the native romantic hero type. But there is little doubt that the average Jewish businessman, unhampered by sentimental ties and traditions hostile to business, was more mobile, agressive, and forward-looking than the average of his German competitors. Here again, distaste, envy, and antagonism against Jews was a logical result.

The financial success of the Jews as traders, merchants, middlemen, financiers, and the like, was only one of the reasons why Jewish activity in these occupations aroused anti-Semitism. In addition, as already mentioned, in the traditional German view all these occupations were "unproductive." They served to increase the price of the goods without increasing their value, and they enriched people who did no "real" work. Essentially, these occupations were considered immoral. And even worse was mere dealing in money itself or trading in the stock market. It follows that the Jews, who were extensively engaged in these occupations, were regarded as economically unethical per se, and this became a fixed stereotype. Contrasted with these unproductive, parasitical occupations were the "honest" and "honorable" ones, even if low paid: farming, the handicrafts, manual labor, soldiering, marine, service to the state; but the Jews could not be found in any of these. The dubious economic activities of the Jews seemed to threaten basic traditional values; and most Germans closed their eyes to the fact that the Jews had merely advanced into the normal economy of the twentieth century, whereas most Germans were still clinging to economic concepts of a past age. At the same time, the low German regard for traders, middlemen, and financiers made it easy for the Jews in Germany to succeed in these less-crowded occupations and, proportionately, to acquire greater wealth than any Jewish group of that period in any other country. Their wealth did not endear them to the Germans.

Jewish business activity was considered "immoral" also in another sense. German literature abounds in tragic stories of farmers losing the old homestead to an ugly grasping Jew who foreclosed a mortgage on the farm. The picture of the German hero type, rooted deep in the native soil, being uprooted and expelled by an alien money-conscious Jew was one of extreme distaste and repulsiveness to millions of Germans.

f. THE JEWS AS THE VISIBLE ENEMY

Some have contended that one reason why National Socialism promoted anti-Semitism was that it needed a "visible enemy." "By heaping all hatred, all resentment, all misery upon one enemy who can easily be exterminated and who cannot resist, Aryan society can be integrated into a whole."[169] "A confrontation with a live enemy, with someone personally guilty, is always more satisfying than to feel oneself as a mere victim of an anonymous, historic, irresistible force."[170] It may be that the need for a visible enemy actually existed in the early days of National Socialism when the Movement desperately struggled for power against many odds. In an early speech (February 27, 1925) Hitler did, in fact, say: "For a people like the German people, it is particularly necessary to indicate one sole enemy, to march against one sole enemy."[171] But later, National Socialism had (and wanted) many enemies, most of whom were quite as visible as the Jews and against whom every bit of the available latent group hostility could be discharged. These enemies proved to be less easy to extermi-

[169]Neumann, *Behemoth*, p. 125.

[170]Ehrlich in Thieme, (ed.), *Judenfeindschaft*, p. 232.

[171]Quoted in Poliakov, *The Weapon of Anti-Semitism*, in Baumont (ed.), *The Third Reich*, p. 833.

nate (and some could not even be subdued), but then National Socialism kept the extermination of the Jews a secret in any event and
never exploited it for propaganda purposes. Clearly, Hitler did not
really need the Jewish visible enemy very long. It would be misleading
to explain German anti-Semitism as a device to manipulate the masses
or as a mere tool of realpolitik. This anti-Semitism was primarily an
ideological obsession. It was believed in sincerely, and its function
as a political tool was purely secondary, if that.

It is something else to say, however, as Mosse does, that "For the
image of the Jew to arouse any feelings, pro or con, he had to be gener-
alized, abstracted, depersonalized. . . . [The Jews] had to be converted
into objectified symbols so as to become other than human beings."[172]
Naturally, this process, and anti-Semitism in general, made the Jews
more visible, but this was not its real purpose. The process of de-
personalization and objectification had been largely accomplished in
the minds of most Germans long before Hitler entered the scene,
except that the conversion into "other than human beings" was mostly
left to him and his associates. Eva Reichmann believes that the
national socialist idea of the Jew was a personification of an "anti-
symbol" which, however, in her view, was of mere subordinate significance.[173] Generally, she is quite correct in taking the view that
"anti-Semitism played no decisive part in the workings [*Wirkung*] of
national socialist thought processes,"[174] particularly if we consider
the total scope of the ideology and the extensive political aims of the
regime.

g. THE SCAPEGOAT THEORY

Somewhat related to the theory of the Jew as the visible enemy is
that of the Jew as the scapegoat. This dates back to the Middle Ages,
and there is hardly a book on the history of anti-Semitism which does
not mention it as a persistent cause of anti-Jewish attitudes. Whenever some disaster occurred, bad times, pestilence or the like, the
local rulers or the population itself found it convenient to put the
blame on the Jews. A good many individual and mass frustrations
could be projected to them. They were a readily identifiable and weak

[172]Mosse, *Crisis*, pp. 301–302
[173]Reichmann, *Flucht in den Hass*, p. 282.
[174]Ibid.

minority group with weird customs, of whose guilt for all kinds of happenings the masses could rather easily be convinced. The Jew "was tangibly present, . . . easy game which even the police had made available, and he was reassuringly weak."[175] In external affairs, the Jews could even look like a medieval "fifth column." There seems to be a general human tendency, in any event, to try to relate all current misery and discontent to *one* cause only.

It is safe to say, however, that at least in Germany the scapegoat theory had ceased being a significant causative factor in anti-Semitism long before World War I. (Some semblance of it could still be found in the so-called *Gründerschwindel*, a major economic scandal and crisis in the 1870s, in which Jews actually had a hand.) The scapegoat theory might indeed never have been resurrected if it had not received an enormously powerful specific impetus at the end of World War I, in 1918 and early 1919. Hitler and others exploited this to the full in later years and never ceased exploiting it until the death of the Third Reich in 1945.

The immediate cause for this resurrection of the scapegoat theory lay in the events surrounding the defeat of imperial Germany at the end of World War I and the concomitant revolution. What happened was that the German nation was psychologically almost wholly unprepared for the defeat when it came on November 9, 1918. Neither the government nor the people had been adequately informed of the worsening military situation. For all anyone knew, the front lines in France were holding reasonably well. It was not until September 29, 1918, that General Ludendorff confidentially notified the Kaiser that an armistice was urgently required.[176] The government still hesitated for several weeks, and it was not until shortly prior to the actual collapse, "five minutes before twelve," that the German public began to realize that its army, which for four years had been steadily proclaimed as victorious, had in fact been defeated. The result was a severe trauma for the entire nation. Nobody could believe that this disaster could have happened without foul play, and an explanation, a scapegoat, was desperately needed.

It was at that dramatic point that the Jews entered the scene, and very visibly so. Revolution broke out all over Germany, and while

[175]Huss and Schröder, *Antisemitismus*, p. 98.
[176]Fritz Fischer, *Griff nach der Weltmacht*, p. 557.

many of its leaders were not Jewish, many others, including important ones, were Jews, for example Kurt Eisner, Rosa Luxemburg, and Klara Zetkin, the latter the wife of Karl Liebknecht, the top communist leader. Eisner set up a soviet-type government in Munich and, for a while, was its prime minister. Other Jewish activists were Edgar Jaffe, Gustav Landauer, Ernst Toller, Eduard Bernstein, Otto Landsberg, Ruth Fischer, Oscar Cohn.[177]

Walter Laqueur summarizes the matter of Jewish participation in left-wing politics in Eastern and Central Europe more broadly:

> In left-wing politics . . . Jews provided the ideological leadership in 19th century Germany; . . . Jews were among the leaders of the revolutionary wing. . . . The leadership of Austrian socialism . . . and Hungarian Communism was almost entirely Jewish, and there was not a single non-Jew in some East-European delegations at the congress of the Second International before the first World War. . . . Most of the founder-members of the German Communist Party in 1918, including the most prominent among them, were of Jewish origin.[178]

The association of so many Jews—previously hardly known— with the left or communist extremists who, in fact, set up mutinous "soviets" (councils) on the Russian pattern in the German army and navy in 1918, led countless Germans to believe that the Jews were traitors and were principally or wholly responsible for the collapse of the German armed forces, which otherwise remained unexplained. It was here that the *Dolchstosslegende* was born, that is, the legend that the army and navy were defeated only because they were stabbed in the back by traitors.

In the end, the extreme revolutionary regime collapsed, many of the Jewish leaders and others were assassinated by conservatives, but incalculable damage had been done to the cause of *all* Jews in Germany. Later, in memory of that fateful November, 1918, Hitler branded the Jews as the "November criminals," and he never ceased calling them by that name. It is probably safe to say that the majority

[177]For these and many other persons, see *Juden im Deutschen Kulturbereich*, pp. 556–573.
[178]Laqueur, *Out of the Ruins of Europe*, p. 472.

of all Germans of his time agreed with him. The Jews thus became the scapegoats for much of the blame for the German defeat in World War I, and the Weimar Republic never made a serious effort to clarify the historical record.

As Mosse says, "The birth of nazism was greatly facilitated by these developments in Munich [in 1918–1919]."[179] No other single event did more to promote anti-Semitism in Germany than the soviet-type premiership of the Jewish Kurt Eisner in that city for a few months. Even calm and reasonable Germans were deeply resentful and distressed.

The German masses, of course, were ready to accept the legend of the "stab in the back." Not only did it explain something for which they had no other explanation, but it also enabled them to project all guilt for the debacle to the Jews. Specifically, it relieved nearly every returned soldier of a feeling of responsibility. It also enabled everyone to give vent to his misery and unhappiness by hating the Jews and other "November criminals" who were believed to have been associated with them. It helped to restore some semblance of German self-respect, which basically had never been very strong and had cruelly suffered from the loss of the war. At the very least, everyone still seemed to have the right to feel that the glorious army was essentially "undefeated." It is a measure of the extent of the German sense of national insecurity that a theory based on such flimsy grounds could be so readily accepted.

Hitler and later the national socialist propaganda machine never ceased to hammer away on the legend of the "stab in the back," and to them it was, of course, a veritable gold mine of exploitable political and emotional issues. The people who naturally suffered most were the Jews, at least at short range. In the long run, however, the enormous self-deception, which the legend of the stab in the back implied, proved to have been of fatal significance to Hitler and all Germans.

h. THE JEWS AS ROOTLESS COSMOPOLITANS AND INTERNATIONALISTS

In the chapter on German Romanticism we shall consider the strong emphasis in the German romantic and neo-romantic movement on

---

[179]Mosse, *Crisis*, p. 237.

being rooted in nature or in the soil, on experiencing the German landscape, on the fusion of landscape, *Volk* and its "soul," on mystical ties with nature, on folk singing, and so forth. The prevailing antitheses were: being rooted in the soil against the urban life with its industrialization, mechanization and, generally, the dilemma of progress; healthy German peasantry against diseased alien urbanism; robust, old, or even primeval times against decadent modernity; genuine *Kultur* against the civilization of the cities; "soul" against intellectualism; decent, meaningful work of the individual against factory labor of the masses. All this was essentially not very different from reactions of a great many people to "modernity" in other countries, but in Germany the reaction was far more intense and assumed the dimensions of a *Weltanschauung*, frequently clothed in a mantle of swooning mysticism, or even a pseudoreligious faith.

In the present context of the factors which caused German anti-Semitism, the important aspect of these tendencies was that the Jews were considered the very embodiment of the modern city person, of rootlessness, of remoteness from the German "soil," of international mass civilization. And it is true that the great majority of all German Jews did live in the cities. They had, indeed, for centuries been forced to do so by laws prohibiting Jewish ownership of land and confining Jews to certain occupations, such as moneylending and commercial trading. Before Emancipation, they had not been permitted to be farmers, and thereafter, following centuries of life in cities and towns, they could hardly be expected to take up farming. (It is noteworthy that countless Jews actually were farmers in Poland under a more liberal land policy; and the kibbutzim in Israel today need hardly be mentioned. In Poland and Soviet Russia, in fact, the occupying German Army and the *Einsatzgruppen* had to make considerable efforts to concentrate the *Landjuden* in the cities before shipping them to the extermination camps.)

But the historical origin of Jewish city life meant nothing to the Germans, and they were largely unaware that "country Jews" existed in other countries. It is probably true, at any rate, that the mere location of the Jews in the cities was not what the Germans necessarily objected to: it was rather the metropolitan spirit and the modernity in all its decadence that city life engendered. All the Germans could see was that the peace and quiet of "the good old days" was increasingly being replaced by a hectic, competitive commercialism, by facile intellectualism, and by materialism. The traditional culture pattern was being threatened, the old values were being destroyed. The farmers moved into the cities and lost their roots; a huge urban proletariat came into existence and lived in ugly slums. And the city people who brought all this about were evidently the rootless Jews who had no feeling for the "old values," who were clever, smart, and materialistic and liked that city life and quickly grew rich in it at the expense of the Germans and of German *Kultur*. The Jewish "alienness [Adorno says] seems to provide the handiest formula for dealing with the alienation of society."[180]

To many Germans, the Jewish communities in the cities meant also an intrusion by the distrusted, suspect "Western" world, the world of the French Revolution and of democracy, into "Germanic" life in which that world was unwanted. Typically, the leader of the Pan-German League, Heinrich Class, said that the "strongest weapon of Judaism is the democracy of the non-Jews."[181] Many Germans felt that the Jews were nothing but a troublesome, malevolent menace, and these feelings "culminated in projecting the Jews as the only real obstacle to the attainment of the ideal society."[182] At least, the developments reached that point under the later propaganda fire of the national socialist regime.

What the Germans closed their eyes to was the fact that many of the miseries of modern life are present in any industrialized country with a rapidly expanding population, whether it includes Jews or not, and that these miseries were to engender ever-increasing discontent in many countries, down to our present day. (But it has now become more customary in various countries to put the blame for the loss of the idealized paradisiacal past, not on the Jews, but on the Americans as leaders and innovators in modern life.)

The German Jews, by and large, understood little of this resentment against them, even though it was seething not far from the surface. This was hardly surprising. The Jews had been city people and rational, sober businessmen for hundreds of years. To them, the "good old days" of the gentiles usually meant a less desirable period in

[180] Adorno, *The Authoritarian Personality*, p. 619.
[181] Quoted in Pulzer, *The Rise of Political Anti-semitism*, p. 311.
[182] Mosse, *Crisis*, p. 243.

Jewish life, and they were glad that it was vanishing. They saw no real objection to an industrial society and to progress, which created the "good life" for them. To be sure, they, too, liked the country, but it was enough to enjoy it on weekends and holidays. One did not *have* to maintain mystical ties to nature and the soil. The Jews were in their element in the lively intellectual life of the cities. It gave them an excellent opportunity to put their intellectual gifts to use. They liked the clever journalism of the metropolitan newspapers and magazines, many of which, indeed, were written by their own people. They would not have known where to live, if not in the cities, and what to be other than city people.

Pulzer says that the

> . . . influence of the closed Jewish community . . . continued to haunt the *déraciné*, however much he might try to exorcise it. It endowed him . . . with an exaggeratedly intellectual and cerebral view of the world's problems, derived from the enforced, undilutedly urban culture of Jewish life and the Talmudic scholasticism which was the mainstay of ghetto education.[183]

It is not surprising, then, that the Jews flocked to Berlin and other big cities in large numbers. In 1933, the year Hitler came to power, 160,500 Jews, that is, 32 percent of all German Jews, lived in Berlin,[184] and most of the remaining Jews lived in Frankfurt and other large cities. It is clear that their heavy representation in the cities and the prominent part they played in city life, brought about far greater visibility of the Jews in German life in general than their small number would otherwise have justified. Leschnitzer believes, in fact, that if there had been a proportionate number of Jewish farmers, sailors, fishermen, soldiers, and postmen, the relations between Jews and Germans and the role of the Jews in German life would have been altogether different.[185] This might indeed have resulted in a considerable reduction of anti-Jewish feeling, but we must bear in mind that anti-Semitism in Poland, for example, was very intense in spite of the fact that millions of Jews in that country were farmers, factory workers, artisans, etc.

[183] Pulzer, op. cit., p. 262.
[184] Adolf Leschnitzer, *The Magic Background of Modern Anti-semitism*, p. 18.
[185] Ibid., p. 35.

There were a few perceptive Jews who understood the German resentment against "city people" and particularly the Jewish variety, and it is interesting to see what one of them said. In 1933, shortly before he was killed by the National Socialists, the German-Jewish philosopher Theodor Lessing (who identified himself as Zionist, German and Communist) wrote an impassioned pamphlet about German-Jewish relations from which a few statements may here be quoted:

> And so I believe that, if there ever was a sound instinct behind the persecutions of the Jews, it was only this instinctive impulse of the blood against the city and its business deals.
> The Jew is the mind which has left nature. . . . The nations, and in the first place the German people, perceive in "the Jew" the sinister genius of abstraction, estranged from nature, in whom the gay colors and pleasing forms expire, and the peoples' souls and landscapes die: the myths, images, native costumes, festivals, and old customs. Jewish (in that sense) would be anything that overpowers and puts in chains the very own kind and peculiarity of the souls of the peoples.[186]

Lessing understood and expressed very well—in fact, in the typical German romantic style—what most Germans felt only vaguely and seldom could express at all.

Much later, in a very different context, Ben-Gurion accused non-Zionist Jews in these terms: "They have no roots, they are rootless cosmopolitans—there can be nothing worse than that."[187]

Being cosmopolitan was even worse to the Germans than being metropolitan, a city person. And there was no doubt that many German Jews were internationally minded or were supranational, or, as Erich Kahler puts it, represented a combination of particularity and universality. Their international tendencies were indeed the natural result of centuries of Jewish history and of their entire particular situation in the world. Since the Middle Ages, the Jewish banking houses had maintained extensive international business and familly connections. In medieval times of tensions and wars when official communications between nations were ruptured, it was the international Jewish bankers through whom negotiations could still be carried

[186]Lessing, *Deutschland und seine Juden*, pp. 11, 12.
[187]Quoted in Beloff, "Rootless Cosmopolitans?" in *Encounter*, November 1969, p. 36.

on. Life in the diaspora itself was, in a sense, international or supra-national. The Jews in one country naturally took an interest in the fate of the Jews in another. In fact, Jewish aid for other Jews across European borders was often needed; refugees from persecutions elsewhere had to be received; and conversely, a watch for possible less onerous living conditions in other countries had to be maintained.

Kahler says that

... the Jewish character combines narrowest particularity with true universality. Indeed *the substance of its particularity is universality.*

This combination made for an existence that was fraught with peril. Both these extremes, separately and jointly, alter-nately and concurrently, acted as a constant challenge to the peoples of the world; they were the source of that persistent hostility . . . toward the Jews. . . .

And when we examine the arguments raised against the Jews by modern anti-Semites, we find again the crucial point to be the . . . connection of Jewish internationality with the sur-vival as a special folk group; the claim to be citizens of modern nation-states and citizens of the modern world, while at the same time remaining Jews. . . .[188]

Similarly, Walter Laqueur has said that "To justify their uprooted existence they had to become universalists, to dispute the view that every people had an individual character and assignment."[189] Heine contended more than a hundred years ago that ". . . cosmopolitanism truly sprang up from the soil of Judah, and Christ, who . . . was a real Jew, truly founded a propaganda of cosmopolitanism."[190]

But modern Germany certainly was one country where Jewish internationalism was regarded with deep suspicion.[191] International Marxism, which involved many Jews, was only one aspect of this, long before Hitler appeared on the scene. As far back as 1887, an anti-Jewish periodical, *Antisemitische Correspondenz*, described as the "crucial point" the fact that the Jews place themselves outside

[188] Kahler, *The Jews among the Nations*, p. 11, 27. (Italics quoted.)
[189] Laqueur in *Encounter*, August 1971, p. 48.
[190] Heine, op. cit., p. 1131.
[191] See also Mosse, *Crisis*, p. 23.

of the German nation *(Volkstum)*, that they form a single international brotherhood and, within it, assume an attitude of segregation and hostility against all non-Jews.[192] "International" came to be equated with "antinational," "unpatriotic," "un-German," "anti-Germanic." To the average German, the desirable people were those who, in the then current jargon, held "national convictions" *(nationale Gesinnung)* or who "thought nationally." The extreme tendency of millions of Germans to regard anything foreign as odious was astonishing, and the Jews suffered from it.

Hitler intensified all this to fever pitch. In one of his earliest speeches, in 1920, he began to elevate Jewish internationalism to the center of his accusations against the Jews.[193] It was to become a "dirty word" throughout the Hitler years. *Mein Kampf* contains countless references to international Jewry, Jewish world finance, Jewish world domination, Jewish world bolshevization, etc.[194] In fact, Jewish internationalism was more and more equated with world communism. Hitler's confidential speech to the officers candidates of May 30, 1942, which probably contained the most complete and earnest summary of his ideology, referred to "the entire international world Jewry" as the enemy.[195] The same clichés thread their tiresome way through thousands of speeches and writings by Hitler and other National Socialists. Even in Hitler's "Political Testament," which he dictated in his underground bunker in Berlin in the full awareness that he would kill himself a little later, he still spoke of the paramount need to "resist mercilessly the universal poisoner of all peoples, international Jewry."[196] To the very end, it was an obsession.

It is quite possible, also, as Bettelheim suggests,[197] that there was a psychological need for the invention of an "international Jewish conspiracy," in other words, of a sinister power of considerable strength, because the persecution of the very small helpless Jewish group in Germany would otherwise have been incompatible with German self-esteem. The idea of the conspiracy, moreover, became

---

[192]*Antisemitische Correspondenz*, February 1887, pp 5–6, cited in Müller, *Die Entwicklung des Rassenantisemitismus*, p. 62.

[193]See Eberhard Jäckel, *Hitlers Weltanschauung*, pp. 63–64.

[194]See, for instance, pp. 702–704, 751–752.

[195]Reprinted in the appendix to *Hitler's Table Talks*, p. 502.

[196]*TMWC*, Vol. 41, p. 552.

[197]Bettelheim and Janowitz, *Dynamics of Prejudice*, p. 34.

particularly important as justifying the extermination of all Jews in the occupied European countries, none of whom ever offered significant resistance to the German armies [198] and who, in fact, even cooperated with their own killers. [199]

i. JEWISH DESTRUCTIVENESS—THE "TUCHOLSKY SYNDROME"

We now come to a causative factor of anti-Semitism which loomed large in the German mind. This was called *Zersetzung* in German. Recently, in a brief, brilliant analysis, Walter Laqueur called it the "Tucholsky syndrome." [200] Both terms require explanation.

The German word *Zersetzung*, in its application to the Jews, has no real English equivalent. It is a word that is widely used in chemistry and biology and means approximately "decomposition," "decay," "putrefaction." When used in relation to the Jews, the word was intended to mean that they worked toward destruction or decomposition of all "genuine values," of everything that was sacred to the Germans—Germanic and German traditions, culture, their position in the world, their patriotism, their patriotic symbols. The use of the word in this sense actually dates back more than a hundred years. In 1848, for example, the patriotic German poet Ernst Moritz Arndt wrote quite typically: "Jews and their associates, baptized and unbaptized, are working tirelessly and are participating in the extreme radical Left to bring about the destruction [*Zersetzung*] and dissolution of that which to us Germans has until now encompassed our humanity and our sacred things." [201] Arndt's style was better than Hitler's, but in content this could have been a statement made by Hitler seventy years later.

Ten years after Arndt, the prominent German historian Theodor Mommsen, in his *History of Rome*, called the Jews of the ancient world "an effective ferment of cosmopolitanism and national decomposition." [202] (This, in fact, was to become a national cliché, and Hitler

---

[198] See, for instance, Arendt, *Eichmann*, p. 122.
[199] See, for example, Hilberg, *The Destruction of the European Jews*, p. 666.
[200] Laqueur, "The Tucholsky Complaint," in *Encounter*, October 1969, pp. 76–80.
[201] Quoted in Cornelia Berning, *Vom "Abstammungsnachweis" zum "Zuchtwart,"* p. 213.
[202] Vol. II, p. 530.

was to repeat the words "ferment of decomposition" in *Mein Kampf* seventy years later.[203] By 1878, the fanatic German anti-Semite Paul de Lagarde had greatly intensified the accusation of Jewish destructiveness and had called for action: ". . . it is undoubtedly imperative to do away [*beseitigen*] with those who, even in the judgment of the notable Theodor Mommsen, have, since time immemorial, promoted decomposition. . . ."[204]

A little later, another well-known German historian, Heinrich von Treitschke, attacked "Jewish radicalism" and called the Jews "destroying and destructive."[205] Radicalism was only one of the various aspects of the more general accusation of Jewish destructiveness.

This accusation is thus very old, and, in various degrees of intensity, it can be found throughout the German-Jewish relationship of about a hundred years preceding Hitler. The intensity of the accusation increased sharply during the Weimar Republic, and under Hitler it became official dogma. But Hitler, in this instance, hardly had to make much of an effort to augment the existing German resentment. There was a sufficient supply of it on hand to serve as a basis for any anti-Jewish policy.

In his *Table Talks*, Hitler once discussed Jewish destructiveness in a fairly philosophical manner, even though he also showed his normal violent reaction:

Many Jews . . . were not aware of the destructive nature of their existence. But anyone who destroys life exposes himself to death, and nothing else will happen to them! . . . We don't know what meaning there is in this arrangement of things [*Einrichtung*] that we see the Jews destroy the nations. Is it that nature has created them [the Jews] so that they, by their destructiveness, may stir up other nations? If so, Paul [St. Paul] and Trotzky would be the most estimable Jews, because they made the greatest contribution to this. By their actions they generated resistance.[206]

[203]*Mein Kampf*, pp. 498 and 743.
[204]Paul de Lagarde, *Deutsche Schriften*, p. 24.
[205]Treitschke, *Deutsche Geschichte im 19. Jahrhundert*, 1879, Vol. III, pp. 703–704.
[206]*Hitler's Table Talks*, p. 152.

Evidently, Hitler, as usual, was looking for a law of nature—even behind Jewish destructiveness. But it is clear also that such a law, if he had found it, would not have saved the Jews. Another law of nature would have required the killing of the Jews to prevent their destructiveness.

One reason for the increased intensity of the accusation of destructiveness during the Weimar Republic has already been stated in the section on the "Scapegoat Theory." It was the legend that the "undefeated" German Army in 1918 had been "stabbed in the back" by predominantly Jewish traitors, and that the loss of World War I was thus due to Jewish treason. It will be recalled, moreover,[207] that many of the leaders of the Revolution in 1918 actually were Jewish; that they organized mutinous "soviets" of the Russian type in the army and navy; and, above all, that the Jewish Communist Kurt Eisner actually set up a soviet-type government in Munich of which he was prime minister for a few months in association with other Jews. All this caused millions of Germans—even reasonable ones—to believe that the Jews were indeed destructive traitors to whom German values and traditions meant nothing and who, in fact, deliberately set out to destroy them. Hitler states his own reaction in *Mein Kampf*. He describes how he received the report of the German collapse, mutiny, and revolution while recovering from gas poisoning in an army hospital: "What followed were dreadful days and still worse nights . . . . In those nights, my hatred grew, hatred against the authors of this deed [the Jews]."[208]

As stated earlier, no other single event did more to promote anti-Semitism in Germany after World War I than the soviet-type government with its Jewish prime minister Kurt Eisner in Munich, although it lasted only until February 21, 1919. Strong anti-Jewish sentiments were, however, aroused also by Jewish Communist leaders in the north, such as Rosa Luxemburg. None of these leaders, including those who were not Jewish, seemed to understand that the establishment of a Communist soviet-type government system represented so violent and rapid a break with 2,000 years of German tradition that it could not be acceptable to the vast majority of the people,

[207] See pp. 131–133, above.
[208] *Mein Kampf*, p. 225.

including even, as it turned out, the millions of German socialists. The monarchy, after all, had disappeared only a few weeks, in some instances a few days, earlier. The sudden sight of the red flag with the hammer and sickle over the palaces and government buildings was repulsive to nearly all Germans, even to those who had previously regarded themselves as anti-monarchist. The prevailing feeling was (and this against the background of the military defeat, the harsh Versailles Treaty, and a severe business depression) that the whole country was falling into chaos and was being taken over by a small malevolent alien minority.

The Jewish leadership, on the other hand, was evidently untroubled by considerations of German tradition, sentiment, and the like, and they seemed able and eager to make the rapid, radical adjustment, to root out and to destroy the old governmental system and to replace it literally overnight by a system which, in its essentials, had been imported from Soviet Russia. In their call for revolution and even anarchy, these leaders resembled such recent American revolutionaries as Jerry Rubin and Abbie Hoffman, who also may be unaware of the fact that the vast majority of the people do not have the remotest intention of accepting fundamental revolutionary changes. At any rate, the result in Germany was disastrous. Most of the revolutionary leadership was assassinated by right-wing Germans within a few months, but the Jews, in general, even those who had nothing to do with these events, could never completely free themselves of the stigma of reckless destruction of German tradition and values. As Max Beloff has said, "revolutionary activity by Jews is playing with fire." [209] But this is something that, it seems, few Jews have ever been able to understand or sense. Walter Laqueur has described the situation better than anyone else:

Traditionally, they [the Jews] have shown great ability on the level of abstract thought, but politics also involves instinct, common sense, wisdom, and foresight, and in this respect their record has not been impressive. The inability to understand the imponderables in the life of peoples has been a great handicap. It has led them time and again into belittling national traditions,

[209] Beloff, "Rootless Cosmopolitans?" in *Encounter,* November 1969, p. 40.

one of the main reasons for the failure of the radical Left every-where.[210]

Twenty-five years later, in 1933, when the time came for Hitler's own seizure of power, he proceeded far more cleverly than the revolutionaries of 1918. He had, if not wisdom, at least instinct, common sense, and foresight. He realized clearly that a people like the Germans may not be made to feel that its age-old traditions have been abandoned from one day to the next, and he understood that political innovations require psychological preparation. Hitler, in fact, in the early days of his regime, made strong efforts to link it ideologically to the venerable Field Marshall von Hindenburg, to the glories of the Prussian Army and even to the House of Hohenzollern. Outstanding among these efforts was the so-called "day of Potsdam," March 21, 1933 (the anniversary of the opening of Bismarck's Reichstag in 1871), when Hitler staged an impressive spectacle in the historic Garrison Church in Potsdam, at the coffin of Frederick the Great. Hindenburg and the Crown Prince were present—and an empty chair for the Kaiser. The historian Friedrich Meinecke later called this quite aptly a "pathetic comedy."[211] In fact, it was worse: it was, in effect, a masked funeral of much honorable Prussian and German tradition. But the German people (and possibly Hitler himself) were deceived into believing—in large part contrary to the facts—that their traditions and values were being maintained and not destroyed, that National Socialism represented historical continuity and not radical change. Even the black-white-and-red flag of the old monarchy, which the Weimar Republic had abandoned, was reintroduced and became one of two of the nation's flags. The other, the swastika banner, for which there was no tradition, was thus made more acceptable. All these actions stand in strong contrast to the revolutionary tactics in 1918, which abruptly broke with the past and had much of the appearance of an alien graft.

Hitler and National Socialism in general never ceased equating Jewry and Communism or Bolshevism and speaking of both the Rus-

[210]Laqueur, *Out of the Ruins of Europe*, p. 479.
[211]Meinecke, *Die deutsche Katastrophe*, p. 25.

sian and German revolutions as "Jewish." Already in *Mein Kampf*[212] Hitler had called Bolshevism "this Jewish disease" and had declared that the Soviet Union had been completely conquered and was being ruled by Jews and was unable "to shake them off." He, in common with most Germans, drew liberally on the fact that the leadership of the Russian Revolution in 1917 included a considerable number of Jews (Trotzky, Kamenev, Zinoviev, Radek, Litvinov, and others). Pinson says that it ". . . remains a fact that during the entire period between 1918 and 1939 the blazing fire of anti-Semitism in the world was fed more fuel from the bogey of 'Jewish Bolshevism' than from any other single charge against the Jews" and "while it is obviously not true that all Jews were Bolshevists, the presence among the leaders of the Russian Bolshevists of many Jewish figures gave a semblance of authenticity to this anti-Semitic change. . . ."[213] To Hitler and most other Germans, it looked like more than a mere "semblance" of authenticity, and they felt confirmed in their opinion by the fact that Karl Marx himself was Jewish as were other early German socialists or Marxists, such as Ferdinand Lassalle, Max Adler, and Rudolf Hilferding. The fact that Lenin, Stalin, Molotov, and others were not Jewish did not fit into the accepted stereotype and was something to which Hitler and other Germans closed their eyes. At any rate, the correctness of the entire premise of Jewish domination of Soviet Russia was never examined, let alone questioned, by the national socialist regime, in spite of the significance it had for various important policy decisions.

We are, of course, concerned not only with Jewish political radicalism but also with what we might call Jewish cultural radicalism in Germany, though the two, in any event, can hardly be separated from each other. This leads us to what Walter Laqueur has called the "Tucholsky syndrome"[214] which refers to Kurt Tucholsky, a German-Jewish writer, essayist, and journalist (1890–1935), who was a

[212] Pp. 277, 743.

[213] Pinson (ed.), *Essays on Anti-Semitism*, pp. 8–9.

[214] See his article "The Tucholsky Complaint," in *Encounter*, October 1969, pp. 76–80, which compresses numerous facts and a penetrating analysis into five pages. See also his article *A Look Back at the Weimar Republic* in *New York Times Magazine Section*, Aug. 16, 1970, pp. 12ff.

fairly typical representative of the Jewish intelligentsia of the Weimar Republic, even if he was far more extreme and articulate than most.[215] His "Collected Works" were published in 1960 in four large volumes,[216] a total of about 5,000 pages, and these do not even include certain special books. He might be described as essentially a "feuilletonist." Most of his writings deal with politics, social problems, literature, the theater, and film; and they consist, to a large extent, of his weekly contributions to the left-wing magazine *Weltbühne*. As Laqueur says, the majority of the contributors and, no doubt, most of its readers were Jews.[217] Tucholsky can be considered its star contributor. The magazine and Tucholsky's writings were, in varying degrees, a mirror of the thoughts and tendencies of the Jewish intelligentsia during the Weimar Republic.

Looking now through Tucholsky's writings with the advantage of about forty-five years' hindsight, one can easily see why he was utterly unsuccessful in his efforts to exert political influence and why he lacked any social impact, except perhaps in provoking more anti-Semitism. Most of his writings, in fact, make for monotonous and tiresome reading, at least today. They produce, strangely enough, a sensation not wholly unlike the one experienced in reading Hitler's *Mein Kampf*, although Tucholsky, of course, wrote a far better style and was generally a vastly more skillful writer than Hitler. But what tires the reader is the consistently vituperative, abusive, raging, sneering quality of most of these thousands of little articles, reports, and reviews, their largely negative, sterile, and destructive character. In looking through the "Collected Works," one is struck with the impression that there was hardly anything in Germany which Tucholsky did not hate and which did not incite him to violent tirades and diatribes. Much of it seemed sterile criticism for no purpose other than criticism.

As Deak says, Tucholsky condemned collectively "Princes, barons, Junkers, officers, policemen, judges, officials, clergymen, acade-

[215] For detailed literature on Tucholsky and other intellectuals of that period see Harold L. Poor, *Kurt Tucholsky and the Ordeal of Germany, 1913–1945;* Istvan Deak, *Weimar Germany's Left-Wing Intellectuals;* and Peter Gay, *Weimar Culture.*

[216] Tucholsky, *Gesammelte Werke.*

[217] See also Deak, op. cit., p. 24.

micians, teachers, capitalists, *Bürger*, university students, peasants, and all Bavarians."[218] He was critical even of the Jews and "perhaps held the Jewish middle class in even greater contempt than the anti-semitic Gentile bourgeoisie."[219] He said on one occasion, after express-ing agreement with a statement by a German humorist that nothing much is likely to come of anti-Semitism unless the Jews take it in hand: "That is entirely correct, because every wise Jew, who has seen through the bad characteristics of his race, could cite much better and more effective things against Jewry than all German-national grey-beards together.[220] On another occasion, he wrote that ". . . from my earliest youth, I have had an inextinguishable loathing for those unctuous rabbis—because I sensed, more than I understood, the cow-ardice of that group."[221]

As early as 1919, Tucholsky wrote that "the remotest black Zulu is closer to us" than German traditionalists.[222] He directed especially fierce attacks against the German judiciary, but the kind of person he probably hated most was the Prussian drill-sergeant type. Strangely enough, as in the case of so many German Jews, his attacks against Hitler were comparatively rare and mild. Somehow, the rather sloppy, bohemian Hitler who had made his way from a Viennese flophouse into German politics, did not quite fit into Tucholsky's stereotyped picture of Germany and the Germans. At any rate, Tucholsky had boundless disbelief in Hitler's political future and, like so many Jews, he could not see Hitler as a genuine revolutionary,[223] but rather saw him as a comical man, a contemptible fool. His voice, Tucholsky said, "smells a little of the seat of a man's trousers, of man—unappetizing,

[218]Ibid., p. 43.

[219]Poor, op. cit., p. 91.

[220]Tucholsky, op. cit., Vol. I, p. 789. Tucholsky's hostility against his own people did not, however, come anywhere near the hostility which today's American Jews of the New Left entertain against other Jews and Israel. See, f.i., Seymour Martin Lipset, "The Left, the Jews and Israel," in *Encounter,* Dec. 1969, pp. 24–35; Arnold Forster, "American Radicals and Israel," in *The Wiener Library Bulletin,* 1969, Vol. XXIII, pp. 26–28; *The New York Times,* Nov. 29, 1969, and Dec. 17, 1969. Lipset reports that in the Russian Revolution of 1917 Jewish revolutionary leaders called for a pogrom against the Jews.

[221]Tucholsky, *Ausgewählte Briefe,* p. 333.

[222]*Gesammelte Werke,* Vol. I, p. 379.

[223]Ibid., Vol. III, p. 439.

but otherwise all right."[224] (But ridicule enraged Hitler, who said years later, "The Jews once laughed about me; I don't know whether they are still laughing or whether they have run out of laughter."[225]) Tucholsky never understood that a new era had begun in which skillful mass propaganda and politics by terror were to dominate the country and in which his targets, such as drill-sergeants, barons, and capitalists, were fading into the background.

In the meantime, however, Tucholsky continued his ragings against nearly all Germans, their way of life, traditions, institutions, and patriotism. His intense group hostility was, to his misfortune, directed against almost the entire ingroup. He did not seem to care that he represented a very small outgroup, and he often showed a great deal of courage. In 1926 he wrote:

> To us, moral condemnation by the patriots sometimes represents praise, but mostly it is immaterial to us, because the country which I am supposedly betraying is not my country; this state is not my state; and this legal order is not my legal order. I am as indifferent to the colors of their flag as I am to their provincially limited ideals. I have nothing to betray here because no one has entrusted me with anything.[226]

And two years later, he wrote:

> . . . I declare here, fully conscious of what I am saying, that there is no secret of the German Army which I would not deliver to a foreign power, if this seemed necessary for the preservation of peace. . . . . We are high traitors. But we betray a country which we repudiate, in favor of a country which we love, for the sake of peace and for our true fatherland: Europe.[227]

Clearly, Tucholsky saw Germany and the Germans as his enemy long before Hitler came to power, and implicit in much of his writings is a strong wish to destroy the Germans. It did not really matter to him of what political persuasion the current government was at any given time: he opposed them all. He hated and raged against the So-

---

[224]Tucholsky, *Ausgewählte Briefe*, p. 247.
[225]Speech of 1943 quoted in Golo Mann, *Der Antisemitismus*, p. 34.
[226]*Gesammelte Werke*, Vol. II, p. 496.
[227]Ibid., p. 1086.

cialists, the Democrats, the Nationalists, the Conservatives, the middle class, the upper class, the Youth Movement, the Army, the Bavarians, the Communist leadership, the National Socialists. He did concede, at one point, that "collective indictments are always unjust" but he added that "they ought to be and have the right to be unjust, because we have the right, in judging society, to regard the lowest type of a group as representative of it, that is, the one whom the group just barely still tolerates, whom it does not expel."[228] This determination to look for the worst, to close his eyes to anything good in a group, and to blame the group for any tolerance, was what governed Tucholsky's philosophy throughout. He himself had no tolerance whatever and seemed entirely unable to understand someone else's different point of view. He saw life solely as a friend-foe situation. Harold Poor believes that Tucholsky "was far more radical" than either Communists or National Socialists,[229] but this may be exaggerated.

Laqueur calls special attention to a book which Tucholsky published in 1929 under the title *Deutschland, Deutschland über Alles*[230] This was also the title of the German national anthem, and there was little doubt about the purpose of this title for a book which was a ferocious all-out attack on everything German, the middle class, the upper class, the veterans, the judiciary, the church, the army, the President, and the way of life of all of them. It was perhaps the most tiresome of all of Tucholsky's tiresome diatribes, and its literary merits are limited. Included in the book is a picture of eight elderly gentlemen, most of them in some kind of uniform, presumably generals and admirals. The caption under the picture is "Animals are looking at you." As Laqueur says, these eight men are "a pathetic sight, but there is nothing particularly animal or evil about them."[231] The matter would not be worth mentioning here if Tucholsky had not said with regard to eight normal-appearing German men that "animals are looking at you" while Hitler and other National Socialists were at that time making it a practice to equate the Jews with animals, swine, rats, and vermin. Each group's equation of the other group with animals was symptom-

[228] Ibid., p. 773.
[229] Poor, op. cit., p. 146.
[230] Berlin, 1929 (not included in the *Gesammelte Werke*).
[231] In *Encounter*, October 1969, p. 78.

atic of the irreconcilability of these two intensely hostile groups. Important segments of both groups were unwilling or even unable to recognize anything but the worst in the other group, and could no longer see beyond rigidly fixed stereotypes of evil.

Near the end of the book Tucholsky said: "For 225 pages we have said "no"—"no" out of pity, "no" out of love, "no" out of hatred, and "no" out of passion. And now, we also want to say "yes"—to the landscape and to the countryside of Germany."[232] But this merely underlined his negation of everything German, because obviously the Germans did not create their landscape and countryside.

Actually, however, Tucholsky was not totally negative and destructive. In other writings, in the Jewish tradition, he frequently made quite clear that he loved the downtrodden, the proletariat, "the poor,"—even abortionist mothers, prostitutes, convicted criminals, any defenseless minority. He espoused their causes on many occasions. In much of this, his difficulty was, like that of his colleagues, that he knew so little of "the poor" and the proletariat. He lived in some degree of affluence and in a kind of intellectual seclusion. His practical experience was confined largely to his kind of life, and everything else was theory. In a letter he wrote to a socialist friend in 1926, he said, "I shall always remain a stranger [to the proletariat]; there is something that separates us."[233] And the proletariat, in turn, treated him with indifference, if not hostility.

But he never ceased striving for some kind of not clearly defined utopian society similar to the utopian society of the New Left of our time, which Laqueur has wittily described as

> . . . political constructions firmly rooted in mid-air, . . . in which governments and political authority in general are replaced by communes of free and equal individuals, in which society exists without repression, and domestic policies require no sanctions, diplomats always tell the truth, . . . and a foreign policy is pursued in which the wolf lies down with the lamb, and the leopard with the kid, under the supervision of Prof. Noam Chomsky.[234]

[232]*Deutschland, Deutschland über Alles*, p. 226.
[233]Quoted in Deak, op. cit., p. 161.
[234]"A Look Back at the Weimar Republic," *New York Times Magazine Section*, August 16, 1970, p. 28.

All this discussion of Tucholsky should not, of course, be interpreted to mean that all German Jews took as radically negative and destructive a view of Germany as he did. He was certainly an extreme case and not representative of German Jewry in a general sense. Yet, in his exaggerated way and in high concentration or magnification, he expressed a spirit and tendencies which, varying in extent from person to person, nearly every German Jew could call his own. There was probably *no* Jew without at least a little bit of the "Tucholsky syndrome," even if he never gave expression to it. Essentially, the Jews in general, who read the magazine *Die Weltbühne* in large numbers, stated no disagreement or opposition. Some non-Jews also were no strangers to the syndrome.

Nor, of course, was Tucholsky the only Jewish writer of that period who gave expression to the spirit of negation and destructiveness. There were a good many of them on the staff of the magazine *Die Weltbühne* itself, and, what was more important, there were far more who wrote for the large Jewish-controlled daily newspapers in the big cities. The visibility of these men was thus very high, and they were anything but reticent. In the perfectly free atmosphere of the Weimar Republic, these men felt entirely at liberty to lambaste and ridicule the German way of life and values; and they never seemed to realize how deeply this was resented by the Germans. To millions of Germans, the reading of some of the daily papers became a source of annoyance and anger at "the Jews" who "in the eyes of the public . . . represented the urge to negation and destruction."[235] The average German, like the citizens of most countries, saw many good and positive things in his country. In many ways, the Germans were proud of it, and they were not wholly pessimistic about its future. The negative, destructive attacks by men like Tucholsky caused them to regard anti-Semitism and the suppression of the Jews as a kind of "national self-defense." They felt that the Jews were a definite "threat," politically and socially as well as culturally, and it is surprising to note, in this connection, that Adorno's investigation in 1950 of anti-Semitism in the *United States* disclosed a feeling of being "threatened" by the Jews:

[235]Laqueur in *New York Times Magazine Section,* Aug. 16, 1970, p. 25.

While the specific surface opinion [of the anti-Semites] covers a great variety of topics, there seem nevertheless to be certain unifying ideas or themes underlying the opinions and giving them coherence and structure. Perhaps most central is the idea that the Jews are *threatening*. . . . Jews are described as a *moral threat;* that is, as violators of important standards and values. These values include: cleanliness, neatness, and conformity; also opposition to sensuality, extravagance, prying, social aggressiveness, exhibitionism. The imagery of Jews as value-violators makes them not only offensive but also very disturbing. [236]

To a considerable extent the complete freedom of expression during the Weimar Republic and the extreme tolerance of the regime proved to be the undoing of the Jewish intellectuals. They did themselves much less damage in the controlled intellectual climate of the Soviet Union.

The intellectual German Jews were almost exclusively critics rather than builders, and this at a time when the tender flower of the Weimar Republic desperately needed whatever constructive care and help it could get from any source. Instead of that, the intellectuals "continued to attack the political structure much as their predecessors had attacked the imperial order, except that now they were more bitter and intense." [237] It was in the liberal atmosphere of the Weimar Republic that the Jews could have flourished as never before, but their intellectuality contributed materially and masochistically to its destruction. [238] They were never willing to place themselves within the existing political institutions and to accept their philosophy, not even by some sort of compromise. Nor could they ever truly attach themselves to a genuine political mass movement. They merely mistook the uprising against the old regime and against the war in 1918 for a symptom of readiness of the German people for a Bolshevist type of revolution, and in doing so, they fatally alienated themselves

[236] Adorno, *The Authoritarian Personality*, p. 95.

[237] Poor, op. cit., p. 4.

[238] Deak, op. cit., pp. 225 and 228, differs from this conclusion, as does Poor, op. cit., pp. 83–84, at least with respect to Tucholsky himself. Poor, a biographer in love with his subject, even says (p. 259) that "the use of the term *zersetzend* [destructive] was inexcusable" in relation to Tucholsky. Evidently, Poor was greatly impressed with the fact — and it *was* a fact — that Tucholsky was a well-meaning, good-natured, decent individual.

from the people. They never understood that, in spite of defeat in World War I and the termination of the monarchy, the great (largely silent) majority of the people was still highly conservative in its political and social outlook, and that, in fact, intense glorification of the "good old days" was underway. But it seems that the failure of revolutionaries to obtain a following merely increases their bitterness and radicalism.

The nearly complete political irrelevance of Jewish intellectuals became apparent when the disaster struck. When Hitler came to power, or for that matter before, they furnished no inspiration to any possible resistance movement. Whatever little Jewish leadership there was became vested in such persons as Rabbi Leo Baeck. Even the rough and brutal men of the national socialist regime who were in charge of anti-Jewish actions, like Adolf Eichmann and Reinhardt Heydrich,[239] did their limited "negotiating" with men like Rabbi Baeck for whom they seemed to feel some small measure of respect. They may have vaguely sensed that such Jews represented age-old dignified traditions, much older than the oldest German traditions.

It may be interesting to examine the reasons for the destructive tendencies among German Jews, because they came to mean so much in the causation of anti-Semitism and in the final disaster. These reasons are by no means clear, and the available literature shows no systematic effort to make them clearer. Non-Jewish German writers usually did no more than to state the phenomenon, brand it as evil, and propose that a stop be put to it. Jewish writers have undertaken only very limited discussions of the subject, and they differ widely in their opinions. What is needed most, but does not exist, is a thorough motivation survey among Jews, of the kind which Adorno and his collaborators, and Bettelheim and Janowitz have undertaken among non-Jews regarding anti-Semitism. By far the best contribution to an analysis of the problem has probably been made by Walter Laqueur in his aforementioned brief article "The Tucholsky Complaint."[240] He says that the problem is "one aspect which is usually neglected or glossed over, perhaps because it is so delicate and yet it is one of the key issues." In describing it as "so

---

[239]Heydrich seems to have been of Jewish descent himself. See Fest, *Das Gesicht des Dritten Reiches,* pp. 142ff, also Hans Bernd Gisevius, *Adolf Hitler,* p. 165.

[240]In *Encounter,* October 1969, pp. 76–80.

delicate," Laqueur presumably means that the Jews do not like to discuss it or hear it discussed because it is an area in which they feel vulnerable and embarrassed. At any rate, few Jews are ever inclined to look at themselves as a social phenomenon, and most of them, in fact, detest being singled out or talked about as a group by non-Jews. Their "touchiness" is extreme. But there is no doubt that, as Laqueur says, Jewish destructiveness is one of the "key issues."[241] It is also of great historical significance. Certainly, in any intelligent consideration of the German-Jewish relationship, this issue will have to be discussed.

There are bits and pieces of opinions on the problem—usually wary, cautious, and discreet—which Jewish writers have expressed. Some of these writers have been obviously and understandably puzzled. The reasons for the tendency toward destructiveness, radicalism, etc., among Jews, which these writers have indicated, range from the implausible to reasonably convincing. None seems completely persuasive in itself. They will here be discussed in what may be no more than a kind of vague order of implausibility.

Seymour Martin Lipset says (largely incidentally) that "participation in the Socialist and Communist world meant, for many Jews, a way of escaping their Judaism, a way of *assimilating* into a universalistic non-Jewish world."[242] Along similar lines, Pulzer believes that "Above all the ideologies of the Left, which promised to emancipate men from restrictive or divisive loyalties, also helped the Jew to reidentify himself with society."[243] Actually, on the face of things, this might have been true of Germany (before 1945), because it is a fact that the majority of Germans rejected, de facto though not de jure, even a limited assimilation of most Jews, so that acceptance of the Jews by Socialists and Communists could be regarded as some measure of assimilation into the German body politic. But the same cannot be said of the Jews in other countries, particularly in the United States; and it seems probable, therefore, that this reasoning is wrong also in relation to the German Jews. In the United States, there is little or no objection to general Jewish assimilation, but assimilation via the American Communists would be vastly more difficult. Participation in the communist world, of which Lipset

[241] Ibid., p. 76.
[242] Lipset, *The Left, the Jews and Israel*, in *Encounter*, December 1969, p. 28.
[243] Pulzer, *The Rise of Political Anti-Semitism*, p. 262.

speaks, would, in fact, definitely place the Jews in an outgroup in the United States. During the period of National Socialism, moreover, the Germans tended to throw both Jews and Communists into one outgroup, frequently called the "Jewish-Bolshevist menace."

Another very astute analyst of the German-Jewish relationship, E. L. Ehrlich, looks elsewhere for the causes of Jewish destructiveness:

> The Jews who entered the European intellectual world from their mental ghetto, beginning only in the middle of the nineteenth century, had to achieve in a few decades a development for which the Christian world had taken centuries, through Renaissance, Reformation, and Enlightenment. Some Jews did not live through this enormous abridgment of a process of intellectual development without psychological damage which manifested itself in many an excess and in the propensity to extreme opinions. [244]

But here again, experience in the United States seems to negate this reasoning. American Jewry has had more than one hundred years of free intellectual development outside of any ghetto, and it has, indeed, for a long time been as well adjusted as anybody to Western intellectual life, if not better, but without apparent "psychological damage." Yet it is the present Jewish-American youth who produce most of the radical leadership among students and the New Left. It seems unlikely, therefore, that German Jews became radical for a different reason, namely because of a psychological damage which they are supposed to have suffered from an accelerated intellectual development of their parents and grandparents. In fact, the adjustment of the German Jews to modern intellectual development seemed just as effortless as that of the American Jews. It is also worthy of note that even the radical German (and French) students of a recent era had a Jewish leader, Daniel Cohn-Bendit.

Closer to the truth may be certain reasoning which can be found in writings of other Jewish authors. They point to the Jewish religious tradition and argue that an ethical idealism grew out of it, which replaced the original religion and ultimately turned into radicalism.

[244] In Thieme (ed.), *Judenfeindschaft*, p. 225.

Jewish monotheism meant a social conscience imbued with personal responsibility and a love for one's fellow man. . . . For many
young Jews this commitment to a left-wing idealism provided a
new religion. . . .

The specific Jewish religious heritage was transformed
into ethical idealism and directed toward bringing about a change
in present society. . . .

For many a Jew the rejection of traditional Judaism led to
this new religion. [245]

Mosse, in fact, reports that the German-Jewish revolutionary
anarchist Gustav Landauer (a colleague of Eisner) believed "in a
general revolutionary tradition which supposedly derived from Jewish
prophecy and which made the Jew especially suited to transform
existing reality." [246] Similarly, Pulzer calls the Jew "the heir to that
legacy of the puritanical visionary, the Hebraic tradition, embodied
by the Jew who does not feel comfortable unless the prophet's cloak
is warming his shoulders. . . ." And he thinks that, if the "prophetic
impulse" is added to the critical view of the Jewish intellectual concerning the status quo, "it is easy to see why a Jew . . . should be
driven to radical Liberalism in the middle of the nineteenth century
and Socialism at the end. We can see, too, why more often than not,
the Jew is likely to be associated with the extreme wing of his party." [247] Laqueur holds a similar view: "One explanation of the Jewish
inclination toward left-wing radicalism several generations after
Börne and Marx, is that it is an outgrowth of messianism." [248]

Related to the derivation of Jewish radicalism from the religious tradition and ethical idealism, is the Jewish concern with
humanity, which in part is presumably religiously based but may
originate also in the Jews' own experience of persecution and suffering over thousands of years. There is no question of the Jewish
compassion for the oppressed and underprivileged wherever they
may be. The Jews "feel . . . every folly and every misery of mankind
as if they were personally affected." [249] "Having been an oppressed

[245]Mosse, *Germans and Jews*, p. 206.

[246]Ibid., p. 90.

[247]Pulzer, op. cit., p. 262.

[248]Laqueur, *Out of the Ruins of Europe*, p. 478.

[249]Laqueur, in *Encounter*, October 1969, p. 80. See also Mosse, *Germans and Jews*, p. 205.

minority and the victim of persecution for so long, it may be only
natural for them to show sympathy for and give support to other
unfortunate groups. . . ."[250] Kahler says that he knows of no other
people who possess in their revered writings a declaration like this
in a Jewish Midrash: "Any distress concerning Israel and the people
of the world is a distress. Any distress concerning Israel alone is no
distress."[251]

But above all, it was, of course, the Jewish Old Testament itself
which—probably for the first time in history—proclaimed God's own
deep concern for the poor, the powerless, and the downtrodden. They
were his really chosen people, and the indifferent rich who lacked
compassion were damned. It was there that social justice originated,
and, in fact, in dispensing that justice, the biblical Jews boldly regarded themselves as partners with God. This whole Jewish concept
of a relationship of social justice between God and man, and among
men, was indeed a vast step forward in the history of human civilization. And clearly, compassion for, and identification with, the oppressed and suffering humanity is something entirely positive. No one
would want to call it destructive. Yet when it becomes passionate and
obsessive, it can turn destructive against those who are believed to be
the oppressors and those who are thought not to be active enough
in the fight against oppression. The Jewish mind could, indeed, develop a degree of righteousness and intolerance that was astonishing.
And it is a strange manifestation of the workings of tradition in human
attitudes that the revolutionary actions of people like Kurt Eisner,
Rosa Luxemburg, and Kurt Tucholsky, or Abbie Hoffman and Jerry
Rubin, might ultimately be traced back to biblical precepts.

It may be mentioned in passing that the German Jews, unlike
the American Jews, never made a serious "public relations" effort
to acquaint the non-Jewish public with their religious traditions and
fundamental ethical idealism. Nothing was done, for example, to put
a friendly Chanukkah alongside Christmas. It may be that German
anti-Semitism was so deep-seated that any such effort would have
been in vain, but it is also possible that it would have narrowed the
gap.

Also important in the motivation of Jewish destructiveness may
have been the uprooting of the Jews from a native soil, combined

---

[250]Laqueur, *Out of the Ruins of Europe*, p. 479.
[251]Kahler, *The Jews among the Nations*, p. 25.

with the conscious, but really unsuccessful, effort of many Jews to shed all Jewish traditions—traditions which they apparently were unable to replace by those of the host country. Pulzer believes that it "is in the main those Jews who attempted to cut themselves loose most completely from their environment [group?] who became the Socialist leaders, such as Adler and Bauer in Austria, Singer and Kurt Eisner in Germany, Rosa Luxemburg in Poland [Germany?], and Trotsky and Zinoviev in Russia. . . ." "The ideology of protest [he said] is natural to the uprooted intellectual . . ."[252] Eva Reichmann feels that the Jews, "in slowly loosening their bonds from their group, quite generally tend to be destructive toward general bonds," and she continues (perhaps too broadly) that "with the release from the chains of Jewish tradition, all tradition will in itself be easily rejected."[253] Jakob Wassermann said, "We know them and we suffer from them, those thousands of so-called modern Jews who gnaw at all foundations because they themselves have no foundations, who condemn today what they conquered yesterday, who befoul today what they loved yesterday. . . ."[254] At any rate, two thousand years of being a people without a state and country of its own and frequently being merely an unwanted guest in a succession of host countries is apt to create an attitude which rejects any of the local traditions and values and may even want to destroy them.

Other transplanted minority groups seem to have had no similar difficulties. The White Russian refugees in Germany and France and the Huguenots in Germany, for example, did not furnish revolutionary leaders in their host countries and did not become destructive of their way of life. But it is true that these minority groups were not really comparable to the Jewish group, particularly as regards rejection of their assimilation by the host country, history of Jewish suffering, degree of intelligence, intensity of feeling, and Jewish exuberant restlessness in general. One noteworthy phenomenon in the Jewish situation is that what occurred was not merely a purely negative failure to replace Jewish traditions by the traditions of the host country, but also affirmative active attacks by the Jews on the host's

[252]Pulzer, op. cit., pp. 261-262.
[253]Reichmann, *Flucht in den Hass*, p. 41.
[254]Wassermann, *Vom Judentum*, p. 5, quoted in Kampmann, *Deutsche und Juden*, p. 438.

traditions. In other words, the Jews did not simply remain indifferent to, or acquiesce in, the traditions of the host, but actively opposed them. Walter Laqueur says that ". . .unable to establish a state of their own, reduced to a marginal, parasitic existence among the peoples, Jews developed over the centuries an overwhelming destructive urge. If they had no fatherland, why should anyone else have one?"[255]

One theory which has not previously been suggested but may be presented here, is that Jewish destructiveness against German traditions, values, and institutions was simply an expression of Jewish group hostility against the Germans, somewhat analogous to the group hostility of the Germans against the Jews discussed above. It will be recalled that Freud saw "in this whole human behavior . . . a readiness to hate, an aggressiveness . . . to which we might ascribe elemental character." No doubt, Jews were as much capable of this hate and aggressiveness as Germans were. And the Jews, too, like the Germans, may have developed interethnic hostility as (to quote Bettelheim's statement once more) "the individual's effort to maintain balance in his psychic economy." Moreover, the Jews certainly knew of the general German hostility against them (even though until the end they never realized the depth of it), and this could hardly have failed to arouse some measure of reactive counterhostility in them. Finally, as a purely racial matter, the Germans were as alien to the Jews as they to the Germans and, therefore, presumably odious. But the Jews, being a small, weak minority in the midst of a large, pugnacious nation, could not safely give direct overt expression to their hostility against the Germans in the manner in which the latter could berate the Jews. The Jewish manifestation of group hostility was, therefore, more subtle. It consisted largely of destructive intellectual attacks against the country's traditions, values, and ways of life, and also of leadership in political radicalism directed against established institutions.

But whatever the motivations for Jewish destructiveness may have been, the Germans of that period could not really have cared less what they were. All that concerned the Germans was the fact that articulate Jews had destructive tendencies and that such Jews

---

[255]Laqueur, *Out of the Ruins of Europe*, p. 475.

owned or wrote for numerous newspapers, magazines, theaters, the film industry, etc. These Jews were highly visible and looked to millions like a menace to the German way of life. The really articulate destructive Jews represented a small percentage of the Jewish group, which itself was small; but this tiny segment of the entire population assumed an importance wholly disproportionate to its numerical strength. And this little group of articulate men caused anger and resentment against *all* Jews—anger and resentment which was greatly aggravated by the feeling, ineradicable among the Germans, that the Jews were aliens who were unable really to understand the German spirit and had no right to attack the German way of life, let alone try to change it.

In all this we should not close our eyes to the possibility that some destructiveness can also be good and may, in fact, have to be at the base of bold, innovative, constructive thinking. It was perhaps no mere accident that three Jews—indeed three German or Austrian Jews—Freud, Einstein, and Marx, were the men who, in our time, tore down some of our basic premises and replaced them by radically new ones.

j. JEWISH PENETRATION OF GERMAN LIFE

One of the most remarkable facts in the German-Jewish relationship was, on the one hand, the smallness of the Jewish group in proportion to the German population and, on the other hand, the great importance which that small group acquired in the cultural, political, and commercial life of the nation. According to Scheffler, in 1933, the year Hitler came to power, there were 503,000 Jews in Germany (not including Austria). This amounted to only 0.76 percent [256] of the total population of about 66 million. The majority of these Jews lived in the big cities and about one-third of them in Berlin. Clearly, this was a very small minority. The United States today, with its approximately 5,870,000 Jews, [257] has more than eleven times as many Jews in a population about three times as large. But the influence exerted by this small minority on German life and the attention that it received were astonishing. This influence evidently was due, in large measure,

[256] Scheffler, *Judenverfolgung im Dritten Reich*, p. 13.
[257] *New York Times*, Nov. 8, 1970.

to the very high degree of Jewish intelligence and education, to ambitious drive, and to the fact that the Jews had penetrated deeply into communications media, that is, the press, the periodicals, publishing, etc. "A great proportion of cultural institutions, like newspapers, publishing, music, and theatre, became Jewish enterprises."[258] The important film industry might be added to the list. "Jews were responsible for a great part of German culture. . . . Their participation in literary criticism and in literature was enormous: practically all the great critics and many novelists, poets, dramatists, essayists of Weimar Germany were Jews."[259] Jewish penetration in Austria may have been even greater. Friedrich Heer suggests that as early as the nineteenth century, nine-tenths of "Viennese culture" was "promoted, nourished, or even created" by Jewry.[260] Pulzer speaks of "their complete domination of Viennese cultural life in the generation before 1914"[261]; and it should be recalled that it was during that period that Hitler spent the miserable years of his early manhood in Vienna. One thing is clear, in any event (regardless of all implications which this Jewish penetration had for the German-Jewish relationship): these developments represented a Jewish cultural flowering and achievement in a host country as the world had never seen before and, quite likely, will never see again.

Jewish ownership or operation of much of the daily press and of the German news agency was, of course, of particular importance. "The 'liberal' press . . . owed its origin almost entirely to Jews."[262] The three most influential newspapers in Berlin and Frankfurt were Jewish owned or operated. In intellectual standards and readability they towered head and shoulder over most other German papers. The most influential national political and cultural magazines were also Jewish. Cultural and political public opinion was thus exposed, day in, day out, to a steady outpouring of Jewish thinking; and many of the publications, moreover, had no hesitation at all in attacking what the Germans considered their sacred values, their national

[258] Arendt, *Origins*, p. 52.
[259] Deak, *Weimar Germany's Left Wing Intellectuals*, p. 28; also Scheffler, op. cit., pp. 13-14.
[260] Heer, *Der Glaube des Adolf Hitler*, p. 141, also pp. 127-128.
[261] Pulzer, op. cit., p. 13.
[262] Ibid., p. 13.

interests. In those days, there was little separation between facts and editorial opinion anywhere in the German press. The Jewish newspapers and magazines were internationally minded, and this in itself, in the eyes of the Germans, made them "un-German" *(un-deutsch)* and evil. A great many Germans read these papers with rising anger. Many Germans also felt anxiety that large numbers of unwitting Germans might become "infected" by Jewish ideas and by the Jewish way of thinking. They came to consider anti-Semitism, as we have said before, as a kind of "national self-defense."

The Jewish penetration into the free professions (lawyers, doctors, dentists, scholars) was also very considerable. Kahler says that ". . . the percentage of the Jewish population in the professions became three times the percentage of the non-Jewish population so occupied, and in some branches the disparity was even greater. There were proportionately fifteen times as many Jewish as non-Jewish lawyers, about eight times as many writers and scholars, and about six times as many physicians." [263] In business, too, Jews had acquired enormous influence. Most of the department stores and most of the clothing industry were Jewish owned. The metal trades were 57 percent Jewish. A few Jews controlled 18.7 percent of the banks. [264] Some Germans viewed the ownership of the department stores and banks as a "Jewish conspiracy." [265]

The Germans of that period created a word for all this: *Überfremdung*, which means approximately "overalienization." Goebbels in a speech early in 1933 complained of "the overalienization of the German intellectual life by international Jewry." [266] But very few Jews of that period saw the danger, and even if they had seen it and had wanted to act, it might have been like trying to hold back the tide. The most they could have done was to advise the use of tact and reticence. The German-Jewish philosopher Theodor Lessing, as usual a lone voice, understood what was going on and expressed himself with his customary exaggerated vigor: "Nothing is more disgusting,

[263] Kahler, *The Jews among the Nations*, p. 85.

[264] For these data see Neumann, *Behemoth*, p. 113. See also Pulzer, op. cit., pp. 12-13. For certain figures relative to Jewish penetration in Austria, see Heer, op. cit., pp. 127-128, 141.

[265] See Mosse, *Crisis*, p. 221.

[266] Berning, *Vom "Abstammungsnachweis" zum "Zuchtwart,"* p. 185.

nothing is more brazen and shameless than this [Jewish] urge to lead and advise." [267]

It was only *after* the catastrophe that a prominent German Jew, Robert Weltsch, then in exile, *began* to see the problem of the past:

> . . . the Jews pushed on toward higher education and into the academic professions. We know that this Jewish preponderence [in the professions] caused strong discontent in German intellectual circles. The literature of the nineteenth and twentieth centuries abounds in examples which show that even important and liberal minds in Germany took a dubious view of this phenomenon. Even if we Jews do not share many of the opinions that reject Jewish writers or intellectuals, it is, nevertheless, not adequate for us to shrug off so striking a manifestation of antipathy as mere petty narrow-mindedness. Objective historiography must take a somewhat more profound view of these things. It will have to be conceded that a problem exists, and that the history of this problem may not be evaded if the history of the German Jew is to be written. [268]

Weltsch does not indicate that there might have been a solution for that problem (and, indeed, there may have been none), but he does go on to suggest that the aim of an interpretation of the past "will frequently demand self-restraint and special intellectual candor" (presumably on the part of Jews who engage in this interpretation). He does not distinguish between what we might call the "quantitative" and the "qualitative" aspects of the situation, that is, the problem of the very large size of Jewish representation and its success in German intellectual life, and the problem of the "destructive" use which the Jews were believed to be making of their heavy representation in that life. The latter problem was discussed in the preceding section.

As far as the quantitative aspects are concerned, it is easy to recognize the problem, but was there any practical solution for it? Should the numerous gifted Jewish journalists have refrained from publishing newspapers and magazines, and should they have gone into some other business instead? Should there have been a *numerus*

---

[267] Lessing, *Deutschland und seine Juden,* p. 26.
[268] In *Deutsches Judentum,* pp. 18–19.

clausus to keep the young Jews out of medical and law schools? Should Einstein have stayed away from physics and done something else so that non-Jewish physicists might have taken over the leadership? Should the Jewish owners of department stores and banks have tried to be less successful in business? It is not easy to see how Jewish intelligence and drive could have been suppressed or self-policed in any field in a free capitalistic society which had achieved complete Emancipation of the Jews in 1869. Even if the Jews had seen the problem (which they generally did not), they could hardly have been expected to submit to such extraordinary restrictions, and this would, in fact, have been repulsive even to a great many liberal Germans. Ultimately Hitler found what was for him the simple remedy of (in the beginning) forcing the Jews to emigrate and (later) of killing those who were left. But this does not assist our consideration of the problem of what the Jews themselves might have done much earlier to avoid or reduce this source of anti-Semitism. The problem was probably beyond solution.

It was, as Kahler says, "the sad spectacle of the Jews pressing or being pressed [?] so deeply into German existence as to provoke violent repulsion,"[269] or it was, as we said earlier, like a rejection of a transplant by the body. The Jews had dreamed too German a dream. Kahler, in this connection, quotes Bernhard Guttmann's statement that "German Jewry perished because it did not stay alien enough. Its *hubris* consisted in the desire to assimilate completely." But the second part of this statement is not correct. German Jewry never did, and never wanted to, assimilate *completely*. True enough, Jewish doctors, lawyers, bankers, businessmen wanted to participate and did participate fully in German life, which indeed furnished the life blood for their outstanding success. But the Jews, as a whole, nevertheless, remained an alien group; and many did not want to or were unable to become totally German. This was manifest, above all, in the Jewish owned or operated communications media, some of which, in fact, were not merely indifferent to German values but actually attacked them and tried to destroy them, thus becoming one of the main causes of anti-Semitism. Jewish efforts to be assimilated, indeed, looked to some Germans like something suspicious. Assimilation to them was no solution but a threat. To them, intimacy with Jews was

[269]Kahler, op. cit., p. 109.

a disease that one had to be careful not to catch. It is interesting, in this connection, that Adorno found in his investigations in the United States that "Jews who attempt to assimilate are apparently even more suspect than the others" and that "most anti-Semites seem to feel that the basic 'Jewishness' is permanent." [270]

In a sense, Kahler is right in saying that there was "a relationship that had reached too deep." [271] But in another sense, it had not reached deep enough. It may have been too deep in the Jewish-German symbiosis, discussed earlier, and also in the quantitative penetration of German cultural and commercial life by the Jews. But it was not deep enough in the Jewish failure or inability to absorb the old German historical and political traditions. And it was this very juxtaposition of depth here and lack of depth there that caused profound antagonism.

No comparably complex relationship between Jews and gentiles seems to have existed in France and Britain, where Jewish influence on cultural and social life was not nearly so great and where no extensive symbiosis ever developed.

National Socialism, on the whole, placed no great emphasis on the disproportionate representation of the Jews in the cultural life of the nation. It might have been embarrassing to mention that the Jews, whose influence on Germany was constantly branded as highly dangerous, amounted to no more than 0.76 percent of the total population. Propagandistically, it was safer and more effective to take refuge behind the nebulous concept of a fight against "World Jewry," which day after day was proclaimed to be Germany's real enemy. But the so-called "Jew-press"—German and international—was, of course, condemned. If any explanations were offered for the obvious success of the German Jew in science, medicine, law, and business, it was that the Jews were utterly deceitful brazen swindlers who ruthlessly pushed everyone else out of their way. In his confidential *Table Talks* Hitler once said:

The Jews are tough like rats, a race of creatures who penetrate through the whole world and make money in every climate because of their boundless brazenness. . . . This is the only ex-

---

[270] Adorno, *The Authoritarian Personality*, pp. 97, 99.
[271] Kahler, op. cit., p. 119.

planation for the fact that Jewish lawyers, without a trace of brilliancy, could win the upper hand during Germany's most shameful era—by deliberately lying. [272]

At any rate, it did not take the regime very long to put an end to all Jewish cultural life in Germany. [273] As early as May 20, 1933, soon after Hitler's seizure of power, the non-Jewish physicians, for example, published this demand: "We German physicians demand the exclusion of all Jews from the medical treatment of ethnic Germans." [274]

The enormously extensive penetration of German life by the Jews thus became, in itself, a cause of anti-Semitism, in addition to giving visibility to, or intensifying, the other causes heretofore discussed.

k. MISCELLANEOUS CAUSES OF ANTI-SEMITISM

Long as our catalogue of the causes of German anti-Semitism has been, it is still not complete. There are other causes, but they, on the whole, may have been minor, even though to some people they may have had major importance.

There is, for example, the simple presence of sadistic drives in Hitler and in other Germans—drives aimed at unrestricted power over other people, including the Jews. Erich Fromm discusses these at some length in *Escape from Freedom*. [275] "Racial and political minorities within Germany and eventually other nations which are described [by the National Socialists] as weak or decaying are the objects of sadism upon which the [German] masses are fed." For Hitler, Darwinism with its theory of the survival of the strongest was "an expression of and simultaneously a justification for his own sadism" which he projected upon "Nature who is 'the cruel Queen of all Wisdom.' " [276] His ideas were "addressed to people who, on account of their similar character structure, felt attracted and excited by these teachings and became ardent followers of the man who expressed what they felt." [277]

---

[272] *Hitler's Table Talks*, p. 415 (indirect speech transposed).
[273] See the "timetable" in Scheffler, *Judenverfolgung im Dritten Reich*, pp. 118–122. For details, see Buchheim et al., *Anatomie des SS-Staates*, Vol. II, pp. 316 et seq.
[274] Buchheim et al., *Anatomie*, Vol. II, p. 317.
[275] Fromm, *Escape*, pp. 221–239.
[276] Ibid., p. 227.
[277] Ibid., p. 236.

The Jews naturally were an ideal object and a readily available "licensed" victim for the practice of sadism. They furnished, above all, the possibility of respectable rationalizations for an ugly instinctual drive. Here was the sadist's chance to work off his cruel fury, to take revenge for whatever irked him, to indulge in the ecstasy of hatred. The German novelist Ernst Jünger must have had this in mind when he wrote that the National Socialists "then abandon themselves to the relish of killing; and this drive to mass murder was what compelled them forward, torpid and confused, from the start. . . . Now they emerge into the open under a mantle of ideology."[278]

Also, as Huss says, one could free oneself of something "evil" and be left clean and be the cleanser.[279] The German Jews, moreover, were deliciously weak antiphysical people who represented a challenge even to any half-developed sadist. The ecstasy of hatred could be a kind of opium for small people, for the frustrated, the semieducated, the crackpots. It is surprising, too, how many passionate followers of extreme national socialist dreams were to be found among food faddists, body builders, opponents of vivisection, and the like.

Moreover, anti-Semitism was a great "leveler" for all groups and classes other than the Jews themselves; it provided an excellent emotional meeting ground. For the unsuccessful, the loafers, the good-for-nothings, being a non-Jew was at least one asset with which they were born and of which they could not be deprived. In this respect, they were equal to the highest—Hitler himself—and he appreciated this asset. It was satisfying to them to be able to look down upon someone else, no matter how low their own status was. Also, their own failure in life could often be explained by Jewish machinations and swindles.

As a political tool, anti-Semitism was highly useful to a totalitarian government. The exercise of terror is essential to such a regime; and the complete brutality of the anti-Jewish terror was, from the very start, the model which could teach every German that his government was prepared to stop at nothing. The fate of the Jews could be a lesson to all in terror, subjection, and submission. What the regime obtained by its anti-Jewish action was a prototype of the contrast

---

[278]Jünger, *Strahlungen*, 1950, p. 73.
[279]Huss and Schröder (eds.), *Antisemitismus*, p. 98.

between absolute power and absolute submission that any totalitarian system needs. Moreover, the brutal confinement and treatment of millions of Jews (and non-Jews) in concentration camps and, finally, the murder of about six million Jews was regarded by the regime not only as necessary action against the powerless Jews themselves but also as a preparatory exercise or practice rehearsal *(Vorübung)* for much larger enslavement operations against the more resistant Slavic race. Himmler, for one, always took this view and emphasized that the experience gained in anti-Jewish actions was to make his SS "harsh" *(hart)* and steel them for their tasks.

Another political purpose of active anti-Semitism (which, however, was probably never consciously understood by the leading National Socialists) was that maligning the "international Jewish" group contributed to building up national self-assurance in the German nation, which historically had never had much of it.

Finally we might briefly mention a theory of the Austrian ethologist Konrad Lorenz. He discusses the basic instinctive aggressive drives of animals and men and says:

> For a chimpanzee and even for a man of the early stone age it was undoubtedly valuable and necessary, for purposes of preserving himself, his family and species, that his inner stimulative production of aggressive behavior was adequate for, let us say, two great fits of rage per week. . . . it is not surprising . . . that modern man, in his police-protected life, does not know where to discharge these rhythmically occurring fits of rage. . . . The increased readiness to commit aggression, which is a result of this very . . . damming up of energy, is undoubtedly the cause of the easy *incitability* of the people. To a certain extent, everyone is glad if he can find a "legitimate" substitute object for his frustrated aggressiveness, and he lets himself be taken in by any sham which a skillful demagogue may dangle before him. I maintain that, in the absence of this purely physiological foundation, there would basically have been no possibility of the occurrence of such demagogically induced mass cruelties as, for instance, witch-trials and persecution of Jews. [280]

[280]Lorenz, *Über tierisches und menschliches Verhalten*, Munich, 1965, Vol. II, pp. 188-189.

D. Some Final Considerations Concerning Anti-Semitism in the Ideology

The foregoing discussion of the causes of German anti-Semitism makes clear that there were enormous tensions in the German-Jewish relationship during the fifty years before Hitler. The catalogue of causative factors was, indeed, extraordinarily large, and some reached down to the very basics in human attitudes and relationships. There was hardly a German non-Jew who was not affected by at least one, and probably by far more, of these factors. The tensions were such and of such long standing that it seemed nearly impossible for the average German not to harbor some form of anti-Semitism, and there is no doubt that it represented accepted tradition and even a way of life. It was certainly "not dependent upon any single crisis,"[281] nor upon stimulation by rabble-rousers, demagogues, and the like.

Adorno said (of American anti-Semitism), ". . . what one has to deal with here is not a single specific attitude but a *system* that has content, scope and structure."[282] If it was not a system, it was at least a syndrome. The Jews could be accused of an astonishing multitude of sins, and they could be hated by a large multitude of groups and combinations of groups. Their sins were not necessarily all compatible with each other—such as ruthless capitalism and radical socialism; disproportionate wealth of businessmen and dirty poverty of the Eastern Jewish immigrants; international war-mongering and effete pacifism. At any rate, ever since long before Hitler the Jews somehow could be offered up as common enemy to all kinds of diverse groups, and this ultimately assisted Hitler in uniting a nation that historically had rarely been united. One fairly common meeting ground for most anti-Semites was the simple broad proposition that the idealized imaginary German world of the past no longer existed because the Jew had destroyed it, and that the utopian German world of the future had not as yet become reality because the Jews stood in its way.

Adorno says that "the usual 'self-contradictions' of the [American] anti-Semite can . . . frequently be explained on the basis that they

[281]Mosse, *Crisis*, p. 301.
[282]Adorno, *The Authoritarian Personality*, p. 42.

involve different layers of reality and different psychological urges which are still reconcilable in the over-all *Weltanschauung* of the anti-Semite," and his "fantasies occur whenever stereotypes 'run wild,' that is to say, make themselves completely independent from interaction with reality."[283] He calls them "emancipated stereotypes." It is probably fair to say that the Germany of the pre-Hitler and Hitler periods gave birth to a larger arsenal of emancipated stereotypes than any other country in history, and this not only in the field of anti-Semitism. Presumably, this array of emancipated stereotypes assisted many Germans in finding their "place in the world" and in overcoming their inherent feeling of national insecurity.

The arsenal of anti-Semitic arguments had been almost fully assembled by 1914. Practically the only accusation against the Jews, which was greatly intensified thereafter, was that of Jewish destructiveness, which for the reasons discussed here earlier received enormous impetus beginning in November, 1918. They became the "November criminals." Hitler, at any rate, had no difficulty in finding a solid ideological basis for his own anti-Semitic policy. But it is true also that very little in German anti-Semitism that preceded Hitler can explain or make comprehensible the ultimate action of murdering six million Jews, which he and Himmler set into motion. There was still a considerable gap between the anti-Semitic *thought* of the nineteenth and early twentieth century and the determined *action* that built the gas chambers of Auschwitz and Treblinka. The probabilities are that only psychiatry could supply explanations to bridge that gap. And the difficulty in finding these explanations may lie not so much in an analysis of Hitler's and Himmler's own emotional condition as in the effort to understand how perhaps 50,000 or 60,000 seemingly normal Germans could be made to become executioners on behalf of the two chief murderers, under an apparently complete paralysis of moral scruples.

It is true, however, that the tensions and hostility between Jews and non-Jews were so strong that some sort of explosion might have occurred even if there had been no Hitler and no National Socialist Movement, although it is most unlikely that such an explosion would ever have approached the proportions of the actual holocaust.

[283] Ibid., p. 613.

In the case of Hitler and Himmler, the intensity of the anti-Jewish obsession—probably pathological—manifested itself most clearly in the fact that, even in the most difficult days of the German-Soviet war, railroad transport trains carrying Jews from the West to the extermination camps in Poland were given priority over trains for urgently needed troops and war supplies. Moreover, skilled Jewish laborers, desperately needed in the munitions plants in occupied Poland, were carted off to the extermination centers, in spite of strong objections by the plant managers.[284] Tens of thousands of able-bodied German men were engaged in the business of killing Jews instead of fighting in the front lines which at times lacked all reserves. All this might be regarded as a triumph of ideology over self-interest; it was, in a sense, idealism, not opportunism. Clearly, Hitler did have principles of a sort. But it is possible that Huss is right when he says: ". . . linked to the complete destruction of the Jews, the victims who symbolized the totality, was the magic hope that even the war, lost as he knew it to be, had to lead to victory . . . on a higher plane on which it meant the ultimate fight against evil."[285]

Of course, even if the Jews had been guilty of every one of the numerous crimes, transgressions, immoral behavior, etc., of which they were accused, this would not, either legally or morally, have justified the punishment they received: total extermination. But this disproportion is quite in line with Adorno's investigations of anti-Semitic attitudes in the United States. He found a

> . . . fantastic disproportion between the Jewish "guilt"—even as conceived by the anti-Semite himself—and the judgment that is pronounced. . . . Where the Jews are concerned . . . the transition from accusations which are not only flimsy but unsubstantial even if they were true, to suggestions of the severest kind of treatment seems to work quite smoothly. . . . The outgroup, the chosen foe, represents an eternal challenge. As long as anything different survives, the fascist character feels threatened, no matter how weak the other being may be. . . . the Nazis went

---

[284] Hilberg, *The Destruction of the European Jews*, p. 298; Jäckel, *Hitlers Weltanschauung*, pp. 79–80; Buchheim et al., *Anatomie,* Vol. II, p. 441; Bracher, *Die deutsche Diktatur*, pp. 467–468. The vast anti-Jewish propaganda is well summarized in Hilberg, pp. 653–658.

[285] Huss and Schröder, *Antisemitismus*, p. 50.

far beyond their official anti-semitic program. . . . The extreme anti-Semite simply cannot stop. . . . Psychologically, the idea of eternal Jewish guilt can be understood as a projection of the prejudiced person's own repressed guilt feelings; ideologically, it is a mere epiphenomenon, a rationalization in the strictest sense. . . . The disproportion between the guilt and the punishment induces [the anti-Semite] . . . to pursue his hatred beyond any limits and thus to prove to himself and to others that he *must* be right.[286]

Hitler, for one, was an anti-Semite who "could not stop" but had to "pursue his hatred beyond any limits." The ultimate decision to exterminate the Jews, however, does not seem to have been arrived at until fairly late. In the summer of 1940, for example, Eichmann was still given instructions to work out a plan for the resettlement of four million Jews in Madagascar.[287] The exact date when Hitler definitely decided to execute, rather than deport, the Jews is unknown. It was probably early in 1941.[288] The entire anti-Jewish scheming was very much a one-man operation at the summit or, at most, a two-man operation between Hitler and Himmler. And the whole sinister enterprise could not really be undertaken before the remote silence and darkness of occupied Poland had become available.

Jäckel believes that there was a "world-missionary trait" in Hitler's anti-Semitism and that the extermination of the Jews became his "most important war aim, the gift which National Socialism was making to the world."[289] This was hardly true *before* the war or in its early stages. It did become true only when Hitler began to realize that his other war aims were beyond his reach and that all he could still accomplish was the destruction of the Jews. Jäckel quotes a statement made by Hitler to Martin Bormann shortly before his death that the world "will be grateful to National Socialism into eternity for having

[286] Adorno, op. cit., pp. 632–633.

[287] Arendt, *Eichmann*, p. 76.

[288] See Hilberg, op. cit., pp. 261–262; also Bracher, op. cit., pp. 460–461, and Maser, *Adolf Hitler*, pp. 334, 415.

[289] Jäckel, op. cit., pp. 83–84.

wiped out the Jews in Germany and Central Europe."[290] In April, 1945, in his Berlin bunker, that was the only "accomplishment" of which he still could boast and which defeat indeed could not take away from him. The Jews were dead.

One of the strangest aspects of the German-Jewish relationship was the extent to which the Germans succeeded in tricking the Jews — in Germany and most other occupied European countries — into going to their death without resistance or, in fact, with their active cooperation. For centuries, the Jews had bested the Germans in millions of commercial transactions, and the Germans had always been ready to concede (with some disgust) that the Jews were superior to them in many aspects of commercial life. Jewish lawyers, too, were generally regarded as being able to "trick" many of their non-Jewish colleagues. There was, in any event, little doubt as to the quickness and acuteness of the mind of the average Jew. Yet, in the confrontation of the Final Solution, the Germans had no difficulty at all in tricking and deceiving the Jews into going to their doom, and this by very simple schemes employed over and over again in dealing with the Jews of all occupied European countries. Constant repetition did not seem to reduce the effectiveness of these schemes.

Briefly, the Germans took full advantage of two elements in the Jewish state of mind. One was, as Bettelheim has pointed out, that the Jews believed National Socialism to represent historically no more than the worst "wave" of anti-Semitism and that they therefore reacted to it in ways which in the past had enabled them to survive.[291] The experience of more than 2,000 years of persecution had shown the Jews that appeasement, bending with the wind, and lack of all active resistance, even active cooperation, was the best policy in the diaspora to assure survival of the larger part of the Jewish groups. The Jews had usually had their losses, but as a people they had never been destroyed. They were "used to understanding their own history, rightly or wrongly, as a long story of suffering"[292] and, indeed, as Pinson says, "we elevated and hypostatized our history of suffering

[290] Ibid., p. 84.
[291] Bruno Bettelheim in F. A. Krummacher (ed.), *Die Kontroverse — Hannah Arendt, Eichmann und die Juden*, p. 104.
[292] Arendt, *Eichmann*, p. 153.

into a destined role imposed upon us, as the servants of the Lord, for the sanctification of His name."[293]

The second element in the Jewish state of mind, of which the Germans took full advantage, was that the Jews simply could not understand or believe that the Germans really intended to exterminate all of them. This is hardly surprising. It was, after all, the first time in world history that anyone had planned the systematic annihilation of six million people (or, rather, far more than six million, as far as the *plans* went). It is likely, in fact, that even most Germans, if informed of the proposals for the Final Solution, would not have taken them seriously, in spite of the vast official anti-Semitic propaganda and the long anti-Jewish tradition. And from the point of view of the Jews, who naturally did not see themselves as the incarnation of evil, the existence of such monstrous plans on the part of the Germans must have seemed extremely unlikely. Jews and Germans had, after all, been closely associated with each other for more than a thousand years, and German culture and civilization was still something the Jews admired. Clearly, the big truth was harder to believe than the big lie. A high SS officer said after the war that "it was the blind confidence of the Jews themselves [in the Germans] which was a great obstacle to preventive action.[294]

The Germans thus had to deal with people whose natural resistance had not been aroused by an expectation of the worst but who were willing to appease, obey, comply, and even actively cooperate, usually in the hope that they might ride out the storm. The Jews rather quickly became reconciled to the fact that they would have to lose all their property and homes and would have to "resettle" in some new place, for instance, a ghetto in Poland. "Resettle" *(umsiedeln)*, in fact, became a very useful word in the vocabulary of the executioners. The Jews became reconciled also to the fact that they would have to do forced labor under severe conditions in the ghettos or in camps. Thus, the Jews, all over occupied Europe, prepared lists of persons

---

[293]Pinson (ed.), *Essays on Antisemitism*, p. 45. By far the most comprehensive study of this subject, Isaiah Trunk, *JUDENRAT: The Jewish Councils in Eastern Europe under Nazi Occupation*, New York, 1972, was published after this book had gone to press.

[294]Erich von dem Bach-Zelewski in *Aufbau*, (New York), Sept. 6, 1946, p. 40. See also his more detailed statement quoted in Hilberg, op. cit., p. 663.

for the Germans, published German instructions, registered their property and delivered it, reported at the designated place for deportation, boarded the cattle cars, and finally dug their own mass graves or marched naked into the gas chambers. They became, as Arthur Koestler once suggested, accomplices in their own destruction.

The German technique of dealing with the Jews was, then, quite simple. Basically, the Germans saw to it that the Jews were left with some hope, until the certain knowledge of imminent death could no longer be avoided. Eichmann testified in Jerusalem that he employed all possible means of deception to make the Jews believe that they were not being sent to their death.[295] They were assured that all measures were "temporary."[296] Above all, various "categories" of Jews were usually established, some of whom would initially be exempted from "resettlement." The Jewish leadership with all their relatives would be exempted, as would be the aged, invalids, persons in forced labor, war veterans, and others.[297] Or, if the operation took place in Germany itself, only Polish Jews were initially to be deported, or Jews who had evaded military service, and so on.[298] Hilberg reports that in Vienna a "deportation agreement" with the Jewish leadership was concluded, providing that six categories would not be deported, and that in the Warsaw ghetto the Jews argued in favor of the deportation of 60,000, if hundreds of thousands could remain. Hilberg calls this the "bisection phenomenon."[299] The Jews who stayed for the time being could argue, of course, that some had to be sacrificed to save the majority. But, from the German point of view, it was merely deportation by stages; the numbers of those who were left bec..me ever smaller, and in the end they all went.

In Germany itself, and perhaps elsewhere, the group-by-group method found support in social reaction patterns of the Jews themselves. Adorno says that

In Germany, at least, the "autochthonous" Jews used to discriminate heavily against refugees and immigrants from the East and

[295] Krummacher (ed.), *Die Kontroverse,* p. 227.
[296] Arendt, *Eichmann,* p. 197.
[297] See f.i., Hilberg, op. cit., pp. 279–280, 668.
[298] Arendt, *Eichmann,* p. 132.
[299] Hilberg, op. cit., p. 668.

often enough comforted themselves with the idea that the Nazi policies were directed merely against the *"Ostjuden."* Distinctions of this sort seem to promote gradual persecution of Jews, group by group, with the aid of the smooth rationalization that only those are to be excluded who do not belong anyway. [300]

It appears that the Germans were highly successful in promoting such rationalizations among the doomed Jews.

There were also minor tricks in the arsenal of deception. In difficult late negotiations with the highly (and rightly) suspicious leadership of the Jewish community in Hungary, for example, Eichmann and his men deliberately acted as if they were corrupt [301] in order to calm Jewish nerves and to create the illusion that the worst could be avoided by bribery. On another occasion, early arrivals at Auschwitz were forced to write encouraging postcards to relatives at home, with datelines from *Waldsee* ("Forest Lake"). [302]

One of the most astonishing acts of deception was a printed form of contract which was to induce affluent German Jews to agree to their deportation to the Theresienstadt concentration camp. [303] The contract followed in general the legal form used for the purchase of a place in an old-age home. In it, the Jew assigned his bank accounts and securities in return for "the obligation to grant [to him], for his lifetime, shelter in the institution *(Heim)*, as well as board, to have his laundry washed, to look after his medical care and to furnish medications, if necessary, and to provide for necessary hospital care." The Theresienstadt camp was bad enough, but the contract contained a "reservation of the right to provide accommodation [*Unterbringung*] elsewhere," by which the Germans presumably meant accommodation in one of the extermination camps where the contractually specified "lifetime" of the "sheltered" Jew would be rather limited. Apparently only 16 percent of the inmates of Theresienstadt survived. [304] A great many wealthy German Jews seem to have signed this agreement.

The Jewish failure to see through all these deceptions and ruses

[300] Adorno, op. cit., p. 624.

[301] Arendt, *Eichmann*, p. 196.

[302] Hilberg, op. cit., p. 538.

[303] This form of contract is reproduced in full in Buchheim et al., *Anatomie*, Vol. II, pp. 400–402.

[304] Bracher, op. cit., p. 464.

should perhaps not be too surprising. Not only were there the basic traditional Jewish attitudes, discussed earlier, but there was also the fundamental fact that a largely helpless person who finds himself in terrible, perhaps mortal, danger will grasp at straws and will be eager to believe in the truth of almost anything that might avert the danger, even temporarily. It is perhaps only this natural reaction that can be the ultimate explanation of the Jewish failure to resist, and their cooperation with Eichmann in Hungary, the country reached last by the executioners. There the Jews *knew* that about five million Jews of other countries had previously been killed, and they were quite aware of the purpose of deportations to Auschwitz and other camps. Yet the Jewish leadership "fell for" courteous treatment by Eichmann and for his assurances that they had nothing to fear. They cooperated. [305] We are not concerned here with individual cases of Jewish dishonesty, selfishness, or treason. They are to be expected in situations of extreme human tension in the face of death.

There was also the fact that active resistance was useless (except as a matter of saving Jewish pride and honor). One of the very few important episodes of armed opposition was the uprising in the Warsaw ghetto, but, as Hilberg says, "measured in German casualties," even this really heroic action "shrinks into insignificance." [306] On the German side, there were no more than 16 dead and 85 wounded, including collaborators. The Jewish losses were naturally very much heavier, but they would have been losses in the gas chambers in any event.

There is, however, a great deal of difference between failure to resist and affirmative cooperation, and this brings us to the severe criticism of the Jewish leadership in almost all European countries, which Hannah Arendt presented in *Eichmann in Jerusalem*. [307] She said, for example, that "to a Jew this role of the Jewish leaders in the destruction of their own people is undoubtedly the darkest chapter of the whole dark story," [308] and her most frequently quoted and criticized statement is:

[305] See details in Hilberg, op. cit., pp. 529-531. See also Gerald Reitlinger, *Die Endlösung*, pp. 480-481, and Isaiah Trunk, *JUDENRAT: The Jewish Councils in Eastern Europe under Nazi Occupation* (published after this book had gone to press).

[306] Hilberg, op. cit., p. 663.

[307] F.i., Arendt, *Eichmann*, at pp. 117-119, 124-125.

[308] Ibid., p. 117.

The whole truth was that if the Jewish people had really been unorganized and leaderless, there would have been chaos and plenty of misery but the total number of victims would hardly have been between four and a half and six million people. [309]

This criticism has resulted in a violent controversy among contemporary Jews and in considerable literature. [310] The subject matter of that controversy is rather outside of the scope of the present book. It should be said, however, that no matter whether Miss Arendt is right or wrong, it would be ludicrous to question the integrity of this eminent scholar, one of the outstanding minds of our time. And it might be added that much of the German success in rounding up the Jews was due to the simple fact that the Jewish community leaders throughout Europe did seem to have reliable up-to-date records of the addresses of all local Jews—a remarkable accomplishment after 2,000 years of life in the diaspora. Had there been no such records, there might have been no effective roundup of the Jews. But it is true also that without records no cohesive Jewish groups might have been preserved throughout the diaspora, and quite likely the Jews would not have survived as a people at all.

With the actual systematic extermination process, we descend into the black abyss at the bottom of national socialist ideology. But the utter brutality of the process was not really a necessary or logical result of this ideology. It did logically call for the killing of the Jews and other "subhumans," but it did not require the use of inhuman methods. It is true that the SS, which was in charge of most executions, had been systematically trained never to have pity and to be harsh *(hart)*, but even this would not necessarily have meant the use of torture, unspeakable daily cruelties, slow killings, and so forth. Motivations in addition to those induced by ideological training were presumably present, even if the ideology furnished rationalizations for all of them. Primitive sexual drives no doubt were frequently active as were generally sadistic drives. Perfect satisfaction of these drives could be obtained by having complete mastery over the Jews (and others),

[309] Ibid., p. 125.

[310] F.i., F. A. Krummacher (ed.), op. cit.; Jacob Robinson, *And the Crooked Shall Be Made Straight,* who preposterously calls attention (p. 10) to Miss Arendt's "concern with Eichmann's defense."

making helpless objects of them and torturing them. To a sadist, the pleasure of inflicting pain is even greater than that of finally killing the victim.

The result, then, was cruelties as the world has seldom seen: beatings, public and private, whippings into unconsciousness or death, starvation, freezing to death, stand-up cells, doghouse-size cells, cells without light, choking, castor-oil treatment, working to death, stomping to death, smashing the head of a baby against a wall in the mother's presence, all forms of severe torture ("intensified interrogation"), and many more. For twelve years, these were daily occurrences. Death in the gas chambers was far more humane (almost mercy killing), and this method of killing was actually adopted by the leadership for "humanitarian reasons." The gas used was *Zyklon B*, a gas that had for many years been employed for fumigation, delousing and, generally, the extermination of vermin.[311] Its use was a macabre but strangely logical climactic result of national socialist ideology which had always described the Jews as vermin.

Earlier killing methods, which were in extensive use in 1941 and 1942, were vastly more cruel. One was described in an affidavit at the main Nuremberg trial by a German civilian construction engineer, Hermann Friedrich Gräbe, who was stationed in the Ukraine in 1942:

> . . . The men, women, and children, who had gotten off the truck, were ordered by the SS man, with horsewhip or dogwhip in hand, to take off their clothes and to put them in certain places, separated according to shoes, outer clothes, and underwear. I saw a pile of shoes which I would estimate at 800 to 1,000 pairs. . . . I stood before the immense grave. Closely pressed together, the people were lying on top of each other so that only their heads could be seen. Blood ran from almost all the heads to the shoulders. Some of the shot people were still moving. A few lifted their arms or turned their heads to show that they were still alive. The ditch was already three-quarters full. I would estimate that by that time it contained about 1,000 people. I looked around for the rifleman. He—an SS man—was sitting on the edge of the narrow side of the ditch on the bare ground, his legs dangling into the ditch, with a submachine gun on his knees. He was smok-

[311]See Hilberg, op. cit., p. 567.

ing a cigarette. The completely naked people went down a stair-case which had been dug into the clay wall of the ditch, and then slid across the heads of the lying people to whatever place the SS man designated. They lay down on top of the dead or wounded people; some stroked people who were still alive and spoke quietly to them. Then I heard a series of shots. I looked into the ditch and saw how the bodies jerked or the heads were al-ready quiet on top of the bodies which lay under them. Blood ran from their necks. . . . The next group was already approach-ing, climbed down into the ditch and was shot. . . .[312]

What happened after killings was described in a report by Kurt Gerstein, a former SS officer, concerning an execution he witnessed on August 18, 1942:

. . . Two dozen dentists were using hooks to open the mouths [of the corpses] and were looking for tooth gold. The ones with gold [were placed] to the left, without gold to the right. Other dentists were using pliers and hammers to break the gold teeth and crowns from the jaws.
Captain Wirth was running around among all of them. He was in his element. — Some workers were examining the genitals and the rectums for gold, diamonds, and valuables. Wirth called me over: "Just lift this can of tooth gold. This is only from yes-terday and the day before. . . ."[313]

It was in such ditches that the German-Jewish relationship of a thou-sand years came to a definite end, and that German civilization itself went under, at least for a time.

We have devoted a good deal of time and space to a discussion of the German-Jewish relationship and of anti-Semitism as an ideological component of National Socialism. Anti-Semitism has always been the most visible and, in all its ramifications, perhaps the most interesting of the various components. But all this should not be taken to mean that anti-Semitism was also the most important component. It would not be correct to say[314] that the ideology "centered around" anti-

---

[312] *TMWC*, Vol. XXXI, pp. 447–448, doc. 2992-PS.

[313] Full text reproduced in Walther Hofer, *Der Nationalsozialismus: Dokumente 1933–1945*, pp. 307–311.

[314] Arendt, *Origins*, p. 3.

Semitism. If it centered around anything, it was more likely to be the restoration of Germany's place in the world, the imperialistic aims of an aggressive world policy, the enlargement of the Lebensraum, the rightful domination of others by the Germans as a superior race, and the like. The "great Germanic trek" toward the East was probably the very center of Hitler's and Himmler's dreams. Anti-Semitism in itself was, after all, an essentially negative component of an otherwise largely "positive" ideology. Hitler would never have been satisfied with merely gloating over six million Jewish corpses, important as they were to him. It is not at all certain, moreover, that if the elimination of the Jews had required a war with millions of German casualties, Hitler would have undertaken such a war, whereas he was quite prepared to sacrifice a great many German lives to obtain Lebensraum in the East.

Basically, the existence of the Jews (including the imagined Jewish domination of the Soviet Union) was regarded as an obstacle to the creation of the idealized utopian German *Volk* community and of an expanded German empire. *After* elimination of the Jews, it would become possible to tackle the more positive ideological aims. This is reflected, for example, in the marching song of the storm troopers (SA):

> *Erst müssen Juden bluten,*
> *Erst dann sind wir befreit.*
> (First the Jews must bleed,
> Only then shall we be free.)

The fight against the Jews was, thus, only the first step in a rather extensive ideological scheme. It was in this sense that extreme anti-Semitism can be regarded as an ideological component of National Socialism at all and not as a mere rationalization of pathological drives.

It is true, however, that as a matter of "ideological timetable," the actual taking of this first step had to await the availability of occupied Poland, where the dark and remote extermination camps could be constructed, where there were no foreign embassies, no Red Cross, and no communication with the rest of the world, except for strictly controlled contacts with Germany itself.

Chapter 5

The Cult of the Germanic

A. The Origins

Closely associated with the racial theories, as a component of national socialist ideology, was the Germanic cult, an intense glorification of the ancient Germanic forebears, the Teutons. This was part of the historical understructure on which the theories of German racial superiority, even of the right to more Lebensraum, could be based. In a negative sense, the Germanic cult was related also to anti-Semitism, because the Jew was the antiperson to the Germanic hero. Clearly, he was out of place in the ideal homogeneous Germanic folk community. Romanticism, too, belonged in this picture. Obviously, only a romantically irrational imagination could indulge in this cult at all. At times, it reached semireligious proportions.

As in the case of the race theories, the Lebensraum doctrine and anti-Semitism, the Germanic cult was far from being an invention of national socialist ideology. On the contrary, National Socialism merely made use of a cultural heritage which was ready when the Movement began to assemble something resembling a coherent ideology. The Germanic cult seems to have developed rather fast within a period of about seventy years before the ascendency of National Socialism.

While a good deal of pride in the Germanic heritage was present in various periods of German history, it was probably not until the second half of the nineteenth century that the glorification of the Germanic forebears could be said to have reached the proportions of an intense veneration of the blond, blue-eyed, tall, erect men and women, pure of soul, who were thought to have inhabited the old, dark German forests. In the generally accepted stereotypy, these Germanic men were heroic warriors and hunters; the full-bosomed women were good mothers and wives. All of them had close ties to nature. They worshipped the sun (perhaps because it was seen infrequently in the German rain and mist). They wrote in mystical rune symbols. They represented the ideal person; their value was absolute and could not be questioned.

To a minor extent, the development of the cult may have been a concomitant of the efforts of that period to bring about unification of the numerous German states into one Reich. A common tribal heritage may have been called for to unify them and to keep them unified. But this was not by any means a major motivation.

An early milestone in the development of the Germanic cult was an enormously popular novel, published in 1867. It was *Kampf um Rom* (Fight for Rome) by Felix Dahn, a fertile historian and imaginative writer who specialized in early German history. The novel remained popular well into the twentieth century, particularly among adolescents. It was an enthusiastic, idealized tale of the sufferings and triumphs of the Germanic forebears.

Not long thereafter, in 1876, another milestone, Richard Wagner's opera cycle *Der Ring des Nibelungen*, was added. There is no question that Wagner was a most important force in the glorification of the Germanic past. He left to the Germans and to the world a great deal of magnificent music, but the effect he had on other aspects of German cultural, political, and social life is in dispute.[1] Some see in his *Ring* merely a resurrection of the old barbaric gods of fury, vengeance, and lust, the drive of the German mind toward horror and chaos,[2] and an "inability [of the German mind] to deal with reality except through murky symbolism."[3] But George G. Windell, for example, considers this a gross misunderstanding of Wagner and contends that "Taken as a whole, the message of nearly all his works, and especially the *Ring*, is that love and sacrifice alone can redeem the world from its agony of hatred and corruption."[4]

If this was, in fact, the message, then it was indeed vastly misunderstood by most Germans. What they saw in the *Ring* cycle was

[1]For a discussion of this, see George G. Windell, "Hitler, National Socialism and Richard Wagner," in *Journal of Central European Affairs*, Vol. 27, 1962-1963, pp. 479-497; also Hans Kohn, *The Mind of Germany*, pp. 189-212.

[2]Kohn, op. cit., p. 193.

[3]Windell, op. cit., p. 487.

[4]Ibid., p. 490.

a kind of gospel of the Germanic race, with Wagner as its prophet, a resurrection of their ancestral heroic myths which were an inspiration for the fight against unheroic modern Western civilization. Here on the stage, stepping out of the mists, engulfed in stirring music, were their ancient heroic forebears, Siegfried, Brunhilde, Kriemhild, the Valkyries, and all the others who were part of the national heritage. Whatever the deeper meaning of these operas may have been, there was in them a powerful message of unique Germanic values which was addressed to the emotions.

At any rate, if there was a message of redemption through love and sacrifice, not much of it was discernible in Wagner's other writings. They were, for example, pervaded with strong hostility against the Jews, and the simultaneity of his writings concerning the glorious Germanic hero and the evil Jew is significant in itself. In 1869 he published the highly anti-Semitic essay "Das Judentum in der Musik" (even though he accepted numerous Jewish disciples, supporters, and admirers). The essay already contained the stereotype, extensively used later, of the uncreative, parasitical Jew who is a demonic adversary of the Germanic hero. "Emancipation from the yoke of Judaism appears to us the foremost necessity [Wagner wrote]. . . . Now we shall never gain this strength from abstract concepts, but only . . . from our feeling an instinctive repugnance of the Jewish character. Thus . . . it will become plain to us what we hate. . . ." Much earlier, Wagner had said in a letter that he had "cherished a long repressed resentment about this Jew business, and this grudge is as necessary to my nature as gall is to the blood."[5] He hated not only the Jews but also the French, and indeed his general hostility was boundless. Like Hitler, he was one of history's great haters.

Wagner naturally was to become a gift from heaven to the national socialist propaganda machine. His music alone, quite apart from all desirable associations with the Germanic past, was highly effective in creating an overwhelming emotional atmosphere at mass meetings and on the radio. His operas conjured up the old heroes and roused new ones to action. Some of the music, in the proper setting, was "music to hate by and to kill by." The Bayreuth Festival, which Wagner himself had established to give a semireligious environment to

[5]For these quotations, see Kohn, op. cit., pp. 203–204.

the performance of his operas, was to become, to an extent, a temple for the rites of National Socialism. The swastika flag flew over the building. Here the prehistoric Germanic age *(Urzeit)* came to life; the very roots of German power and strength could be seen and felt.

The Germanic cult was heavily promoted, for many decades, in every German school, in every village, town, and city. There was not a single school child who was not exposed to a steady drumfire of "Germanic thought" throughout his school years. The educational rationale was explained, for example, in a teachers' magazine of 1892, *Zeitschrift für den deutschen Unterricht* (Journal for the Teaching of German):

> Without doubt, the saga of our ancient heroes has high educational value, even if we completely disregard the national [patriotic] background which in itself justifies extensive consideration of the heroic mythology in the teaching of German. What could be more suitable than the shining images of Dietrich, Hildebrand, Beowulf, Siegfried and Kriemhilde, Herwig and Gudrun, in giving to the child a vivid picture of the ideals, encountered daily, such as loyalty of men, courage, tender devotion, and perseverance? In these figures, elevated to the superhuman, the youthful imagination will see images equal to those of its own creation. It absorbs them eagerly, and from these and from hero types of the classical age . . . , it creates images to which all the glorious qualities of men and women usually attach themselves. But while the heroes of Greek and Roman mythology will always remain alien to our native soil, the images of our German mythology are to this day linked to our emotions by many ties.[6]

The Germanic hero figures of whom that writer spoke became indeed the historic guiding images for countless millions of German children and adults. With them as a basis, the heroic fight and war were glorified as a purpose in themselves. History books for use in the schools emphasized the idea (with reference to Tacitus) that among the Germanic forebears "there was no greater disgrace than to survive the leader of a unit *(Gefolge)* in battle" and that "to fight for him without asking for reasons and without regard to danger —

---

[6]*Zeitschrift für den deutschen Unterricht*, 1892, p. 544.

that was German loyalty."[7] It represented early conditioning for the much later demand by National Socialism that the Führer be given unquestioning loyalty and obedience into death. National Socialism merely continued an unbroken tradition of many decades. At a minimum, this kind of education or indoctrination was totally incompatible with the development of democratic or peaceable attitudes.

Significant, also, in the teaching of history, was the constant emphasis on the fights between the Germanic tribes and the Romans before, during, and after the Great Migrations. These tribes were thought to have brought the spirit of a young virile civilization to a declining, effete, and contemptible world. A heroic people was carrying out a historic mission. Without this infusion of young unspoiled blood, without the discipline of the Germanic warrior in this collapsing civilization, there would have been no Middle Ages of note, no Renaissance. But the Germanic tribes had to be on guard against the debilitating and corrupting influence of that ancient effete civilization on their own decent unsuspecting men and women. There were slighting references to Germanic women who adopted the fashions and customs of the degenerate Romans. (Later, the image of the frivolous degenerate Roman female was to merge with that of the "western lady" for whom many Germans expressed contempt.) What all this amounted to was a projection of modern antiwestern German attitudes back to the days of the Germanic invasions of Rome, and these attitudes were then regained in modern times, particularly by National Socialism, as Germanic heritage.

Efforts to promote the Germanic cult in the lower schools bordered on the ridiculous. Mosse reports, for example, that in 1905 a group of 273 teachers condemned the teaching of the Old Testament because it allegedly acquainted the children with the ideas of Syrian-Arabic Bedouins instead of the more vital Germanic heritage.[8]

But it was again Houston Stewart Chamberlain, the racial theorist, who, as far back as 1900, helped to build the theoretical understructure for the Germanic cult. He was an important proponent of the dogma of the significant rootedness of the Germans in their Ger-

---

[7]Ernst Weymar, "Geschichte und politische Bildung," p. 93.
[8]George L. Mosse, *The Crisis of German Ideology*, p. 154.

manic past.[9] He quoted Tacitus, who had said that "the various tribes of Germania, uncontaminated by marriage with foreign peoples, have always constituted a special, unmixed people which resembles no one else," and Chamberlain regarded this as a recognition of the "great relationship between phenomena."[10] According to him, "it had been high time" that the Germanic tribes appeared on the scene to become the saviors of culture and civilization.[11] The only thing he regretted was that the Teutons "did not exterminate more thoroughly wherever their victorious arm forced its way," and Chamberlain felt that "only sordid mental laziness or shameless historical lies can regard the Germanic entry into world history as anything other than the rescue of an agonized humanity from the claws of the eternal-bestial."[12]

It is also significant that "unexampled loyalty" *(Treue)* to the leader was repeatedly mentioned by Chamberlain as one of the outstanding virtues of the Germanic tribes.[13] Loyalty to the Führer was to play a great part in the attitudes of the army, SS, and others. This subject will be discussed again later.

Chamberlain was followed by other writers in the pre-Hitler years who espoused the Germanic cult and became increasingly irrational. One of them was "Ellegard Ellerbeck," which was the Germanic sounding pseudonym of an extremist who was actually named Erich Leiser.[14] Becoming prominent in Germany around 1919, he contended that Germanic blood signifies a blood relationship with the ancient gods, and he asked his audience, "Do you know that you are gods?" He accused the Jews of being malevolent exterminators of the Germanic and said that they prevented the Aryans from assuming their godlike stature. The Jews, therefore, must be eradicated. He was almost too ludicrous to be mentioned here, if it were not for

[9]See, f.i., the chapter "The entry of the Teutons into World History" in Chamberlain's *Die Grundlagen des 19. Jahrhunderts,* pp. 549–632. Of course Chamberlain's opinion that the Teutons *(Germanen)* comprised not only the Germans proper but also the Celts and Slavs was totally incompatible with subsequent teachings of National Socialism which conveniently overlooked it.

[10]Ibid., p. 551.

[11]Ibid., pp. 550–551, 371–372.

[12]Ibid., p. 550.

[13]Ibid., pp. 599–604.

[14]See Mosse, op. cit., pp. 82–83, and generally pp. 67–87 for a review of these writings.

the fact that among Ellerbeck's associates there was the "ideologist" of National Socialism, Alfred Rosenberg, as well as Dietrich Eckart, who was Hitler's early mentor and had a profound ideological influence on him.[15] (The second volume of *Mein Kampf* was dedicated to Eckart.)

Another equally grotesque protagonist of the Germanic cult was Alfred Schuler, a resident of Munich, whom Hitler is likely to have met during his early days in that city, about 1922. Schuler "rejected all academic scholarship in favor of an inner correspondence with Germanic antiquity." He could "see with his soul." Mosse believes that Schuler's views had much effect on Hitler, but this may be doubtful since Hitler himself, as will be pointed out later, took a dubious view of various aspects of the Germanic cult.[16]

In the universities, it was, above all, the professors of Germanistics and of history who promoted the cult. Among these, one of the most fanatic and articulate (and a very good speaker) was Prof. Gustav Roethe. Here is a quotation from one of his numerous addresses to students:

> The science of Germanistics professes the German word. Hold the German word in honor! . . . Goethe, a friend of peace, yet was also a determined prophet of creative action. The false doctrine that action is sinful . . . is un-German through and through. . . . The call of the science of Germanistics is to proclaim through you the German spirit, the German thought to our whole German people through the German word. The great task is waiting for you, German youth, who once were leaders, to let creative German action rise from German thought, the crowning achievement as it was with our forefathers. May God grant it![17]

In another speech, Professor Roethe urged that "every disciple of Germanistics be imbued with its great patriotic significance!" and he said that "my science once led me . . . to the conviction that the Germans are a people of noble birth, called to special missions. . . ."[18]

[15] See Werner Maser, *Hitlers Mein Kampf*, pp. 17, 71.
[16] See Mosse, op cit., pp. 75-77.
[17] Roethe, *Deutsche Reden*, Berlin, 1927, p. 456 (speech of 1923).
[18] Ibid., pp. 440-441 (speech of 1923).

As early as 1906, Professor Roethe had complained that "the days of the hero seem gone" and that there was "little call for him," but he nevertheless stated "the conviction that a new heroic ideal will be born if we Germans remain Germans."[19]

In 1921 a university president, Martin Spahn, in an address to faculty and students, described the contemporary situation (three years after World War I) as a fight of the Germanic people against the Latin people and the "intellectual world of the West."[20]

Related to the adoration of the Germanic hero and an outgrowth of the heroic ideal in general was the image of the front fighter *(Frontkämpfer)*, which arose after World War I. This was the hero image of the returned soldier who had spent four years fighting in the trenches (and then was "stabbed in the back" by communist-Jewish traitors). It was an image which pervaded the adult world as well as the schools. Many school teachers, between the two wars, were old front fighters themselves and were not averse to propagating this heroic image in their schools. As Weymar has pointed out, this image "prevented a free development of democratic opinions, bourgeois ethics, and peaceable attitudes."[21] Like the hero image in general, it promoted the exclusive "friend-foe" view, as well as the sole alternatives of victory or defeat, with no room for compromise. The admiration for the front-fighter image was, in fact, so general that even the German Left, in the interwar years, felt constrained to call itself "Red Front" *(Rotfront)* and "Iron Front" *(Eiserne Front)*. That image was still an inspiration to the German fighting soldiers of World War II.

The cult, in its more advanced stages, had little or nothing to do with serious research into the history of the old Germanic tribes. The interest in actual historical detail was at a minimum. At any rate, comparatively few details of the ancient dim Germanic past were available even to scholars. But this was just as well because the lack of concrete knowledge could only be advantageous to the great majority who did not want facts but "feeling" and wanted to have faith in something esoteric, magical, and irrational. Some groups carried

[19] Ibid., p. 18.

[20] Reported in Hans Peter Bleuel, *Deutschlands Bekenner — Professoren zwischen Kaiserreich und Diktatur,* p. 117.

[21] Weymar, *"Geschichte,"* p. 94.

the cult to extreme lengths. Wotan, Thor, and other Germanic gods were venerated; some worshipped the sun, and there were solstice cults. Few Germans let themselves be carried away to this extent, but it is also true that few remained wholly unaffected. (Even a good many Jewish Germans, touchingly enough, tried to participate.) There was hardly a school boy who was not deeply impressed with the mystery of the Germanic rune writing.

Astonishing as it was, large numbers of intelligent and educated Germans, especially of the middle class, were willing, in varying degrees, to accept ideas of the Germanic cult. It was, in fact, the respectable solid bourgeois who was its foremost spokesman. In part, the cult amounted to a quite conscious rollback of contemporary ideology to a primitive ancestral age, of which little was known and which was probably thoroughly misinterpreted, but into which one could project whatever human qualities were currently considered desirable. These qualities, having thus become venerable character-istics of the race, could then be regained and paraded not only as cur-rent ideals but also as inherited characteristics of which no German could divest himself. National socialist propaganda was to make much use of this whole process. The process, moreover, represented also a flight into the irrational, a flight from modern urban life, from pro-gress and daily pressures, and as such it was part of the general pat-tern of German Romanticism.

B. The Cult in National Socialist Ideology

a. HITLER'S POSITION

Hitler's own position in relation to the Germanic cult was rather ambivalent. In *Mein Kampf* he still spoke of "the Germanic mother of all life, which has given our world its cultural image,"[22] and there is no doubt that to the end he remained convinced of the creative force of the Germanic element in any race wherever present. But his unshakeable faith in the Germanic race did not lead him to admire the ancient Germanic culture. In fact, he took a very sober view of it, and this may have been due to his having grown up in the somewhat

[22]*Mein Kampf*, p. 742.

more rational southern atmosphere of Austria. There were occasions, in fact, when he made quite derogatory remarks about the old Germanic tribes, at least in the privacy of his *Table Talks.* "At the same time when our forebears made the stone vessels and clay jugs which our archaeologists have made so much fuss about, an Acropolis was being built in Greece. . . . The real upholders of culture, not only in the few thousand years before Christ but also in the 1,000 years after him, were the Mediterranean countries."[23] "[The Teutons] were on no higher cultural level than [today] the Maoris [of New Zealand]."[24] Albert Speer reports similar statements by Hitler:

Why do we force the whole world to know that we have no past? As if it was not enough that the Romans were already constructing great edifices while our ancestors were still living in clay huts, Himmler is now starting to dig up those clay villages and becomes enthusiastic about every clay potsherd and every stone axe he finds. The only thing this proves is that we still threw stone hatchets and squatted around open fires at a time when Greece and Rome had reached the highest cultural level. We really have every reason to be quiet about that age.[25]

Hitler ridiculed the people who "swoon over old Germanic heroism, over dim prehistoric times, stone axes, spears and shields . . ." and who "wave around . . . tin copies of Germanic swords. . . ."[26]

But, as a racial matter, Hitler took the position that the ancient Greeks had actually been Germanic *(Germanen)*, [27] something that he probably based on certain statements by Chamberlain.[28] (Hitler's sober views about the Germanic culture were seemingly inconsistent with his veneration of Wagner's operas, discussed later, but it may be that his reaction to the operas was a purely emotional one to the music per se.)

[23]*Hitler's Table Talks*, p. 446 (indirect speech transposed).
[24]Ibid., p. 173.
[25]Speer, *Erinnerungen*, p. 108. See also *Mein Kampf*, pp. 395–396, and Maser, *Hitler's Mein Kampf*, p. 192.
[26]*Mein Kampf*, p. 396.
[27]Ibid., p. 166.
[28]*Grundlagen*, p. 836, however, does not go that far.

In any event, Hitler seems to have looked at the Germanic cult as something that could be politically and propagandistically advantageous, especially in winning over other "Germanic" countries (such as Holland, Denmark, Norway) to the cause of Germany. Thus, he said, "I welcome Axmann's[29] attempt to open up the minds of the youth in the Germanic countries more and more to National Socialism and to the Germanic idea"[30] and "the thing to do [in the Germanic countries] is to give the Germanic idea an increasingly big buildup."[31] He even thought that "it would be well to give particularly strong impetus to these efforts by renaming . . . Berlin 'Germania,'"[32] It might be added that the official greeting "Heil (Hitler)" accompanied by a raising of the outstretched right arm had its origin in (assumed) customs of the Germanic tribes.[33]

Hitler himself was profoundly affected by Wagner's operas. During his wretched years in Vienna, he saw countless performances and was deeply moved by the music.[34] Apparently he could recite entire passages of the *Lohengrin* text.[35] Throughout his life, he remained a fanatic admirer of the operas. He had a large bronze bust of Wagner in his house, frequently played Wagner records, and made annual visits to the Wagner Festival at Bayreuth[36] where even the general atmosphere filled him with elation *(ein fabelhaftes Leben dort).*[37] "I could live in a town like . . . Bayreuth."[38] (Typically, he declared that he had been "very much annoyed about the Jew Schorr singing the part of Wotan! For me, this amounted to desecration of the race."[39]) About his feelings toward the music, he said, "When I hear

[29]Artur Axmann, leader of the Reich Youth Organization.
[30]*Hitler's Table Talks,* p. 397 (indirect speech transposed).
[31]Ibid., p. 475.
[32]Ibid., p. 398.
[33]Ibid., pp. 197–198. More about the outstretched arm will be said later in the chapter on Hitler's sex life.
[34]According to the memoirs of his childhood friend August Kubizek, *The Young Hitler I Knew,* pp. 187–192.
[35]According to an anonymous report by Ernst Hanfstaengl, *Adolf Hitler,* unpublished typescript dated Dec. 3, 1942, PPF 5780, in President's Personal File, Franklin D. Roosevelt Library, Hyde Park, N.Y.
[36]Speer, op. cit., pp. 104–105, 145.
[37]*Hitler's Table Talks,* p. 187.
[38]Ibid., p. 180.
[39]Ibid., p. 187.

Wagner, I feel as if these are the sounds of the prehistoric world *(Vorwelt).*"[40] Presumably he meant the age of the Germanic tribes. Obviously, as in the case of millions of other Germans, that world had tremendous emotional appeal for Hitler, even if, as stated earlier, he took a dim view of its cultural achievements. It was fitting that when Hitler's death was announced over the German radio, the announcement was framed within solemn Wagner music.

One rather important result which Wagner produced for National Socialism was that the greatness of his music tended to narrow the gap between the regime and those groups of the German intelligentsia who were hostile to it. The music was acceptable to nearly everyone, and it furnished some common meeting ground.

It is curious to observe the interaction between the main protagonists of the race doctrines which were to become the most important component of national socialist ideology. These protagonists were Gobineau (1816–1882), Wagner (1813–1883), Chamberlain (1855–1927), and Hitler (1889–1945). Much of this interaction centered on Wagner. Gobineau, who was the first substantial proponent of Nordic superiority, met Wagner in Rome in 1876 and had much influence on him and his circle. Gobineau may, in fact, as Heiden says, have provided a kind of "biological basis for the twilight of the gods."[41] The German Gobineau Society, in turn, was strongly supported by the Richard Wagner Circle. Chamberlain was also greatly influenced by Gobineau, but even more so by Wagner, whose circle he joined and whose daughter Eva he married. He lived for years in Wagner's holy ground, Bayreuth, and published a book entitled *Richard Wagner.* Hitler was born too late to meet Gobineau and Wagner in person; but through the years, he had many meetings with Wagner's ambitious widow, Cosima. In 1923 in Bayreuth, Hitler met the aged Chamberlain, whom he adored.

These four men—a Frenchman, an Englishman, a German, and an Austrian—were a quartet of astonishing variety. But they did have a good deal in common. They were all dilettantes as philosophers, but were, nevertheless, completely certain that they possessed the truth; and all were tedious preachers of what they knew to be true.

[40]Ibid., p. 168.
[41]Konrad Heiden, *Der Fuehrer—Hitler's Rise to Power,* p. 227.

They were also supreme egotists, and their insolence was frequently boundless. They were highly emotional; at least three of them, Chamberlain, Wagner, and Hitler, were great haters. They reacted violently to anything they regarded as interference with their mission. All of them, even Hitler, were direct products of the European culture of the nineteenth century.

b. THE GOOD FIGHT AS A GERMANIC VIRTUE. A RATIONALE FOR WAR

An important part of the cult was the glorification of the good fight as a Germanic ideal (and, in the hands of the national socialist propaganda experts, this—like much else of the Germanic saga—lent itself well to propagandistic exploitation). Ever since the early days of the cult, the image of the heroic warrior, among others, had been projected back into the Germanic past to be retrieved from it as an inherited German racial virtue. It was a precious heritage: the virtue of the lusty fight—*Das Volk in Waffen* (a people armed), then and now. It was an inspiring heritage, too: Had not the Germanic tribes conquered the Roman Empire?

The postulate of the fight as a Germanic and German virtue was carried to extremes by National Socialism. The 1939 edition of *Meyers Lexikon*, a comprehensive encyclopedia published in revised form during the Hitler years, defined *Kampf* (fight) as ". . . a basic condition of all reality, which neither has a derivation nor needs proof."[42] The word *kämpferisch* was introduced into the language, an untranslatable term meaning approximately "filled with fighting spirit." The encyclopedia defined *kämpferischer Mensch* as "the Nordic-Germanic ideal of man and his way of life, subject to the ethos of fight . . . ."[43] Oswald Spengler said that "fight is the basic fact of life, is life itself."[44] Wendula Dahle (1969) cites numerous examples of laudatory references to "fight" and the Germanic or German "fighting spirit" in serious scientific and literary works, such as "the typical German way of life of the eternal fighter" or the demand that the science of Germanistics become a "Fighting League for Education to Folkdom."

Dr. Goebbels, the chief propagandist, even required art to be

[42]Cited in Wendula Dahle, *Der Einsatz einer Wissenschaft*, p. 31.
[43]Ibid., p. 33.
[44]Spengler, *Jahre der Entscheidung*, p. 14.

"close to the people and [to be] filled with fighting spirit."[45] But the most extreme example of an exclusive identification of the heroic quality of *Kampf* (fight) with "German" was a wartime request, addressed by the High Command of the Armed Forces to the Press, that "in the future the term *Kampfflugzeuge* (fighter planes) be used only in relation to *German* planes and that those of the enemy be described only as 'bombing planes,' 'reconnaissance planes' . . ." etc.[46] The enemy presumably was unable to fight like a German. "Fight in the human sense is . . . possible only between equals," said the encyclopedia.[47]

The ethos of fight received its strongest expression in the SS. While organized along military lines, the SS men did not look upon themselves as soldiers but as fighters. Being a soldier was a mere profession, but being a fighter was something infinitely higher. It was an attitude toward life. The fighter fights for the sake of fight; he fights as a matter of principle. The essential question is not about the purpose of the fight, but it is rather how well the fighter fights, no matter for what cause. In fact, fighting well for a cause the fighter knows to be lost is the best test of the real fighter. Faith in the fight as such distinguishes the fighter from a mere soldier. Heinrich Heine saw far into the future when he said in 1835:

[The nature philosphers] . . . will be frightful because . . . they conjure up the demonic powers of the ancient Germanic pantheism and because that lust for fight comes alive in them which we find in the ancient Germans and which does not fight in order to destroy but only in order to fight. Do not smile about the visionary who, in the realm of action, expects the same revolution that has taken place in the region of the mind. Thought precedes action as lightning precedes thunder. A spectacle will be performed in Germany, compared with which the French Revolution may look like an innocent idyll.[48]

---

[45] Quoted in Cornelia Berning, *Vom "Abstammungsnachweis" zum "Zuchtwart,"* p. 111, a useful dictionary of national socialist terminology.

[46] Ibid., p. 111.

[47] *Meyer's Lexikon*, 1939, Vol. 6, p. 765, cited in Dahle, op. cit., p. 34.

[48] From Heine's essay "Zur Geschichte der Religion und Philosophie in Deutschland."

To some extent, Hitler already indicated his ideas of the value of the fight per se in *Mein Kampf:* "Yes, we can say that the strength [of a movement] and hence its right to live will grow only so long as it acknowledges the principle of fight as the basis of its development. . . ."[49]

The SS excelled in the entire Germanic area. Its training curriculum included Germanic studies. The identification with the Germanic forebears is shown dramatically in the following quotation from a guide book published by the SS Main Office in Berlin:

> . . . But what the Goths, the Vikings, and the single wanderers of Germanic blood could not achieve, in this we, a new Germanic migration, and our Führer now succeed, the Führer of all the Germanic people. Now the onslaught from the Russian plains is being beaten back, now Europe's eastern boundary is definitely being made safe, now comes the fulfillment of the ancient dreams of the Germanic fighters in the plains and forests of the East. Today, a chapter of 3,000 years of history receives its glorious ending. The Goths are riding again — since the 22d of June 1941 — each of us a Germanic fighter! . . .[50]

The Goths were riding again. Clearly, they were intoxicated with their Germanic historical image.

At any rate, the whole Germanic cult tended to create a feeling that an inescapable line of descent tied every German to the heroic tradition, even the political tradition, of his tribal forebears. The emphasis on German uniqueness, on a destiny different from that of the rest of the world, was dangerous in itself. Ultimately it contributed heavily to the arrogance of national socialist Germany and to the conviction, on the part of National Socialists and other Germans, that there was no purpose in even trying to make the rest of the world understand what German aims were.

Earlier in this chapter, we discussed the important role played by the Germanistics scholars in the development of the Germanic cult before World War I and in the interwar years. Their efforts, and also those of other writers, reached a screaming crescendo after

[49]*Mein Kampf,* p. 385.
[50]Quoted in Walther Hofer, *Der Nationalsozialismus: Dokumente 1933–1935,* p. 250. (June 22, 1941, was the date of the invasion of the Soviet Union.)

1933 when Hitler came to power. It was then that every vestige of restraint could be abandoned. Dozens of prominent scholars published a veritable flood of books and articles during the period from 1933 to 1945, and particularly in the early years, under such titles as:[51]

War as Destiny of a People in German Literature
German Poetry in the World War 1914-1918
The War as Creative Experience
The Task of Our War Poetry
Poets and Warriors
The Image of the War in German Thought
Heroic Ideology in the Historic Novel of Our Time
War Poetry in the Schools
The Teaching of German and War Poetry
The Soldier in the German Poetry of Our Time
The Image of the War in German Literature
Coming to Terms with War in the National War Novel

Wendula Dahle's remarkable study reports that in July 1940 a so-called "Conference for War Action of German University Teachers of Germanistics" was held at Weimar upon suggestion of the Reich Science Ministry, and that this resulted in the publication of a 5-volume work containing 46 articles by 43 Germanistics scholars on the subject "The German Character [*Wesen*] in the Mirror of German Literature."[52] These 43 authors appear to have constituted practically the entire body of Germanistics scholars, and their participation in this work must be evaluated as an expression of their approval of their proposed "war action."[53] Miss Dahle quotes the following from the preface by Prof. Franz Koch explaining the task of Germanistics in "total war":

The *total* war, as we are experiencing it, is not only a military but at the same time also an intellectual-cultural controversy of largest dimensions. What is involved is not any individual aims but the collapse [*Untergang*] of an outdated and diseased condi-

[51]The foregoing titles were selected from Wendula Dahle's list, op. cit., pp. 129-134. They could be multiplied many times.
[52]Ibid., p. 66.
[53]Ibid., p. 66 and fn. 203.

tion and the creation of a new and healthy Europe, . . . Germany faces the immense task of giving to this new Europe also a new spiritual order, of spiritually penetrating what the sword has conquered.[54]

The same Professor Koch spoke of the "key position" of Germanistics "in taking part in the war in its own way."[55]

Much space in the murky, bombastic writings of the Germanistics scholars during the Hitler period (as before) was devoted to the Germanic ideal of the heroic man, his fight, etc. Here are some quotations from the writings of Germanistics scholars and others in Miss Dahle's study:

Man proves himself in fight but the strength for such proof comes to him from the example with which he aligns himself. For the German man, this example is the Germanic hero as he manifests himself to us in the figures of Arminius, Siegfried, Widukind, Prince Eugen, Blücher, or Hindenburg. . . . The heroic songs of the German people were born in times of fateful fights. . . .[56]

. . . we still sense the tragic greatness of those Germanic heros . . . as being related to us and as exemplary even today.[57]

. . . it is the task of the German writer as member of a people whose history, in splendor and darkness, grows so much out of a life's foundation of heroism, to sense the basic heroic trait in the character of the German people, to give artistic expression to it, and to have it enter the live consciousness of the people. We do not ever want to forget it: the heroic thought is the great forceful thought of German history. . . .[58]

Miss Dahle presents 113 pages of such quotations, most of them from publications of Germanistics scholars. Almost all of them are written in a bombastic, rapturous, overloaded style, characteristic

---

[54]Ibid., pp. 66–67.
[55]Ibid., p. 151.
[56]Ibid., p. 42.
[57]Ibid., p. 43.
[58]Ibid., p. 171.

of much German writing. But in fairness, it should be said also that Hitler himself and many national socialist leaders spoke and wrote a German language which, bad as it was in many instances, seldom descended to the level of that of the Germanistics scholars. (And this is true even more of the reports of the High Command of the Armed Forces.) Much earlier, in *Mein Kampf*, Hitler himself objected strongly to "this tossing around of ancient Germanic expressions which neither fit into our time nor represent any definite meaning . . . ," and he said that "this is a real nuisance which, however, can today be observed on countless occasions."[59]

It is quite clear that the science of German linguistics had gone far beyond the purposes and aims of a mere science. For many decades, it propagated the Germanic cult, heroism, and the fighting spirit, and it fought everything "un-German." If it was not a genuine precursor of National Socialism, at least it furnished important ideological elements. In the end, it became a fighting ideological ally of the National Socialist Movement and, later, of the Hitler regime itself. It did whatever it could to lend support to his wars. It was a "fighting science," and there is no doubt that its contributions to German belligerence, pugnaciousness, and general arrogance were considerable over a period of many years.

It does not seem that the fighting attitudes of the Germanistics scholars and their effect have so far received much systematic attention. Wendula Dahle says merely in a footnote that "regrettably, the science of Germanistics has not as yet conceived of itself as a historical problem," and that "therefore, these important questions, which concern the history of science, can only be alluded to."[60] Another modern Germanistics scholar goes a little further. He criticizes the scholars of the past for a good many sins, including their "evaluation of literature . . . with the help of the adjectives *völkisch*, racial, German, nordic, tribal, heroic, tragic, soldierlike" and others. He reaches the conclusion (rather strangely formulated) that "in its rejection of bourgeois security and in its propagation of the heroic and the tragic, which no longer has any relation to guilt and purification but finds fulfillment only in total senselessness, the science of Germanis-

[59]*Mein Kampf,* p. 395.
[60]Dahle, op. cit., p. 41, fn. 121.

tics reached its most extreme inhuman position and became a pro-claimer of national socialist messages of perseverance."[61] Still another modern Germanistics scholar says that this "science was corrupted by its fixation on a phantom of the German, by its confusion of re-search with reactionary patriotic pedagogics." He speaks of Ger-manistics having "promoted the intoxication of the nation, probably without even noticing it," and he says quite correctly that it "is im-material whether we select our examples from the fascist or the Wilhelmine Germany. One of each will do."[62]

An important practical result of the Germanic cult, and specifical-ly of the worship of the Germanic hero, was that this probably con-tributed greatly to instilling in the German soldier the remarkable fighting qualities which he displayed in all German wars from 1870 to 1945. He had been taught from early childhood that his ancestors were magnificent fighters, and he tried to live up to the tradition. He had been taught also that fight was the traditional Germanic and German way of life, that fight is good and is, in fact, life itself. That this could easily be converted into a desirable soldierly behavior pattern is not surprising. Acceptance of the hardships and privations of fighting a war was part of this pattern, as was self-discipline, obedience, harsh-ness, and, finally, the willingness to die a "hero's death." Moreover, the consciousness of being a prospective or actual hero was an emo-tional condition which laid the soldier open to easy additional manipu-lation by a regime whose propaganda was frequently based more on emotion than reason. This, in fact, applied not only to soldiers but, to a lesser extent, to a great many Germans who saw themselves as possessing hereditary qualities of the Germanic hero and thus were emotionally vulnerable to propagandistic manipulation.

Another practical result of the cult of the Germanic fighter was that it put the fighting of wars against France, Poland, and Russia in the light of an honorable tradition and furnished a kind of historical rationale for them. Wars against the East and West were what the Germanic tribes had always carried on; they were a German heritage, a historical mission. The French were the "hereditary enemy" back to the days of the Gauls; the Slavs had always had to be pushed back

[61]Paul-Gerhard Völker, "Die inhumane Praxis einer bürgerlichen Wissenschaft," in *Das Argument*, Heft 6, December 1968, pp. 448–449.

[62]Walter Boehlich, "Aus dem Zeughaus der Germanistik," in *Der Monat*, No. 217, 1966, pp. 56–68.

to the East to make more room for the expanding Germans. Even before World War I, the German Chancellor Theobald von Bethmann-Hollweg said that war between the Germanic peoples and the Slavs was inevitable,[63] and in this he merely expressed sentiments traditionally held by large parts of the German middle and upper classes. Hitler, who stated the same view many times and acted on it, merely continued in the venerable tradition. "Now comes the fulfillment of the ancient dreams of the Germanic fighters in the plains and forests of the East. . . . The Goths are riding again," wrote the SS Main Office when the Germans invaded Soviet Russia.[64]

No Germanic tradition of wars against Great Britain existed, and it is significant that, to the last, Hitler made strong efforts to avoid that war. Even the airplane flight of the mentally disturbed Rudolf Hess to Scotland in the middle of the war seems to have been motivated by the conviction that "two Germanic nations" should not fight each other.

c. GERMANIC LOYALTY, THE FÜHRER PRINCIPLE, THE OATH

Another practical result of the Germanic cult flowed from the (actual or imagined) Germanic principle of *Treue*, that is, loyalty, faithfulness, fidelity, giving allegiance and obedience to a Führer or a cause. The loyal vassals or followers of a Germanic Führer were his *Gefolgschaft*, and it is significant that during the national socialist regime this term loomed large and was used even to describe the labor force of industrial plants. The idea of loyalty was carried to extremes in the SS,[65] and indeed the motto of the SS was "Our Honor Means Loyalty."

The so-called "Führer principle" permeated the political, social, and even cultural life of the entire nation, and it was readily accepted by the great majority of Germans as something desirable, indigenously German, stemming from the mythological Germanic past. The Führer principle stood in direct antithesis to democracy as a way of life, and in this respect it was welcomed also as being anti-Western, as belonging to the German "blood and soil."

The postulate was unquestioning obedience to the Führer. There was widespread use of the slogan "Führer command us—we shall

[63] Andreas Hillgruber, *Deutschlands Rolle in der Vorgeschichte der beiden Weltkriege*, p. 38.

[64] Quoted in Hofer, op. cit., p. 250.

[65] See, f. i., Himmler's speech in *TMWC*, Vol. XXIX, Doc. 1919-PS, p. 149.

follow!" Any order that was officially identified as *Führerbefehl* (Führer's order) took precedence over everything else, no matter whether it conflicted with law or moral principles or reason. It was not subject to question, doubt, or open criticism. This became apparent, for example, in the testimony of the defendants in the so-called *Einsatzgruppen*-trial in Nuremberg, [66] dealing with the murder of about 900,000 Polish Jews and others by SS task forces, based on a "Führer order."

Loyalty, in short, had become a concept of mythological origin whose value was absolute and was not really to be measured in terms of the merits of the person to whom the loyalty was due. It had become a purpose in itself which needed no other rational basis. It was not unlike what T. W. Adorno has called other concepts — an emancipated stereotype."

The loyalty oath, which was required of all members of the Armed Forces, the SS, SA, the civil service, and the cabinet, was an oath to Adolf Hitler in person (not, for example, to the Constitution as in the Weimar Republic nor to Germany or the German people). The wording of the soldier's loyalty oath was: "I swear to God this holy oath, that I shall give unconditional obedience to the Führer of the German Reich and people, Adolf Hitler, the Supreme Commander of the Armed Forces, and that as a brave soldier I shall be ready at any time to risk my life for this oath." [67] The oath was not unlike that sworn in Imperial Germany to the person of the Kaiser, [68] and the latter oath, in turn, was probably derived historically from the old Prussian army and state. Ultimately, this type of loyalty oath to a person may stem from the days of the Germanic tribes.

At any rate, the oath to Hitler was to assume vast and fateful importance. While many of the leading army officers felt strong objections to Hitler and his policies, they nevertheless agreed, difficult as this is now to understand, to serve him faithfully because of their oath, sometimes after severe conflicts of conscience. The former Chief of the General Staff, General Ludwig Beck, a reluctant

[66] *TWC*, Vol. IV.

[67] Quoted in Manfred Messerschmidt, *Die Wehrmacht im NS-Staat — Zeit der Indoktrination*, p. 51. Other oath formulas are quoted in Franz Neumann, *Behemoth: The Structure and Practice of National Socialism*, p. 85.

[68] See, in this connection, Klaus-Jürgen Müller, *Das Heer und Hitler — Armee und nationalsozialistisches Regime 1933-1944*, p. 135.

participant in the assassination conspiracy of July 20, 1944, felt restrained by his oath, and to the end he called the day when he gave that oath "the blackest day of my life." Mutiny and revolution, he once said, are words "which do not exist in the vocabulary of a German soldier." [69] The conspirators of that unsuccessful assassination attempt on Hitler encountered no greater obstacle in their efforts to recruit coconspirators than that loyalty oath. As Fest says, "the effective idea manifestly was that a soldier may betray his country, his people, his honor, his responsibility for the life of his subordinates, in short everything except a man, guilty of a thousand broken promises, to whom he had sworn an oath." [70] By and large, in spite of the subsequent assassination conspiracy, Dr. Goebbels was not really wrong in saying in his diary in 1943: "Treason, such as the Italian generals have committed against Mussolini, would be quite out of the question [in Germany] in view of the entire mentality of the German generals and above all the Prussian generals." [71]

For most of the officers, the religious implications of this oath meant little or nothing. Their reluctance to disregard their oath to a person whom many of them knew to be a criminal was so irrational that it seems impossible to understand unless we resort to seeing in this attitude a survival of residual principles of loyalty deeply rooted in the unconscious from the Germanic tribal days. It was only a tiny group of conspirators—fifty or sixty courageous men—who were able to free themselves of these chains and could see other higher principles and goals than loyalty to a criminal Führer and who at the same time had the courage to act. But even these conspirators may have been severely troubled by their oath to Hitler. Fest believes that their lack of success may have been due in part "to that lack of final determination to commit a deed, running counter to all principles instilled in them, which fundamentally made strange modern Hamlet characters of them all—those brooding, broken, incessantly debating conspirators, deeply entangled in reasons and counterreasons." [72]

It may well be, also, that perverted principles of loyalty, the

[69]See Joachim C. Fest, *Das Gesicht des Dritten Reiches,* p. 330. (For statements of other generals, see Müller, op. cit., pp. 136-137.)

[70]Fest, op. cit., p. 331.

[71]*The Goebbels Diaries,* entry of Sept. 23, 1943.

[72]Fest, op. cit. p. 330.

oath, and obedience have to this day prevented the Germans in general from elevating their own resistance fighters of the Hitler years to the status of heroic historical images. Resistance against authority and the established order of the state has never been among German traditions.

Of course, there were undoubtedly a great many Germans to whom the oath meant no more than a convenient and comfortable refuge to avoid all conflicts of conscience, all need to show moral courage, and all personal responsibility for actions that they knew to be wrong. The oath, in their view, enabled them to remain morally decent or even legally innocent. Eichmann, for one, at his trial in Jerusalem, tried to take shelter behind the oath: "An oath is an oath," he testified, and breaking your oath "is the worst crime of which a man can ever become guilty."[73] Only comparatively few men of remarkable moral stature seemed able to recognize or, at least, admit that it cannot be wrong to break an oath and commit high treason against a regime essentially criminal in nature that has violated the rights of hundreds of thousands of its own citizens, not to speak of the rights of the people of other countries. It is strange to observe the very high position of the oath in the scale of moral principles of a nation which, for many decades, was politically dominated by Machiavellian principles and realpolitik.

These were the main results of the Germanic cult. Their importance was considerable. The cult came into being long before Hitler was born or National Socialism was conceived, and Hitler himself, as pointed out, did not really have much faith in it. But to most Germans, it was a powerfully motivating force. National Socialists, moreover, recognized it as the potent political and propagandistic tool that it proved to be. As in the case of the other ideological components, National Socialism intensified the existing thought patterns and the emotional content of the cult, fused them with others and acted upon them.

The strong effect of the Germanic cult brings to mind Sigmund Freud's statement that "every piece that returns from oblivion gains acceptance with special power, exerts an incomparably strong influ-

---

[73]Quoted in Helga Grebing, *Der Nationalsozialismus — Ursprung und Wesen,* p. 123.

ence on the human masses, and asserts an irresistible claim to truth, against which any logical objection remains without power."[74] A parallel is Erik H. Erikson's finding, in his investigations of today's Sioux Indians, that to them "the prehistoric past is a powerful psychological reality."[75]

[74]Freud, *Der Mann Moses und die monotheistische Religion*, in *Gesammelte Werke*, p. 190.
[75]Erikson, *Identity, Youth and Crisis*, p. 48.

Chapter 6

German Romanticism

A. Nature and Origins

The Romantic Movement covered all of Western civilization, and it did not, of course, originate in Germany. The contribution which Romanticism has made to civilization is enormous, and it may seem incongruous, therefore, to associate this culturally fertile movement with National Socialism. But there is little question that a special German version of Romanticism became important in the evolution of National Socialism. If Romanticism was not actually one of its ideological components, it functioned at least as a kind of bond holding together other components; and, in any case, it did much to pave the way for the general acceptance of various elements of national socialist ideology.

The early German Romanticism was essentially no different from that in other European countries, particularly France. As elsewhere, it represented a reaction and antithesis to classicism and Enlightenment. It had for its aims, among many other things, a return to nature, the dominance of emotions and senses over reason and intellect, a revolt against rationalism, emphasis on nostalgia, yearning, dreams and magic, a tendency toward the infinite and the inexpressible mystery of spirit. Oswald Spengler—himself a romanticist—once said that "Romanticism is characterized by a faith which is stronger than all proof."[1] By its very nature, Romanticism is hostile to being defined, and historically it consisted of many different, even conflicting, aspirations and ideas.

It may well be that the amorphous, nebulous character of Romanticism had (and has) particularly strong appeal to the *German* mind

[1]Spengler, *Jahre der Entscheidung*, Munich, 1929, 1933, p. 7.

and emotions. The most "natural" products of German thought seem to stem from the romantic; and there is no doubt that the Romantic Movement was extraordinarily influential, if not dominant, in the development of German civilization, at least from 1800 to 1945. Basically the Germans, perhaps more than any other people, seem naturally open to a romantic sense of mystery and wonder, to the excitement of purely intuitive experience close to the sources of nature, and to a high valuation of the unconscious and irrational. In fact the German mind does not always object to murky reasoning, formlessness of thought, sentimentality in argument, and extensive symbolism. Intuition, "soul," and dreams often nourished it for a century and a half, and not infrequently these were combined with a disregard, even conscious contemptuous disregard, for cold facts that could not be made to fit into the dream. All this was probably good for the creation of much remarkable poetry and music (Hölderlin, Rilke, Beethoven, Schubert, Liszt, Schumann, Wagner, Brahms, etc.), but it was less good, and sometimes disastrous, in social and political affairs.

At any rate, one trait of the Germans during the last 150 years seems to have been a strong reckless tendency to carry an idea, once seized, to extremes and to lose themselves intellectually and emotionally in what they themselves call *das Uferlose, das Masslose* (the boundless, the uncontrolled, the "oceanic")—and this without much thought as to what the future practical consequences might be. German Romanticism was seldom compatible with intellectual prudence, circumspection, and moderation. Some Germans have criticized their native urge toward *Übersteigerung* of ideas—a rather untranslatable term meaning approximately "overintensification."

It was early in the nineteenth century that German Romanticism began to turn away from the West and to set out on a course of its own. One reason for this may have been that the numerous disunited sovereign states of which "Germany" was then composed were occupied by the Napoleonic French army and that the Wars of Liberation, which resulted in freedom in 1813, had to be preceded by a vast patriotic German effort. This seemed to imply revulsion against any Western thought, including much of Western Romanticism. The humanism of the earlier Romanticism was increasingly replaced by nationalism. There was as yet no German nation, but there was a German *Volk*, and this concept, romantically embroidered, became dominant. German Romanticism turned inward toward the uniquely German. Slowly, the so-called German *Sonderbewusstsein* began to develop, that is, the consciousness of being unique and different from the West. In this, as in various other ways, the German divergence from Western thought was to have major consequences. The love of Volk came to imply hatred of other nations or even races. Humanism came to be felt as an alien coating on the genuine German substance. What had been a natural liking for the German way of life grew into an intense belief in being a "chosen people," in a German mission in the world.

All kinds of strange cultural and political antitheses developed: healthy German peasantry against diseased alien urbanism; robust primeval times against decadent modernity; the Germanic principle of allegiance to a leader against western parliamentarianism and democracy. The romantic antithesis which was strangest but was quite generally accepted was culture against civilization, that is, German *Kultur* against Western civilization. "Culture," in the German sense, was the sum of the creations of an organically and historically grown mind and soul of a people, that is, art, literature, philosophy, etc. Civilization, on the other hand, was by and large regarded as meaning not much more than improvements in a nation's mode of living, which the modern technical mind has produced. Quite typically, *Meyer's Lexikon*, an encyclopedia, in an edition issued in the pre-Hitler period (1930), said under *Zivilisation:* "Any intelligent nation can understand and imitate the products of civilization, f.i. airplanes, laws; but not every nation can understand and produce the' creations of culture, for example, Goethe's *Faust*, German music, German philosophy. Cultural values can be damaged by civilization."[2] The inclination to identify cultural creations with Germany was apparent. As a minimum, there was a strong tendency on the part of the Germans to look upon themselves as being capable of a more "profound culture" because they were less "civilized" than the West (and less "barbaric" than the East). In the German romantic conception, civilization was cultural decline; and, in fact, *pure* civilization would be the end of culture. Oswald Spengler spoke of "civilization beginning where culture has been brought to a close.[3] A great many saw a ro-

[2]Vol. XII, p. 1836.
[3]Spengler, op. cit., p. 12.

mantic contrast between the German soul as a basis of true culture and Western intellectualism as the essense of decadent civilization. Jews were regarded as incapable of creating true culture and even as a danger to it, because they were thoroughly permeated with civilization.

Romanticism of a kind even extended into economics. The prominent German economist Werner Sombart, a man of considerable stature, published a book in 1915 under the title *Händler und Helden* (Merchants and Heroes) in which he contrasted western merchant and trader nations with the German heroic people.

German Romanticism had a profound effect on the German language, and nowhere is the divergence from Western thought more clearly apparent than in this sphere. To some extent, we dealt with the language in our discussion of the part played by the Germanistics scholars in the development of the Germanic cult (which essentially was part of German Romanticism). The language did, in fact, come to reflect the romantic dominance of emotions and senses over rationality, and all the lack of clarity, certainty, and definition which this implies. Much of German terminology is formless, emotionally soft, untidy, brooding, dreamy, even intellectually anarchic. It defies definition. Sometimes, the language seems to be anxious to advance beyond the outer limits of what is still sayable, or it acts as if it does not want to be understood but merely felt. It seems to make an effort, in fact, to bypass the mind and to push on toward the emotions. But it is doubtful whether such efforts are not futile, and their results may at times be absurd, except in poetry and music.[4] At a minimum, the price paid in lack of form and clarity is high. At the same time, there can be immense force, weight, and beauty in this language when it is used with measure and sense. In any event, the divergence of German from, for example, English and also from French is very great, in spite of all their etymological connection, and equally great, therefore, are the difficulties of translating German into English or French. The long striving for German uniqueness did achieve considerable success in the language.

---

[4]All this may be largely meaningless to anyone who does not have a thorough knowledge of German. For a few examples of largely incomprehensible and untranslatable German terms, we might mention *das Werdehafte, die Seinsgerechtigkeit, volksbedingt, Volkheit, Erbwörtliches,* and generally the prefix *Ur,* as, for instance, in *Urwort.* There are hundreds of such terms.

There were two special movements within the Romantic Movement, which originated early in the twentieth century and ultimately led directly into National Socialism. One was the *Völkisch* Movement and the other the *Jugendbewegung* (Youth Movement). The German word *völkisch* means approximately "pertaining to the *Volk*—the people or nation." But Volk really connotes more than just "people" or "nation."[5] German Romanticism endowed this word with a transcendental sense, and it came to mean a group of people fused together by their race, individuality, and cultural heritage and, above all, by their common experience of their own landscape. In addition, the word had or acquired strong overtones of "patriotic," "nationalistic," "racially pure," and "anti-Semitic." The Movement, on the whole, was no more than a loose alliance of likeminded people, mostly young, who had typically romantic ideas of a German national rebirth or rejuvenation. It was in many ways a direct ideological forerunner of National Socialism in whose development it was no doubt of the greatest importance.[6] Significantly the name of the official Party newspaper was *Der Völkische Beobachter* (The *Völkisch* Observer).

The other special movement, the *Jugendbewegung* (Youth Movement), was a highly romantic movement which originated around 1900.[7] Starting perhaps primarily as a kind of hiking society *(Wandervögel)* of young nature lovers, the movement became a focus of a mild youth rebellion against modernity, industrialization, mechanization, and urbanization, against mass existence, the hypocrisy and prejudices of the old generation, the rigidity of rational thought, and so forth. It promoted close, frequently mystical ties with nature, a revival of old music, folk singing, careless dress, liberation from strict schools, opposition to bourgeois morality. Unwilling or unable to face its own time and the future, youth turned to the past or to what it

[5]For a brief history of the world *völkisch* see Cornelia Berning, *Vom "Abstammungsnachweis" zum "Zuchtwart,"* pp. 192–193.

[6]George L. Mosse devotes practically his whole book *The Crisis of German Ideology* to an exposition of what, in an anglicized adaptation, he calls "volkish" thought, and he uses his term "volkish" in an extremely broad sense to cover practically all aspects of national socialist ideology. We are not here following him in this usage.

[7]For a discussion of this movement see Walter Z. Laqueur, *Young Germany— A History of the German Youth Movement;* also Theodor Litt, *The National-socialist Use of Moral Tendencies in Germany,* in M. Baumont (ed.), *The Third Reich,* pp. 439–446; also Mosse, *Crisis,* pp. 171–189.

imagined the past to have been. (Many of these tendencies bore a surprising resemblance to those of American youth today. Even the immense popularity of the German novelist Hermann Hesse of that period is now repeated in the United States.)

The Youth Movement had no violent tendencies until National Socialism assumed control. The movement, in fact, was largely turned inward, and its inclination was to live in a romantic utopia. There were efforts to find the utopian better world in the structure of medieval society (as it was imagined to have been); there were antiauthoritarian and, later, mildly procommunist tendencies, some revulsion against the democratic system of the Weimar government, etc.

Uniquely German in the Youth Movement was the overriding emphasis on the need of a deep sense of identity with the German *Volk* and landscape. These romantic aims were not politically motivated. Yet they were something that, in many members of the Youth Movement, could turn into patriotism or nationalism; and they slowly did take such a turn in various subgroups and splinter movements. At the very least, the Youth Movement had created an emotional climate quite favorable to the reception of various elements of national socialist ideology; and to an extent the movement even manifested early symptoms of the later Hitler Youth and the SA and even the SS. The Youth Movement itself had laid the foundation for its own subversion, and National Socialism was not slow in taking advantage of it. All in all, it did not take much of a push to convert overwhelming numbers of the Youth Movement to Hitler's cause, and this without arousing too much awareness that the original, quite valuable ideals of the Youth Movement had been lost in the process.

The attitude of the Youth Movement toward the Jews had been rather ambivalent. In some groups, there was anti-Semitism from the start; in others, Jews were accepted—probably always with some reluctance. The emphasis in the movement on identification with the Volk naturally presented problems as to the Jews, who in Germany never ceased being regarded as alien or un-German. Also, the generally accepted stereotype of "the Jew" as devoid of spirituality and deep feeling, as distinguished from intellectualism, was hardly compatible with any romantic movement. But the Jews were eager to join, because, as usual, they were attracted by the elements of liberalism and rebellion against established order which were present in the movement. Some Jews formed a youth movement of their own, but it did not become important.[8]

B. Romanticism in Hitler and National Socialism

Hitler himself did not by any means personify the typical German romanticist; he never epitomized the mystical German soul. This may have been due to the fact that he grew up in the more sober southern atmosphere of Austria-Hungary (and we saw before that he had misgivings also about the Germanic cult). It may have been due, further, to the fact that, by nature, he was too much of a calculating practical politician. His own attitude was indicated rather clearly in a speech in 1938:

> What ranks first in our program is not some mysterious sensing but a clear understanding. . . . It would be a misfortune if, as a result of the creeping in of mystical elements, our Movement or the government were to give unclear orders. And it would be enough if the lack of clarity were in the wording. It can even be dangerous to give instructions for a so-called "cult sanctuary" [*Kultstätte*] because this will imply the necessity of later on inventing so-called ritual games and ritual acts. Our sole "cult" is devotion to that which is based on nature, and this implies that which is God's wish.[9]

Earlier, in *Mein Kampf,* he had treated the *völkisch* idea with considerable contempt, although it was dear to the heart of his German followers. He objected to the *völkisch* concept on the ground that it was "limitless" and, therefore, "no possible foundation for a [political] movement," that it was "indefinable" and subject to such "many-sided interpretations" that it could not be used in a political fight where discipline was needed.[10] He added that "all kinds of people, whose essential opinions are in complete disagreement, roam around under cover of the word *völkisch*," and he pointed out that while "accumulated knowledge" of "the most eminent importance" is implied in this term,

[8]For a discussion of the Jewish Youth Movement, see George L. Mosse, *Germans and Jews,* pp. 77–115.

[9]Max Domarus, *Hitlers Reden und Proklamationen 1932–1945,* p. 894.

[10]*Mein Kampf,* pp. 397–398.

it "can rise above the value of a more or less acceptable opinion only if it can be fitted, as basic element, into the framework of a political party."[11] He emphasized that political demands do not materialize as a result of "pure feeling," "inner desires," or "general yearning."[12] He spoke of "*völkisch* sleepwalkers."[13] All this was decidely unromantic. What Hitler really seemed to promote was a complete equation or fusion of the *völkisch* concept with his racial views.[14]

But the National Socialist Movement paid little or no attention to such warnings by its Führer; it indulged in a great deal of pure feeling and many cult sanctuaries and ritual acts. The official propaganda machine, which knew what it was doing, adhered largely to the traditional *völkisch* ideas of the German people. These ideas had penetrated too deeply into the national consciousness to be lightly abandoned or modified. *Völkisch* thought, after all, was the heir to about a hundred years of development of Romanticism. It is true, however, that, under National Socialism, more emphasis than before was placed on the specific anti-Semitic content of *völkisch* thought, and that no one could really be *völkisch* without being anti-Semitic.

At any rate, it seems that, in spite of Hitler's more sober politically oriented views, ultimately he made no real objection. He may have reached the conclusion that his propaganda machine could indeed make good use of the emotional power of these ideas. Nevertheless, this was one of the instances in which national socialist ideology diverged from Hitler's and assumed a leadership role of its own. In the end, within the blurred terminology of that period, the terms *völkisch* and "national socialist" may have become more or less synonymous.

All this is not to say that Hitler himself did not also espouse some quite romantic ideas. He started out as a romanticist particularly in relation to industry, commerce, and agriculture, of which he knew nothing. He and his party program demanded, for example, that the so-called "money-interest servitude"*(Zinsknechtschaft)* be abolished.[15] This was probably the most naïve of all the romantic economic ideas.

[11] Ibid., pp. 415, 417.
[12] Ibid., pp. 417–418.
[13] Ibid., p. 399.
[14] See his description of what a real *völkische Weltanschauung* is or should be, in *Mein Kampf*, pp. 420–422.
[15] Ibid., pp. 232–233.

Apparently it related back to the days when Jewish moneylenders financed the German peasants between harvests at usurious interest rates and then foreclosed the mortgages on their farms. The sinister image of a fat cigar-smoking Jew looking at an emaciated farmer, hanging dead from a tree branch, had for decades played a large part in German romantic fiction.

Peasantry and agriculture generally occupied a very favored position in the romantic compartment of the ideology, at least initially. In *Mein Kampf*, Hitler had already proclaimed:

> . . . The maintenance of a healthy peasantry as a foundation of the entire nation can never be valued highly enough. . . . Industry and commerce are to withdraw from their unhealthy leading position. . . .[16]

> The first result [of German pre-World War I policy] of the gravest significance was . . . the weakening of the peasant class. To the same extent to which that class declined, the masses of the proletariat in the big cities steadily increased, until finally the equilibrium was lost entirely.[17]

The agrarian Romanticism was carried very far. The peasantry was venerated as the tree of life, the future of the nation, its biological source of renewal. Laws were enacted to "safeguard the inseverable ties between blood and soil." The words "blood and soil," at any rate, played an enormous role in the national socialist vocabulary.

Hitler, at least originally, took a naïve, romantic view also of the evils of corporate ownership in the modern economy, and this in a country which at that time was already highly industrialized by numerous large corporations: "A grave symptom of economic decay [he said] was the slow disappearance of individual ownership and the gradual transfer of the entire economy into the ownership of corporations."[18] But in the end the romantic approach to agriculture and industry had to yield to modern economic realities. (Moreover, Hitler needed the financial support of big business.) The demands for abolition of "money-interest servitude" and for reduced corporate owner-

[16]Ibid., p. 151.
[17]Ibid., p. 255.
[18]Ibid., p. 256.

ship were silently abandoned. It may be that Hitler never really had his heart in them and raised them merely because he had heard of them from his early more romantic mentors. In Germany, as elsewhere, the migration from the farms to the factories of the cities continued at an ever-increasing pace. It is true, however, that the farmers, under various laws, continued to be favored by the regime.

Some believe that Romanticism and violence are close neighbors or even that violence can flow from Romanticism. Thus, Mosse says, the "'New Romantics' accent upon the internal became, in the end, a blatant praise of force, of the necessity of struggle to realize the new utopia."[19] But actually the relationship of Romanticism to violence is not so readily apparent. At least, it does not seem likely that German Romanticism would have produced violence unless the race theories, the Lebensraum doctrine, and the cult of the Germanic heroic fighter had been added to it. However, some support for the compatibility of violence and Romanticism—even in a very literal sense—might be found in the collections of letters from the front by German students killed in the two wars.[20] Many of these beautiful, sensitive letters of young soldiers speak again and again of reading Hölderlin's romantic poetry, a volume of which these soldiers evidently carried in their backpacks. The letters speak also, however, of fighting the war.

Romanticism has always had the strongest appeal to youth, and German youth was no exception. We have already discussed the highly romantic aspirations of the German Youth Movement, beginning about 1900, and of the later *Völkisch* Movement, which was also dominated by the young. It was inevitable that National Socialism, with its own romantic aspirations, would again have strong appeal to youth, and the leadership saw to it that it did. A highly idealistic Reich Youth Leader, Baldur von Schirach, was appointed. Here is part of a speech by him to his young charges, which represents nearly classical romanticism:

> We interpret the National Socialist Revolution as the rising of German feelings [*Gemüt*] against the arrogance of cold intellect.

[19] Mosse, *Crisis*, p. 65. See also Joachim C. Fest, *Das Gesicht des Dritten Reiches*, pp. 65, 241.

[20] *Kriegsbriefe gefallener Studenten*, Munich, 1928, and Stuttgart, 1952.

Its victory signifies the triumph of the soul over everything that is only mechanic. . . . Faith has overcome doubt. It rules the lesser forces that dared to deny it. The motto of our lives must be Adolf Hitler's most profound saying "Woe to the one who has no faith!"[21]

Able propaganda work did much to create the impression that the National Socialists were the party of the young. Some of the official slogans were "Make room, you old ones!" *(Macht Platz, ihr Alten!)* and "National Socialism is the will of organized youth" *(organisierter Jugendwille)*. Millions of fanatical and faithful young Germans believed it. Fron the start, National Socialism succeeded, to a surprising extent, in making youth think that what was taking place was a revolution of the young and that the young were receiving what they demanded. As we shall see later, there was no generation gap between Hitler and them, and Hitler himself was, in fact, an eternal or "unbroken" adolescent (Erik H. Erikson). The Youth Movement was smoothly incorporated into the new regime, without apparent break with too many of its old ideas. But it is true also that, in actual fact, the political leadership itself was extraordinarily young. The average age of the members of Hitler's Cabinet was around 40, whereas it was about 56 in the United States and 53 in Britain.[22] The Reich Youth Leader was 26 in 1933. (Hitler himself was 44 in 1933, and he started his agitation much earlier.) More than 37 percent of the party membership was less than 30; more than 65 percent, less than 40; those over 50 represented barely 15 percent.[23] Seldom, however, has youth been more wrong in believing that the ideology of its movement was something new and a break with the past.

National Socialism derived many benefits from Romanticism: the myth of blood and soil; the faith of the people in a coming political utopia and their unwillingness to settle for anything less; the propensity of the Germans to approve extreme solutions; readiness of the nation to go oñ its "uniquely German way" as opposed to "Western," liberal, democratic ways; the dislike for the rational big-city Jew.

[21]Quoted in Hermann Huss and Andreas Schröder (eds.), *Antisemitismus— Zur Pathologie der bürgerlichen Gesellschaft*, p. 103.
[22]Karl Dietrich Bracher, *Die deutsche Diktatur*, p. 299.
[23]Ibid., p. 256.

Much of the basic mood of Romanticism and (at least early) National Socialism was alike, even if Hitler himself had some misgivings about this mood. Countless ideas and slogans, which served national socialist propaganda with great effect, were derived from romantic literature and poetry, such as "blood and soil," the "singing of the blood" *(das Singen des Blutes)*, "dark voices of the blood," etc., which could make pleasurable shudders run down the spines of German romanticists. The fact that such nebulous slogans were able to exert their tremendous attraction on the masses was the result of German Romanticism.

Moreover Romanticism tended to unite the nation behind the regime because its ideology had strong romantic elements in it. Every German of nearly every social level had been brought up on a solid diet of romantic literature, music, and art. Almost everyone had read, in school or elsewhere, the romantic novels of the late nineteenth and early twentieth century, including the romantically anti-Semitic novels, historical novels of heroism, and novels of rural nostalgia. A great many had read Rilke and Spengler. Every child had had courses in *Heimatskunde* (lore of the native land) and *Volkskunde* (lore of the German people). They had learned to commune with nature and — to repeat what has frequently been said — had sat on mountain tops, dreamily gazing down on old castles and medieval towns. And this was equally true of the members of the opposition to the regime, who faced considerable emotional difficulty in disentangling their own roots and motivations from those of the average National Socialist. To many Germans, it seemed, at least initially, as if the Party program was designed to fulfill their own cherished dreams.

An important practical result of Romanticism, in the present context, was that it created a general climate of inexact thinking, an intellectual and emotional dream world, and an emotional approach to problems of political action to which sober reasoning should have been applied. With the help of shrewd propaganda work that exploited German Romanticism to the full, the loss of sober reasoning power became a formidable phenomenon. Failures of judgment, self-deception, and miscalculations abounded. Information derived from romantic dreams and preconceived ideas was officially accepted as superior to available objective evidence. Even German diplomats abroad, insofar as they were national socialist believers, sent reports home to Berlin which were strongly colored by assumptions inherent in their official ideology and had little relation to the facts they could observe.

In a larger sense, as has been pointed out by various writers, Romanticism—in any Western country—represents a rejection of the contemporary dehumanized technological world and an effort to escape into a less complex, more innocent ancestral world of a trans-figured past where relations between men, and between men and things, were assumed to have been simpler and more decent. It seems that this rejection and effort to escape is a process through which each new generation in the West has had to go for about a hundred years, in varying degrees of turbulence, but that each new generation regarded its own efforts as unique and unprecedented. (The lack of awareness of the earlier efforts may be a psychological necessity to the young.) The fact of the constant repetition of the process is in itself an indication of the great difficulties mankind faces in adapting to the modern technological world. In this sense, National Socialism was in part what we might call a convulsive romantic revolution against modernity—but only in part, because, as we have seen, it was motivated also by many other factors. [24] Hitler himself essentially was not a romantic person, and, to a large extent, he merely used the romantic emotions of the German people and of his underlings, as well as the romantic content of the German cultural heritage, in order to achieve his own purposes. Much true idealism, particularly of the young, was thus abused and led astray.

Hitler said: "What luck for governments that people don't think. Thinking may be done only when an order is given or executed. If this were different, human society could not exist." [25]

[24] For a discussion of related questions see H. A. Turner, Jr., "Fascism and Modernization," in *World Politics*, Vol. 24, July 1972, pp. 547-564.

[25] *Hitler's Table Talks*, p. 159.

Chapter 7

Nationalism

A. The Nature and Development of German Nationalism

The type of nationalism with which we are here concerned is that which prevailed in Germany from approximately 1806 to 1945, with some interruptions. This was what we might call aggressive or extreme political nationalism, frequently identified also by the less descriptive term "integral nationalism."[1]

There is no agreement as to the causes of nationalism. Some writers (for instance, Hans Kohn and Kenneth R. Minogue) seem to believe that it is a fairly recent European invention, but it seems doubtful whether the nationalism of ancient Athens, Sparta, Rome, and Carthage, and of Japan was really much different from the modern European variety. To this author, it seems likely that nationalism, in a broad sense, has existed ever since the first family of humans encountered another family, and that modern nationalism represents merely an extension and expansion of a feeling of loyalty to the family group, proceeding from it to progressively larger units, such as hordes, tribes, principalities, provinces, and nation states.

In the course of history, nationalism has had many ups and downs. At times when strong transnational loyalties emerged, nationalism

---

[1]Other types of nationalism have been called "Jacobin," "humanitarian," "liberal," "traditional," "cultural," etc. For discussions of nationalism, see Carlton J. H. Hayes, *The Historical Evolution of Modern Nationalism;* Hans Kohn, *The Idea of Nationalism;* Hans Kohn, *The Age of Nationalism;* Hans Kohn, *Prophets and Peoples — Studies in Nineteenth Century Nationalism;* Frederik Hertz, *Nationality in History and Politics;* Barbara Ward (Lady Jackson), *Nationalism and Ideology;* Hans Buchheim, *Aktuelle Krisenpunkte des deutschen Nationalbewusstseins;* M. Rainer Lepsius, *Extremer Nationalismus;* Kenneth R. Minogue, *Nationalism;* Louis L. Snyder, *The New Nationalism.*

was weakened and receded, but it never disappeared. It may have been weakest in medieval Europe, where it seems to have been effectively repressed by transnational Christianity, and it was relatively weak also in Europe between 1650 and 1750. Its strength depends on its relation to other coexisting forces. Today, "everything that has happened since [World War II] has helped to confirm the impression of nationalism's driving and undiminished force."[2] Even so typically a transnational movement as international Communism is now disrupted by the nationalism of some of the communist states.

Today, extreme or aggressive nationalism is a condition of mind characterizing groups of people who have a strong sense of belonging to a nation and to their native soil, an intense feeling of loyalty and attachment to them, as well as a passionate eagerness to see the prestige and power of the nation enhanced. Their loyalty to it exceeds most or all of their other loyalties. They are convinced of the general excellence of the nation and regard it as superior to all others. With respect to such people, it is possible to speak of national egotism and national egocentrism. Their state of mind is apt to lead to a high degree of conformity to the ingroup and to the demand that all members of it conform. It creates also a tendency to exclusiveness of the group. In the more advanced stages, a tendency to aggressiveness against outgroups can develop, one reason for this being an urge to prove the nation's superiority over others. Adorno says that "A primary characteristic of ethnocentric ideology is the *generality* of outgroup rejection. It is as if the ethnocentric individual feels threatened by most of the groups to which he does not have a sense of belonging; if he cannot identify, he must oppose; if a group is not 'acceptable,' it is alien."[3] A simpler way of stating the proposition might be to say that love of country easily turns into hatred of the alien.

There can be aggressiveness also against nonconforming members of the ingroup. The intensity of this type of nationalism can vary considerably not only from nation to nation but also within the same nation, from period to period, depending on a great many circumstances. At its most intense, nationalism of this type can be comparable to a deeply felt religion.

[2]Barbara Ward, op. cit., p. 99.
[3]T. W. Adorno (and others), *The Authoritarian Personality*, p. 147.

Such attitudes have, from time to time, come to the surface in a great many countries, large and small; and it is hardly correct to say, as Buchheim does,[4] that "irrational nationalistic feelings" are a "typically German matter."

In a psychological sense, Minogue probably oversimplifies and exaggerates when he speaks of the "notion of nationalism as a collective grievance against foreigners . . ." and when he says that a nation consists of all those people who have been persuaded that they share in this grievance.[5] But nationalism is no doubt an important manifestation of elemental group hostility, and it implies extreme loyalty to the ingroup. Nationalism may, in fact, be the most significant and frequent rationalization of group hostility. Adorno (who seems to equate nationalism and patriotism) takes that view that

> The term "patriotism" . . . does not mean "love of country." Rather, the present concept involves blind attachment to certain national cultural values, uncritical conformity with the prevailing group ways, and rejection of other nations as outgroups. . . .

and

> The ethnocentric "need for an outgroup" prevents that identification with humanity as a whole which is found in anti-ethnocentrism. . . . The inability to identify with humanity takes the political form of nationalism and cynicism about world government and permanent peace.[6]

Lepsius has pointed out that it was always the German middle class which was "particularly vulnerable to nationalistic tendencies" and that its claim to social recognition is tied to the position of the

---

[4]Buchheim, op. cit., p. 10. As for recent events, we need only recall the soccer match between Honduras and El Salvador which resulted in a small war between the two countries, or the Italian attack against Ethiopia in 1935, or Senator Joseph R. McCarthy's campaign against the communist outgroup in the United States in the 1950s. Surface phenomena of nationalism are more conspicuously visible in the United States than elsewhere, for instance the daily pledge of allegiance to the flag by the school children, and the veneration of the flag in general.

[5]Minogue, op. cit., pp. 29, 31.

[6]Adorno. op. cit. pp. 107, 148.

nation. He says that the self-confidence of the middle class will always become shaken when its political position within the nation and the international position of the nation do not come up to the expectations held by that class.[7] But, as a phenomenon in nationalism, this was not uniquely German.

Historically, extreme German nationalism did not exist until 1806, the year Hans Kohn rightly calls the "turning point."[8] At that time, "Germany" consisted of hundreds of small or even tiny principalities and free cities, few of them large or powerful enough to permit more than the pettiest kind of nationalism. Their horizon, as Kohn says, was strictly parochial. There was no real striving for national power. The leading minds of that period in Germany opposed political nationalism. Herder promoted merely "cultural" nationalism. Schiller wrote that an interest in a fatherland was important only for immature nations. Goethe felt himself to be a citizen of the world and took comparatively little interest in Germany. Kant was hostile to any form of nationalism, and he, too, regarded himself as a world citizen. He spoke of "national mania." It is fair to say that between about 1650 and 1800 German civilization was and wanted to be genuinely European.

But much of this was changed rather abruptly, largely as a result of the invasion of the German states in 1806 by Napoleon I and by the humiliating Peace of Tilsit of 1807. Thereafter, a vast patriotic effort was undertaken to prepare the German states for the Wars of Liberation, which finally resulted in freedom in 1813. That patriotic effort naturally stimulated intense nationalism. The philosopher Johann Gottlieb Fichte (1762–1814)—originally strongly pro-French and an internationalist—made a remarkable about-face when Napoleon I invaded Prussia. In 1807 and 1808 he delivered his famous *Addresses to the German Nation (Reden an die deutsche Nation)* which were to exert great spiritual, intellectual, and moral force on several generations of Germans. As he saw it then, the Germans had a great moral and spiritual mission to fulfill for the benefit of mankind. He praised the German language as superior to French, English, and others. A people with national character was a manifestation of the divine. Only the German spirit was capable of true patriotism, and to him this

[7]Lepsius, op. cit., pp. 17–18.
[8]Kohn, *The Mind of Germany*, p. 69.

was a religious sentiment. The German mind was superior, and Germans, therefore, had every right to fight Western "overalienization" (*Überfremdung*, a term on which Dr. Goebbels was to rely 130 years later). Only the Germans were capable of depth and originality. It was the beginning of the theory of a German *Kultur* of higher value than that of the superficial, uncreative Western *Zivilisation;* and it was a hymn to German uniqueness as well as to the idea that the German people as a people must take precedence over the individual. The latter, in fact, must be willing to die for his people, if its superior interests demand this.

It should be emphasized, however, that Fichte himself never directly promoted an aggressive type of nationalism. While he welcomed the Wars of Liberation in 1813, he did not glorify war as such or political power. He did not want conquests and, indeed, the German people of that period merely wanted to liberate themselves from Napoleonic rule. In many ways, Fichte remained a civilized, detached philosopher. Nevertheless, his *Addresses* with their intense glorification of the German mind, its creativeness, superior culture, and uniqueness, could not fail to supply powerful stimulants for the development of aggressive nationalism and of that ominous state of mind which the Germans call *Sonderbewusstsein*, that is, the consciousness of being someone different and special. The *Addresses* became a German classic.

Another German philosopher of the same period, G. W. F. Hegel (1770–1831), also made a certain contribution. He was far from being a nationalist—in fact, he was a great admirer of Napoleon—but some of his ideas became essential to the nationalism of the future, particularly the glorification of the state as against the individual, and the idea of nations with a divine mission.

A more genuine political nationalist of that period was F. von Schlegel (1772-1829), although he was primarily a romantic poet. He contributed much to the veneration of the German soil, and his poems sought to make the Rhine a symbol of the German people. He promoted German mysticism, was anti-French, and seemed to desire "total annihilation" of that "corrupt nation."

But a patriotic poet and pamphleteer of very practical influence on his own and succeeding generations was Ernst Moritz Arndt (1769–1860). To him, Germany was the sacred heart of Europe. He sounded the call for the Wars of Liberation from the Napoleonic yoke and made nationalism into a religious experience. He was very much what the divided German states needed to unite and to rise against the oppressor. He cursed Jewish cosmopolitanism. The influence of his poetry was to continue all through the nineteenth century and into the Hitler era. As the poet of the Wars of Liberation and as a great patriot, he became, in fact, one of the guiding historical images of modern Germany. Other such images were the generals who led the German armies in the Wars of Liberation, particularly Scharnhorst, Gneisenau, and Blücher. It is significant that cruisers of the German navy were still named Scharnhorst and Gneisenau in World War I and that battle cruisers of the same names still fought for Hitler in World War II.

Another leading mind whom we should mention was the prominent historian Heinrich von Treitschke (1834–1896). He was one of the "fighting professors" whom we encountered before in our consideration of the role played by professors in the propagation of the Germanic cult. (It is significant that no comprehensive scholarly treatise on the subject of nationalism, such as those by Carlton J. H. Hayes, Hans Kohn, and F. Hertz in the United States and Britain, has ever been written in Germany. To the German professors, the subject seemed to be one of current politics which was more suitable for "books of passion" than for an objective scholarly approach.) Treitschke seemed to conceive it as one of his tasks in life to imbue the Germans with the proper patriotic and nationalist views, and as a prominent professor of history he had immense influence. His efforts, combined with Bismarck's intoxicating political successes, did much to create the basis for modern German nationalism. His attacks on other countries (even South German states) were violent. He was, above all, fanatically anti-British and saw in the British much of the source of the frustration of German territorial expansion. He wanted Germany to become the greatest naval power. Hans Kohn says that Bismarck and Treitschke "firmly and finally established in nineteenth-century Germany the cult of might and of the hero."[9] Treitschke declared it to be "a cruel truth that we live in an age of wars."[10]

[9]Kohn, *Prophets and Peoples*, p. 108.
[10]Ibid., p. 115.

Extreme nationalism in the second half of the nineteenth and early twentieth century was, of course, by no means confined to Germany. That period was generally one of those in history which were distinguished by much intense nationalism and by a repression of transnational tendencies. France, too, had its own considerable share of nationalism. There were, for example, Maurice Barrès (1862–1923) and Charles Maurras (1868–1952), the latter the leader of l'Action Française (and finally convicted of collaboration with the Germans). Both Barrès and Maurras were intense nationalists, anti-Semitic, antidemocratic and antiforeign. Both believed in a "cult of the soil," and they also talked a good deal about "pure blood."[11] Some of their statements resemble those of much later writers of National Socialism. It is unlikely, however, that the blood-and-soil philosophers of National Socialism were directly influenced by Barrès or Maurras. For one thing, National Socialists generally had profound contempt for the "decadent" French mind. But it is conceivable that some thoughts of these two and other French nationalists found their way into National Socialism by way of Italian fascism.

The Germans, however, were far less able than the French to cope with their own nationalism after the German unification in 1871 and the successful wars of 1864, 1866, and 1870–1871. André Malraux has said that "Germany is a country in which the idea of the nation seems to be specially dangerous" and that "it is harder in Germany than in France to control the national idea. . . ."[12] George F. Kennan attributes this to the lateness of the hour when the Germans acquired a national identity:

By and large, it seemed to me, only those people had been able to cope successfully with the emotional power of national feeling who had known national identity in the dynastic era—in the period before the Napoleonic wars—before the currency of the romantic linguistic nationalism of the nineteenth century. For those who acquired the sense of national identity after that time, for the Germans in particular, national feeling was heady wine. Prior to the establishment of the German Reich in 1870, the

[11] As for Barrès, see f.i. his *Les Amitiés Françaises,* pp. 266–267, where he describes himself "as an act of the soil . . ., as one of the secrets of our race."
[12] Interview in *Encounter,* January 1969.

Germans had been no more and no less of a problem to their neighbors than anyone else in Europe. It was their attempt, beginning at that time, to think of themselves as a single national community, unified on the primitive basis of a common tongue, and competing in this quality with the older established powers of Europe, that had caused the trouble.[13]

The word "national," as used in German, has always had a much higher emotional content than, for example, in English.

As in the case of other components of national socialist ideology, Houston Stewart Chamberlain was important also in the development of nationalism. It is true that his main work *Die Grundlagen des 19. Jahrhunderts* (1899) places the emphasis on the accomplishments, not of the Germans only, but of the Teutons *(Germanen)* of Northern Europe generally. In fact, Chamberlain expressly said in that book that "failure to distinguish between Germanic and German is awkward; it confuses everything."[14] But the German readers of the book took it nevertheless as a hymn to Germany (which in countless ways it was), and in any case they regarded the Germans as the leading element among the Teutons. It is true also, at any rate, that in later writings Chamberlain went much farther in his praise of the Germans:

And one should recall the great German battle lords from Frederick [the Great] to Moltke to Hindenburg, and one should compare them with others: what culture, what ethical foundation!

At this time I merely want to suggest that I would have to say the same of the scholars, the researchers, the inventors, the leaders in everyday life. It is manifest that no country in the world is able to show anything even remotely similar. . . .[15]

Germany is destined — or, let us say, *would* be destined — to become the heart of mankind. . . .[16]

[13]Kennan, *Memoirs 1925-1950*, Boston, 1967, p. 416.

[14]*Grundlagen*, p. 866.

[15]Chamberlain, *Deutsches Wesen* (1915) quoted in *Houston Stewart Chamberlain der Seher des Dritten Reiches. Das Vermächtnis Houston Stewart Chamberlains an das Deutsche Volk in einer Auslese aus seinen Werken,* edited by Georg Schott, p. 27.

[16]Chamberlain, *Politische Ideale* (1915), in ibid., p. 120.

Today, the Lord relies on the Germans alone. That is the knowledge, the certain truth which has filled my soul for years. To serve it, I have given up my peace; for it, I shall live and die. [17]

It was during the period from the German unification and the foundation of the Reich in 1871 to the outbreak of World War I in 1914 that Germany developed its brassy, coarse, aggressive nationalism on an ever-increasing scale. In fact, in order to achieve unification, Bismarck played on a spirit of German nationalism, and after unification, he promoted nationalism to hold the individual states together. The very fact of the lateness of the unification was in itself an unhealthy stimulant of excessive nationalism. A great many Germans felt that now that unification had finally been achieved, it ought to lead to much greater German power and prestige in the world. Colonies and a strong navy were among the demands.

It is true that Germany was not the only country in that period that generated intense nationalism; but, as the historian Friedrich Meinecke says, it was "the candor and baldness, the intensity in principle, and the awareness of it, the joy in the ruthless consequences . . . which were so specifically German in it and which, at the same time, were so serious for the future. . . ." [18] There was also great indifference to the requirements of European coexistence, as well as unscrupulousness in the selection of political means. The *Alldeutsche Bewegung* (Pan-German Movement) — which we encountered before in the evolution of other components of national socialist ideology — contributed greatly to the development of this nationalism.

One surface manifestation of the coarse, immature kind of nationalism was the much-discussed saber rattling of Kaiser Wilhelm II during various international crises. His carefully posed picture hung in every German public office, schoolroom, etc. It showed him in cavalry uniform with spiked helmet (sometimes on horseback), his hand on the saber, his prominent moustache boldly turned up. His expression was proud and fierce. While all this seemed naïve and simple minded, for millions of Germans — probably the majority — the Kaiser

[17] Chamberlain, *Briefe*, Vol. II (1901), in ibid., p. 29.
[18] Meinecke, *Die deutsche Katastrophe*, p. 28.

was a symbol of their own nationalism. To an extent, they could identify with him as they could later identify with Hitler, whose pictures
also often showed him with a proud and fierce expression. In his case,
there was likewise much emphasis on the moustache, though a different kind. But these were merely superficial resemblances, even if they
might suggest that the German people had an immature desire for a
certain type of brassy leader. Nothing, however, would be more wrong
than to regard Wilhelm II as a historical precursor of Hitler or to
consider Hitler's Third Reich a continuation of Wilhelm's Germany.
Wilhelm II, unlike Hitler, did not have the personality of a real leader.

The German nationalism of the years before World War I slowly
degenerated into political irresponsibility and finally into the destructiveness that is war. It culminated in a veritable orgy of nationalist
feeling during the first few months of that war, when proud military
victories seemed to promise complete German hegemony in Europe,
including Russia. And much of this high-flying nationalism was kept
alive during the war years by the efforts of the so-called *Vaterlands-
partei* (the fatherland party), which continued to propagate far-
reaching ambitious war aims, no matter how unrealistic they were.

One might have thought that the defeat of Germany in that war
and the flight of the Kaiser would have put an end to or at least diminished, nationalism, but this did not become true. After a rather brief
stunned silence, nationalism reemerged, hardly the worse for wear.
The main reason for this phenomenon—apart from the astonishing
vigor of the German people—was the *Dolchstosslegende* (heretofore
discussed), that is, the legend that the undefeated German Army had
been stabbed in the back by Bolshevist-Jewish traitors. In this view,
German strength, at its very zenith, had been cruelly and unjustly
broken; the German position in the world had been ruined by traitors.
It was the classical situation which incites large groups to intense
nationalism. Few Germans could reconcile themselves to what they
regarded as an extreme injustice of national fate, and most were
determined to restore the national and international position of the
country. The situation was clearly a fertile field for the leadership
which Hitler was to offer a few years later.

In the years between the two wars it was German middle class
youth that stood in the forefront of the nationalistic commotion, although the older generation, particularly of the middle and upper

classes, also contributed its share. This youth was activist if not revolutionary minded, and it had a rough, militant vocabulary. It spoke
of "national revolution," by which was meant the fight for nationalism
and against democracy at home, for the reassertion of German power
in international relations, the breaking of the "chains of the Treaty
of Versailles," and other related purposes. This revolutionary element
of German youth had been lost to the Weimar Republic from the very
start and never ceased fighting it. It was one of the reasons for the
precarious existence led by that republic for all of its brief life of fifteen years. There were few young people in the nation who supported
Weimar.

A second group of nationalists in the period between the two
wars centered on the old conservatives, mostly the middle and upper
middle class, former army officers, public officials, and the nobility.
They wanted to restore the old glories, perhaps even the monarchy.
They were, and had always been, highly nationalistic, and the defeat
in the war had been a deep trauma to them, although the legend of
the "stab in the back" helped to establish some order in their psychological households. They were not really revolutionary, but they, too,
saw nothing good in democracy and the Weimar Republic. They were
as eager as anyone else to reestablish German power and prestige;
and to this end a great many of them were willing to support Hitler's
politics of power, even at the expense of common decency.

It was during that period of the interwar years that Oswald
Spengler published his *Decline of the West* and other books which
predicted, on the basis of a romantic philosphy, the development of
nationalistic dictatorships as something organic, natural, and inevitable. He envisioned the future Europe as ruled by a "Greater Germany," which was to be vastly expanded by annexations. His books
had profound effect on the German mind.

The final form of nationalism in Germany, as it developed before
Hitler, elevated the concept of the nation, the state, the fatherland
to the level of a high ethical value, independent of any other value.
It outweighed all humanitarian and normal ethical considerations.
Extreme nationalism—not only in Germany but wherever it appears
—creates a gulf between personal ethical precepts and those applicable in politics, particularly the politics of foreign relations. The power
of the nation and its welfare take unquestioned precedence over any

ethical postulate. "My country right or wrong!" said the British. The Italians spoke of the *sacro egoismo* of the nation. In Germany, the historian Treitschke coined the much-repeated phrase that the essence of the state was power and again power and, for the third time, power. The dual morality, once called Machiavellism and confined to a narrow ruling group in whose secret archives it reposed, now paraded openly, even proudly, under the mantle of nationalism— a kind of Machiavellism of the masses. What was uniquely German about all this aggressive nationalism and lack of political morality was that they were loudly proclaimed alongside equally loud proclamations (sometimes by the same people) of romantic German attachment to classic humanism and humanity, understood as part of German *Kultur*. Putting it a little differently, the modern German sociologist Ralf Dahrendorf speaks of "the great stillness in the face of inhumanity in Germany [which] appears coupled with limitless idle talk about humanism and humanity as no other country knows it." [19]

B. Nationalism under Hitler

It may be that German nationalism was developed to the highest intensity during the Hitler period. It was then that the last surviving principles of elementary political morality atrophied and nationalism became completely vicious. Any intrusion of moral principles into foreign policy (unless tactically advantageous) was condemned as the morality of weakness, flabbiness, and resignation. A person who proposed such a morality was ipso facto a *Versager*, a term meaning approximately a "despicable failure." Harshness was what was required for dealing with other nations (and, in fact, if anyone within Germany opposed this, then harshness was needed also for dealing with him). When Neville Chamberlain went to Munich in 1938 to plead with Hitler, he looked to Hitler like a laughable contemptible type of politician because he was willing to make concessions and did not show British strength.

It is possible that historically German nationalism in the Hitler era reached the all-time high ever reached by nationalism anywhere.

[19] Dahrendorf, *Gesellschaft und Demokratie in Deutschland*, p. 394.

At any rate, there is no question that it was a component of considerable importance in national socialist ideology. Buchheim even contends that "the hypostatization of the national community was one of the main roots of the totalitarian development."[20] Nationalism was of course related to other components of the ideology. The firm belief in the superiority of the nation, which is inherent in nationalism, found its counterpart and further ideological confirmation in the doctrine of German racial superiority. Both stamped other nations as inferior. In the German situation, race and nation were natural co-partners; what was good for the one almost necessarily had to be good for the other. Eva Reichmann says, moreover, that it is "no wonder that nationalism and Darwinism were well suited to each other and, later, in imperialism and race doctrines, entered into a fateful alliance."[21] And if the race doctrines and nationalism were close relatives, the Germanic cult was necessarily a third one. It furnished a romantic ideological foundation for both. Even anti-Semitism fitted into the entire picture, though again only in a negative sense. Few Jews were inclined to be extreme German nationalists, no matter how much they liked the country. The Germans—for this and other reasons—regarded them as internationalists, as rootless cosmopolitans, and, therefore, as enemies of everything for which true nationalism stood. Adorno says that "wherever a certain kind of militant and excessive nationalism is preached, anti-Semitism is, as it were, automatically supplied with it."[22] Even to those Germans, moreover, who may have had doubts about the race theories or the Germanic cult or anti-Semitism, the legitimacy of extreme nationalism was traditionally beyond question, and nationalism could thus be used as an attractive wrapper in which the entire ideological package could be sold.

Extreme nationalism was one of the most effective propaganda tools—perhaps the most effective of all. At countless meetings, with hundreds of banners and flags in the light of torches, the nationalistic feelings of the masses were whipped into a frenzy. There were throaty

[20] Buchheim, *Aktuelle Krisenpunkte,* p. 18.

[21] Reichmann, *Die Flucht in den Hass—Die Ursachen der deutschen Judenkatastrophe,* p. 97. What she meant was not the original Darwinism but the later social Darwinism.

[22] T. W. Adorno, "Zur Bekämpfung des Antisemitismus heute," in *Das Argument,* May 1964, p. 89.

mass recitals of oaths, pledges, dedications to Germany, and so forth. One observer, Joachim Fest, speaks of the "arousal of a state of ecstasy" at these meetings.[23] Albert Speer describes "raging masses who were guided to ever-increasing fanatic furies of rapture and hatred—a witch's cauldron of unleased passion," which, he says, disgusted him.[24] The crowning achievement was the annual "Day of the Party" in the Nuremberg stadium, a gigantic assembly of about 100,000 people. For this, Speer—evidently repressing his disgust— requisitioned 130 high-powered searchlights (of antiaircraft units) with which he surrounded the stadium at intervals of 30 feet, each searchlight sending its cone of light vertically into the night sky for a distance of more than 4 miles. Speer calls the effect "grandiose" and speaks of the creation of a "cathedral of light"[25]—an apt setting for this huge pseudoreligious ceremony of delirious nationalism, racism, and self-adoration.

The overwhelming emotional experience of nationalism at such meetings represented, moreover, the very essence of what the sadomasochistic character needs. On the masochistic side, the individual could totally immerse and lose himself in the oceanic mass of like-minded, equally inspired party members, all of whom, in unison, yelled the identical responses and slogans. He could surrender his individuality but, at the same time, could take deep satisfaction and pride in his membership in a group of vast strength. He was given security. At the same time, on the sadistic side, he could feel superior to all enemies and all those who possessed less power, and he could find gratification in the promise of his masters that these enemies would be attacked and destroyed. (In fact, in the early days of National Socialism, such meetings were not infrequently followed by immediate violence against Jewish shops, Communists, etc.) And all this could be accomplished, moreover, by an efficient process of rationalization, executed so smoothly that it avoided any awareness by the individual that sadomasochistic drives were involved or that he even had any. Nationalism of this intensity could heal many psychological wounds.

Moreover, mass meetings of this sort could satisfy the normal

[23]Fest, *Das Gesicht des Dritten Reiches,* p. 120.
[24]Speer, *Erinnerungen,* opposite p. 112.
[25]Ibid., p. 71.

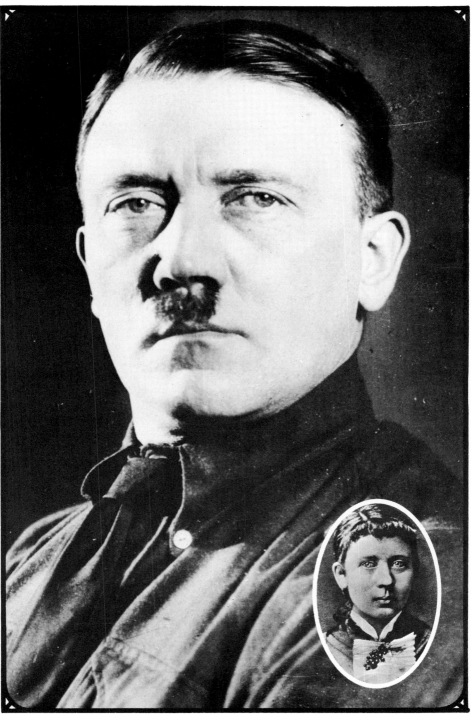

Hitler, probably in the early 1920s
BROWN BROTHERS

Hitler's mother (date unknown)
ACME NEWSPICTURES

Hitler in the early days of the Movement.
BROWN BROTHERS

Hitler at Nuremberg, 1927
BROWN BROTHERS

Hitler and Joseph Goebbels (in civilian clothes) 1933? <small>UPI</small>

Mass meeting at Zeppelin Field, Nuremberg, 1933.
<small>UPI</small>

Hitler with a group of youths at a Munich cafe (1933?)

Hitler and Hindenburg campaign poster, 1933
UPI

Hitler relaxing (1933?) UPI

Party ceremony for Rudolf Hess, the "Deputy Fuhrer" in 1933.
UPI

**Salute to Hitler in the Reichstag in 1934 on first anniversary of
Hitler's seizure of power.**
UPI

**Hitler's dramatic appearance in Munich beer cellar among
Party veterans in 1934 on 14th anniversary of launching of Movement.**

President Paul von Hindenburg with Hitler after "Rohm-Putsch" in 1934.

Back row (l. to r.): Joachim von Ribbentrop (German Foreign Minister), Neville Chamberlain, Hitler, Paul Schmidt (interpreter), Sir Neville Henderson (British ambassador) at conference in 1938.

UPI

UPI

Neville Chamberlain and Hitler (with interpreter Paul Schmidt behind them) after Godesberg conference on Sudeten-crisis in 1938.

Mussolini, Hitler, Goring, Hess (1939?)

Hitler Youth saluting, 1938.

Hitler receiving flowers
from a child believed to
be Eva Braun's niece
(date uncertain)

Heinrich Himmler with Hitler at maneuvers, 1939

**Hitler with Albert Speer (at his left) and others taking
a walk in conquered Paris, 1940.**

Hitler speaking, 1942.
UPI

Hitler during a speech (date uncertain).
UPI

strivings of the young (who made up a large percentage of the participants) to conform to the ideas and customs of their own group and to substitute the security of group membership for that no longer wanted from their parents.

Hitler himself, in a sense, might be said to have outgrown conventional nationalism and to have held certain transnational views. If Hermann Rauschning can be believed, Hitler, in private confidential conversations, expressed a strong conviction that nationalism was a thing of the past and was being replaced by the "race concept." Rauschning's book *Gespräche mit Hitler* (Conversations with Hitler) devotes two pages to a recital of such statements by Hitler, some of which are sufficiently important to be quoted here:

> The concept of the "nation" has become empty. I still had to start with it for reasons of contemporary history. But from the outset I was clear in my own mind that this could make only temporary claims to validity. The "nation" is a political expedient of democracy and liberalism. We must break up this false concept and replace it by the race concept which is not politically exhausted yet. The historically grown peoples [nations?] will not be the determining concept in the future; but the race concept, which is hidden behind it, will be — and all the rearranging of boundaries and settlement areas is idle activity. . . .
>
> . . . I, as politician, need a concept which permits the dissolution of the historically established order and the forcible establishment of an entirely new antihistorical order, a concept that furnishes intellectual support for this order. . . . I have to liberate the world of its historical past. The nations are the manifest shapes of our past history. I must, therefore, melt the nations into a higher order, if I want to eliminate the rubbish of a historical past which has become absurd. And for this I find the race concept useful. It dissolves what is past and gives the possibility of new bonds. With the concept of the nation, France led its great Revolution beyond its borders. With the concept of race, National Socialism will carry its revolution through to a new world order.
>
> . . . our revolution . . . is the final step . . . toward recognition of purely biological values. And throughout Europe and the whole world I shall set in motion that new [biological] selection

that National Socialism represents in Germany. . . . Nothing much will then be left of the customary local nationalism, not even among us Germans. In place of it, there will be comprehension among the members of the same valuable master-race, though they speak different languages.[26]

As is often the case with Rauschning's reports of Hitler's statements, it is unlikely that Hitler actually said *all* of this or that he actually said it in this precise way. Some of it sounds quite unlike Hitler's usual style of speaking or sounds more like something that Rauschning *thought* Hitler *wanted* to say. Nevertheless, it seems probable that Hitler did make statements to the general effect of those reported by Rauschning. Even in his early years, in *Mein Kampf*, Hitler had vaguely suggested the primacy of race,[27] although he still spoke of the need for national pride, national feeling *(Nationalisierung)* and national education.[28] The word "nationalism" itself remained unmentioned. That word likewise does not seem to appear in *Hitler's Table Talks* (in spite of misleading index listings). He did refer to "nationalism" in his secret speech to officer candidates of May 30, 1942,[29] but then only as something that stands in contrast to international socialism, which, of course, he condemned. It is perhaps significant also, as being in line with Hitler's transnational views, that in a decree he prohibited the further use of the description "German race" as it would lead to the "sacrifice of the racial idea as such in favor of a mere nationality principle."[30] Incidentally, the historian Friedrich Meinecke reports that the German general Ludwig Beck said to him about Hitler: "This man really has no fatherland."[31]

On the whole, it seems likely that Hitler did in fact accord primacy to race over nation, at least late in his career.[32] But what did

[26] H. Rauschning, *Gespräche mit Hitler*, pp. 218–220 (printed in France).

[27] See, f.i., p. 272, *Mein Kampf*, and the elaborate index listings under *"Rasse"* on p. xxi.

[28] *Mein Kampf*, pp. 31, 34, 123, 370, 473.

[29] Appendix to *Hitler's Table Talks*, p. 502.

[30] Decree of Aug. 9, 1941, *Verfügungen, Anordnungen, Bekanntgaben* cited by Hannah Arendt, *The Origins of Totalitarianism*, p. 412.

[31] Meinecke, *Die deutsche Katastrophe*, p. 89.

[32] Buchheim, op. cit., p. 13, agrees. Alan Bullock, *Hitler, a Study in Tyranny*, p. 41, however, sees fanatical nationalism throughout Hitler's life.

this really mean? In the end, it would have meant nothing other than the formation of a larger *German* empire *(Grossdeutschland)* in which the racially Germanic countries, such as the Scandinavian countries and Holland, would at best have been nonsovereign states in a federation whose capital would have been Berlin renamed "Germania."[33] Naturally, Hitler would have welcomed it if the Germanic countries had voluntarily joined the Reich. In his *Table Talks*, he said:

> We must, of course, proceed very cautiously in discussing these questions [of political incorporation] with the Dutch and Norwegians. . . . I always pointed out [to the Austrians] that I wanted to unite them with Germany in a greater German Reich. In the same way, we must again and again make clear to the Germanic people of the Northwest and North that what is involved is the Germanic Reich, simply "the Reich," which merely finds its strongest source of ideological and military power in Germany.[34]

Austria, it will be recalled, had been simply annexed in 1938. The ultimate fate of the countries of the "Northwest and North" would hardly have been much different. In other words, Hitler's primacy of race over nation essentially amounted only to the substitution of broader, more flexible criteria for the determination of the nation-state, and it represented also a device for a more effective imperialist policy. Hitler was pushing his frontier forward from the narrow one of the nation to the much more distant one of the race. The frontier of the race, moreover, had the advantage of being nebulous and movable. "Race [Hitler had said] is . . . not a matter of language but of blood. . . ."[35] His ideas, thus, were not genuinely transnational but represented, in effect, an extreme form of nationalism. As he told Rauschning, the race concept was to enable him to establish a new world order, and we can take it for granted that Germany was to be the master of that order.

At the same time, while this racial type of nationalism had for its purpose a union of all Germanic peoples in one greatly enlarged

---

[33] *Hitler's Table Talks*, p. 398.
[34] Ibid., p. 254 (indirect speech transposed).
[35] *Mein Kampf*, p. 428.

Reich, it was hostile to other, non-Germanic races. Some of them, like the Latin race, it might have tolerated, but others—those regarded as inferior or even subhuman, like the Slavs—it planned to enslave. Their countries were to be German protectorates or colonies in Europe itself.

National Socialism carried nationalism *ad absurdum.* In Germany, as the philosopher Karl Jaspers has said, "the consciousness of the nation-state grew into a more dreadful disaster than at any other time in history." [36]

[36]Jaspers, *Freiheit und Wiedervereinigung,* Munich, 1960, p. 55.

Chapter 8

Militarism

A. The Nature of Militarism and Its Place in National Socialist Ideology

For at least a hundred years, militarism has been the central target of criticism of German behavior up to 1945. The image of the marching columns, in goose step and eyes left, has been pervasive and lasting throughout the non-German world, and this image was readily transferred from the imperial armies to those of Hitler. It seems that picturesque images of this sort are easily absorbed and retained, and their death is slow. In actual fact, however, the type of militarism of which the goose-stepping columns might have been symbolic was very different from the kind developed under Hitler; and, indeed, militarism was by no means the essence, or even a very important component, of national socialist ideology.[1]

This is not to say that militarism and the militaristic tradition of the old Prussia and of Imperial Germany did not play a considerable role in the organization, structure, and numerous thinking processes of national socialist Germany. Clearly, the old ingrained militarism greatly facilitated the military mobilization of the entire nation, the creation of an effective fighting force, and the acceptance of Hitler's aggressive plans by the existing army leadership. To many Germans, national socialist early emphasis on a military way of life looked like a return to an accepted life style—a welcome return after fifteen years of the soft, unmilitary ways of the Weimar Republic. Few, if any, were

[1]In connection with this chapter, see particularly: Gordon A. Craig, *The Politics of the Prussian Army 1640–1945;* John W. Wheeler-Bennett, *The Nemesis of Power;* Alfred Vagts, *A History of Militarism;* Heinz-Erich Fick, *Der deutsche Militarismus der Vorkriegszeit;* Gerhard Ritter, "Das Problem des Militarismus in Deutschland," in *Historische Zeitschrift*, Vol. 177, 1954, pp. 21–48; Gerhard Ritter, *Staatskunst und Kriegshandwerk.*

aware that the warriors of the SS and, to an extent, of the regular army were to be made into an infinitely more cruel and unscrupulous fighting force than the best-trained Prussian soldiers had ever been. Thus a relationship between Prussian and imperial German militarism, on the one hand, and Hitler's wars of conquest, on the other, may seem obvious, but, to an extent, this is deceptive.

Before we proceed further, however, we should examine what militarism really is. Alfred Vagts is the one who has gone into the matter most thoroughly. He offers no exact definitions but confines himself to descriptions.

> Militarism . . . presents a vast array of customs, interests, prestige, actions, and thought associated with armies and wars. Its influence is unlimited in scope. It may permeate all society and become dominant over all industry and arts. . . . Militarism displays the qualities of caste and cult, authority and belief. . . .[2]

> Militarism has connoted a domination of the military man over the civilian, an undue preponderance of military demands, an emphasis on military considerations, spirit, ideals and scales of value, . . . the imposition of heavy burdens on a people for military purposes, to the neglect of welfare and culture, and the waste of the nation's best man power in unproductive army service. . . .[3]

> [Militarism] covers every system of thinking and valuing and every complex of feelings which rank military institutions and ways above the ways of civilian life, carrying military mentality and modes of acting and decision into the civilian sphere.[4]

It has been said elsewhere, with some malice and a little exaggeration, that militarism is the supremacy of the specialists in violence.[5] According to Vagts, moreover, "the prime characteristic of militarism" is a loss "of all sense of the proportions among things and of the limitations on human power."[6] Writing before World War II, he cited Napoleon I as an example.

[2] Alfred Vagts, op. cit., p. 11.
[3] Ibid. p. 12; see also Fick, op cit., p. 7.
[4] Vagts, op. cit., p. 15; see also Fick, op. cit., p. 13.
[5] M. Baumont (ed.), *The Third Reich*, p. 742.
[6] Vagts, op. cit., p. 135.

In wartime, the entire nation can be militarized. In peacetime, in a truly militaristic country, militarism may turn strongly narcissistic; and the military establishment may exist largely for its own sake. There will be countless flattering parades, honor guards, ceremonies, military honors of all sorts, splendid uniforms, and so forth. An extreme of this kind of attitude was expressed in the pronouncement of a Russian prince: "I hate war because it ruins the armies."[7] But some narcissistic attitudes are present in any army even in wartime, and they probably have their uses.

The militarists are the great ritualizers in nations. They are the specialists in grand public ceremonies, and also the funeral directors for the powerful. When a king or president dies, his coffin is carried off on a caisson. An army bugler blows taps.

Napoleonic France, Japan, Prussia, and Germany before 1945 are the main examples of extreme militarism. In Germany, the military came to be regarded as the highest form of human existence. Conventional German militarism reached its apex, as we shall see, not under Hitler but during World War I. (Hitler, in fact, in his later years, represented a turning point away from true conventional militarism.) It should be understood also that even a military dictatorship (which Hitler's regime was not) is by no means synonymous with militarism. Various Latin-American countries with military dictatorships, for example, are hardly militaristic. Nor would it seem that heavy armaments of a country can necessarily be equated with militarism. Fascist Italy under Mussolini never became a nation of soldiers. Conversely, militarism is possible in a country with a very small army. This was true, for example, among large population groups of the Weimar Republic (though not its governments), but it was, of course, a carryover from the highly developed militarism of the preceding Imperial Germany. Militarism, in other words, is largely a state of mind; and it is likely that this state exists chiefly in countries where the authoritarian character structure, with its simultaneous presence of sadistic and masochistic drives, is prevalent.

Apart from all the disastrous consequences which militarism can have in the disruption of the peace of the world, there is the additional fact, pointed out by Gordon A. Craig in his brilliant *The Politics of the Prussian Army*, that a strong army can be "the most effective and

[7]Fick, op. cit., p. 44.

inveterate opponent of political change."[8] Similarly Fick calls the army officer "a factor in the guaranty of the old political order in domestic political life."[9] And it is a fact that in nineteenth-century Prussia the army contributed a great deal to the prevention of political liberalization and the establishment of democratic institutions. On the other hand, in the Weimar Republic, when democracy had actually been introduced, the army not only abandoned its traditional role of being the guarantor of the established order but, on the contrary, played an important part in 1932 and 1933 in enabling Hitler to come to power. The reasons for this, however, were very special and will be discussed here later.

On the face of things, the place of militarism in the national socialist ideology is self-evident. Obviously, militarism is closely tied to nationalism, and, in fact, it is difficult to envision true militarism without a strong nationalistic understructure. Moreover, the glorification of fight for the sake of fight in the Germanic cult and its worship of the heroic were related to aspects of militarism, and so was the doctrine of the eternal struggle for the survival of the stronger in the racial theories which, indeed, proclaimed war to be "the father of all things." Obviously, the general fight ideology of National Socialism had no difficulty at all in linking up with traditional German militarism. And as far as the romantic component of the ideology is concerned, Fick even contends that without a certain "romantic light the militarism . . . [of the years after 1870] is entirely unthinkable."[10] Clearly, militarism fitted well into the package.

It seems likely that militarism is one manifestation of the sado-masochistic character structure of the authoritarian personality, previously discussed in relation to other components of the national socialist ideology. On the masochistic side, it is clear that the armed forces are typically a body of overwhelmingly strong power to which the individual can submit himself completely, and this with public approval. The soldier largely annihilates himself as an individual self and thereby overcomes the unbearable feeling of powerlessness of the masochist.[11] At the same time, he becomes part of a powerful, glamor-

[8] Craig, op. cit., pp. XV–XVI.
[9] Fick, op. cit., pp. 32–33.
[10] Fick, ibid., p. 26.
[11] See, in this connection, Erich Fromm, *Escape from Freedom*, pp. 152 et seq.

ous institution, and he participates in its strength and glory. Fick (without mentioning masochism and perhaps with some exaggeration) refers to "the utter absorption [of the Germans before World War I] in the moral duty to serve the people" and to the fact that "the average German would a thousand times prefer to be a slave with no responsibility at all, and an unseeing but conscientious machine that executes orders, rather than a man who is free but carries heavy responsibility and has to rely on his own judgment." [12] This attitude, in Fick's view, was in fact the essence of Germany military discipline. [13]

Similarly, Vagts (also without mentioning masochism) speaks of "the desire . . . to be put in one's right place from above, as members of military bodies seem to be placed, under a venerable head. . . ." The isolated individual, Vagts says, may find "relief in the mass movements and processions in which the equal step, the music of bands, and mass chanting drown out, temporarily, the dissensions of ordinary life." [14] All these devices, unconsciously designed to aid the masochistic personality to submerge itself into a stronger power, were later carried to extremes in the totalitarian countries, Germany, Italy, and Soviet Russia. They were, in fact, introduced into civilian life in such uniformed organizations as Hitler Youth, SA, Black Shirts, Komsomol, and others. Marching in columns became a style of life.

On the sadistic side, it is obvious that militarism is well suited to satisfy sadistic drives of the sadomasochistic character. The very essence of militarism is the creation and maintenance of the power to subdue and dominate other nations. The mere thought of humiliating a foreign nation, making a helpless object of it, inflicting pain on its citizens, is a source of pleasure to the sadist. In wartime itself, this pleasure reaches fulfillment. There are also other smaller sources of sadistic satisfaction in army and navy life. Except for the lowliest private or seaman, everyone has a chance to humiliate and lord it over someone else. Stories of cruel, vicious drill sergeants abound in many armies. In the United States Marine Corps on Parris Island, recruits have died from mistreatment. The extreme degree of discipline in the German SS was legendary. Every last remnant of individualism and human dignity of the SS men was systematically extirpated by humili-

[12]Fick, op. cit., p. 12.
[13]Ibid. p. 48.
[14]Vagts, op. cit., p. 21.

ation and inhumanity. Hans Buchheim, in *Anatomie des SS-Staates*, [15] quotes from the memoirs of a former member of the *Waffen-SS* who during training accidentally dropped a cartridge. He was ordered to pick it up with his lips, twice refused to do so, was ordered to do fifty knee bends with his rifle in his extended arms, but in the middle of this exercise broke into convulsive sobbing and, crying, did pick up the cartridge with his lips. Abusive insults and other punishment followed.

B. The Historical Development of German Militarism

To understand the specifically German type of militarism, it is necessary to go back rather far in history. The origin of much of the exalted position of the Prussian and German officer corps can really be found in the medieval feudal relationship between the hereditary monarch and his knights, the nobility. The knight and his followers rendered military services to the ruler in return for land ownership or other advantages. They developed into a monarchal retinue. They owed allegiance to the monarch and not to the nation. Their business was war, and they had no overriding interest in the peaceful adjustment of conflicts. They looked down upon the merchants, tradesmen, and others who depended on their military protection and who, in turn, looked up to the noble warrior class that systematically excluded them.

It is surprising to what extent traditions of feudal military organization and thought processes continued to live on in Prussia and Germany through the centuries down to World War I and, to an extent, down to the Hitler era. The officer corps of the Prussian and, later, the German army remained a military caste that swore unconditional obedience to the person of the monarch, an obedience which had "no legal limits." [16] They were the "knightly servants of the monarch" and only to a lesser extent of the nation. The army remained essentially a monarchal retinue, and its position as an institution of the state was hazy. (Malicious critics of old Prussia have said that it was not a country that had an army, but an army that had a country.) After the inter-

[15] Vol. I, pp. 254-255.
[16] See Wheeler-Bennett, op. cit., pp. 4-5.

lude of the Weimar Republic, the army oath to the person—to the person of Hitler—was reintroduced in 1934, and it was to become crucially important.

Up to the end of World War I and to a lesser extent until Hitler made himself Supreme War Lord, the army remained under the domination of the nobility. Being an army officer was *the* way of life to a large part of the nobility. It was an acceptably chivalrous occupation. Only members of the nobility were admitted to officership in the "good" regiments. Non-nobles were relegated to newly created infantry and artillery units and to the engineer batallions on the Polish frontier. The tradition of the knight on horseback found expression in the placing of noble officers exclusively in the cavalry regiments. The horse and horsemanship still had a very special traditional meaning. An officer's post in the infantry or artillery, not to speak of the engineers, was entirely intolerable to a nobleman and could at best be accepted as a temporary demotion for punitive purposes. The great majority of this officer caste was inclined to be anti-intellectual.

It is significant in this connection that, under the constitution of Imperial Germany, officers of the highest ranks could be appointed only by or with the approval of the Emperor.[17] As a practical matter, the officer corps—like the knights of the Middle Ages—was the basis of the ruler's power. And he, in turn, was fully aware of the debt he owed them. The Hohenzollern dynasty, through the centuries, remained thoroughly loyal to the officers and accorded them many advantages. The Prussian kings and later the German emperors, in fact, always regarded themselves as members of the army family. In Prussia and Germany the officer corps occupied an extraordinary position of power and social advantage, though not financially, for about two centuries before Hitler. The situation, at least up to 1918, was typified by the fact that the affluent bourgeoisie knew no higher ambition than to win the title of "reserve officer."

When Hitler became Supreme War Lord, the army—seemingly automatically—sought to renew with him the highly personal relationship of loyalty and obedience which had traditionally existed between army and monarch. In fact, it seems that the army's oath to Hitler's person was something that the army volunteered. There was actually

[17]Ibid. p. 9.

no need for such an oath, since an oath to "people and fatherland" was already in effect. The new oath formula was drafted by General Werner von Blomberg. [18] Gordon Craig rightly calls it a "careless commitment," [19] but it was, nevertheless, in line with an old and revered German tradition. The tradition was evidently merely "suspended" during the Weimar Republic, and the fourteen years of that republic were not long enough to break it.

Historically, there is little doubt that militarism was the dominant fact of Prussian history. In retrospect, as Fick suggests, [20] this may have been almost inevitable in a country which geographically occupied an endangered inner position, being surrounded by larger, more powerful neighbors. "The historical development of a remote hinterland into a European great power, above all by military accomplishment, is one of the most essential factors in the rise of militaristic thinking in Germany." [21] The idea of being encircled and having to break out of encirclement by force was one of the most pervasive concepts in the German mind (and this idea was extensively relied on in government propaganda in both world wars). The psychiatrist Erik H. Erikson, himself a refugee from Hitler Germany and an expert on the German psyche, says:

> It is impossible to characterize what is German without relating Germany's familial imagery to her central position in Europe. For . . . even the most intelligent groups must orient themselves and one another in relatively simple subverbal, magic design. Every person and every group has a limited inventory of historically determined spatial-temporal concepts, which determine the world image, the evil and ideal prototypes, and the unconscious life plan. These concepts dominate a nation's strivings and can lead to high distinction; but they also narrow a people's imagination and thus invite disaster. In German history, such outstanding configurations are encirclement versus *Lebensraum*. . . . (N)othing can be more fatal in international encounters than the attempt to belittle or to argue another nation's mythological

---

[18] See, in this connection, Craig, op. cit., pp. 479-481.
[19] Ibid., p. 481.
[20] Fick, op. cit., pp. 77-79.
[21] Ibid., p. 78.

space-time. The non-German does not realize that in Germany these words carried a conviction far beyond that of ordinary logic.[22]

The Prussian kings were the great educators in militarism, starting with the "soldier king" Frederick William I (1713–1740) and, above all, his son Frederick II (the Great, 1740–1786). These two were followed by a long, tenacious line of Prussian kings and German emperors, able generals, and statesmen who unyieldingly continued the promotion of the militaristic way of life. Prussia became a *Militärstaat*, that is, a state which was thoroughly permeated with the military spirit. It was characterized, as Fick says, by "the primacy of the military over the political, . . . our ecstatic faith in blood and iron— that was our school, our philosophy, our whole life, down to the silly imitation of military gestures by the civilians."[23] Even the small railroad-station master had to stand on the platform at military attention whenever the daily express train to Berlin rushed by. Every policeman and even the post-office clerks adopted the manners of an army sergeant in dealing with the public. There was a certain stern facial expression *(Amtsmiene)* of a strict disciplinarian, which most public officials assumed. And all this was not forced upon the civilian population by the military; it was a voluntary and natural style of civilian behavior, growing out of centuries of admiration of the military way of life. In part, it may have been the result of a feeling of being inferior to the soldier, which historically many German civilians had.

Planning for war and saber rattling thus became a generally acceptable and desired method of dealing with other nations. Even war itself, while probably not wanted by most, was accepted as a necessary evil. The war against France in 1870–1871 was, in fact, deliberately used by Bismarck for *domestic* political purposes, that is, for the unification of the various German states into one Reich in a spirit of militaristic and nationalistic solidarity. It was an action that indicated the considerable extent to which political and military thinking had merged. And it is historically possible that without the intense spirit of militarism, without strong military force, combined with an

---

[22]Erikson, *Childhood and Society*, p. 345.
[23]Fick, op. cit., p. 11.

indomitable pride, Prussia-Germany would never have achieved great power status in Europe.

As was to be expected, the spirit of militarism was given the necessary philosophical foundation by German historians, philosophers, and others. The historian Leopold von Ranke saw Christianity as "the spirit which transforms peoples into orderly armies." The philosopher G. W. F. Hegel spoke of war as a "moral bath of steel" *(moralisches Stahlbad)*. Some regarded war as a "historical necessity" or as the "destiny" of the nation. Few saw anything desirable in a peaceful advance of a spirit of equality and democracy. "The scheme of the armed society," Vagts says, "owes . . . much to Germany" and "the most radical practitioners and thoroughgoing theorists of social embattlement are German."[24] But he wrote this in 1937. Thereafter a good deal of militarism became manifest also in Japan, and even in the United States. At least superficially, there seems, indeed, to be much resemblance between the militarism of Prussia-Germany and of Japan, although for centuries they developed independently or even without knowledge of each other.

In practice, the consequences of Prussian-German militarism were aggravated by the fact that anti-intellectualism was a frequent concomitant of it. It seems that, by and large, the "military man" is not expected to be well educated or intelligent or to take an interest in things of the mind. In Germany, an officer's candidate was not required or even expected to have finished the last two years of high school *(Gymnasium)*, and apart from army manuals, many of them never touched a book again after leaving school. Of course there were exceptions, and indeed many officers of the General Staff were highly intelligent and well-read men. But the average officer, particularly of the nobility, took an interest primarily in horses, women, and wine, and if he had intelligence, he tried not to show it. All this was probably no disadvantage, and perhaps an advantage, in a mere fighting man, but it should be remembered that these men were the demigods of large parts of the population and set cultural and social standards for a great many civilians. There is no doubt that the officer corps had far-reaching influence on the life style of the nation. The result was, as the historian Friedrich Meinecke has pointed out, "a danger-

---

[24]Vagts, op. cit., p. 443.

ous narrowing of the intellectual and political field of vision" as also "a naïve self-admiration of the Prussian character."[25] "Many a richer source of life was caused to die," and Meinecke adds that "under the mantle of an outward discipline all ugly drives and passions could rage."[26]

In a sense, militarism reached its apex during World War I. It was then — under an ineffective, unintelligent, but vain monarch — that the military established real dominance over the political leadership of the country. To a considerable extent, this was due to the extraordinarily strong personality of General Erich Ludendorff, which was in no way counterbalanced on the civilian side. Gerhard Ritter calls him "the archetype of the militarist of the purest water."[27] It was Ludendorff's claim that with the outbreak of hostilities the Supreme Command became an agency which shared responsibility with the Chancellor of the Reich (Bethmann-Hollweg), the highest civilian official; and as Gordon Craig says, the Chancellor "unfortunately, never contested this claim, but himself drifted into an acceptance of the idea that, in political as well as military matters, the Supreme Command's views must be considered on the same level as his own. . . ."[28] In cases of conflicts, Emperor Wilhelm II had to function as arbiter between the two, but he himself was strongly inclined to take the military view, and, at any rate, he was no match for the formidable Ludendorff. The result was a catastrophic abrogation of political reason and sense in favor of considerations of purely military expediency.

In terms of popular enthusiasm, too, militarism was never stronger in Germany than during World War I, at least in its early stages. In 1914, the average German took an intensely positive attitude toward the war. Most Germans felt that this war was desirable, necessary, and just. The civilians streamed, happily singing and laughing, into the mobilization centers; the troops crossed the Rhine bridges to the throaty, stirring song *Die Wacht am Rhein* (The Watch on the Rhine). They carried flowers in the barrels of their rifles. Church bells rang, and the clergy of all faiths blessed the German arms. It was one of the sublime moments of German history. The soldiers felt

[25] Meinecke, *Die deutsche Katastrophe*, p. 25.
[26] Ibid., p. 24.
[27] Ritter, "Das Problem des Militarismus in Deutschland," p. 44.
[28] Craig, op. cit., p. 327.

then that they and the entire army represented a high moral value. In contrast to these feelings of 1914, the mood was subdued in 1939. True enough, the great majority approved of Hitler and National Socialism, but there was disappointment that Hitler had not disposed of the problems without war, as he had miraculously done earlier in the case of the Rhineland, Austria, and Czechoslovakia. The army seemed no longer a value in itself, but an instrument for a purpose. And there probably was an unconscious realization by many that the war would ultimately lead to a German disaster.

Returning now to 1918, one might have assumed that when the Emperor, the Supreme War Lord, fled to Holland, when the long and utterly exhausting war had ended in defeat, when a democratic republic had been established, the spirit of militarism might have vanished, but this proved not to be true. There were several reasons for the survival of militarism. One was that the great majority of Germans refused to believe that their proud army had really been defeated in the field. They preferred to believe in the previously mentioned *Dolchstosslegende*. No military defeat was, therefore, seen as negating the proud Prussian-German tradition of militarism. A tradition of 200 years does not die easily, in any event. Moreover, the old tradition was effectively carried forward by the professional army of 100,000 men which the Treaty of Versailles permitted the Weimar Republic to maintain. That small army, led as it was by very able generals, particularly General Hans von Seeckt, became a source of pride to most Germans. The army was supplemented by small illicit army forces and certain small *Freikorps*. But above all, the important thing was that the youth of Germany, particularly the students, took up the spirit of militarism. They carried on secret military drills in many places under the guidance of old officers. Rifles were transported in cello cases, and so forth.

As National Socialism grew into a political movement in the Weimar Republic, the paramilitary activities were vastly increased. The SA, the Hitler Youth, and the SS developed. Marching in uniformed columns behind flags, obeying barked commands, singing aggressive (or sentimental) marching songs, yelling *Sieg Heil* in unison, became the style of life of the leisure hours for large numbers of Germans; and even larger numbers stood along the sidewalks and admired the marchers. The narcissism and self-admiration which seem to be inherent in militarism were on the rise again. And so were the masochistic drives of millions to submerge themselves into a mass organization and to participate in its glory. The regimes of the Weimar Republic never became strong enough to absorb such drives. The guiding image of the front fighter—the man who had fought in the trenches for four years—was and remained strong. Even the militant groups of the Left, *Rotfront* (Red Front) and *Eiserne Front* (Iron Front), marched in columns.

Finally, it was the generals of the small professional army, particularly General Kurt von Schleicher, who contributed a great deal to inducing the aged President von Hindenburg (himself a former general) to appoint Hitler as Chancellor of the Reich on January 30, 1933. This was the beginning of what Hitler himself liked to call his "seizure of power." There is no doubt that General von Schleicher and other generals were intimately involved in the negotiations preceding Hitler's elevation to the chancellorship[29] and that without their support it would have been far more difficult for him to seize power. In fact, if the army had actively opposed him then and later, he might never have succeeded, at least not without a very difficult civil war.

Actually, General von Schleicher and the other involved generals had little liking for Hitler, and President von Hindenburg was deeply suspicious of "the private first class from Bohemia" as he called him.[30] But the generals thought that he would be a useful, if turbulent, ally of the army, a kind of "captive" Chancellor of the Reich who would agree with their plans for secret rearmament and other plans. Above all, they held the cynical view that they would be able to handle him. They could not, of course, have been more wrong in their judgment. As it turned out, Hitler knew how to handle them as well as the aged President; and, in the end, he was to deprive the generals of all their power and to dishonor them. It was one of the many instances of a fatal underestimation of Hitler's ability by others. To be

[29] The available literature on the contribution of the generals is voluminous. The matter is summarized in Craig, op. cit., pp. 453–467, and J. W. Wheeler-Bennett, op. cit., pp. 182–285, and *passim*.

[30] The German army rank *Gefreiter,* which Hitler held, has frequently been mistranslated as "corporal," probably due to confusion with the British rank "lance-corporal." The German rank is the equivalent of private first class.

sure, in various details Hitler fulfilled the expectations of the generals—and exceeded them. He did greatly expand the army, air force, and navy—and not secretly but quite in the open. All the money the armed forces could desire was suddenly at their disposal. The causes for the traditional controversies between the military and the civilian government about money had vanished. It was the fulfillment of all the normal daydreams of a professional militarist. Moreover, for the first time in decades the country seemed united, or mostly so, behind a strong leader; and the young officers and soldiers, many of whom were National Socialists, were content. But in the end, the generals and all Germans had to pay a very high price for all this in blood and hardship, millions of lives, a ruined country, and their own dishonor.

C. Hitler and Militarism. The Decline

Hitler's own attitude toward the army, its leadership, and militarism in general underwent a considerable transformation in the course of his life, and this was probably the result of the interplay of his political rise, his own participation in the leadership of the armed forces, and certain developments in his sadomasochistic drives. As a young man of twenty-three, he did not seem at all enthusiastic about the *Austrian* army. He tried to dodge service in it by taking refuge in Germany. It was an incident that understandably he later did not wish to be known, and for this purpose he went so far as to falsify in *Mein Kampf* the date of his departure from Vienna for Munich by one year.[31] The reasons for his draft dodging are unknown but, in view of the fact that about two years later he volunteered for service in the *German* army, it may be fair to assume that the Austrian army did not seem glamorous enough to satisfy his masochistic strivings. That army did not then have much of a reputation in Europe. Hitler, at any rate, "detested the [Austrian] racial conglomeration. . . . this whole hodgepodge of people, Czechs, Poles, Hungarians, Ruthenians, Serbs, Croats, and so forth, . . . Jews and more Jews."[32] He called

[31] See Franz Jetzinger, *Hitlers Jugend—Phantasien, Lügen und die Wahrheit*, pp. 249–272, particularly p. 257; also Alan Bullock, *Hitler, a Study in Tyranny*, pp. 46–47; Karl Dietrich Bracher, *Die deutsche Diktatur*, p. 69; Joachim C. Fest, *Das Gesicht des Dritten Reiches*, pp. 27–38.

[32] *Mein Kampf*, p. 135.

Austria "a cadaver of a state."[33] He did say, in connection with the outbreak of World War I, "I did not want to fight for the Habsburg State."[34]

On the other hand, initially he had the highest admiration for the *German* army. In *Mein Kampf*, he called it "an element of the greatest value," "the most tremendous school of the German nation," and he said, "What the German people owe the army can be briefly summarized in a single word: everything."[35] (In part, this, like many other Hitler statements, echoed Houston Stewart Chamberlain, who had declared that "The German army is a magnificent school of the German way of life. . . ."[36]) A few years later, in 1928, in Hitler's then unpublished *Zweites Buch*, he went into greater detail:

> . . . all in all, around the turn of the century, the German army was still the most grandiose organization in the world, and its work was more than a blessing for our German people. . . . [The army] was the breeding ground of German discipline, German efficiency, decent convictions, plain courage, bold daredeviltry, tough tenaciousness and rocklike honesty. The concept of honor, held by one caste, slowly and imperceptibly became the common property of an entire nation.[37]

Obviously, this was sincere praise of various aspects of militarism. Hitler himself possessed some of the qualities which he praised, such as discipline (even if not at all times), courage, daredeviltry, and tenaciousness. But he lacked others, particularly honesty and, above all, any comprehension of honor. In the end, it was he who dishonored the army and the nation.

At the outbreak of World War I in August, 1914, Hitler immediately volunteered for service in a Bavarian regiment (though still an Austrian citizen). His enthusiasm is described in detail in *Mein*

[33] Ibid., p. 141.

[34] Ibid., p. 179. (See also Werner Maser, *Adolf Hitler—Legende, Mythos, Wirklichkeit*, p. 117.)

[35] *Mein Kampf*, pp. 305, 306.

[36] Chamberlain, *Deutsches Wesen* (1915), in *Houston Stewart Chamberlain der Seher des Dritten Reiches. Das Vermächtnis Houston Stewart Chamberlains an das Deutsche Volk in ciner Auslese aus seinen Werken* (edited by Georg Schott), p. 25.

[37] *Hitlers Zweites Buch*, p. 64.

Kampf. ". . . My jubilation and gratitude [at being accepted] were boundless."[38] "Even today, I am not ashamed to say that, overwhelmed by passionate enthusiasm, I sank to my knees and thanked Heaven from an overflowing heart. . . ."[39] "The only worry which tormented me in those days, as it did so many others, was whether we would not arrive at the front too late."[40] But his most significant statement about joining the army probably was that "To me, those hours seemed like a deliverance from the troublesome emotions of my youth."[41] Presumably this meant that he could now finally find satisfaction in annihilating himself as an individual and could free himself of the feeling of powerlessness, unbearable to the masochist, by submerging himself in the glamorous and powerful army.[42] Also, as we shall see later, it was his joining the army that finally rescued him from his years of existence as a purposeless drifter.

Hitler spent nearly four years at the front as a regimental runner or courier, and it does not seem that he ever applied for a promotion. He became an excellent soldier. The official statements of his superior officers concerning his extraordinary bravery, perseverance, diligence, etc. gave him the highest possible praise.[43] As a result, he was awarded the Iron Cross second and first class, an unusual honor for his rank of private first class. With pride, he habitually wore the Iron Cross on his jacket to the end of his life.

There is little doubt that Hitler's participation in World War I was his most important formative experience. Many years later, he still spoke of "the stupendous impression produced upon me by the war—the greatest of all experiences" and in keeping with his masochistic strivings, he mentioned that at that time "individual interest —the interest of one's own ego—could be subordinated to the common interest."[44]

In many ways World War I was never decided and never ended for Hitler, and it is perhaps symbolic that he was told the news of the

[38]*Mein Kampf,* p. 179.
[39]Ibid., p. 177.
[40]Ibid., p. 180.
[41]Ibid., p. 177.
[42]See, in this connection, Fromm, *Escape,* p. 155.
[43]See Maser, op. cit., pp. 136, 141-142, who quotes these statements.
[44]Speech of Aug. 17, 1934, quoted in Bullock, op. cit., p. 53 (not in Max Domarus, *Hitlers Reden und Proklamationen, 1932-1945*).

German capitulation while he was in a hospital, temporarily blinded by a British gas attack. He could not read. "I groped and staggered back to the dormitory, threw myself on my bed, and dug my burning head into the blanket and pillow."[45] Fundamentally, he never really understood or wanted to understand that Germany had lost the war. The army, to him, had not been defeated. It had been stabbed in the back by all sorts of un-German elements, Jews, Marxists, and other traitors. The psychiatrist Erik H. Erikson says that "If Hitler . . . denied the defeat of this army with all the weapons of self-deception and falsehood, he saved for himself and for German youth the only image that could properly belong to everybody."[46] At any rate, when Hitler started World War II, it was to him essentially nothing but a continuation of the earlier war, which emotionally he had never finished. In a late speech he connected the two wars very definitely:

> It is simply the old eternal struggle and the old eternal fight. It did not come to an end in 1918 . . . it was only the beginning, the first piece of this drama. The second piece and the ending are now being written, and this time we shall obtain what we were defrauded of at that time. . . . We shall be able to proclaim . . . at the graves of our soldiers of the World War [I]: *Comrades, you have been victorious after all!*[47]

Mein Kampf contains no criticism of the conduct of World War I by the generals. When Hitler wrote that book, he was presumably still emotionally submerged in the glory of the old army and had not freed himself from his masochistic relationship to it. He still admired the old generals and had, in fact, made the retired General Erich Ludendorff his political ally. But Hitler's political rise and his seizure of the office of Supreme War Lord for himself was to bring about a profound transformation. It was, indeed, to alter radically the face of German militarism in general or even to put an end to it. The remarkable leap in rank from private first class to commander-in-chief naturally meant that Hitler had emerged from the great mass of faceless soldiers, had become an individual again, and very much so. His

[45]*Mein Kampf*, p. 223.
[46]Erikson, *Childhood*, p. 352.
[47]Speech of Nov. 8, 1941, Domarus, *Hitlers Reden*, p. 1781.

masochistic drives had to look elsewhere for satisfaction, for something higher, something even more powerful (and, as we shall see later, he substituted such powers as the "laws of nature," "historical necessity," "Providence," "fate," and so forth). What now came to the fore, however, was the sadistic side of Hitler's sadomasochistic character structure; and it expressed itself in a thousand ways, including ways of extreme destructiveness, ranging from the murder of the Jews to the final scorched-earth order to blow up all German industrial plants, utilities, monuments, bridges, etc. And included in the course of the sadistic, destructive process was the utter humiliation of the generals and, indeed, the dethroning of traditional Prussian-German militarism itself. On the other hand, almost to the end Hitler maintained his admiration and even a sense of comradeship for the lower ranks. It was not until March, 1945, that he told Albert Speer that the German people—by which he must have meant primarily the army—"had proved to be the weaker one, and the future belongs exclusively to the stronger Eastern people *(Ostvolk)*."[48]

It is not correct to say, as Gerhard Ritter did,[49] that Hitler was the "most extreme of all militarists." To him, at least in his later years, the army was merely a tool to obtain more Lebensraum, to subjugate inferior races, and to establish Germany's political hegemony in Europe (and, later, perhaps the world). If the army had not been useful for these purposes, he might well have dissolved it and might have relied on the SS for ceremonial and other purposes. The "military way of life" in the Prussian and imperial German sense had no genuine meaning to the Hitler of the late 1930s and 1940s, even if, for purposes of public morale or other reasons, he might have professed the contrary. He had probably never heard of the feudal tradition of mutual loyalty between dynast and knight (but he did insist on absolute obedience). And, in any case, the chivalrous attitude of the old German officer was incomprehensible and merely distasteful to Hitler, or, as General Walter Warlimont puts it in his memoirs, ". . . Hitler regarded chivalrous conduct . . . as a moral infirmity and a sign of weakness. . . ."[50] In a fight he was a man of vicious violence, a slugger,

[48]Speer, *Erinnerungen,* p. 446.

[49]Ritter, "Das Problem des Militarismus in Deutschland," p. 47.

[50]Warlimont, *Im Hauptquartier der deutschen Wehrmacht 1939–1945,* Frankfurt, 1964, p. 205.

a killer. In his view, a successful war could be conducted only by terror and deliberate brutality against the enemy. "One must have no pity for the people who have been destined by fate to perish."[51] And as he saw it, fate had destined a great many of his enemies to perish, particularly the "inferior races."

Actually, even quite apart from Hitler's emerging sadistic drives, some hostility on his part against an officer corps of the Prussian type (composed mostly of Protestants) was something entirely natural and had to be expected. He was, after all, an Austrian (and Catholic), and there had always been a great deal of aversion between the careless, less disciplined, more easygoing, more "southern" Austrians and the bemonocled, heel-clicking, highly disciplined, arrogant, "correct," conscientious officers of the German army. Friedrich Heer (an Austrian Catholic) says quite aptly that Hitler was "infinitely strange to them, and they infinitely strange to him."[52] Moreover, an officer corps that was composed largely of "gentlemen" (or at least thought it was) did not basically fit into the national socialistic system, whose hierarchy consisted mainly of political adventurers, revolutionaries, and others unsuccessful at their earlier pursuits, few of them being particularly interested in bourgeois or military respectability. If this hierarchy was interested in honor, it was only the honor which success could bring. Also, specifically as between Hitler and the German officer corps, the basic aversion was bound to be increased by the social prejudices of the officers. Even in Austria, Hitler's family had been a social zero; he came from a background of the lowest middle class, and his speech and appearance corresponded to this background. In other words, he was no one with whom a self-respecting German (or Austrian) officer of the old school would normally have maintained social relations. And all this naturally was something that Hitler, being as highly sensitive in human relations as he was, must have sensed very clearly; and the rejection, which was implicit in this relationship, must have aroused this hatred.

It is not surprising, then, that the generals were gradually excluded from his group of intimates (which was limited, in any event). His resentment of the generals grew steadily into hatred and hostility,

---

[51] *Hitler's Table Talks*, p. 247 (indirect speech transposed).
[52] Heer, *Der Glaube des Adolf Hitler*, p. 386.

from the time he first assumed power in 1933 to the end of his life. But this was something which he could express only in confidence to his closest associates because he needed the generals. Thus, Dr. Goebbels, in his diary, reported remarks by Hitler that "he cannot stand the sight of the generals any more" and that "he feels like a total stranger to this class of people and, in the future, would stay away from them more than ever."[53] Another high national socialist official, Hans Frank, wrote in his memoirs:

> . . . if there was anyone in the world to whom the Führer, within himself, was hostile in German history, then it was those circles of the General Staff who "long ago betrayed, forgot and sold out Moltke and Schlieffen" (as he said again and again) and "who had become a special caste of particularly stuck-up junker-type fatheads and national mischief-makers, completely unproductive, barren of any ideas, cowardly and correspondingly conceited." On another occasion he said: "Sometimes those gentlemen with the purple stripe on their trousers[54] strike me as more repulsive than the Jews. . . ."[55]

Much of this sounded like the traditional Austrian view of the "Prussians." In any case, the contempt which Hitler developed for the generals was extreme.

Goebbels' diary reports the following:

> The Führer's judgment concerning the generals is exclusively negative. He says that they swindle him whenever they can. Besides, they are uneducated and don't even know their own job of conducting a war, which is the least one might expect of them. Of course, you can't blame them for having no higher culture because this is not what they were trained for. But what speaks absolutely against them, he said, is that they know so little also about the purely material things of warfare. Their education has been wrong for generations. He said that we can now see the products of this education in the corps of our high officers.[56]

[53]Goebbels, *Tagebücher 1942-43*, pp. 336-337 (May 10, 1943), Zurich, 1948.
[54]The members of the General Staff were distinguished by a purple stripe on their trousers.
[55]Hans Frank, *Im Angesicht des Galgens*, 1953, p. 243.
[56]Goebbels, op. cit., p. 255 (Mar. 9, 1943).

General Adolf Heusinger reports in his memoirs that Hitler made these statements to him in 1944:

> I made a big mistake. I left the integrated education and alignment of the officer corps to these gentlemen [the generals]. I thought they would act according to my own principles. But when I took over the leadership of the army myself, I saw more and more how they had swindled me. I have often deeply regretted the fact that I didn't purge my officer corps as Stalin purged his. [57]

Hitler's hatred and contempt for the generals was, indeed, founded in part on the fact that his early enormous military successes had been obtained with ease in spite of dire prophecies by the generals of the dangers which his proposed undertakings involved and the calamities in which they were likely to result. The generals had warned him not to have the army march into the Rhineland, not to occupy and annex Austria, not to proceed against Czechoslovakia, and not to attack Poland. Yet each one of these undertakings was spectacularly successful in no time at all; and later even the French army was crushed within a few weeks. In fact, even in the Soviet Union the early German military campaign was successful almost beyond belief. The warnings of the generals and their predictions of failure must have worried Hitler greatly, although he did not mention this, and, at any rate, he never forgave the generals for trying to discourage him and for showing poor judgment. He never regained faith in them. He could not, of course, bring himself to admit later that from a long-range point of view the generals had been right at least in trying to dissuade him from starting the war against Poland (and France and Britain) and, thereafter, the Soviet Union. As far as he was concerned, the failure of these wars was due to the inability of the generals to conduct war.

And Hitler's unshakable faith in his own abilities, at least as a strategist, does not seem to have been wholly unjustified. The British military expert, Sir B. H. Liddell Hart, had quite high regard for Hitler as a strategist:

[57] Adolf Heusinger, *Befehl im Widerstreit. Schicksalsstunden der deutschen Armee 1923-1945*, Tübingen-Stuttgart, 1950, p. 367.

... Hitler was far from being a stupid strategist. Rather, he was too brilliant—and suffered from the natural faults that tend to accompany such brilliance. He had a deeply subtle sense of surprise, and was a master of the psychological side of strategy, which he raised to a new pitch. Long before the war he had described to his associates how the daring coup that captured Norway might be carried out, and how the French could be manoeuvred out of the Maginot Line. He had also seen, better than any general, how the bloodless conquests that preceded the war might be achieved by undermining resistance beforehand.

No strategist in history had been more clever in playing on the minds of his opponents—which is the supreme art of strategy. . . .

. . . in the Russian campaign his defects became more potent than his gifts, and the debit balance accumulated to the point of bankruptcy.

Even so, it has to be remembered that Napoleon, who was a professional strategist, had been just as badly dazzled by his own success, and made the same fatal mistake in the same place. . .

Hitler was quicker to spot the value of new ideas, new weapons, and new talent. He recognised the potentialities of mobile armoured forces sooner than the General Staff did, and the way he backed Guderian, Germany's leading exponent of this new instrument, proved the most decisive factor in the opening victories. Hitler had the flair that is characteristic of genius, though accompanied by liability to make elementary mistakes, both in calculation and action. . . .

. . . By Hitler's success in demonstrating the fallacy of orthodoxy he gained an advantage over the military hierarchy which he was quicker to exploit than to consolidate.[58]

Any layman reading the stenographic transcripts of Hitler's daily discussions of the military developments with his generals and admirals[59] cannot help being impressed by his apparent knowledge of strategic and tactical considerations, his enormous memory, and his ability to make quick decisions.

[58]Liddell Hart, "Hitler as War Lord," in *Encounter,* January 1968, pp. 69–71.
[59]*Hitlers Lagebesprechungen,* edited by H. Heiber.

Hitler's lack of orthodoxy—often deliberate—his failure to play according to the rules, his amateurish boldness, did indeed account for much of his military (and political) successes. Albert Speer no doubt described it well in his memoirs:

> Dilettantism was one of Hitler's characteristic peculiarities. . . . Unencumbered by deeply ingrained ideas, his highly receptive intelligence sometimes developed the courage for extraordinary actions which would not even have occurred to an expert. The strategic successes of the first few years of the War can be traced back quite directly to Hitler's unwillingness to learn the rules of the game and to his laymanlike eagerness to make quick decisions.[60]

But Hitler's difficulty evidently was that psychologically his deep-seated contempt for other people, particularly "inferior" races, did not permit him to make an objective assessment to the effect that the enemy's military situation was really more favorable than that of his own units at any given time. Also, his narcissism (of which more will be said later) was such that he always felt sure that the enemy would do what he expected him to do.

Hitler's vendetta against the generals actually got underway later than one might have assumed. It started in earnest in 1938, five years after his seizure of power (disregarding, in this connection, the murders of Generals von Schleicher and von Bredow in 1934, which, as part of the "Röhm Blood Purge," were differently motivated). Hitler needed that "honeymoon" of five years to consolidate his power in general and to strengthen his relations with the rank and file and the lower officers of the army. His behavior toward the army and even the generals still was respectful, cautious, and accommodating. He staged the "Day of Potsdam" (heretofore discussed). He put an end to the jurisdiction of the civil courts over the armed forces. He spoke of the "inviolability" of the army and designated it as "the sole bearer of arms in the nation."[61] Above all, he abolished the rival SA and killed its leader, the aggressive Ernst Röhm. (The army, of course, was

---

[60] Speer, op. cit., p. 244.
[61] See Craig, *The Politics of the Prussian Army*, p. 480.

unaware that the SA was to be replaced by the SS, a rival infinitely more effective and dangerous to it.) [62]

The generals, on their part, initially fell all over themselves to demonstrate their loyalty to Hitler, and their conduct was cheap and sordid. When, as part of the Röhm Blood Purge on June 30, 1934, Hitler had the innocent Generals von Schleicher and von Bredow murdered, an order of the day by Field Marshall Werner von Blomberg informed the troops that "The Führer has personally attacked and wiped out the mutineers and traitors with soldierly decision and exemplary courage," and Blomberg said that the army "pledges anew its devotion and fidelity." [63] (Even President von Hindenburg expressed to Hitler his "most profound thanks and sincere appreciation." [64]) An additional example, in August, 1934, was the oath of unconditional obedience to Hitler in person which, as mentioned earlier, the generals voluntarily offered to Hitler, who had not even asked for it. Such actions could hardly fail to lower Hitler's own respect for the generals. Weakness and cowardice were always repulsive to his sadistic character structure and, in fact, were apt to provoke his hatred.

The Army continued to go out of its way to "coalign" *(gleichschalten)* its policies with those of the regime. Without any urging, it introduced regulations which made the anti-Jewish personnel requirements applicable to the military. [65] Generally, a vast national socialist indoctrination effort was undertaken by the High Command in cooperation with, or even under censorship of, the Party propaganda organization. [66]

In spite of all this, Hitler's resentment of the generals grew in the years after 1934. Their baseless warnings of impending disasters seemed designed to frustrate his ambitious schemes and to be obstacles in the way of a gratification of his sadistic, destructive drives. In January, 1938, he finally struck against the top leadership of the

---

[62] For details of the whole relationship between the national socialist regime and the armed forces, see Manfred Messerschmidt, *Die Wehrmacht im NS-Staat — Zeit der Indoktrination;* also Klaus-Jürgen Müller, *Das Heer und Hitler — Armee und nationalsozialistisches Regime 1933-1940.*

[63] Quoted in Wheeler-Bennett, *Nemesis,* p. 325.

[64] Ibid., p. 326.

[65] Messerschmidt, op. cit., pp. 40-47.

[66] Ibid., *passim.*

army. He summarily dismissed Field Marshall and Minister of Defense Werner von Blomberg on the ground that he had recently married a woman with a police record (and this, indeed, did greatly impair Blomberg's usefulness). Hitler dismissed also the Chief of the Army Command, Colonel-General Werner von Fritsch, on a purely trumped-up charge of homosexuality, for which Himmler and Heydrich produced a seedy "witness." Other high generals, whose removal followed, were Gerd von Rundstedt and Wilhelm Adam. In the course of the next few years, the purge of generals became monstrous. It seems that of 17 Army Field Marshals, 10 were sent home. Of 36 colonel-generals, 18 were sent home and 5 died as a result of the assassination attempt on Hitler on July 20, 1944, or were dishonorably discharged. Only 3 colonel-generals survived the war in their positions. More than 35 commanders of divisions and corps were sent home.[67] The futile assassination attempt itself took the biggest toll in lives. Wheeler-Bennett's "List of Victims" indicates that 18 generals, 1 admiral, and 48 lower officers were killed or committed suicide.[68]

In the fifteen years of his rule, Hitler subjected the generals to a long series of humiliations, such as no Prussian king or German emperor would have dared to inflict upon that once proud and willful group. Anyone who disagreed with his views and dared to say so might be insulted and summarily dismissed. During the campaigns of World War II, a suggestion of retreat, a shortening of some front line under severe attack by superior enemy forces, could result in disgraceful dismissal of a general with an excellent earlier record. Hitler exercised tight control even over quite small phases of the conduct of the war; and the generals were expected merely to carry out (or anticipate) his orders, no matter whether these made military sense or not. The only type of general whom Hitler was able to stand was the completely servile lackey type, such as Generals Wilhelm Keitel and Alfred Jodl. Neither of them belonged to the Prussian aristocracy; both were worshippers of the Führer. They lasted to the end and, had, in fact, the honor of signing the instruments of surrender or capitulation.

[67] Wheeler-Bennett, op. cit., p. 526.
[68] Ibid., pp. 744–752.

Between 1938 and 1944, Hitler had accomplished what the liberals and antimilitarists of a century or more had been unable to achieve. He had brought the army under complete control of the civilian government. In fact, as Gordon Craig says, Hitler compelled "the obedience of [the Army's] officers even to commands which violated their historical traditions, their political and military judgment, and their code of honour."[69] Never before in German history had the army been in such a relationship of subordination and subservience to the political government as under Hitler. The difference between the relative position of the army in World War I and World War II was astonishing In the first war, as mentioned earlier, General Ludendorff demanded and received political equality with the Chancellor, and he was, in fact, the most powerful person in the state. In the second war, no general carried any real prestige or authority remotely comparable to Hitler's. His dictatorship was essentially civilian, and the terror by which it ruled dominated the army no less than the whole country. The army, which once had amounted to a state within the state under the leadership of the nobility, had degenerated into a group of mere technicians, into an obedient tool of power of an irrational dictator who was indeed an enemy of the officer corps. The militaristic societies of Prussia and imperial Germany, dominated as they had been by the aristocracy, were worlds apart from the national socialist society, which was dominated by the lowest middle class headed by a former resident of a Viennese men's lodging house. Essentially, the Prussian-German tradition of militarism was largely distasteful to Hitler, and, in effect, he suppressed it. When in 1945 the Allied Powers ordered the dissolution of the State of Prussia to destroy the base of Prussian militarism, their action was really no longer necessary. Hitler had degraded and destroyed that militarism far more effectively than this could ever have been done by an outside power. (It could also be said that unintentionally Hitler, an Austrian, was Austria's revenge for the defeat of the Austro-Hungarian Empire by Prussia in the war of 1866.)

Gerhard Ritter may be right in pointing out that under Hitler, "the natural relationship between the politicians and the military

[69] Craig, op. cit., p. 469.

was turned exactly upside down."[70] The generals were the ones who, again and again, tried to be an element of moderation in Hitler's policies, whereas normally the politicians have to restrain the generals. Hitler himself, in fact, was quite conscious of this reversal of the normal traditional roles:

> Before I became Reich Chancellor, I had thought the General Staff was like a butcher dog whom one had to grab firmly by the collar because he was threatening to attack everyone else. After I became Reich Chancellor, I was forced to discover that the German General Staff is anything but a butcher dog. This General Staff has always been a hindrance to me in doing what I considered necessary. The General Staff objected to the rearmament, to the occupation of the Rhineland, to the march into Austria, to the occupation of Czechoslovakia, and finally even to the war against Poland. The General Staff advised against the offensive in France. . . . I am the one who always had to goad that butcher dog into action.[71]

But it may be questionable to what extent the generals would have tried to restrain Hitler if they had felt that the army was strong enough for his adventures. Their warnings against rash political and military undertakings were based, after all, more on considerations of military weakness than on ethical doubts. But it is true that most of the generals would have been satisfied with far fewer conquests than Hitler planned. The generals do, in fact, carry a heavy guilt. Gordon Craig takes a most severe view of the actions or inaction of the great majority of the commanding officers.[72] They failed to live up to their political, military, and moral responsibility. They shirked their obligations to the German people. Craig points out that for three hundred years the army had claimed to be the ordained protector of the national interest and, in return for this position, had obtained special privileges. In the course of fighting for its preferred position, the army had vitiated all attempts to create a democracy, which would

---

[70] Ritter, "Das Problem des Militarismus in Deutschland," p. 47.
[71] Domarus, *Hitlers Reden*, p. 1753 (Sept. 24, 1941).
[72] Craig, op. cit., p. 497.

have been the most effective defense against a dictatorship. In Craig's view, it was the army's obligation to protect Germany against Hitler's dictatorship; but instead of doing so, it contributed greatly to bringing Hitler to power in 1933, and it cooperated with him thereafter.

Much of this is true, but what Craig does not mention, in this connection, is that the Weimar Republic, unstable as it was, was actually a functioning democracy and that Hitler was, in effect, lawfully and constitutionally voted into power by the German people, even though it is true that some army generals gave President von Hindenburg the final push to appoint Hitler Chancellor. In spite of the description "seizure of power," which Hitler later was fond of using, there is no question that he had worked his way up within the system and had submitted to the electoral process. There is also little question that even if some generals had not supported his appointment in 1933, he could ultimately still have become Chancellor by lawful means, though perhaps a year or two later. What Germany faced was a vast, popular movement. Had the generals attempted by military force to prevent a lawful appointment of Hitler, they would also have done severe damage to the democratic principles of the Weimar Republic, though surely not as much damage as Hitler was soon to inflict on that unhappy Republic.

But the generals are subject to much more serious criticism regarding their subsequent cooperation with Hitler in thousands of large and small ways. These ranged from their daily military work to such dishonorable acts as furnishing (at a minimum) logistic support to the *Einsatzgruppen*, the special task forces that killed about 900,000 Jews, Soviet commissars, etc., behind the front lines in Poland and the Soviet Union. There is also the sordid matter of the army's failure to prevent the death of three to four million Soviet prisoners of war from starvation and neglect. True, there were doubts and even protests by some generals against some actions; but apart from one or two resignations the great majority of the entire officer corps complied and cooperated. The conspirators in the assassination attempt of July 20, 1944, were, of course, a different breed, although some of them had seen the truth only very late. They were true heros; they paid with their lives; and many of them, after torture, died a slow, cruel death, hanging naked from a thin string attached to a meat hook. But their total number was only about 250, and this included many civilians. As Craig has said, the "most significant aspect of the officers' revolt was that it failed, and it did so because the great majority of the army's leaders refused to participate in it."[73] Nevertheless the conspirators by their act did preserve a small residue of honor of the old German army.

Most of the generals and lower officers seemed psychologically quite incapable of raising their voices against Hitler. A good many were sincerely troubled by their oath to him; others took refuge behind it. The old tradition of unconditional obedience to the monarch as supreme war lord was transferred to Hitler. The enormous significance of the oath was quite well described by a high national socialist official, Hans Frank, in his memoirs:

> Hitler, after all, was chief of state and supreme commander of the armed forces, and the oath to his person was an oath like every oath, that is, binding without any reservation before God and people. Moreover, there was war, and this put everyone under a duty to dedicate himself to people and fatherland. I am aware that hundreds of thousands of men, who were Hitler's deadly political enemies at home, such as communists, loyally did their soldier's duty under their oath in this war as German soldiers. Many of them were decorated and promoted for bravery. Many of them were killed fighting. . . . All this was characteristic of a true, old, loyal military nation of honor![74]

In the SS, the motto was: "Have faith, obey, fight—nothing else!", and for many it was not much different in the army. They called it "doing their duty."

But perhaps even more important, Hitler, in some strange way, seems to have induced a reaction of fear among the generals. Groups of them, for example, who intended to persuade him to take a different course in some matter, would fail to say much to him when they met him, and they would leave the meeting cowed, submissive, and silent. They did not really know how to deal with him; a person of his type was outside of their experience. By and large, they were

[73]Ibid., p. 470. See also Helmuth Groscurth, *Tagebücher eines Abwehroffiziers 1938–1940,* Stuttgart, 1970.
[74]Frank, *Im Angesicht des Galgens,* p. 398.

accustomed to dealing with "gentlemen," but here they faced a *Gewalt-mensch*, a man of violence, fury, and hatred. General Walter Warlimont reports in his memoirs that "[Fieldmarshall Walter von] Brauchitsch, in particular, seemed actually to suffer physically in meeting with Hitler, so that he could often give an impression as if he were paralyzed."[75] Instant dismissal of an uncooperative general was always a possibility, and not the worst. In a speech to the high military leadership on November 23, 1939, Hitler made himself clear: "I shall recoil from nothing and shall crush anyone who is against me."[76] In their general reaction, the generals probably did not differ much from politicians, such as Neville Chamberlain, Lord Halifax, and others, who also did not know how to deal with Hitler.

And there were some factors in mitigation of the guilt of the generals, at least in the early years of the Hitler regime. Nearly all of them were patriots and were deeply troubled by the political humiliations to which Germany was subjected by the Allies during the Weimar Republic, by Germany's extreme political, economic, and military weakness, by the seeming incompetence of a long succession of Weimar governments. (They did not see that their own support, instead of indifference or opposition, might have helped these governments, and they had traditionally no interest in a democracy.) In Hitler they believed they saw a man—turbulent and strange as he was—who could set all this right; and in the early years the correctness of this view appeared to be confirmed by his miraculous bloodless successes in the Rhineland, Austria, Munich, and Czechoslovakia, as well as by the full economic recovery. Naturally, the generals were pleased also with the enormous build-up of their own army. And finally, they realized that thousands of the young officers and even larger numbers of young enlisted men, whom this rapid build-up had suddenly injected into the army, were strong National Socialists and worshipped Hitler. Open opposition by the generals against him might have split the army apart. In later years, when the officer corps became aware that there would be disaster, many nevertheless continued to cooperate with Hitler in some vague, unrealistic hope that this would "avoid the worst."

[75] Warlimont, *Im Hauptquartier der deutschen Wehrmacht 1939-1945*, Frankfurt, 1964, p. 76.
[76] Ibid., p. 104.

Also, in general, it had been traditional in the Prussian-German army that an officer is an "unpolitical" person. He did his military duty and did not meddle in the affairs of the government. To an extent, therefore, J. C. Fest is correct in pointing out that the army became an "aristocratic form of emigration" for those who disagreed with Hitler but did not dare or wish to make their objections known.[77] By and large, apart from a few exceptions, the officer corps seemed totally unable to develop the initiative and moral courage or, indeed, the *genuine* patriotism necessary to disobey and to forestall disaster; and strangely enough, the officers still fought on and died in the ruins of Berlin. The reliance of the generals on a tradition of obedience became irresponsible and unconscionable.

To what extent, then, may militarism be regarded as a component of national socialist ideology? No matter what Hitler's personal reactions to the traditional Prussian-German militarism were and no matter what he did to destroy that militarism, there is no doubt that the great majority of Germans held on firmly to their militaristic traditions and to the values of the military way of life. Without this faith in militarism and without a highly effective army born of militarism, Hitler could never have accomplished as much as he did, though he may not have known this. It is ironic that he was to be the one who, in fact, brought about the decline and fall of German militarism.

Finally, in conclusion, we should not fail to remember that militarism had also a good side, at least in its German setting. It once was so intense that its spirit permeated a large portion of the civilian side of life, particularly the civil service, the world of the public officials. This had some bad results, as discussed earlier, but it also resulted—down to this day—in a body of dedicated public servants of unexcelled conscientiousness, integrity, incorruptibility, and disciplined working habits. To a considerable extent, the same spirit can even be found in German business and industry; and this probably goes a long way to account for the country's economic success. But the price paid for all this was very high.

---

[77]Fest, *Das Gesicht des Dritten Reiches*, p. 325. See also the discussion of the obedience of the generals by A. Hillgruber, "Die 'Endlösung' und das deutsche Ost-imperium . . . ," in *Vierteljahrshefte für Zeitgeschichte*, Vol. XX, 1972, pp. 149-150.

Chapter 9

A Summing-up

A. An Ideological Edifice

We have considered the main components of the national socialist ideology—the race theories, the Lebensraum doctrine, anti-Semitism, the Germanic cult, Romanticism, nationalism, and militarism. Taken as a whole, it was an ideological edifice of considerable size—an edifice in which the average German found ample room to move around and expand. He could feel at home and secure in it. To him, the ideology was a real *Weltanschauung*, that is, a comprehensive orderly conception of the scheme of things and of his relation to it—the all-embracing conception in which most Germans seem far more interested than other people. The ideology told the average German authoritatively what he wanted to know: where he came from, where he stood, where he was going, and also what was expected of him in order to get there. His search for identity—to use the jargon of our time—had come to an end. He had "found himself."

To the average German, it did not seem too difficult to accept the irrational premises on which many of the ideological components were based, even if they were what we might in retrospect call an "integrated system of delusions." And once they had been accepted, the whole bundle appeared to have an interior logic of its own—reasonably definite and seemingly irresistible. (In this respect, as in others, the ideology resembled some of man's great religious systems.) Of course, even a convinced National Socialist might have balked at one or two of the ideological premises or components here or there, but, all in all, he could close his eyes to these, because enough was still left that was traditional and respectable to justify accepting the entire package. In his view, excesses could be overlooked because the ultimate purpose of the ideology was a very high one indeed. And by and large it seemed to the faithful that anyone could quite comfortably embrace every one of the ideological elements. As we have seen, all of them were interrelated, and at times it is even difficult to separate one clearly from the other.

One reason for the ready acceptance of the whole ideology was that it forged a link between the faith in the imaginary laws of nature and history and the belief in a coming utopia. These laws guaranteed that the utopia would be achieved in our time, and, moreover, Hitler promised that it would last a thousand years. The result was a popular movement of quasi-religious fervor on a seemingly rational historical foundation. And again like a religion, the ideology consciously dispensed with a serious attempt at verification of its basic contentions. Faith was enough.

But the main reason for the ready acceptance of the ideology was the fact that basically it presented what millions of Germans thought they believed in anyway; and it has indeed been one of our chief purposes here to show that, to a large extent, they were right. There was almost nothing that was new in the fundamental teachings of National Socialism. Every one of the components represented tradition, doctrine, or even dogma, which had long been common ideological property of the nation, its *Gedankengut*, its cultural heritage. One might well say that it was an anonymous *German* ideology which was merely vulgarized for the tastes of the petty bourgeois, intensified and put on a pedestal by national socialist propaganda. It had trickled down, through the generations, to the lower middle class which was to be the backbone of National Socialism and was to furnish most of its leaders. Much of the ideology, as we have seen, dated back to the nineteenth century, some to an earlier time. The ideas of the twentieth century had hardly reached that petty bourgeoisie, and the few that had, had made no significant impact or had been rejected. The staleness or obsolescence of the old ideas seemed to go without notice. Some have said that National Socialism was a last attempt to prolong the nineteenth century.

Of course, what Hitler did with these old ideas was no mean accomplishment. He presented them in fresh glory, dramatized and exalted them, intensified or magnified them, and skillfully wove them into a living whole which contrasted a coming utopia with all the then current misery and frustration that nearly every German felt. He was

able to articulate what the average German, more or less unconsciously, sensed and desired. He sanctioned old prejudices and gave
strength to mere uncertain longings. He rationalized human drives
and made them seem respectable or even desirable. All the old ideas
became "larger than life," and yet they were dragged down to a lower
intellectual level. Much was vulgarized and adapted to the needs of
mediocre men and of the young.

And above all, in Hitler's hands, the conglomerate of the old ideas
became a program for action. He was the one who had the courage of
everyone else's convictions and infused that courage into a great many
others. (As we have seen, he would have liked to scuttle a few of
the old ideas, but the average German was too deeply attached to
them to permit him to do so.) In any case, except for Hitler's driving
force toward action, National Socialism was not a sudden irrational
disaster that struck Germany, but it was a product of German intellectual history. National Socialism had been born long before Hitler
emerged and long before his National Socialist German Workers Party
was founded. The thoughts that later showed revolutionary power had
looked fairly tame in the thinking processes of the bourgeoisie of the
nineteenth century. They did not receive their explosive power until
Hitler came along.

With this ideology, a German could see his country's greatness
come to its long overdue fulfillment. Working for this fulfillment and
for these ideals could give intense happiness; it could be almost intoxicating. Helga Grebing[1] quotes from the memoirs of former dedicated National Socialists who describe their feelings of elation and
euphoria. They speak of being "filled with the happiness of being
allowed to participate and being so proud of carrying responsibility
in spite of our youth and inexperience," of an "almost ascetically radical self-sacrifice and devotion to the Reich," of "standing there as
Germany's trustee, which gave us . . . mysterious protection," of
"surpassing oneself in the service of something believed great, growing into a kind of infallibility," of "a cold, almost intoxicating feeling
of being superior" (in Poland). Achieving Germany's greatness would
be a little rough on some non-Germans (and even some Germans),
but this was inevitable under the "laws of nature and history."

[1]Grebing, *Der Nationalsozialismus — Ursprung und Wesen*, pp. 124-125.

At the same time, the ideology provided release for the vast reservoir of accumulated group hostility of many Germans, born of frustration and defeat. It provided also, as we have seen, satisfaction for the prevalent sadomasochistic drives, as well as easy rationalizations of these drives. All the boundless hatred and destructive tendencies, which previously could be indicated only to one's most intimate friends or within the family, suddenly turned out to be official policy, and, far from being objectionable, they were actually regarded as desirable. The rationalizations, which the ideology furnished, prevented the realization that the release of these drives amounted, in effect, to a reversion to primitive cultural levels.

Clearly, the great bulk of the ideology was uniquely German and had no counterpart elsewhere. It was truly *sui generis* and understood itself as such. Even nationalism and militarism, in their particular German setting, were of a special German kind. The ideology, except for one of its components, was never fit for export and was, indeed, never intended to be exported except perhaps to the "Nordic" countries. Hitler himself strongly objected to "all attempts to export the national socialist ideology."[2] (In this respect, the ideology differed sharply from Communism.) The sole exportable component was anti-Semitism. The national socialist rulers did make considerable efforts to propagate anti-Semitism in the occupied countries, and they did so with some degree of success, for example in France. But there was, of course, considerable latent anti-Semitism in most of these countries in any event. The fact that, on the whole, the ideology was so uniquely German accounts for much of the difficulty which other nations experienced at that time in trying to comprehend the motivations for German actions; and it still can be a source of difficulty to historians today. As Erik H. Erikson has said, the non-German did not realize that in Germany certain ideological concepts, such as the need for Lebensraum, "carried a conviction far beyond that of ordinary logic."[3]

Another result of the uniquely German character of the ideology may be that it passed into history without leaving a significant imprint on contemporary or subsequent ideologies of other nations.

[2] *Hitler's Table Talks*, p. 356. See also Albert Speer, *Erinnerungen*, p. 136.
[3] Erikson, *Childhood and Society*, p. 345.

Dictatorships in the Latin-American countries seem to have remained essentially what they have always been. It is possible, however, that in Greece the use of terror as a political instrument may have been more extensive than it would have been without the German example. It is conceivable, also, that this example gave some stimulus to such atrocities as American massacres of civilians in Vietnam. On the other hand, in at least one respect the German example, because of its monstrous radicalism, has had a deterrent effect. Anti-Semitism has been widely discredited and may now be at a historical low point.

In the face of this substantial ideological edifice, it seems impossible to agree with those historians and other writers[4] who contend, with varying degrees of emphasis, that National Socialism was not based on an ideology at all. Some see nothing but plain greed for power, a simple raw desire to rule the world, an overt discharge of low drives or other similar motivations. It is, in fact, tempting to take this view because one normally likes to associate "ideology" with some measure of respectability or even with "ideals." Moreover, if there was no ideology, the entire historical picture would be greatly simplified.

Other writers do not go quite that far. They do admit—sometimes grudgingly—that there was an ideology but say that it was used cynically merely as an instrument of power, for the manipulation of people, and as a mantle for the discharge of hostile drives.[5] J. C. Fest is clearly the most vocal and articulate protagonist of this line of thought. He speaks of "the cynicism of the practitioners of power . . . who had no faith in the ideologies but used them";[6] "ideological constructions as mere attractive window display or as means of concealment"; and "ideologically concealed discharges of drives."[7] At one

[4]For example Alan Bullock, *Hitler, A Study in Tyranny*, pp. 382, 806; K. Sontheimer in *The Path to Dictatorship 1918-1933*, edited by Fritz Stern, p. 34, and H. Krausnick, in ibid., pp. 134-135; Franz Neumann, *Behemoth: The Structure and Practice of National Socialism*, p. 467.

[5]More or less to this effect: Joachim C. Fest, *Das Gesicht des Dritten Reiches, passim.*; Grebing, op. cit., pp. 75, 87, Eva Reichmann, *Flucht in den Hass—Die Ursachen der deutschen Judenkatastrophe*, p. 229; perhaps also M. Broszat, "Soziale Motivation und Führerbindung des Nationalsozialismus," in *Vierteljahrshefte für Zeitgeschichte*, Heft 4, October 1970.

[6]Fest, op. cit., p. 408.

[7]Ibid., p. 403.

point, Fest almost seems to doubt that any genuine ideology existed because he says that "An epigrammatic formulation would be that National Socialism was propaganda which posed as ideology—that is, a will to power which formed its ideological theorems corresponding to their greatest psychological usefulness at a given time and which derived its postulates from superbly sensed moods of the masses and the directions of their drives."[8] Yet elsewhere Fest admits that National Socialism "was both, the exercise of domination and, at the same time, doctrine, each superimposed on the other and often intersected by it," and that the "decisive manifestations of power [by the regime] cannot be understood without an ideological motive, cursory and highly elusive as it sometimes was."[9]

At any rate, Fest makes very high intellectual demands on something that was never intended for intellectuals. As we have said, it was designed by mediocre men for mediocre people. The intellectual standards of the leadership were, on the average, very low indeed. Fest views what essentially was or had become a "beer-hall philosophy" of the lowest middle class through the eyes of a German *Akademiker* of a very high intellectual level, and he cannot stand what he sees. (At one point Fest speaks very aptly of an "intolerable, almost physically noticeable odor emanation" which rises from the ideological concepts of National Socialism—"an obscene ideological poor-people's odor."[10]) And above all, Fest's whole brilliant book is predominantly a biographical analysis of fifteen individuals, Hitler and fourteen other leaders, (resembling in some ways, a collection of case histories by a psychiatrist), and Fest thus looks primarily at these leaders and not at those whom they led. In most of the leaders the ideology took indeed second place to cynicism, lust for power, and considerations of expediency of mass domination. On many occasions the ideology was used as a tool for mass propaganda (but this is hardly anything very unusual in numerous countries even today). Göring once said that he had "joined the party because it was revolutionary, not because of that ideological stuff."[11] And Goebbels spoke of the typ-

[8]Ibid., p. 119.
[9]Ibid., p. 226.
[10]Ibid., p. 371.
[11]Douglas M. Kelley, *22 Cells in Nuremberg*, p. 64.

ical National Socialist as someone who "has in his heart and, what is most important, *in his fist*, whatever he does not have in his brain."[12] The climate was definitely anti-intellectual.

It should not be overlooked, however, that there were occasions when even some of the leaders, especially Hitler, Rosenberg, and perhaps Himmler, put ideological considerations above those of power and expediency. Rosenberg, the official "ideologist," carried no weight. But it should be recalled, for example, that upon Hitler's or perhaps Himmler's order railroad cars urgently required in Soviet Russia at the height of the war were diverted to transport Jews to the extermination camps; also, that Jewish laborers who were desperately needed in ammunition plants were shipped off to the camps; and that, in spite of all warnings by the "Eastern experts," the civilian populations of Poland and the Ukraine were treated so abominably as subhuman that they lost all interest in collaboration with the Germans. Another example is Hitler's extreme reluctance in 1941 to authorize Speer to use 30,000 construction workers for the urgently needed rebuilding of the destroyed railroad system in Russia, his reluctance being due to the fact that these construction workers were busy erecting his long-planned triumphal buildings and monuments in Berlin.[13] All these actions were ideologically motivated and ran counter to political or military expediency. They were by no means opportunistic.[14]

Hitler himself, in fact, attached the greatest importance to a solid ideology *(Weltanschauung)* as a foundation for political action. As early as in *Mein Kampf* he said that "Any power which does not spring from a firm intellectual foundation, will be wavering and insecure. It will lack the stability which can be found only in a fanatical ideology."[15] Speaking of his extensive reading in his early years in Vienna, he reported that "In that period there took shape in me a picture of the world and an ideology *(Weltanschauung)* which became a rocklike foundation for my subsequent actions."[16] Two of the chapters of his book were, indeed, entitled "Ideology and Party" and "Ideology and

---

[12]Reported by Fest, op. cit., p. 124. The indicated source is not clear.
[13]A. Speer, op. cit., p. 200.
[14]Fest, op. cit., p. 365, seems to disagree with this view.
[15]*Mein Kampf*, p. 188.
[16]Ibid., p. 21.

Organization." The whole book abounds in references to national socialist or *völkisch* ideology. In his inexpert and bombastic ways as a writer, Hitler made a strong attempt in *Mein Kampf* to forge an ideology for the German people. That he did not really succeed in presenting a coherent exposition of it does not detract from the importance which it had to him. (And if the outside world had taken the ideology seriously from the start, much distress might have been avoided later.)

The ideology thus remained largely "uncodified," but it was nevertheless very much alive in the unconscious and conscious of the German people, including the national socialist leadership, no matter how cynically they used it for political purposes.[17] The ideology was, in fact, what one took for granted. It was common property and, with few exceptions, was commonly accepted, at least as an imprecise, vague, blurred body of thoughts. To some, it represented idealism; to others, it amounted to a convenient arsenal of rationalizations of human drives, or the discharge of piled-up hostility, or it became this later. And with its inherent pugnaciousness and aggressiveness, it lent itself well to this purpose. In practical application, cruelty and brutality were a very likely result. To the leaders, the ideology was, in addition, a tool for manipulating the masses, for example, by an emotional statement of what the masses vaguely felt and wanted to hear more clearly expressed. Youth was particularly susceptible to the ideology's temptations because it paraded in the mantle of something revolutionary and new and, as presented by the leadership, it included a call for action. To the young, it looked like pure idealism, and they seemed impervious to the odor of the intellectually poor. Erikson speaks of the German "imagery of ideological adolescence."[18]

Frederick Hertz says that

A fully developed ideology comprises not only distinct political doctrines but also a particular interpretation of history and a specific philosophy. The substance of the national ideology con-

---

[17]Karl Dietrich Bracher, *Die deutsche Diktatur*, p. 22; George L. Mosse, *The Crisis of German Ideology*, pp. 1–2; and Eberhard Jäckel, *Hitlers Weltanschauung — Entwurf einer Herrschaft, passim.*, seem to be more or less in agreement with the views here stated.

[18]Erikson, *Childhood*, p. 344.

sists in ideas on the character of the nation and that of other nations, on the past, present and future of the nation, on its mission in the world, on the tasks of the state and on the duties of the individuals towards the nation.[19]

The national socialist ideology met all these tests. It makes no difference whether its reasoning and its ideological premises, aims, and objects were intelligent or not, or whether they were good or evil.

In the face of this extensive ideology and the actions based on it, it seemed naïve on the part of the prosecution and the courts at the Nuremberg trials to have characterized the defendants as mere "war criminals" and National Socialism as a mere "conspiracy to commit aggression," even if this may have been a "legal handle" by which the defendants could then be reached. As Edmund Vermeil puts it, "We are dealing not with a mere conspiracy, but with a conception of life, with a *Weltanschauung*."[20] The concepts of the war criminal and of a conspiracy still represented a conventional lawyer's approach to a case, the real nature of which was then not understood at all and which was, in fact, much too exceptional, vast, and amorphous to fit into any legal category. Also, as Hannah Arendt says very aptly, "never had a conspiracy, if such it was, needed fewer conspirators and more executors."[21] With respect to most actions, in fact, Hitler quite probably was the lone plotter. Sometimes Himmler may have plotted with him; the others were largely henchmen.

B. The Missing Elements

It is important to note also what elements the ideology did *not* contain. There was, above all, the astonishing total absence of sympathy, compassion, or humanitarian feelings for the peoples of other countries or for alien groups within Germany. Toward them the average German seemed to feel merely a vast group hostility. He appeared unable to identify with any outgroup. There was only "the great quiet in the face of inhumanity," as Ralf Dahrendorf has called it.[22] The

[19] Hertz, *Nationality in History and Politics*, p. 45.
[20] In M. Baumont (ed.), *The Third Reich*, p. 95.
[21] Arendt, *Eichmann in Jerusalem*, p. 153.
[22] Dahrendorf, *Gesellschaft und Demokratie in Deutschland*, p. 394.

forging of the new Reich took precedence over any humanitarian considerations. Any cruelty could be excused by the old German saying, repeated a thousand times, "Where timber is being planed, the shavings will fly" *(Wo gehobelt wird, da fliegen die Späne)*. Sympathy and compassion for other nations would, of course, have been incompatible with an ideology, the very essence of which was the promotion of power, force, and pugnaciousness as high ethical values.

There was also, generally speaking, contempt for education. According to Hitler, "the goal of . . . education" was to make selected children "physically tough, strong in character and mentally elastic,"[23] and "it makes much more sense to let . . . [children] spend as much time as possible in the fresh air."[24] "In some fields, any professional knowledge will have devastating results: it will lead away from the instinct. Man will be talked out of his instinct."[25] "The conflict between mind and physical strength will always be decided in favor of physical strength," he declared,[26] and this might well have been the motto of the semieducated petty bourgeoisie that represented the core and furnished most of the leadership of National Socialism. Real education had no place in the ideology. It would have been incompatible with the caliber of the leadership material who then dominated the country and more of whom were systematically being trained in special schools and in the Hitler Youth. It was better to be a fighter than a thinker. Moreover, unconsciously, the ruling group may have feared genuine education as a dangerous source of doubt which could undermine its questionable ideological foundations.

Another thing which, naturally, was completely absent from the ideology was democracy. It was incompatible with the Führer principle and was held in thorough contempt. Hitler declared in *Mein Kampf* that democracy "sins against nature's basic aristocratic principle"; that the majority "always represents not only stupidity but also cowardice"; that "Only the Jew can praise an institution [democracy] which is as dirty and dishonest as he is himself."[27] Twenty years later, he still said that "if the other countries adhere to their demo-

---

[23] *Hitler's Table Talks*, p. 275.
[24] Ibid., p. 423.
[25] Ibid., pp. 178–179.
[26] Ibid., p. 170.
[27] *Mein Kampf*, pp. 87, 89, 99.

cratic systems, they are certain to head for ruin."[28] The average German would have chosen less extreme formulations, but even he would have said that democracy was nonsense, that it would never work, and that Germany needed a strong man.

The picture of the world, and specifically of Germany, which the ideology conveyed was very much simpler than the picture which the democratic system of the Weimar Republic had half-heartedly attempted to form in the German mind. Under National Socialism, one did not have to bother with the complexities of the democratic ideology which, curiously enough, admitted that it was imperfect and which clearly was not functioning in practice in the Weimar Republic. At any rate, it was wholly outside of German traditions. By contrast, the national socialist ideology seemingly represented what one had always believed in; it appeared to link up with all the venerated traditions and guiding historical images.

C. Resemblances to Other Ideological Systems

Considering the uniquely German character of the ideology, it was remarkable how similar the system of national socialist government was to that of the Soviet Union. Here are some of the points of resemblance:

> Both were governed by strong dictators, the cult of personality being extensively developed.
>
> Both were one-party states by law.
>
> Both had parliamentary bodies whose sole function was to approve—and not to disapprove—the acts and proposals of the government.
>
> In both, there was severe party discipline and an extensive party apparatus with functions competing with those of the Administration.
>
> In both, the party maintained in the armed forces "commissars" or similar functionaries.
>
> Both tried to maintain a theory of permanent revolution and warned against any counterrevolutionary activities.

[28] *Hitler's Table Talks*, p. 356.

In both, there was strict censorship, and the government dictated the standards for literature and the arts.

In both, the ideology claimed the status of an infallible dogma, and any nonbeliever was regarded as an enemy.

In both, the government assumed the right of total education and coordination of the entire society, and of total suppression of all opposition by terror or otherwise.

In both, the people had no control whatever over their government which claimed, however, complete identity between its interests and those of the people.

These were, indeed, the hallmarks of totalitarian rule. It is clear that National Socialism had learned much from Soviet Communism — far more than from Italian fascism.[29] And it is not surprising, then, that Hitler had much admiration for Stalin. "We have to have unqualified respect for Stalin . . . In his own way, he is clearly a man of genius!"[30] The *Table Talks* contain various additional flattering references to him.[31] But in calling Stalin a genius in 1942, Hitler, of course, was paying a considerable compliment to himself because he had previously succeeded in deceiving and duping Stalin to an almost incredible extent.

It is true also, however, that the national socialist ideology never developed the severe scholasticism and scholastic rigidity of Communism. Its programs were left more unclear — often romantically blurred — and they were subject to varying interpretations, depending sometimes on the political moods and developments of the moment. But as Broszat has pointed out, most of Hitler's voters hardly regarded this as a disadvantage. On the contrary, to many of them, this seemed to be evidence of flexibility and vitality.[32]

Another ideological system that resembles National Socialism in some respects is Catholicism. Hitler, while filled with hatred for the

[29]Relative to the whole subject, see Les K. Adler and Thomas G. Paterson, "The Merger of Nazi Germany and Soviet Russia in the American Image of Totalitarianism," in *American Historical Review*, Vol. 75, No. 4, April 1970, pp. 1046 et seq.

[30]*Hitler's Table Talks*, p. 468.

[31]Ibid., pp. 200, 270, 332, 465. See also A. Zoller, *Hitler privat*, p. 158, and Werner Maser, *Adolf Hitler: Legende, Mythos, Wirklichkeit*, p. 226.

[32]Broszat, "Soziale Motivation und Führerbindung des Nationalsozialismus," in *Vierteljahrshefte für Zeitgeschichte*, Heft 4, October 1970, p. 395.

Catholic Church (or any Church), nevertheless had much admiration for it. He regarded it as a "highly instructive model" in some respects. He spoke of its "incredibly robust strength," and said that the Church "had very properly understood that its power of resistance . . . was founded . . . on its rigid adherence to dogmas once they have been laid down."[33] He praised particulary the method of electing the Pope and saw in it a model for electing a future German Führer.[34] Adorno says that "Psychologically, fascist hierarchies may function largely as secularizations and substitutes of ecclesiastical ones. It is not accidental that Nazism arose in Southern Germany with its strong Roman-Catholic tradition."[35] (Austria, Hitler's home country, was even more strongly Catholic.) Erik H. Erikson, too, has compared the Catholic Church to totalitarianism. In speaking of the fact that the Church makes its dogma "the exclusive condition for *any* identity on earth," Erikson said:

> The Roman Church . . . made this total claim totalitarian by using terror. In this case (as in others) the terror was not always directly applied to quivering bodies; it was predicted for a future world, typically in such a way that nobody could quite know whom it would hit, or when. . . . As in the case of all terror, the central agency can always claim not to be responsible for the excessive fervor of its operatives. . . ."[36]

The great effect which Hitler's intensely religious Catholic upbringing had on him and on National Socialism will be discussed more in detail in the chapter on Hitler's religiousness. We should here mention, however, that other high national socialist leaders, particularly Himmler, Goebbels, and Höss, had also received a deeply pious Catholic education. It might be worthwhile, someday, to investigate a possible relationship between Catholicism and National Socialism, in a manner similar to Max Weber's investigation of Protestantism and capitalism.

[33] *Mein Kampf,* pp. 481, 512-513.
[34] *Hitler's Table Talks,* pp. 228, 236.
[35] T. W. Adorno (and others), *The Authoritarian Personality,* p. 734.
[36] Erikson, *Young Man Luther,* pp. 181-182.

D. The Practice of National Socialism

Implicit in the entire national socialist ideology was a nearly complete and deliberate destruction of political morality in international as well as domestic politics. Of course, a lack of morality in international politics is scarcely anything new. Machiavellism, realpolitik, and similar doctrines have long been generally acceptable. But it was Hitler and National Socialism who stripped international politics bare of any pretense of morality. "Politics . . . is not only a nation's fight for its very life but . . . it is the art of carrying this fight through."[37] In other words, his politics went for the jugular. Any lie and deception were justified. "The victor is not going to be asked later whether he told the truth or not,"[38] which may have carried some implication that the loser could not ask because he was dead.

Accordingly, assurances of all sorts concerning German peaceful intentions were convincingly presented to other governments, while preparations for war were under way. The famous nonaggression treaty with the Soviet Union was entered into without the remotest intention of keeping it. In fact, until the start of the invasion of the Soviet Union, Germany, as part of the scheme of deception, made extensive shipments of strategic materials to that country. Bracher[39] points out that there was a definite scheme which proved effective on various occasions. It consisted of far-reaching political demands, secret planning, emphatic assurances of peaceful intentions, successful surprise attack—followed by immediate assurances addressed "to the world" that this was the last assertion of German rights and that there were no further demands, the way to friendship now being open. In some respects, that scheme resembled the tactics, discussed earlier, by which the European Jews, in country after country, were induced to go to their death without resistance.

The majority of Germans accepted their Führer's radical realpolitik with a satisfied smile about his cleverness, undisturbed by the total lack of political morality, and not overly concerned by brutalities

[37] *Hitlers Zweites Buch,* p. 47.
[38] Speech of Aug. 22, 1939, Max Domarus, *Hitlers Reden und Proklamationen 1932–1945,* p. 1238.
[39] Bracher, op. cit., p. 333.

and cruelties. After the politically impoverished years of the Weimar Republic and the humiliations then suffered at the hands of the Western Powers, the sudden, astonishingly successful assertion of the German position looked to most Germans very good indeed. Moral scruples were at a minimum or did not exist at all. In place of scruples, there frequently was cynicism and contempt for human rights and dignity.

Moreover, there no longer was an effective counterbalance by the values of classicism and the Enlightenment, humaneness or tolerance. These values, in fact, had for a hundred years receded further and further, and their surviving genuine protagonists were rather few. This, however, was something that neither the British, the French, the German Jews, nor the Germans themselves were ready to see and believe. On the whole, most of them still took a kind of Neo-Hellenistic view of Germany. They still saw the country of Goethean classicism, of *Weltgeist*, of the great philosophers, poets, and composers. Most Germans thought that they had as much *Kultur* as ever, and they talked and wrote about it a good deal.

The amount of self-deception that prevailed in Germany was astonishing, from Hitler down to the most ordinary citizen. Thus Hitler himself said in his *Table Talks:* "The period from the middle of the third to the middle of the seventeenth century was surely the most cruel era of a human low point. Thirst for blood, meanness and lies dominated that period."[40] And he condemned the medieval Catholic Church for its "extreme brutality"—"thousands of burnings of valuable people." "Today, we are much more humane than the Church."[41] Hitler made these statements in January and April, 1942, that is, at a time when the *Einsatzgruppen*, upon his order, were busy killing hundreds of thousands of Jews and others behind the front lines in the Soviet Union, when millions of Soviet prisoners of war had already been permitted to die from starvation and neglect, and when untold numbers of inmates of concentration camps, Jews and non-Jews, had already been put to death. Yet Hitler evidently regarded the Middle Ages as more cruel, brutal, and bloodthirsty than his own era, and there is no reason to assume that in these statements

[40] *Hitler's Table Talks,* p. 167.
[41] Ibid., p. 267 (indirect speech transposed).

he was trying to deceive his dinner companions. This was what he believed. It is clear, also, that he did not see that the brutalities of his era might be doing damage to the German *Kultur* of which he frequently boasted. If anyone at the dinner table had disagreed and had dared to say so, Hitler might have answered that the cruelties of his time, as distinguished from those of the Middle Ages, were directed against subhumans whose destruction was called for by the laws of nature. Nature is cruel, was a frequent answer in the national socialist ideology. Few recognized that a reversion to nature might derogate from, or destroy, their *Kultur*.

Himmler, too, indulged in vast self-deception. He spoke of not wanting to have other countries benefit "from our completely innocent soul with its warmth of feeling [*Gemüt*], . . . our good nature, our idealism," and he said that "We Germans, who are the only people in the world with a decent attitude toward animals, will, of course, take a decent attitude also toward these human animals [Russians and Czechs]."[42] The belief in the risks created by the innocent German soul, *Gemüt*, good nature, and idealism had, indeed, been very common in Germany for a long time; and these qualities had frequently been branded as dangerous by German politicians long before Himmler. It is, of course, a fact that many Germans possessed such qualities, but it is true also that they represented only one side of their character and coexisted with sadomasochism (accompanied by destructive tendencies), strong group hostility, etc.

Under the national socialist regime, even some elementary moral principles of everyday life atrophied quickly—a process which had begun even before Hitler. Thus in the early days of the regime when Jews were still tolerated in Germany but were deprived of the right to sue non-Jews in the courts, non-Jews discontinued paying rent to their Jewish landlords. Jewish businesses were taken over by competitors for nominal payments under the pressure of anticipated emigration. In the police stations, Jews were addressed, not by name, but as "Jewish swine" *(Judenschwein)*. Some public bathing places displayed signs reading "Dogs and Jews are prohibited from bathing." At the reception center of Dachau Concentration Camp, the clerk who recorded the personal data of newly arrived Jews would not ask for

---

[42] Himmler's Posen speech, *TMWC*, XXIX, p. 122, Doc. PS-1919.

"your mother's maiden name" but would ask "What Jew-whore shit you out?"[43] When Jews were forced to emigrate or were deported "to the East," non-Jews did not hesitate to move into their abandoned apartments. It should be noted that none of these actions were required by any law or decree. They were voluntary actions of ordinary citizens in disregard of elementary moral concepts or principles of human dignity. There was in those days much *Schadenfreude,* that is, much glee and gloating over the misfortunes of the enemies of the regime.

But it should be added that these were not the attitudes of all Germans of that period. A good many had preserved ethical and humanitarian standards and felt ashamed of the actions of the government and their fellow citizens. A few even spoke out in the face of the official terror.

While the atrophy of the old values and standards had begun long before Hitler, it was greatly accelerated under him. One reason was that National Socialism succeeded in replacing them by an imaginary world of new values drawn from the edifice of national socialist ideology. The atrophy of the old values was facilitated by the severe censorship of the press and publishing houses, which prevented the people from hearing warning voices from the outside. In fact, by the use of outright lies the propaganda organization and the controlled press could make the people believe that Hitler's ideas and policies found strong approval in various other countries. (One banner headline in a German newspaper read: "U.S. acclaims Hitler.") No true standards of comparison with foreign ethical values were available. And any criticism within Germany was, of course, ruthlessly suppressed.

One myth about National Socialism (and other totalitarian or authoritarian systems) which should be laid to rest is the widely believed theory that the "monolithic" nature of this form of government invested it with a degree of efficiency, orderliness, stability, and speed of action which no democracy could hope to rival.[44] At best, if at all,

[43]Richard Grunberger, *The 12-Year Reich,* p. 330.

[44]Opposed to this theory are, among others, Bracher, op. cit., pp. 258, 505; J. C. Fest, *Das Gesicht des Dritten Reiches,* pp. 175–176, 406; Arendt, *Eichmann in Jerusalem,* p. 152; Arendt, *Origins,* pp. 395–409. Miss Arendt, however, credits the national socialist leadership with a kind of diabolical supercleverness which men of their caliber were hardly likely to possess.

such a comparison was true in relation to National Socialism only during an early brief period, that is, before the democracies were able to catch their breath after the hammer blows of Hitler's initial surprise attacks. But it was a theory easily believed in the more disorderly democracies, particularly in times of crises; and it was indeed a theory that any totalitarian regime finds it useful to spread at home and abroad. Bracher calls it "the lie essential to the life of all authoritarian movements, then as now."[45]

It seems more likely that there can be highly efficient democracies and highly inefficient authoritarian systems and vice versa, depending on the particular leadership, its popular acceptance, the character of the people, and the particular crisis situation in which the country may find itself. But one thing is sure: the national socialist regime itself—after its first few years of life—came close to being a form of governmental chaos. One reason for this was the frequently concurrent and competitive administrative functions of the state and of the National Socialist Party. Many levels of the administration itself suffered from a duplication of officials and of whole departments, appointed from above, whose precise area of competency, as against its rival, was left unclear. Often when some official (or his whole department) fell from favor at the top, he was told nothing, but a new official or department was appointed with a slightly different title— and the two would acrimoniously function in competition with each other. The history of the period abounds in petty quarrels, rivalries, and intrigues, to an extent which is almost unbelievable and makes for tiresome reading. Moreover, there was a feeling of insecurity, or even fear of the general terror, on the part of many officials, which was hardly conducive to governmental efficiency. There was much protective maneuvering, buck-passing, favor-seeking, and the like, which prevented quick and rational decisions.

In the structure of the national socialist hierarchy, Hitler himself seemed to be the only one who could adjust all the countless fights and quarrels among the members of his Party and Administration and who could establish some measure of uneasy peace. Hitler was really the only one who stood above the disorder of conflicting competencies, and his acknowledged right to be the final arbiter greatly strengthened his own position. It enabled him to play off one against the other. Bracher says[46] that Hitler used this principle with virtuosity. Yet Bracher adds that "it will remain in dispute" . . . "to what extent this was fully intended or was rather a manifestation of the fitful moods of the Führer and of his Movement." Bracher calls the whole phenomenon "guided chaos." Similarly, Fest describes the system as "structurally predominately chaotic."[47]

That there might have been some measure of deliberateness in this guided chaos seems indicated by Albert Speer's memoirs. He says that it was "occasionally" Hitler's "principle to appoint two or three competing partners for one job,"[48] and that he "did not like to delimit competencies clearly from each other. Sometimes, he intentionally charged persons or departments with identical or similar tasks. 'Then,' Hitler liked to say, 'the stronger one will prevail.'"[49] Nevertheless, it seems almost unbelievable that Hitler could have intended a governmental chaos of the proportions that did exist. (Speer even reports that occasionally Hitler gave independent instructions to two different people to bid on his behalf at art auctions for the same art object without limit of amount, the result being that their competitive bids caused an enormous increase in the price.[50]) It is more likely that much of the chaos was due to Hitler's highly unsystematic working habits, his dislike of administrative detail, his general sloppiness, laziness, indifference, his reluctance to confront his old collaborators with an announcement of their replacement, as well as to what Speer calls "Hitler's conception of an improvised state leadership by an impulsive genius."[51] Besides, at least some of Hitler's administrative decisions may have been arrived at largely as a result of neurotic processes within himself—fury at being "rejected" by someone, an accumulation of general hostility, sadism stimulated by someone's weakness, and so forth.

One might well ask how this poorly structured, chaotic or near-chaotic Administration managed to succeed so well for some years in subjugating not only the German people but most of Europe and much of the Soviet Union. The reasons are diverse: There was the

[46]Ibid., p. 233.
[47]J. C. Fest, op. cit., p. 406.
[48]Speer, *Erinnerungen*, p. 194
[49]Ibid., p. 225
[50]Ibid., p. 194.
[51]Ibid., p. 224.

use of surprise, unorthodoxy, sheer power, and terror; and there was the fact that the regime, in the lower echelons, had inherited a highly stable and efficient corps of dedicated public servants as well as a highly disciplined, well-organized, effective, loyal army, and, finally, a well-functioning industrial machine. (The latter was kept functioning well or was even improved by one of the regime's few stable personalities, Albert Speer.) Thus, while there was near-chaos at the top, there was excellent organization below. In the early stages, the allied powers were unable to match many of the German advantages, and there were plenty of unsystematic working habits, confusion of competencies, and sloppiness on their side. In fact, the Soviet Union had been most severely handicapped by the purges of the Stalin era. The Russian chaos at the top was then possibly even greater than the German.

And the "guided chaos" or near-chaos at the top also had its advantages from the point of view of a totalitarian regime. The amorphous structure of various government departments and the unending conflicts of competency among them were highly baffling to the individual citizen. He could not always know how to identify the ones who governed and perhaps tormented him. If he was taken away in the middle of the night, neither his lawyer nor his relatives knew where to turn. The general confusion gave the regime a kind of slippery unassailability, even when it was not intended. And sometimes it *was* intended, as in the case of the so-called Night and Fog *(Nacht und Nebel)* Decree.

One attribute of the National Socialist Movement was that it became increasingly radical as time went on and as success piled on success. This became clear, for example, in relation to the anti-Jewish actions, which started mildly with the deprivation of Jews of their civil rights, proceeded to forced emigration, and on to (unrealized) plans for mass resettlement in Madagascar, to concentration in Polish ghettos, forced labor, killing operations by the *Einsatzgruppen*, and, finally, systematic mass murder in the extermination camps. Adorno, in fact, found that "The extreme anti-Semite cannot stop" and "Hatred is reproduced and enhanced in an almost automatized, compulsive manner which is both utterly detached from the reality of the object and completely alien to the ego."[52] But the process of the radicalization

---

[52] Adorno (and others), *The Authoritarian Personality*, p. 633.

of the Movement was by no means confined to the anti-Jewish actions. It extended to the hatred of all designated outgroups, domestic and foreign. Speer reports that Goebbels and Bormann "relentlessly tried to radicalize Hitler ideologically."[53] There was more and more inclination among the extremists to let members of outgroups perish or even to murder them. The treatment in the concentration camps became increasingly worse, and few could survive it. Millions of Soviet prisoners of war were permitted to die. Even quite irrational political decisions were made, seemingly born out of hatred, such as the declaration of war on the United States.[54]

In the end, it seemed that Hitler even came to regard the German people itself as an enemy. He told Speer that "if the war is going to be lost . . . there is no need to pay any attention to the basic requirements of the German people for its most primitive further existence. On the contrary, it is better that we ourselves destroy these things."[55] He issued his "scorched earth order" for Germany, but he was no longer able to enforce it. In general, what Adorno said about the extreme anti-Semite was hardly much less true of the extreme National Socialist: "[He] . . . pursue[s] his hatred beyond any limits . . . to prove to himself and to others that he *must* be right. . . . [He] silences the remnants of his own conscience by the extremeness of his attitude. He seems to terrorize himself even while he terrorizes others."[56]

Tenaciously, even in the face of the approaching catastrophe, the national socialist leadership and its followers held on to their convictions and to their basic dream for the future. They were sure that they, being Germanic, were racially stronger, and they knew that in nature the stronger cannot lose. In *Mein Kampf*, Hitler had predicted victory for the racially conscious "in accordance with almost mathematically definite laws."[57] There could be no doubt that in the end the Germans would be able to subdue or exterminate the weaker and the subhumans, and to conquer the Lebensraum which Nature granted to the stronger. As we have seen, they envisioned in their

[53]Speer, op. cit., p. 136.
[54]See, in this connection, Ernest R. May, "Nazi Germany and the United States," in *Journal of Modern History*, Vol. 41, No. 2, June 1969, p. 207.
[55]Speer, op. cit., p. 446.
[56]Adorno, op. cit., p. 633.
[57]*Mein Kampf*, p. 782.

dream an empire from the Atlantic Ocean to the Black Sea, with its capital "Germania." The most important area in all this immense territory would be Southern Russia, a kind of "Eurasian heartland," which was to be a real German colony, a breadbasket that would furnish untold riches. It would be crisscrossed by vast *Autobahnen* for use by the German conquerors who would live in strings of fortified Germanic settlements. The native population, as Himmler put it, was to be available "as a leaderless working people" and would be "called upon to cooperate in [Germany's] eternal cultural accomplishments [*Kulturtaten*] and monuments."[58] Himmler usually had a special gift in such pronouncements for reaching an even lower level than Hitler could reach, but here it should be noted that Hitler had approved Himmler's Memorandum, finding it "very good and correct."[59]

There was no interest in maintaining the native population. Medical service was, therefore, to be limited, and "I prohibit the introduction of steps for cleanliness, like our own, into those territories." "Vaccination requirements are to be valid there for Germans only."[60] Even dental treatment was to be very limited. On the other hand, Hitler "would personally shoot any idiot" who wants to prevent the sale of means for abortion because "we can only welcome it if women and girls have the largest possible number of abortions."[61] It was a philosophy of hate and utter contempt for the subhumans, "these human animals" as Himmler later called them.

All in all, National Socialism looked at Europe, including Germany itself, as if it were a thoroughly neglected animal farm which urgently needed the elimination of racially poor and unhealthy stock, better breeding methods, etc. It was reminiscent of Himmler's past occupation as a chicken breeder. But all these fantastic schemes were presented in pretentious earnestness and with an expression of sincere concern for the future of Germany and Europe. All of Europe and the East were finally to make biological sense, and Germany, in all this, was to be the *Ordnungsmacht*, that is, the power which would put

---

[58] For this and further details see Himmler's Memorandum concerning the Treatment of Aliens in the East *(Denkschrift Himmlers über die Behandlung der Fremdvölkischen im Osten)* of May 25, 1940, reprinted in *Vierteljahrshefte für Zeitgeschichte* Heft 5, 1957, pp. 194–198. See also *Hitler's Table Talks*, pp. 270–272, 330.

[59] See the Preface to the last-mentioned Himmler Memorandum, p. 194.

[60] *Hitler's Table Talks*, p. 272.

[61] Ibid., p. 469.

order into a chaotic community. It was a measure of the abnormal ideological conceptions of German society in general that a substantial portion of it could succumb to some or all of such ideas.

At the same time, the war was to be the final all-determining fight against Communism as well as the western plutocracies, both of which, strangely enough, in spite of their not inconsiderable differences, were declared to be dominated by international Jewry, the arch enemy. Nearly every nation, plus the Jews, could thus be properly hated as an outgroup.

Altogether, it was a world of fantasy and fabrication, and, in its final concepts and schemes, its distance from reality became enormous. It was probably characteristic of this kind of intellectual milieu that a good many members of the leadership (excluding Hitler) believed in such things as horoscopes and occult knowledge, dietetic and medical fads, nature wisdom, etc. (but these things have always had extraordinary appeal to Germans). Even the swastika symbol, suggesting as it does something ancient, mysterious, occult, yet grimly cruel, fits into this picture of a world distant from modern Western reality. As a national flag, the swastika banner was a symbol of Germany's alienation from the family of western nations, and of the fact that the country represented a different, more cruel and threatening civilization.

Hitler tenaciously held on to his basic tenets to the last day of his life. In his final message, which he handed to Col. Nicolaus von Bredow for delivery to General Keitel, he said that "The aim must still be to win territory in the East for the German people."[62] And in his "Political Testament," which he dictated a little earlier, he still spoke of a future "realization of a genuine racial community" and he said "Above all, I enjoin the leaders of the nation and their followers carefully to observe the racial laws and mercilessly to resist the universal poisoner of all nations, international Jewry."[63] It was all unchanged from *Mein Kampf.* With the Russians fighting in the streets of Berlin, these old aims of Hitler made no sense at all (assuming they had ever made sense).

[62]Col. von Bredow destroyed this message but reconstructed it later. See H. R. Trevor-Roper, *The Last Days of Hitler,* 3d ed., pp. 252–253.

[63]The only publication of the complete German text of the private and political testaments seems to be in *TMWC,* Vol. XLI, pp. 548–554. A faulty English translation can be found in George H. Stein (ed.), *Hitler,* pp. 83–87.

Hitler's death and the collapse of his regime left behind it merely the tracks of millions of senseless murders and of untold misery and suffering. The Jerusalem court in the Eichmann trial said quite correctly that sufferings on so gigantic a scale were "beyond human understanding."[64] It seems that human emotions are structured in such a way that they can be deeply affected only by the suffering of individuals or families or small groups. Anything larger cannot really be comprehended, and figures like six million killed Jews or three million dead Russian prisoners are apt to be mere statistics. We are unable to grasp the total of the suffering which these figures imply. Bettelheim says that "Our feelings are always the feelings of the small community or group. . . . We still have not learned to master the experience of the total mass state. We really can think only in the order of magnitude of individuals and not of magnitudes of millions — at least most of us."[65] Bettelheim thinks that this is the reason why an effort was made in Jerusalem (unsuccessfully) to establish that Eichmann once killed a small Jewish boy with his own hands, even though this would have changed nothing about his guilt in causing the death of millions. "But if they had been able to prove him guilty of one murder with his own hands, then he would have done something that we could comprehend. . . ."[66] Perhaps the Jerusalem court was right in saying also that making us understand these gigantic sufferings was a matter "for great authors and poets,"[67] but it is doubtful whether even they could overcome what may be an elemental human disability.

It should be remembered, in this connection, that Hitler himself never witnessed a single execution in person. He merely gave orders for the killing of "all Jews," "all commissars," "all Gypsies." In human terms, he cannot have comprehended the extent of the horrors he had loosed.

[64] Arendt, *Eichmann*, p. 211.
[65] Bruno Bettelheim in *Die Kontroverse*, p. 93.
[66] Ibid., p. 95.
[67] Arendt, *Eichmann*, p. 211.

Chapter 10

Miscellaneous Theories Bearing on the Evolution of National Socialism

Our discussion of the nature and origins of the various ideological components may have explained a good deal, but it is still necessary to consider certain historical and emotional developments in Germany which may have greatly contributed to the rise and acceptance of the ideology. Some of the miscellaneous assortment of theories, with which we shall briefly deal in this chapter, may indeed approach the more basic reasons why some components of the ideology could have gained acceptance in the first place, either by way of rationalization of emotional drives or otherwise. It is, in fact, possible that parts of the ideology were themselves mere "symptoms" and not ultimate causes or that certain components of the ideology represented mere intermediate stages in a progressive process of development or, as it were, disease.

A. "Spirit of Place"—*Furor Teutonicus*

It has been suggested that the habitat of the old Teutons in the brooding, dark, primeval German forests may be the most important single key to the recent happenings. And while this evidently leads to an inaccessible psychological swamp of a prehistoric age, it is worth mentioning that Lawrence Durrell, a gifted explorer of the "spirit of place," maintains that "human beings are expressions of their landscape" and that "they exist in nature, as a function of place." He speaks of "the hidden magnetic fields which the landscape is trying to communicate to the personality." "I don't believe [he says] the British character, for example, or the German has changed a jot since

Tacitus first described it."[1] And Tacitus, it will be recalled, already spoke of the *furor teutonicus* which gave the Romans considerable trouble.

It is possible that, since pre-Christian days, nature and mythological concepts of folkdom, blood and soil, fight and heroism have always held central place in the German psyche, at least in the unconscious. The mythology has, to an extent, survived in the *Nibelungenlied* to this day. Romanticism and Richard Wagner, in his *Ring*, did much to bring these concepts back into the conscious. We may once more quote Freud's statement: "It should be especially emphasized that every item which returns from oblivion gains acceptance with particular force, carries incomparable weight with the masses, and makes irresistible claims to truth, against which logical objections remain powerless."[2] And the psychiatrist Erich Fromm discusses the return of archaic impulses specifically in relation to the Germans:

> Millions of Germans, especially those of the lower middle class, ... reverted under the leadership of Adolf Hitler to their teutonic ancestors' cult of "going berserk." ... For the majority the archaic form of experience is always a real possibility; it *can* emerge. ... Specific circumstances such as war ... or social disintegration can easily open up the channels, permitting the repressed archaic impulses to surge forward.[3]

Clearly, however, any derivation from a prehistoric ancestry can be hardly more than guesswork and speculation. It is beyond any controllable observation. What was, however, still observable in the recent German character, in public and particularly in private life, was a certain easily induced uncontrolled fury or rage which, in Germany, seemed to be generally regarded as acceptable. This is what Helmuth Plessner presumably meant when he said that ". . . the Germans . . . take pleasure in seeing themselves in the role of a volcano, the eruptive manifestations of which quite normally do include lack of all moderation, and ferocity — an alleged privilege derived from a

[1]L. Durrell, "Landscape and Character," in *Spirit of Place*, New York, 1969, pp. 156–163.

[2]Sigmund Freud, "Der Mann Moses und die monotheistische Religion," in *Gesammelte Werke*, Vol. 16, p. 190.

[3]Fromm, *The Heart of Man*, p. 121.

natural predisposition which the Romans already attested to the Germans as *furor teutonicus*."[4] Going beyond this, Toynbee sees in the extermination policies of National Socialism "a primaeval wickedness and cruelty that were innate in Human Nature," and he makes the sweeping statement that ". . . civilization was no permanent transfiguration of the essence of Human Nature, but was merely a 'brittle cake of custom' precariously plastered over the crater of a live spiritual volcano where it was at the mercy of perennial eruptions of Original Sin."[5] But this leaves open the fundamental question why the "perennial eruptions" took place in Germany and not in other countries of Western civilization.

B. Martin Luther as Spiritual Grandfather

We reach somewhat more solid (though still dubious) ground when we come to consider another theory which has been rather frequently cited as indicating what we might call a "basic cause" of at least one element of National Socialism. This is the theory that German Protestantism, particularly Martin Luther himself, was the real spiritual grandfather of German obedience to the ruler and blind trust in higher authority. It was Luther who propagated St. Paul's dictum that all government is of God. And according to Luther, even bad rulers were appointed by God and were His punishment for the sins of the ruler's subjects. The ruler had to be obeyed, no matter how wicked and unjust he might be. An often-quoted statement by Luther was that it is better that a tyrant do wrong a hundred times than that the people do wrong once to the tyrant. (This, in fact, was rather similar to the pronouncement by the historian Heinrich von Treitschke, centuries later, that the individual has no right to resist the authority of the state, even if he regards it as immoral.) Luther, thus, could be said to have contributed greatly to the firm establishment of an authoritarian type of government in the Protestant sections of Germany. He was a forceful teacher of submissiveness to authority and was what we would today call a strong antiliberal and antidemocratic influence. One might even go so far as to see in Luther's anti-Roman

[4]Plessner, *Die verspätete Nation*, p. 22.
[5]A. Toynbee, *Study of History*, Vol. VIII, p. 273.

struggles an origin of the later German rejection of Western thought in general.

It thus may be tempting to draw a line from Luther to National Socialism, across 400 years of time and across countless intervening events and a vast output of sharply different ideas and ideologies. But one obvious difficulty with this facile theory is that National Socialism was not, in fact, born or raised in Protestant northern Germany but rather in Catholic Bavaria, and that its immediate spiritual father, Hitler, was brought up in Austria as a devout Catholic. The cradle of National Socialism stood in Munich, a thoroughly Catholic city. Not only Hitler but also other prominent leaders of National Socialism, for instance, Himmler and Goebbels, had received a strict Catholic education. No statistics are available as to the number of the original founding members of the National Socialist Party in Munich who were Catholic or Protestant, but it is quite likely that most of them were Catholic.

Hitler probably knew little of Luther. In *Mein Kampf,* Luther is not mentioned at all, though there is a discussion of the regrettable cleavage in the religious denominations. In the *Table Talks,* however, Hitler speaks of Luther as "a mighty man . . . who shook the Church severely in its foundations," but at the same time Hitler derogated from Protestantism in general by saying that Luther's successors were "only undistinguished imitators."[6] His comments on Protestantism were unfavorable throughout. He accused it of paving the way to "moral hypocrisy," and said that "in a controversy with the Catholic Church, the Protestant Church cannot be rated as an opponent of stature." He declared that "a certain protestant sanctimoniousness is even worse than the Catholic Church," and he characterized the Protestant Church as a "northern glacier phenomenon,"[7] Coming from a Southerner like Hitler, this was severe condemnation. The antagonism between the Protestant North and the Catholic South was, in fact, strong at all times in Germany, even apart from religion, as indicated from the Northern end, for example, by Bismarck's (alleged) statement that "a Bavarian is a cross between a human being and an Austrian."

---

[6]*Hitler's Table Talks,* p. 259. On p. 133 his statements seem ambivalent.
[7]Ibid., pp. 335, 260, 153 (indirect speech transposed).

It is thus very unlikely that Hitler's own ideology, and that of his immediate disciples, was affected by Luther or Protestantism in any positive sense. But this is not inconsistent with the theory that Luther's teachings of submissiveness to authority and even to "the tyrant" contributed a good deal to the general North-German willingness to accept the Hitler regime and to give it unconditional obedience. A prominent German historian, Gerhard Ritter, has said that

> It is from Lutheranism that the German derives (at least in part) the inclination not to demand very much political "liberty," once he is in possession of purely spiritual freedom, but to have blind confidence in his rulers and to rely on the "conscientiousness" of the governors rather than on politically organized control by the governed. The aversion of the German intellectuals to too close a contact with politics, their much-discussed trait of unworldliness, is genuinely Lutheran.[8]

But, then, we should not lose sight of the fact that the Catholic Bavarians and Austrians accepted and obeyed Hitler with even greater enthusiasm than the North-German Protestants. Evidently, then, the former's enthusiasm was fed from other springs. This could not have been their Catholicism because Hitler never made this a basis for any of his appeals; and, as time went on, he became increasingly hostile to *all* churches. It seems questionable, under all the circumstances, to what extent, if any, a Lutheran ancestry can be claimed for any element of National Socialism.

C. Napoleon and German Revulsion Against the West

In the chapter on German Romanticism, we discussed the German rejection of Western ideas because they seemed to have been brought to Germany by Napoleon's invading and occupying armies. But this rejection reached far beyond Romanticism, and more need be said about it here. It is a fact that before the Napoleonic Wars—approxi-

---

[8]Ritter, "Die Ausprägung deutscher und westeuropäischer Geistesart im konfessionellen Zeitalter," in *Historische Zeitschrift*, Vol. CXLIX, No. 2, 1934, pp. 247-248. In a later essay, "The Historic Foundations of the Rise of National-Socialism," in A. Baumont (ed.), *The Third Reich*, footnote on p. 388, Ritter takes a rather different position.

mately between 1650 and 1800—the civilization of the numerous small and large German states was genuinely European and oriented toward the West, producing such supranational figures as Bach, Händel, Goethe, Schiller, and outstanding philosophers. Originally the ideas of the French Revolution were, in fact, received by the Germans with enthusiasm, and even Napoleon found a number of accomplices among the German states (including Prussia itself). But revulsion set in very quickly when Napoleon's plans for a permanent division and disunity of the German states were understood, and particularly after he had crushingly defeated Prussia at Jena in 1806 and had imposed the harsh Peace of Tilsit on that country in 1807. In fact, as stated before, the year 1806 was one of the most important turning points in German history. Edmond Vermeil speaks of a "startling change of course which was conceivable only in Germany, from a perfectly genuine lack of interest in things national to a fanatical Pan-Germanism."[9]

In no time at all, nearly everything French was regarded with deep suspicion, and this included the humanitarian and democratic principles of the French Revolution. The Germans saw that the French, far from bringing them liberty and equality, had brought them foreign imperialism. It was a case of a deep German feeling of being rejected and of an intense reaction to it. We discussed before the leading German thinkers turning inwards, Fichte's all-important *Addresses to the German Nation*, the developing consciousness of a German uniqueness, the budding concept of the German Volk as a substitute for a unified state which did not as yet exist. The emotional and intellectual break with the West cut very deep across modern German history, and it was not completely healed until after 1945.

It was that break with the West which was to become of fundamental significance in the much later rise of anti-western National Socialism. And it is startling to discover that someone like Joseph Goebbels was quite aware that National Socialism represented a final break with the principles of the French Revolution. In a radio speech of April 1, 1933 (soon after Hitler's seizure of power), he said with pride that "This means that the year 1789 is being deleted from history."[10] Actually, the break had, of course, been made much earlier,

[9]Vermeil in M. Baumont (ed.), *The Third Reich*, p. 18.
[10]See Goebbels, *Revolution der Deutschen*, Oldenburg, 1933, p. 155.

but, as so often, National Socialism presented warmed-up old facts as fresh ideas of its own, even though with emotional exaggeration and radicalism.

It might well be asked why similar developments did not take place in England as a result of its own involvement in the same war against Napoleon, in which, indeed, it was allied with Prussia. The reason was that the war never had the same emotional impact on the English, because they had never lost an earlier phase of the war as the Prussians had, and the English had not been under French occupation. Moreover—and this may be more important—England itself, on its own, had already turned in the direction of the principles of the French Revolution at the time that Revolution broke out, whereas the Germans were far behind. The acceptance of similar principles in England could no longer be stopped, whereas in Germany they could still be rejected as an alien—and, as it turned out, a hostile alien—transplant. Also the English, being as they were a unified nation with secure, definite borders on their island, did not have to make the enormous preparatory effort for the war which was required of the numerous divided German states.

It is tempting to speculate as to what might have happened in Germany if the ideas of the French Revolution had not been linked to a hostile invader, and if these ideas could instead have been peacefully absorbed as they were in other countries. It is possible that in that event there would have been no turning away from the West but a gradual development toward democracy with sufficient emotional and intellectual strength to resist the temptations of National Socialism, if inded such an ideology could ever have seen the light of day.

D. Disunity and Insecurity

The lack of German political unity, to which we have repeatedly referred, is the central point of another theory which can be advanced to explain the rise and acceptance of National Socialism. In modern times, Germany did not become a united country until 1871 under Bismarck. The last previous date when the Germans might still be regarded as having had a semblance of unity was 1250, the year when Emperor Frederick II of Hohenstaufen died. In the intervening 621 years, there were hundreds of virtually independent German states which were frequently at war with each other. The Peace of Westphalia of 1648 seemed to intend to perpetuate German disunity and the impotence of the German people. Toward the end of the eighteenth century, there were more than 300 sovereign territories under countless princes and nobles. Napoleon, and later the Congress of Vienna, reduced their number to thirty-nine; but the map of Germany still looked like a jigsaw puzzle. Throughout all these centuries of disunity, however, the dream of the recreation of a united German empire remained very much alive. The legend had it that the Hohenstaufen Emperor Frederick I (Barbarossa) never died but was still sitting inside the Kyffhäuser Mountain awaiting German unification, his red beard growing through a table of stone. The legend was one of the guiding historical images for every German. (There may be some significance in the fact that Hitler selected the code name "Barbarossa" for his most important action of the war, the invasion of Soviet Russia.[11])

The overemphasis on the Volk concept, which resulted from the disunity of the country, was in a sense, a mere pitiable manifestation of a political impoverishment. Hundreds of years of emphasis on the Volk seem to have left so deep an impression that the concept continued to live on, practically unchanged, even when unification was finally achieved in 1871 and when a healthy state concept could have been substituted. Instead, in the ideology of National Socialism, the Volk concept, reinforced by the related race theories, was elevated to an even higher place than before in the order of national images. We may again quote Erik H. Erikson who was surely correct when, in speaking of German "familial imagery," he said that

> . . . historically determined spatial-temporal concepts . . . determine [a nation's] world image, the evil and ideal prototypes, and the unconscious life plan. These concepts dominate a nation's strivings and can lead to high distinction; but they also narrow a people's imagination and thus invite disaster. In German history, such outstanding configurations are encirclement versus *Lebensraum;* and *disunity versus unity.* . . . The non-German does not realize that in Germany these words carried a conviction far beyond that of ordinary logic. . . .

[11] Alfred Philippi and Ferdinand Heim, *Der Feldzug gegen Sowjetrussland 1941 bis 1945*, pp. 43–44.

> [The world] persistently underestimated the desperate German need for unity which, indeed, cannot be appreciated by peoples who in their own land take such unity for granted.[12]

An unfulfilled national dream which lasts for 621 years would probably be bad for any nation's emotional condition. In Germany, one result was much irrational political thinking and boundless longings of all sorts, going far beyond unity. The Germans became addicted dreamers in politics. Their dreams became institutionalized; they were taught in schools and universities. The people, in fact, seemed unable to wake up even when unification came. Anyone, who, like Hitler, promised fulfillment of the dreams, could, to use Erikson's words, carry a conviction far beyond that of ordinary logic.

It is possible, in fact, that even for a long time after unification in 1871, the consciousness of the accomplished unity remained weak. There may be a measure of truth in Golo Mann's statement that "national unity, in full, was brought about only under Adolf Hitler."[13]

Moreover, a concomitant of the lack of unity was a lack of security. Not only was there, for centuries, much threatening and fighting among the numerous small German states, but they were threatened and attacked also from the outside by their far more powerful neighbors who were integrated nations of long standing. In the East and West and large parts of the South, Germany never had any natural borders and was wide open to sweeping invasions. The permanent feeling of insecurity overshadowed the normal striving for freedom from harsh local rule. As Eva Reichmann has pointed out,[14] what should have been a demand for freedom from authority often was merely a striving for freedom from foreign enemies. The permanent feeling of vulnerability sometimes gave rise to excessively destructive countermeasures. "Many a German trait which later, in the form of imperialism and ruthless power politics, terrified the world, may have had its origin in old historic conditions."[15] And Erikson says, from the psychological point of view, that Germany, even after uni-

---

[12]Erikson, *Childhood and Society*, pp. 345, 347 (italics added).

[13]Mann, *Deutsche Geschichte des 19. und 20. Jahrhunderts*, p. 1036.

[14]Reichmann, *Flucht in den Hass—Die Ursachen der deutschen Judenkatastrophe*, p. 147.

[15]Ibid., p. 148.

fication, "remained conscious of her vulnerable position, both rationally and irrationally."[16]

E. "The Belated Nation"

The problem of German unity or disunity is connected with another theory that attempts to explain the basic causes of the German calamity. This theory is the subject matter of Helmut Plessner's book *Die verspätete Nation* (The Belated Nation), and the title itself suggests, to an extent, what the theory is. Plessner, so far, is the one who has made the most determined effort to present a coherent theory. Omitting here those of his views with which it is difficult to agree and doing a little violence to some others to fit them into the present study, the theory is that, while France, Britain, and Holland steadily grew in power as nation-states during the seventeenth and eighteenth centuries, the various small splintered German states steadily declined, having been enormously weakened by the Thirty Years' War (1618–1648) and by subsequent disunity and internal conflicts. The political horizon of most citizens of the small states was naturally very limited, and their public concerns were petty. German culture, too, was primarily regional, not national. Many of the princes were only anxious to obtain greater and greater privileges for themselves at the expense of whatever central power there might have been but did not exist. Those were the centuries in which, in fact, the German states became politically and culturally dependent on France.

Other nations, in the course of these centuries, not only were united, but also slowly attained a measure of democracy, largely as a result of the development of an increasingly affluent middle class which acquired political power and began to assert itself in government. In the German states, on the other hand, whatever middle class there was, was far from prosperous; it was powerless and no match for the princes. There was practically no natural growth of democracy as, for example, in England. And later, when some democratic concepts were finally imported from abroad, they failed to take root in the consciousness of the people because they were not home-grown but alien, and the people had not grown with them.

[16]Erikson, *Childhood*, p. 347.

Modern Germany, Plessner says, has "no connection with the centuries that were decisive in the formation and consolidation of the modern world. It is without traditions, when compared with the other great leading nation-states. Germany, unlike France and Britain, has not acquired a secure style of life through its past since the sixteenth century."[17]

It was not until the second half of the nineteenth century that a united Germany became a fact and a political power, but this was really too late, not only for its political development but also for a healthy ideological evolution. What was missing, above all, was a confident, self-assured middle class which could look back on centuries of an established tradition and secure values. Most social and political values of modern Germany, at least until 1918 and to a lesser extent even thereafter, were still determined by the nobility as in the past. There were various traditions which reached back to the era of the small states, such as obedience to and dependence on the ruler, but there were few traditions that could have been a sound foundation for a modern democratic nation-state. And once again, we are led back to the Volk concept because it was on this that the Germans placed vastly exaggerated importance by way of overcompensation, because a healthy nation concept, secure in home-grown values, was still missing.

These, on the whole, are Plessner's views, although with some embroideries, modifications, and adaptations to bring them in line with our present study. They are, more or less, supported by other writers, earlier and later. Oswald Spengler, for one (not normally cited as an authority here), said:

> But we are suffering from our past, from those 700 years of a pitiful system of provincial small states without a trace of greatness, without ideas, without aim. This cannot be made up for in two generations.[18]

> . . . All other great nations were given a character by their past. We had no educational past. . . .[19]

---

[17] Plessner, *Die verspätete Nation*, p. 72.
[18] Spengler, *Jahre der Entscheidung*, Munich, 1933, p. 2.
[19] Ibid., p. x.

The German states—small, weak, and indifferent as they were—failed to participate in what Golo Mann calls "the beginning Europeanization of the world."[20] They missed, he says, the "incalculable education" of "colonizing other peoples" and the attendant enlargement of their own horizon. (It was not until 1884 and 1885 that Germany acquired a few African colonies of small importance.) But no matter whether the colonizing of other peoples is really educationally so valuable as Golo Mann seems to believe, one thing is sure: there was a widespread feeling among the Germans, for about a hundred years before Hitler, that they had come too late to share in the distribution of the spoils of the world. There was much resentful envy of Britain and France for their colonial empires. Hitler himself, in *Mein Kampf*, spoke resentfully of the British Empire "calling almost one quarter of the entire earth's surface its own."[21] This kind of territorial envy may have been one of the motivations of Hitler's deep-seated urge to acquire more Lebensraum in Europe itself. At any rate, Germany's belated emergence as a great power or even as a nation stamped and distorted its entire political and social development thereafter.

Industrialization, too, was far slower to arrive in Germany than, for example, in Britain; and the British middle class which emerged from industrialization was older, larger, and stronger than its German counterpart. It was much surer of its own social standards and better able to impose its political and moral ideas on the rest of the nation. The German middle class still continued to see its social guidance in the army officer and other images created in an earlier age. The German industrial society had the appearance of having been hastily grafted on a preindustrial social and political structure, and it grew in unnatural haste on an unsound base.

The old ruling groups had remained at the wheel after unification, probably even more powerful than they had been before. Bismarck's very strong personality had been instrumental in bringing about unification, but it was almost equally—and tragically—instrumental in preventing significant modernization. He was a member of the highly conservative Prussian aristocracy and saw no reason to terminate or weaken the traditional authoritarian pattern, regardless

[20]Mann, op. cit., p. 35.
[21]*Mein Kampf*, p. 730.

of different contemporary developments in Britain and France. He introduced into the old system just enough modern elements to preserve it and to frustrate its opponents. The proletariat was reluctantly permitted to organize, but it obtained no political power, and its social mobility remained nearly nil. The German historian Friedrich Meinecke, in a belated about-face at age 84, said after World War II that "today we have to admit that formerly, in the brilliancy of . . . [Bismarck's] achievement, we paid too little attention to the hidden dark spots where . . . the disaster could happen later," and he spoke of "the connections between Hitlerism and the preceding social and spiritual development, the intoxication with power on the part of large groups of the bourgeoisie since the days of Bismarck. . . ."[22]

Before World War I, the middle classes, on the whole, appeared satisfied with the status quo in domestic politics, and this was, of course, even more true of the upper classes. It seemed that more than 600 years of trust in, and obedience to, the ruler could not be erased from the German unconscious in a generation—in fact, as it turned out, not in three generations. It might still be there today, if one ruler, Hitler, had not thoroughly discredited the entire principle of authoritarian government.

One might have expected that the rapid and enormous German successes between 1871 and 1914 in politics, industry, and science would have satisfied the drives and the pride of the unified nation, but evidently this was not so. An ambivalent self-estimation, mostly indeed a deep lack of self-confidence, if not of self-respect, did remain as a heavy residue of the past, and it continued to lead to all kinds of acts of overcompensation. At a minimum, all this was not the soil in which democracy could grow.

The belated achievement of political unity in 1871 did have at least one important result. Consciously or unconsciously, a great many Germans felt after unification that they had to make up for much missed history. They had to catch up with the power and glory of France and Britain, and, in fact, had to overtake at least France. It was as if they continuously had to assert their new-found big power status. They built a large navy, acquired whatever colonies were still to be had in Africa and elsewhere, rattled their saber, and threw

[22]Meinecke, *Die deutsche Katastrophe,* pp. 85, 141.

their weight around in various international crises. Generally, they played the part of an objectionable political and social parvenu. Most Germans seemed to believe that their big-power status gave them a natural right to hegemony in Europe. Long before World War I, Germany thus became a disturbing element in the world. National Socialism and World War II were not unnatural or illogical sequels.

But if, by this time, anyone is tired of all the theorizing, he might, with Thomas Mann, blame the devil for the whole calamity. Mann said that "there are no two Germanys, an evil one and a good one, but only one whose best, by the wiles of the devil, turned bad. . . ."

III

A PRELUDE: THE EARLIER GENOCIDE OF THE GERMAN•HERERO WAR, 1904•1905

German South-West Africa was established as a German colony in 1884, and it was the first colony which Germany acquired.[1] In the absence of earlier German colonial experience, the administrative structure of this "crown colony" was modeled on that of the mother country. By 1914, the European population amounted to about 15,000; the native tribes, to a few hundred thousand. Economically the colony was never of any real value to Germany. It was, in fact, largely worthless. If it had any political value, it was one of prestige and principle. The possession of this colony symbolized that Germany, late as it was, had joined the ranks of the colonial powers.

In January 1904, one of the local tribes, the Hereros, revolted against German rule. They murdered about 100 German male settlers and soldiers, destroyed farms, and drove off the cattle herds. German reaction was slow but very strong. Its declared aim was the total extermination of the Herero tribe. This was never completely accomplished, but by 1906 the original Herero population, estimated at 60,000 to 80,000, had been reduced to 16,000. In other words, between 75 and 80 percent of them had died.[2]

In the history of colonization, events of this sort are not, of course, anything very extraordinary. Much larger native population groups have perished elsewhere, the largest being perhaps the population of the Congo, which the Belgians reduced from 20–40 million in 1890 to 8,500,000 in 1911.[3] What is significant, however, in the present context are the reasons given by the German leadership for its radical measures, its motivations, the scraps of an "ideology" which came to the surface and bore surprising resemblance to aspects of the national socialist ideology twenty-five or thirty years later. A small window opens up on the existence of a state of mind in 1904 that was to find much more intense expression under Hitler nearly a generation later.

The basic philosophy was stated simply by the German Chief of Staff, General Count A. von Schlieffen, in a letter to the Reich Chancellor B. von Bülow, in which he defended the local military com-

[1]The present chapter is based largely on the valuable book by Helmut Bley, *Kolonialherrschaft und Sozialstruktur in Deutsch-Südwestafrika 1894–1914,* no significant further research having been undertaken.

[2]Ibid., p. 191.

[3]Hannah Arendt, *The Origins of Totalitarianism,* p. 185.

mander General L. von Trotha: "We can agree with him when he wants to destroy the whole [Herero] nation or wants to drive it out of the country. . . . The *race war* which has broken out can be brought to a conclusion only by the destruction of one of the parties."[4] Trotha had previously written that "This revolt is and remains the beginning of a race war" and that he believed "that the nation [of the Hereros] must be destroyed as such."[5]

The general attitude of the German settlers seems to have been that the natives were "animals" or even "vermin,"[6] as the Jews were declared to be thirty years later. Even the local German newspaper proclaimed that "against vermin no action [can be] strong enough."[7] The German governor wrote to a missionary that "sexual relations between Europeans and Africans" were "not only a crime against the maintenance of the purity of the German race and of German morality . . . but could also endanger the position of the white man here generally."[8] It will be recalled, in this connection, that the national socialist regime prohibited all sexual relations between Germans and Jews because the mere act of sexual intercourse was deemed to destroy the purity of the German race, even when it did not produce children.

The action of the German army against the Hereros lacked nothing in vigor and brutality. Prisoners were taken only with reluctance or not at all. The German commanding general objected to the application of the Geneva Convention to such a colony; and anticipating Heinrich Himmler's maxims in World War II, he said that the introduction of the humanitarian rules of the Convention would "deprive our own fellow citizens of humane treatment."[9] General von Trotha announced that "every Herero, with or without rifle, with or without cattle, will be shot. I shall accept no further women and children, but shall drive them back to their people or shall have them shot. This is my message to the Herero people."[10] And he signed this announcement as "The Great General of the mighty German Emperor."

[4]Bley, op. cit., p. 205 (italics added).
[5]Ibid., pp. 204–205.
[6]Ibid., pp. 297–298, 306.
[7]Ibid., p. 297.
[8]Ibid., p. 249.
[9]Ibid., p. 101.
[10]Ibid., p. 204.

In an order to the troops, Trotha gave details. The troops were to shoot above the heads of women and children to make them run away. He assumed "with certainty that this decree will result in the taking of no further male prisoners, but will not degenerate into atrocities against women and children. . . ."

Later the military operation was proudly described by the General Staff:

> This bold operation shows in splendid light the ruthless energy of the German leadership in pursuing the beaten enemy. No exertions were spared, no hardships avoided, to deprive the enemy of the last ounce of his power of resistance. Like a hounded animal, he was driven from water hole to water hole until finally, having lost all energy, he fell victim to the natural conditions of his own country. The waterless Omaheke desert was to complete what German arms had started: the extermination of the Herero people.[11]

According to Bley,[12] even such prisoners as had been taken and were being kept in camps were subject to a policy of extermination, particularly in the cold, damp camps along the coast. About 45 percent of them died. Tribal chiefs and other important people were executed. The survivors were finally deported to distant parts of the colony to prevent any organized rehabilitation of the Herero people. It is all strongly reminiscent of Himmler's treatment of the Poles and Russians. The extermination of between 75 and 80 percent of the Herero people was a kind of unwitting prelude to the Final Solution.

It is to the credit of Reich Chancellor von Bülow that he strongly objected to the methods employed by the army in South-West Africa. In a formal "intervention" before Emperor Wilhelm II, Bülow described these methods as "running counter to all principles of Christianity and humanity"; and, upon his request, counterorders were issued.[13] This still indicates the continued existence of moral principles in 1905 among some of the upper echelons of German leadership — principles no longer recognized under Hitler, who replaced

[11] Ibid., p. 203.
[12] Ibid., p. 191–192.
[13] Ibid., p. 203.

them by the "cruel laws of nature." The continued existence of ordinary moral principles during the colonization of South-West Africa may be indicated also by the fact that local German courts, in a series of criminal cases from 1911 to 1913, convicted German settlers (men and women) of physical cruelties which resulted in the death of natives. Severe whippings and kicking (even of highly pregnant women and of children) seem to have been the rule.[14] ("It was generally known [Bley says] that pieces of iron were woven into the leather whips."[15]) Of course, while the prosecution of such acts by Public Prosecutors and the courts indicates a continued awareness of moral and legal wrongs on the part of the authorities, one might say that the fact of the apparently general commission of these acts by the settlers indicated an erosion of this awareness on their part.

All in all, German behavior in South-West Africa shows that long before World War I the race doctrines had become well established in the German mind and were already being applied in practice to justify the mistreatment and extermination of a small, weak, racially different group.

[14] Ibid., pp. 294–300, 127.
[15] Ibid., p. 296.

IV

THE
MOMENT
IN HISTORY

Chapter 11

Introduction

The edifice of national socialist ideology, as we have seen, was firmly anchored in the German cultural heritage and tradition. Decades before Hitler, the ideology began to move toward intellectual domination and political action. Yet success had to wait until the right moment in history had arrived. The time for the establishment and acceptance of the radical totalitarianism, implicit in the ideology, did not come until after Germany's defeat in World War I. All the potential totalitarian inclinations of the earlier period had still been outweighed by residual tendencies toward a genuine democracy and humanitarianism—tendencies which, in fact, found brief and weak expression in the establishment of the entirely liberal democratic Weimar Republic.

The historical moment arrived when a certain combination of circumstances arose. The postwar humiliations by the allied powers became insufferable; the business depression, unemployment, and inflation reached staggering proportions; a series of weak governments seemed unable to cope with the difficulties or even to offer hope for improvement, however modest. But above all, one man, Hitler, appeared on the scene to present a reasonably cohesive, highly persuasive picture of the total ideology and to convince millions that, with it and with his program of action, he would succeed in leading them into a better future.

To this extent it is true, as some historians have contended, that the National Socialist Movement owed its birth and public acceptance to a "unique constellation of circumstances." But it is true also that what became national socialist ideology had existed long before the National Socialist Movement was born and that, without the old-established ideas, the Movement would never have become what it was and would never have succeeded. It was precisely the traditional ideological conditioning which furnished the Movement with a receptive, pliable, obedient population, willing or eager collaborators, such as the entire lowest middle class, the professors (including the influential historians), the students, the army. Without all these, or at least most of them, and without an able leader, National Socialism might well have remained the chaotic and ineffective brew of confused radical ideas and immature theories which existed before in a multitude of right wing, more or less radical organizations, parties, *Freikorps, Bünde,* etc. A very special political and social situation was required, in which a strong leader of a certain personality could seem to satisfy the needs, longings, and drives of millions. That situation and that personality will now be discussed.

Chapter 12

The Personality of Adolf Hitler

The existing literature on Hitler is, of course, enormous, and it is still growing at a fast rate. It may suffice to mention here four outstanding writings: Alan Bullock, *Hitler, a Study in Tyranny* (revised edition, 1962), a comprehensive, scholarly biography now somewhat superseded by new source material; Werner Maser, *Adolf Hitler* (1971), the most recent and up-to-date of all the biographies; Joachim C. Fest, *Das Gesicht des dritten Reiches* (1964), pp. 15–100; and Karl Dietrich Bracher, *Die deutsche Diktatur* (1969), particularly pp. 60–72.[1]

We have no intention of repeating here what these and other writers have said about Hitler or of presenting any cohesive biographical sketch of him. At any rate, to a considerable extent, this whole book has already dealt with him. Some special aspects of his personality and of his effect on the Germans do, however, still require discussion.

A. No National Socialism without Hitler

If there is one thing on which nearly all historians of the period agree, it is that National Socialism would have been unthinkable without Hitler.[2] There might conceivably have been some radical national-

---

[1] Among additional books of value are Hans Bernd Gisevius, *Adolf Hitler;* H. R. Trevor-Roper, *The Last Days of Adolf Hitler;* Eberhard Jäckel, *Hitlers Weltanschauung, Entwurf einer Herrschaft.* J. C. Fest and R. G. L. Waite, moreover, are reported to be at work on complete biographies.

[2] Karl Dietrich Bracher, *Die deutsche Diktatur,* p. 140; Helga Grebing, *Der Nationalsozialismus — Ursprung und Wesen,* p. 61; Golo Mann, *Deutsche Geschichte des 19. und 20. Jahrhunderts,* p. 865; Alan Bullock, *Hitler, a Study in Tyranny,* p. 805; Joachim C. Fest, *Das Gesicht des Dritten Reiches,* p. 66. George L. Mosse, *The Crisis of German Ideology,* p. 8, seems to hold a different view.

istic, anti-Semitic mass movement, but without "this one unparalleled individual," as Golo Mann calls him,[3] there could not have been that national dedication to a brutal irrational cause, that vast exaggeration of national, social, and cultural purposes, that fantastic faith in their own strength, which the German people displayed under him. But "there happened to be that man."[4] It was through him that the old ideology, most of which to any thinking German appeared to be largely obsolete, received cohesion, vigor, and reality. He made it the credo of a mass movement, and he—essentially alone—created that mass movement itself. None of his associates could show any comparable combination of ideological teaching ability with practical, cold politics, and his talent to manipulate as well as organize the German masses. That this man appeared on the scene in the early 1920s was indeed by far the most important element of the "moment in history" in which National Socialism could ripen. The German historian Friedrich Meinecke concludes quite aptly that "the Hitler Movement . . . is one of the great examples of the singular and incalculable power of a personality in historical life—in this case a plainly demonic personality."[5] At the same time, the fact that Hitler's career became possible is one of the most alarming phenomena of world history.

It is not surprising, then, that when the Germans heard of Hitler's death, they looked at each other perplexed.[6] It was as if the nation "awakened from a long drugged sleep," Golo Mann says. "The evil magic did not last longer than the magician." Neither the regime nor the Party nor the Movement could really survive the leader by as much as one day, and upon his death they all disappeared like a burst balloon. Even the ideology itself, old as it was, had become so identified with Hitler or, one might say, tainted by him that large parts of it seemed to vanish with him into nothing. For many Germans, even for National Socialists, all that remained was a vast embarrassment.

Was Hitler a pied piper or a drum-beater? Some have called him the former, others the latter. It does not really matter; he may have been both. He himself, very early in his career, described himself as drum-beater and said that "this was the highest; the other things

[3] Mann, op cit., p. 808.
[4] Ibid., p. 809.
[5] Meinecke, *Die deutsche Katastrophe*, p. 141.
[6] Mann, op. cit., pp. 865, 962.

are trifles."[7] What *was* the secret of his attraction, of his enormous seductiveness, to millions of Germans? For one thing, he was, in his way, an excellent, passionate, fanatic orator—and there have been few real orators in German history. There has never been a great tradition of public speaking in Germany as in Britain. Hitler may have been the first real German orator since Luther, and this may in part account for the enormous impact of the thousands of his speeches. Fully aware of his abilities as a speaker, he emphasized on many occasions that the spoken word was far more effective than the written. "From time immemorial, the magic power of the spoken word has been the force which has set into motion the great historical avalanches of a religious or political kind."[8]

The use of masterly propaganda, moreover, was the very essence of National Socialism, and many pages of *Mein Kampf* are devoted to cynically frank explanations of methods of manipulating the masses. ". . . clever and persistent use of propaganda can make a nation believe that heaven is hell and, conversely, that the most miserable life is paradise. . . ."[9] Hitler's propaganda minister, Joseph Goebbels, is reported to have said, "Propaganda has nothing at all to do with truth!"[10] Contemptuously, but frankly, Hitler declared in *Mein Kampf* that "The overwhelming majority of the people are so feminine by nature and attitude that their emotions, far more than sober reasoning, determine their thoughts and actions."[11] And he was sure that he knew how to deal with these emotions. Erik H. Erikson describes this kind of propaganda as "inviting men, collectively and unashamedly, to project total badness on whatever inner and outer 'enemy' can be appointed by state decree and propaganda as totally subhuman and verminlike, while the converted may feel totally good as a member of a nation, a race or a class blessed by history."[12]

But the main source of Hitler's ability to enchant and entrance millions of Germans probably was that his sadomasochistic character structure was so much like their own, no matter that he towered

---

[7]In his plea before the Munich People's Court in 1924, quoted in Walter C. Langer, *A Psychological Analysis of Adolf Hitler: His Life and Legend*, typescript, p. 12.

[8]*Mein Kampf*, p. 116.

[9]Ibid., p. 302.

[10]Fest, op. cit., p. 130.

[11]*Mein Kampf*, p. 201.

[12]Erikson, *Identity, Youth and Crisis*, p. 86.

above them in intelligence and leadership qualities. This has been suggested, above all, by Erich Fromm.[13] Hitler addressed himself "to people who, on account of their similar character structure, felt attracted and excited by [his] . . . teachings and became ardent followers of the man who expressed what they felt." These people were primarily the members of the lowest middle class, and it was almost as if he were someone whom they had long awaited. He was always superbly able to articulate what they felt only vaguely or what was still hidden in their unconscious. In fact, he represented a kind of collective unconscious. He was "one of them," not only in his character structure, but also in family background, manners, mediocre education, longings, and so forth. He was the "unknown nameless soldier"[14] of World War I, as so many millions of others. Yet he now was clearly a superior leader or even big brother whom one could adore and obey. There is no question that everyone could sense the unshakable political determination which Hitler personified.

Moreover, Hitler satisfied the sadomasochistic strivings of the people by creating, as Fromm has pointed out, "a hierarchy . . . in which everyone has somebody above him to submit to and somebody beneath him to feel power over."[15] At the very top, Hitler himself had fate, history and nature as the powers to which he could submit, and he made extensive use of that. Everyone below him, however, could feel sheltered by a more tangible superior power. Helga Grebing quotes a very apt description of this condition from a speech by a high national socialist official: "Why does the German man love Adolf Hitler? Because he feels sheltered by him! The Führer relieves him of his sorrows and gives him strength."[16] Constant emphasis on Germany's diabolical enemies, the Jews, Communists, and others, did much to increase the value of the shelter.

While the lowest middle class always represented the backbone of the regime, the appeal of National Socialism was, as time went on, by no means confined to that group. The psychological suction of Hitler's political successes abroad and of the economic boom at

[13] Fromm, *Escape from Freedom*, pp. 236-237. See also Langer, op. cit., p. 240.

[14] He applied this description to himself, for instance, in his speech to the officer candidates of May 30, 1942 (Appendix to *Hitler's Table Talks*, p. 503).

[15] Fromm, *Escape*, p. 236.

[16] Grebing, op. cit., p. 73.

home soon became so strong that all sorts of population groups found it difficult to resist it. Their own nationalism, their intense wish to see Germany recover its lost greatness persuaded many a reasonable man to close his eyes to the vulgarities and savageness of the regime and to regard Hitler as the savior. His appeal to youth, as we have seen, was especially strong, and deliberately so. The young saw action and the prospect of more of it; and, as usual, they did not inquire into the underlying wisdom. The propaganda, like all totalitarian propaganda, concentrated "on the claim that youth is left high and dry by the ebbing wave of the past."[17] Youth felt sure that its own moment in history had come. "Make room, you old ones" was the attractive slogan which National Socialism gave them.

The delirious enthusiasm, the sincere, boundless love which many millions of Germans felt for Hitler are difficult to understand for anyone who was not physically present in the Germany of that period. Some of its outward manifestations were described rather well by Hitler's chief translator and interpreter Paul Schmidt:

> On the day when Hitler made his big triumphal procession through Nuremberg, it was one of my tasks to ride in an open car with the most prominent French and British guests just a few yards behind Hitler's car. . . . The ride went on almost an hour. . . . crisscross through the old city. It was overwhelming to watch the masses of people who jubilantly greeted Hitler in ecstatic enthusiasm. I was again and again impressed with the facial expression of an almost biblical devotion with which these people looked at Hitler as if in ecstasy and almost bewitched. It was like mass intoxication which overcame thousands upon thousands of people all along the way whenever Hitler came into view. As if in a delirium, these people raised their arms towards him and greeted him with loud screams and *heils*. To ride for an hour in the focal point of this frenetic jubilation was a real physical effort after which one could feel a definite exhaustion. Also, somehow one's power of mental resistance was paralyzed. I almost had the feeling of having to control myself in order not to join in the general jubilation. Fortunately, during the ride my translation work required my frequent attention and distracted me, but I saw Englishmen and Frenchmen who some-

[17]Erikson, *Identity*, p. 89.

times had tears in their eyes because they were deeply moved by what they saw and heard. Even hard-boiled international journalists like Jules Sauerwein . . . or Ward Price . . ., who once rode in my car, were actually groggy when we reached the end of the trip.[18]

One can only guess at the emotional reaction in the man who was the focus of all the love and cheering. But it would hardly be surprising if he had acquired a vastly exaggerated sense of his own greatness and invincibility, not only within Germany but in the world. At any rate, millions of Germans—a normally rather sober and highly critical people—were prepared to be almost purely emotional and uncritical in their views of Hitler and all the irrational theories and promises which he presented to them. Objections and criticism by others were impatiently or angrily shrugged off. Rumors of brutalities were disbelieved. Actual knowledge of brutalities was disposed of with the statement "If the Führer knew this, he would never permit it." The breath-taking career of the former resident of a Viennese lodging house for the homeless and private first class was in itself such as to convince millions of his German contemporaries that he was a genius without parallel.

But Hitler's seemingly magical effect on the Germans does not mean that his contemporaries are blameless and that all guilt can be put on him because he had, as it were, put the Germans into a trance which was not of their doing and from which only his death could free them. The relationship between Hitler, the Germans, and German intellectual history was reciprocal. The history of the German mind shaped him more than he was to shape that mind. He was, as J. C. Fest puts it, ". . . undeniably symptom and result of specific misdevelopments of our [German] history, . . . [he was] much 'in ourselves'."[19] Or, as K. D. Bracher says, "he was no mere accident, he was a 'condition'."[20] The fact that he could rise and be accepted in Germany was due not only to his abilities but at least equally so to his being a specific product of a long German intellectual history. Essentially, as we have seen, he was no ideological innovator but was a

---

[18]Schmidt, *Statist auf diplomatischer Bühne*, 1949, pp. 362-363.
[19]Fest, op. cit., p. 411.
[20]Bracher, op. cit., p. 140.

dynamic adapter of old ideas and traditions and of prevailing theories. What happened was not a rape of the Germans by Hitler, but a seduction. And if a nation is to be successfully seduced, it must possess the proper qualities of seduceability. The majority of Germans had these qualities and thoroughly enjoyed the seduction.

Naturally, Hitler's rise and acceptance was a phenomenon of considerable complexity. It was composed of many factors: the national socialist ideology, his own psychology and that of the Germans, German political and intellectual history, the contemporary political situation, the economic circumstances, and other factors. All these — or most of them — interacted and shaped each other, and Hitler himself represented a personification of the interaction. In a sense, after the start of his political career, he was never merely "himself." But we should also not omit to say that there were millions of thinking Germans who never "interacted" with Hitler or with the national socialist ideology, who never wanted him or what he promised. And there were also millions of others who thought that they did want Hitler but who never wanted to go as far as he was to lead them.

B. Hitler's Psychology

a. IN GENERAL

What is still missing in the available literature and is greatly needed is a thorough analysis of Hitler's personality by a qualified psychiatrist on the basis of all the material now available. For the time being, we shall have to rely on the more important analyses (not all published) heretofore prepared, mostly on the basis of limited source material. It may be best to list them here in chronological order:

1. Erich Fromm, *Escape from Freedom*, 1941, *passim*.

2. W. H. Vernon, "Hitler, the Man — Notes for a Case History," in *Journal of Abnormal and Social Psychology*, vol. 37, 1942, pp. 295-308.

3. Walter C. Langer, *A Psychological Analysis of Adolph [sic] Hitler: His Life and Legend*, with the collaboration of Henry A. Murray, Ernst Kris, and Bertram D. Lewin. Prepared in 1943 for M.O. Branch of U.S. Office of Strategic Services. With *Source Book* of 1,050 pages. Typescript, National Archives, Washington, D.C.; (In

connection with this typescript see Walter C. Langer, *The Mind of Adolf Hitler*, 1972, which professes to be a publication, in book form, of the typescript "as an historical document" (without the *Source Book*), but contains, nevertheless, various additions to, and modifications of, that typescript. It also omits some portions. All page references in the present study are, therefore, to the original typescript.)

4. Henry A. Murray (Harvard Psychological Clinic), *Analysis of the Personality of Adolf Hitler*, October, 1943. Probably commissioned by the Office of Strategic Services for President Roosevelt. Unpublished typescript in President's Secretary File PSF:OSS Box 97A, Franklin D. Roosevelt Library, Hyde Park, N.Y.

5. Erik H. Erikson, *Young Man Luther*, 1962, pp. 105–110.

6. Erik H. Erikson, *Childhood and Society*, 1963, pp. 326–353.

7. Johann Recktenwald, *Woran hat Hitler gelitten?* 1963.

8. Erich Fromm, *The Heart of Man*, 1964, *passim*.

9. Wolfgang Treher, *Hitler, Steiner, Schreber*, 1966.

In addition, there is a psychiatric study by a historian, not a psychiatrist:

10. R. G. L. Waite, "Adolf Hitler's Guilt Feelings: A Problem in History and Psychology," in *Journal of Interdisciplinary History*, vol. l, no. 2, 1971, pp. 229–249.

There is also:

11. An anonymous, unpublished, pseudopsychiatric study by a layman, Ernst (Sedgwick) Hanfstaengl, *Adolf Hitler*, dated December 3, 1942, probably commissioned by President Franklin D. Roosevelt, typescript in President's Personal File 5780, Franklin D. Roosevelt Library, Hyde Park, N.Y. The author probably received assistance from a psychiatrist.

Finally, a brief summary of numerous psychiatric and other statements on Hitler's psychology is offered in Wilhelm Lange-Eichbaum/Wolfram Kurth, *Genie, Irrsinn und Ruhm*, 6th ed., 1971, pp. 381–388. It reveals nearly hopeless confusion and contradictions as to the facts and their interpretation. The physiological aspects of Hitler's various illnesses are dealt with in detail in Werner Maser's biography *Adolf Hitler*, pp. 326–370. Maser does not concern himself, to any extent, with the purely psychological aspects; in fact, he sees the causation of much action or inaction by Hitler in physiological illnesses.

Fromm and Erikson have made a considerable contribution to an understanding of Hitler's psychology, and their theories will be discussed here later in some detail. But the other psychiatrists have also helped greatly to clarify the facts and have added their part to the general picture of a very complex personality. The actual diagnoses vary widely. Dr. Langer concludes that Hitler was "not insane . . . but neurotic."[21] Dr. Murray, on the other hand, says that Hitler "exhibited, at one time or another, all of the classical symptoms of paranoid schizophrenia: hypersensitivity, panic of anxiety, irrational jealousy, delusions of persecution, delusions of omnipotence and messiahship,"[22] He says, further, that Hitler "is a hive of secret neurotic compunctions and feminine sentimentalities."[23] Similarly, Dr. Treher concludes that Hitler was schizophrenic, mentally sick[24] (but some of Treher's diagnostic methods seem absurd). Fromm sees "severe mental sickness" and "potential psychosis," and he suggests that Hitler was "on the borderline between sanity and insanity."[25] Erikson states agreement with the diagnoses of others that, at least at times, Hitler was a "psychopathic paranoid," an "amoral sadistic infant," an "overcompensatory sissy," etc., but says that he "was something over and above it all" and that "it seems inexpedient to apply ordinary diagnostic methods to his words."[26]

One or two of these diagnoses seem to have been based on a minimum of facts and a maximum of conjecture and intuition, but it is surprising to what extent, though not always, the intuition has turned out to be right. We shall now examine some of the underlying facts of Hitler's psychology; but before doing so, it will be well briefly to discuss the neurological findings of Dr. Recktenwald, which are of considerable interest in any consideration of the development of Hitler's personality in his late years.

Recktenwald is a neurologist or neuropsychiatrist. His book rep-

---

[21] Langer, op. cit., p. 128.
[22] Henry A. Murray, *Analysis of the Personality of Adolf Hitler*, p. 14.
[23] Ibid., p. 11.
[24] Wolfgang Treher, *Hitler, Steiner, Schreber*, pp. 86, 263.
[25] Fromm, *The Heart of Man*, pp. 37, 76, 66.
[26] Erikson, *Childhood and Society*, pp. 329–330.

resents primarily a diagnosis of an organic brain disease. He has collected impressive material concerning various aspects of Hitler's physical condition and symptoms, particularly: strong trembling or shaking of his left hand, arm, and leg; lameness of the left foot; protruding eyes; waxy complexion; severe insomnia; sudden rages.[27] All these do indeed make it appear probable, as Recktenwald says, that Hitler suffered from late Parkinsonism. To these symptoms, we might add some mentioned in Werner Maser's biography, (pp. 344, 349, 350–351, 429) namely, trembling of the whole left side of his body, a dragging walk, lack of a sense of balance, drooling from the corners of his mouth, a feeling of falling toward the right. According to Recktenwald, this is likely to have been a final stage of a condition resulting from an early epidemic-encephalitic infection, in other words, presumably a virus infection of the brain. Recktenwald suspects that Hitler's brother died of encephalitis as a child and that Hitler became infected at that time.[28] During Hitler's lifetime, however, medical opinion on the question of Parkinsonism was divided.[29] Hitler himself once said that he was suffering from a "severe nervous disease."[30] (It is a strange fact, in this connection, that Parkinsonism was one of the diseases which, under Hitler's "euthanasia program," called for the "mercy death" of the incurably ill[31] or, as it was sometimes called, the extermination of living beings unworthy of living— *Vernichtung lebensunwerten Lebens.*)

But Recktenwald, like many specialists, sees the answers to *all* questions within his medical specialty. From his quite plausible diagnosis of Hitler's Parkinsonism, an organic nerve disease, he proceeds to the much broader and implausible theory that Hitler suffered only from this organic illness and that all or nearly all of his actions and reactions can be explained on the basis of it. In other words, Recktenwald sees no need for any psychological interpretation. It seems inherently unlikely that Hitler's vastly complicated character and

[27] See, in this connection, also Bullock, *Hitler,* pp. 765-767.

[28] Hitler's brother Edmund died of the measles in 1900. See Werner Maser, *Adolf Hitler—Legende, Mythos, Wirklichkeit,* p. 62. It is worth noting, also, that Hitler himself, according to Maser, p. 389, suffered from a severe case of encephalitic influenza *(Kopfgrippe)* in 1942.

[29] See ibid., pp. 352, 362-364.

[30] Ibid., p. 342.

[31] See Walter Görlitz, *Adolf Hitler,* p. 140.

its manifestations can be explained solely by an organic brain disease. If this were possible, we should keep a most careful watch on all survivors of encephalitis.

b. HITLER'S FATHER

Hitler's father came from peasant stock, had little education, but worked his way up to the position of a minor Austrian customs official at the German border. He was 23 years older than Hitler's mother, his third wife. At the time of Hitler's birth, the father was 52; he died when his son was 13. The only direct evidence we have as to the kind of man the father was and Hitler's relations to him is contained in *Mein Kampf.* Hitler describes the father as a "hard and determined" man whom, however, he claims to have loved and "venerated" *(verehrt).*[32] Quite likely, the claim of love and veneration was nothing but an effort to build a desirable image of himself. *Mein Kampf* does describe a serious conflict between father and son when Hitler, at age 12, informed his father that he wanted to become a painter and not, as desired by the father, a public official.[33] There he describes the father as "ruthless" and himself as "filled with bitterness." Erikson asks, "Is this the naive revelation of a pathological father-hate?"[34]

More important, perhaps, are other passages in *Mein Kampf.* Hitler discusses the wretched family life to which many Austrian children were exposed, but he probably had in mind, by way of projection, some of his own childhood experiences. He spoke of the "battle which is carried on between the parents . . . , and this almost every day, in forms which, for brutality, often leave nothing to be desired." He told of "brutal attacks by the father against the mother, of drunken attacks which someone who does not know such a milieu can hardly imagine."[35] The probabilities are that this had been his own milieu and that he spoke from personal experience. The fact that this may have been a description of life in the Hitler family is, to an extent, confirmed by other evidence, though it is entirely hearsay. An old associate of Hitler, Ernst Hanfstaengl, told an interviewer of the Office of Strategic Services (OSS) in 1942 or so, that

[32]*Mein Kampf*, pp. 6, 8, 16.
[33]Ibid., pp. 7–8.
[34]Erikson, *Childhood,* p. 330.
[35]*Mein Kampf*, pp. 32–33. See also p. 28.

. . . he had a long talk with Brigid Hitler, Alois' [Hitler's][36] wife in London in 1937. She told him that her husband [Hitler's half brother] had frequently talked about his childhood and that he had described his father as having a very violent temper and that he often beat the dog until the dog would cringe and wet the floor. He often beat the children and on occasions when he was in an exceptionally bad temper would beat his wife. . . .[37]

There is further corroboration of such actions by Hitler's father, though again only hearsay. William Patrick Hitler, the son of the above-mentioned half brother, informed the OSS interviewer that

. . . he has heard from his father [Alois] . . . that he [Adolf's father] used to beat the children unmercifully. On one occasion, it is alleged he beat the older son [Alois] into a state of unconsciousness and on another occasion beat Adolph [sic] so severely that he left him for dead. It is also alleged that he was somewhat of a drunkard and that frequently the children would have to bring him home from the taverns. When he reached home a grand scene would take place during which he would beat wife, children and dog rather indiscriminately.[38]

There is corroboration for the report that the children had to bring the drunk father home from the taverns. Many years later, Hans Frank confirmed this as to Adolf in his memoirs. He was given this information by Hitler himself, presumably in a rare unguarded moment.[39] (W. Maser, *Adolf Hitler*, pp. 55, 446, cites evidence to the contrary.)

It does seem reasonably fair to assume, in all the circumstances, as Dr. Murray does, that Hitler's "immeasurable hatred," his "incessant need to find some object on which to vent his pent-up wrath . . . can be traced back with relative certainty to experiences of insult, humilation and wounded pride in childhood" and that the "source of such insults, we have many reasons to believe, was Hitler's father, a coarse boastful man who ruled his wife . . . and his children with

[36] Alois was Adolf's half brother.
[37] P. 913 of *Source Book* to Langer, op cit. See also Maser, op. cit., p. 480, ftn. 90.
[38] Langer, op. cit., pp. 98–99; see also Hanfstaengl (anonymous), *Adolf Hitler*, p. 4.
[39] Frank, *Im Angesicht des Galgens*, Munich, 1953, p. 332.

tyrannical severity and injustice."[40] Hanfstaengl calls the father a "sadist."[41] And we might say at this point that fathers of this general type were not unusual in Austria and Germany, even though few may have reached the degree of brutality of Hitler's father. Erikson, who paints a good composite picture of a pattern of such German fatherhood, says very aptly that

> During the storms of adolescence, . . . when the boy's identity must settle things with his father image, . . . [the German father-son relationship] leads to that severe German *Pubertät* which is such a strange mixture of open rebellion and "secret sin," cynical delinquency and submissive obedience, romanticism and despondency, and which is apt to break the boy's spirit, once and for all.[42]

Two of the psychiatrists, Dr. Murray and Dr. Langer, have adopted the "hypothesis" that Hitler's hatred of his father was intensified by his having witnessed sexual intercourse between his parents as a boy. The present author has found no evidence to this effect, but Dr. Murray claims that the hypothesis is "supported by much evidence" (which he does not specify), and Dr. Langer says that an "examination of the data makes this conclusion almost inescapable" (the data being left unexplained).[43] At any rate, as Dr. Langer says, "from our knowledge of his father's character and past history . . . [this occurrence] is not at all improbable." If it did happen, then the result might well have been a repressed drive and passion for revenge, locked up within the boy under tension, which was released much later when Germany (one of Hitler's mother substitutes) was subjugated and humiliated in 1918.[44]

It follows from Hitler's most unsatisfactory relationship with his father that Hitler—consciously or unconsciously—never aimed to be a father figure to the German people. Also, most of his life he was much too much of a reckless adventurer to be a proper father. What

---

[40]Murray, op. cit., pp. 8–9.
[41]Hanfstaengl (anonymous), p. 4.
[42]Erikson, *Childhood*, p. 332.
[43]Murray, op. cit., p. 9; Langer, op. cit., p. 162.
[44]Murray, op. cit., p. 9.

he unconsciously did aim for was to be an adored elder brother. Erikson, with considerable insight into Hitler's personality, puts it this way:

> Psychologists overdo the father attributes in Hitler's historical image; Hitler* *the adolescent who refused to become a father* by any connotation, or, for that matter, a kaiser or a president. He did not repeat Napoleon's error. He was the Führer: *a glorified older brother*, who took over prerogatives of the fathers without over-identifying with them: calling his father "old while [Hitler was] still a child," he reserved for himself the new position of *the one who remains young* in possession of supreme power. He was *the unbroken adolescent* who had chosen a career apart from civilian happiness, mercantile tranquility, and spiritual peace: a gang leader who kept the boys together by demanding their admiration, by creating terror, and by shrewdly involving them in crimes from which there was no way back. And he was a ruthless exploiter of parental failures.[45]

It is significant that in *Mein Kampf* Hitler himself, speaking of his early school years, said that he "had become a small ringleader who in school . . . was rather difficult to deal with."[46] We shall have more to say about Hitler's "unbroken adolescence" later.

c. HITLER'S MOTHER

"I had venerated my father, but I had loved my mother,"[47] says Hitler, speaking of her death. The shock of this death, he says, was "horrible" *(entsetzlich)*. The attending physician, Dr. Eduard Bloch, said later that "In all my career, I have never seen anyone so prostrate with grief as Adolf Hitler" at the death of his mother.[48] There is no doubt that his love of his mother was an entirely genuine emotion. He describes her in *Mein Kampf* as "living wholly for her household and being devoted, above all, to us children in eternally loving

---

* The word "was" may have been inadvertently omitted at this point.

[45] Erikson, *Childhood*, p. 337 (italics added).

[46] *Mein Kampf*, p. 3.

[47] Ibid., p. 16.

[48] Bloch, "My Patient, Hitler," in *Collier's*, Mar. 15, 1941, p. 39.

care."[49] This was also one of the very rare references by Hitler to the fact that his mother had other children. Erikson is not far wrong in saying that "Hitler never was the brother of anyone."[50] He was probably too narcissistic to tolerate an equal in any relationship.

According to the family physician, Dr. E. Bloch, the mother was a very affectionate woman whose life was centered in her children and particularly Adolf, the youngest, whom she adored.[51] Three of her other children had died within one year, which explains the concentration of all her love and care on Adolf.[52] Without doubt, as Hanfstaengl said, the mother occupied "the central position in his whole erotic genesis."[53] Erikson speaks of Hitler's "pathological attachment to his mother."[54] Dr. Bloch said "I have never witnessed a closer attachment," but he did not believe that it was pathological.[55] She was profoundly religious, and we must assume that she and her favorite son jointly submerged themselves in the overwhelming emotions of countless Catholic church services. (Hitler's religiousness will be discussed here later.) Dr. Murray even believes that "the emotional source of . . . [Hitler's] orgiastic speeches were childhood tantrums by which he successfully appealed to his ever-indulgent mother."[56] He always carried her picture with him in his early days in Vienna,[57] and a picture of this modest woman still hung over his bed in the Chancellery in Berlin,[58] looking down upon some apparently quite abnormal sex acts which we shall go into later.

In the light of Hitler's relations to his father and mother, it is not surprising that psychiatrists have seen an Oedipus complex in this situation. Dr. Murray says that "the evidence is in favor of Hitler having experienced the common Oedipus complex."[59] Dr. Langer describes a "strong libidinal attachment between mother and son."

[49]*Mein Kampf,* p. 2.
[50]Erikson, *Childhood,* p. 338. See also Langer, op. cit., p. 149. It is true, however, that Hitler's half sister Angela kept house for him for a while at the Berghof.
[51]Bloch, op. cit., p. 36.
[52]Maser, *Adolf Hitler,* p. 52.
[53]Hanfstaengl (anonymous), op. cit., p. 5.
[54]Erikson, *Childhood,* p. 333.
[55]Bloch, op. cit., p. 36.
[56]Murray, op. cit., p. 8.
[57]August Kubizek, *The Young Hitler I Knew,* p. 36.
[58]Karl Wilhelm Krause, *Zehn Jahre Kammerdiener bei Hitler,* p. 35.
[59]Dr. Murray, op. cit., p. 10. See also Hanfstaengl (anonymous), p. 5.

"Infantile sexual feelings [he says] were probably quite prominent in this relationship. . . . This is the Oedipus complex. . . . The great amount of affection lavished upon him by his mother and the undesirable character of his father served to develop this complex to an extraordinary degree."[60]

Erikson, however, has some reservations. He suggests that "in Hitler's national as well as domestic imagery, the young mother betrays the longing son for a senile tyrant," but he concludes that a

> . . . seemingly naive coincidence of themes lends itself easily — much too easily — to a psychoanalytic interpretation of the first chapter of *Mein Kampf* as an involuntary confession of Hitler's Oedipus complex. This interpretation would suggest that in Hitler's case the love for his young mother and the hate for his old father assumed morbid proportions, and that it was this conflict which drove him to love and to hate and compelled him to save or destroy people and peoples who really "stand for" his mother and his father. There have been articles in psychoanalytic literature which claim such simple causality. But it obviously takes much more than an individual complex to make a successful revolutionary.[61]

However, there is really no one who has suggested that it was Hitler's Oedipus complex alone which was at the root of his political actions.

Perhaps the most important result of Hitler's attachment to his mother was that, in later life, he replaced this physical mother in his imagery by what Erikson calls "an abundance of super-human mother figures." The extent to which Hitler referred to these abstract mother figures in his writings, speeches, etc., is, in fact, enormous. Erikson himself quotes some examples: "'Fate . . . designated my birthplace.' . . . 'Poverty clasped me in her arms.' . . . 'Dame Sorrow was my foster mother.' . . . 'The Wisdom of Providence.' . . . 'Nature, the cruel Queen of all wisdom.'"[62] All these figures clearly dominated him. Nature, indeed, was probably his most important

[60]Langer, op. cit., pp. 160–161.
[61]Erikson, *Childhood*, p. 329.
[62]Ibid., p. 339.

mother figure, but there were also race (which was part of nature), history, the *Volk*, and, above all, Germany. One of Erikson's conclusions is that Hitler "saw in himself a lonely man fighting and pleasing superhuman mother figures which now try to destroy him, now are forced to bless him." [63] It is at this point that Erikson, to an extent, converges with Erich Fromm's two theories about Hitler, which will be discussed in detail below. In the one theory, Fromm proposes the concept of "incestuous symbiosis" or mother fixation, and in the other he discusses the masochistic striving toward submission to an overwhelmingly strong power, such as nature, Providence, fate, history.

It is quite possible, as is substantially suggested by Langer, that Hitler transferred to his most important superhuman mother figure, Germany, all the emotions he had once felt for his physical mother. On an unconscious level, it was his longing, after the humiliation of Germany in World War I, to come to the rescue of his superhuman mother and to redeem her, which he had been unable to do as a child for his physical mother when his father brutally attacked her (and, perhaps, raped her before his eyes). [64] The Oedipus complex thus merged into nationalism, and this merger may have profoundly affected history from 1920 to 1945.

d. HITLER, THE ETERNAL ADOLESCENT

It is Erikson who suggested that Hitler always remained the "unbroken adolescent," the "one who remains young." [65] It is an important point, and much can be said in support of it. Hitler was, as we have seen, a "glorified older brother" who had vigorously defied his own father's efforts to force him into the respectability of "the system" or "the Establishment" as we might call it today. The "Germans [as Erikson says] acquiesced to his broken pledges, as long as Hitler, the tough adolescent, seemed merely to be taking advantage of other men's senility" and "In Germany, then, we saw a highly organized and highly educated nation surrender to the imagery of ideological adolescence." [66] We might add that this was possible only because a great many Germans themselves were ideological adolescents or nearly so.

[63] Ibid., p. 340.
[64] See Langer, op. cit., pp. 164, 212, 214; Murray, op. cit., p. 9.
[65] Erikson, *Childhood*, p. 337.
[66] Ibid., pp. 338, 344.

The theory of Hitler as the eternal adolescent is supported by a good many facts. One is that he almost never changed opinions which he had acquired as an adolescent, no matter how immature these opinions might have been. Even of his early childhood he says in *Mein Kampf* that "my first ideals were probably formed in those days,"[67] and in high school *(Realschule)* "I became a nationalist . . . I learned to understand and comprehend history in its real meaning."[68] More importantly, during his years in Vienna (approximately from his eighteenth to his twenty-fourth year) "my eyes were opened to . . . the horrible meaning . . . of Marxism and Jewry," and "At that time, there took shape within me a picture of the world and an ideology which became the rocklike foundation for my subsequent actions. I have had to learn little in addition to what I then created for myself; and I have had to change nothing."[69] The theme that he never had to change his early views is repeated over and over. Thus, discussing his early acquaintance with socialism, he said that "in the course of the years, my opinion concerning it was broadened and deepened, but I have had no need to change it."[70] In fact he devoted nearly three pages of *Mein Kampf* to a rationalization of the inadvisability of a change in the opinions of any Führer.[71] Twenty years later, he still told Albert Speer that what he "is now planning and creating is merely the realization of . . . ideas" conceived as a young man.[72] And Speer himself felt that "Hitler's plans and goals had never changed."[73]

There is, then, little doubt that Hitler had a strong and probably abnormal aversion to abandoning any position which he had occupied as an adolescent. (It is strange, in fact, to note the old-fashioned Austrian turn-of-the-century flavor of *Mein Kampf*.) It follows that objective facts, which ran counter to Hitler's established views, were repugnant to him. There was nothing he shied away from more than the fatal danger which an encounter of his fixed opinions with the actual facts could involve. The world had to be as he knew it to be; and he was, on the whole, willing to accept new facts, information,

[67] *Mein Kampf*, p. 3.
[68] Ibid., p. 8. A very similar statement is found on p. 137.
[69] Ibid., pp. 20–21.
[70] Ibid., p. 53.
[71] Ibid., pp. 71–73.
[72] Speer, *Erinnerungen*, p. 134.
[73] Ibid., p. 120.

and advice only if they could be made to fit into his established ideology. Typically he said in an aggressive speech on November 8, 1941, ridiculing President Roosevelt's brain trust: "I have no experts at all. In my case, my own head alone is always enough. I need no brain trust to help me. Therefore, if there really is to be a change anywhere, then that change will be created in my brain and not in other people's brains. . . ."[74]

Like an adolescent, he never had a doubt about the truth of what he knew to be right; and he preferred to live in a world of fantasy and intoxicating dreams, even dreams of a heroic death. Albert Speer says, perhaps with some exaggeration, that Hitler "knew nothing about his enemies and refused to make use of information that was at his disposal; he preferred to rely on his spontaneous . . . inspirations. . . ."[75] In his last year, the steel doors of his bunkers, behind which a mad world of dreams led a troubled existence, were almost totally sealed against the reality outside.

Again like an adolescent, he had a strong aversion to orderly systematic work throughout his life. The fact that he was a poor student in high school is not, of course, of much significance; but his real aversion to work first became apparent when he dropped out of school at age 16 — with the permission of his indulgent mother, his father having died three years earlier — and began a life of doing nothing in his mother's home for about two and a half years. He seems to have filled these years with doing a little drawing, visiting the local theater, walking with his friend August Kubizek, and generally lounging around.[76] There followed about seven years of doing little or nothing in Vienna and later in Munich.[77] Altogether, Hitler had a period of about nine years of a "moratorium" — as Erikson calls such inactive periods in the life of young people — certainly much longer than normal.[78] His volunteering for the German army in August 1914 put an end to it, and at age 25 he became a diligent soldier. It was, in a small way, his first step into history and into heroic history at that.[79] (In

[74] Max Domarus, *Hitlers Reden und Proklamationen 1932-1945*, p. 1778.
[75] Speer, op. cit., p. 180.
[76] See Kubizek, op. cit., *passim*.
[77] Ibid., *passim;* F. Jetzinger, *Der junge Hitler, passim.*
[78] In his *Table Talks*, p. 324, Hitler expressed limited approval of such moratoria.
[79] See his Political Testament, *TMWC*, Vol. 41, p. 548.

1919 he decided to become a politician and seemingly developed what clinicians call an "obsessive compensation." [80]

What is more significant, for purposes of our discussion of Hitler's eternal adolescence, is that his youthful aversion to orderly, systematic work continued or was revived when he became Chancellor and Führer, if not before. This is attested to in the memoirs of many of his collaborators and is perhaps related best by Speer. [81] He describes the course of Hitler's regular day in Obersalzberg and in Berlin, including the interminable midday and evening meals with a large group of more or less the same people. "A meal with Hitler [he says] normally meant a considerable loss of time because we sat at the table until about half past four." The evening and a good portion of the night were spent in largely meaningless conversations, or listening to Hitler's monologues or to phonograph records, or looking at films, the latter for three or four hours. Some of this sounds like a description of a gathering of teen-agers. If television had existed at that time, Hitler would very likely have been addicted to it. At any rate, his pursuits hardly represented the manner in which normal, mature politicians spend their time. Speer summarizes his own reaction as follows:

I was an intensive worker and, initially, could not understand the wastefulness with which Hitler dealt with his working time. It is true that I could sympathize with his bringing his day to an *end* in boredom and entertainment, but this phase of the day, lasting an average of six hours, seemed a little long by my standards, whereas the real workday was relatively short. When—I often asked myself—does he really work? There was little left of the day; he got up in the late morning, then disposed of one or two conferences on official business, but beginning with the midday meal, which followed, he more or less idled away his time until the early evening hours. Infrequent business meetings set for the afternoon were endangered by his preference for architectural plans. [82]

Hitler's "unbroken adolescence" manifested itself also in the

[80] Erik H. Erikson, *Young Man Luther,* p. 45.
[81] See particularly Speer, op. cit., pp. 102-106, 142-146.
[82] Ibid., p. 145.

nature of some of the books which impressed him. They were books of pseudonatural history, pseudoscience, pseudophilosophy, and the like, which were normally read by teen-agers or the semieducated. In his *Table Talks*, in 1942, he still said that he believed in the "world ice theory" which had been developed in 1912 by a dilettante, Hanns Hörbiger, in a book entitled *Glazial-Kosmogonie.*[83] Other German teen-age favorites, which greatly impressed Hitler, were Edgar Dacque, *Urwelt, Sage und Menschheit* (Primeval World, Saga, and Humanity),[84] and, of course, Houston Stewart Chamberlain, *Die Grundlagen des 19. Jahrhunderts.*[85] (But he read also more adult books that fitted into his schemes, such as Philipp Bouhler, *Napoleon,*[86] which compared him and Napoleon, and a book by "Petri" which dealt with the "Germanic" elements in Belgium and Northern France.[87])

Erikson speaks of Hitler's (adolescent) "conviction that no school or occupation within the system could contain him."[88] This is undoubtedly true of his period in high school which he left prematurely, but thereafter he made two quite determined, though unsuccessful, attempts to be accepted as an art student by the Vienna Academy of Arts, and he would have liked also to enter the School of Architecture, being prevented only by his lacking the required high school diploma.[89] If either one of these schools had accepted him, the history of the world might well have taken an entirely different turn. There is no question that art, and particularly architecture, remained his true passions to the end of his life; and to this author his architectural sketches demonstrate definite talent. (For the rest of his life "his orientation" remained "that of an artist and not of a statesman."[90]) The impossibility of entering these schools no doubt left the young Hitler with a traumatic sense of rejection which, in large measure, may have been responsible for his subsequent "moratorium" period of doing almost nothing for about seven years. His old friend Kubizek

[83] *Hitler's Table Talks*, p. 167.
[84] See Mosse, *Crisis*, p. 306.
[85] *Hitler's Table Talks*, pp. 155, 396.
[86] Ibid., p. 199.
[87] Ibid., p. 313.
[88] Erikson, *Luther*, p. 105.
[89] For details, see Maser, *Adolf Hitler*, pp. 76–78, 85.
[90] Langer, op. cit., p. 60.

reports that the rejection by the Academy of Arts "resulted in an ever-growing sense of rebellion."[91] "He fled from the world which knew him."[92] He probably did not know what else to do and what else he could identify with, until the outbreak of World War I solved his problem.

Not only was Hitler himself an eternal adolescent, but as such he was able to exert tremendous influence on the millions of German adolescents, young and not so young. Youth massed around him in enormous numbers. Long before he seized power, countless students at all universities demanded with much noise and conviction that he be made Germany's leader. He was one of them—no father, but an older brother, the gang leader, a tough and noisy adolescent. He "had never sacrificed his will to any father,"[93] had never been part of the Establishment. He, like they, saw everything in black and white, the good people and the wicked ones. He, like they, had all the answers. All one had to do to achieve the German millenium was to beat the wicked people into submission or get rid of them. Naturally, there was no generation gap between Hitler and German youth. They were all willing and eager to be adventurers together. The spirit of adolescence ruled, and in no time it became violent and destructive.

e. HITLER'S SEX LIFE

There is more uncertainty about the nature of Hitler's sex life than about any other aspect of his psychology. The available evidence, apart from one minor exception, is all hearsay. The exception is the diary of Hitler's mistress Eva Braun, but this is brief and tells us little. A good deal has been written about the matter—much of it unpublished—but, in the nature of things, it must be largely conjectural. Nonetheless, some of the conjecture is useful. At any rate, we may never obtain more reliable information than we now have. Other diaries or correspondence of persons sexually involved with Hitler might conceivably still come to light, but this is uncertain.

Some of the conjecture may be motivated in part by the natural temptation to assume ipso facto—and perhaps quite correctly—that the sexual activities of someone as abnormal as Hitler could not have

[91]Kubizek, op. cit., p. 160.
[92]Maser, op. cit., p. 86.
[93]Erikson, *Childhood*, pp. 341, 338.

been normal. It may be motivated further by the tempting assumption that, no matter how enormously strong and powerful this man was in politics and warfare, he was no good at all in bed with a woman.

One reason for the dearth of really reliable information is that, whatever the nature of Hitler's sex life was, it not only began very late but there apparently never was very much of it. (Erikson, however, is wrong in speaking of "Hitler's proclaimed abstinence from . . . sex."[94]) Another reason is that throughout his life he was extremely discreet and reticent in *all* personal matters. The German people, for example, had never heard of Eva Braun until after she and Hitler died. Even his most intimate associates—he had no real "friends"— knew very little about his sex life. In fact, at times he may have intentionally misled them. His general reticence is shown, for example, by the fact that he never allowed anyone to see him in his bath or naked[95] (except his physicians, who examined him freely[96]) and that he did not like to bathe in the open air.[97] Yet there are some facts of his sex life of which we can be reasonably sure, and there are also some others that justify certain assumptions.

It may be advisable first to discuss the question whether he had any *homosexual* tendencies. Everyone appears to be in agreement that he never was an overt or active homosexual, and the whole question might never have been raised, if it had not been for two facts:

1. A good number of the men in Hitler's inner circle, particularly in the early days of the Movement, were homosexuals, for example Hess and Röhm (who did not even hide it); and Hitler clearly liked their company.

2. There was a "large feminine component in Hitler's physical constitution" and he had "feminine tastes and sensibilities."[98] His hips were wide, his shoulders relatively narrow.[99] There is no question that there was something feminine about him.

These facts have resulted in opinions about his covert homosex-

[94]Ibid., p. 342.

[95]See, f.i., Ernst Hanfstaengl's interview in *Source Book*, p. 897, to Langer, op. cit.

[96]Maser, *Adolf Hitler*, p. 436.

[97]Krause, *Zehn Jahre Kammerdiener*, p. 47; see also Speer, op. cit., p. 114.

[98]Murray, *Analysis*, p. 19; to the same effect, W. H. D. Vernon, "Hitler, the Man— Notes for a Case History," in *Journal of Abnormal and Social Psychology*, p. 298.

[99]Langer, op. cit., p. 20.

uality, which differ in degree. Edward Deuss, who had personal contact with Hitler for one and a half years, called him "a man on the borderline of woman."[100] Hanfstaengl believed that "some of his . . . [Hitler's] relationships have bordered on this type. . . ."[101] He saw "possibly even a homosexual streak," and then said more positively, "He is both homosexual and heterosexual; . . . both man and woman."[102] Dr. Murray spoke of "repressed . . . homosexuality."[103] Dr. Langer thought that "he is certainly not homosexual in the ordinary sense of the term."[104]

All these opinions were stated while Hitler was still alive, some on the basis of personal observation, others after long-distance analysis. Today, about thirty years later, it seems difficult to concede more than the presence of a mere "homosexual streak" in Hitler. It is true that there was a rather large feminine component in his physical constitution, tastes, and so forth, but this was nothing unusual in Austrian men, at least of that period—men who were predominantly heterosexual and certainly were far from being overtly homosexual. It is true, also, that there was a rather large homosexual group in the Movement, particularly in its early days, but this does not mean that Hitler selected them for sexual reasons. They "came with" the Movement as indeed did a great many other "dissenters" of various kinds. Some of the homosexuals proved to be among Hitler's most loyal and useful collaborators.

To be sure, later he showed what might be called an excessively strong adverse and therefore perhaps suspicious reaction during the "Röhm affair," when actual homosexuality was discovered in the SA. He told Speer that "the homosexual atmosphere nauseated" him. "In one room we surprised two naked young men."[105] In a public declaration at that time, he again spoke of a "nauseating situation," and he ordered a "ruthless cleaning out of this plague-boil."[106] His order of the day to the SA announced his determination that "in the future every mother shall be able to give her son to the SA, to the Party and

[100]Memorandum of February 1943 in correspondence file relating to *Source Book* to Langer, op. cit., National Archives, Washington.

[101]*Source Book,* p. 912, to Langer, op. cit.

[102]Hanfstaengl (anonymous), *Adolf Hitler,* pp. 29-30.

[103]Murray, op. cit., p. 19.

[104]Langer, op. cit., p. 138.

[105]Speer, op. cit., p. 64.

[106]Gisevius, *Adolf Hitler,* p. 184.

the Hitler Youth without fear that he might be ethically or morally ruined . . . . I want to see men as leaders of the SA, and not ridiculous monkeys."[107]

But strong as his reaction was, it should be remembered that his reactions to a great many things were excessive. And politically this reaction was no doubt useful. As evidence of latent homosexuality, the Röhm-incident is not reliable. It is clearly counterbalanced, more-over, by irrefutable evidence that Hitler was very much impressed by, and attracted to, the beauty and company of women. Here is a quotation from his *Table Talks:*

> What beautiful women there are! We were sitting . . . [in a res-taurant]. A woman came in: you really thought she had come down from heaven! Simply radiant! The guests put down their knives and forks. Nobody could stop looking at that woman.
>
> And then later in Braunschweig! Afterwards I bitterly blamed myself . . . . A blond girl ran over to me in the car to hand me flowers. Everyone remembered the incident but no one thought of asking the girl for her address so that I might have sent her a thank-you note. Blond and tall and magnificent! But that's the way it is: masses of people all over the place. And we were in a hurry, too. I'm still sorry about it today. . . .
>
> [At a reception in Munich] a woman came in—so beautiful that beside her everything faded . . . —Three women, each more beautiful than the other—, that was some sight! During my time in Vienna, too, I saw many beautiful women.[108]
>
> . . . I don't like to be alone anymore and I like best to have a meal with a woman. . . .[109]

These are not the words of a man with really significant homosexual tendencies, and there were many of such statements.

The belief that Hitler was not a homosexual is supported, further, by the views of a *homosexual* physician who x-rayed him before 1939: "I, as a homosexual, was fascinated by Hitler's eyes, his speech and his way of walking; but I felt at once: he is not one of us."[110]

Of course, there is the fact that Hitler did not get married until

---

[107] Domarus, op. cit., p. 401.
[108] *Hitler's Table Talks*, pp. 164–165.
[109] Ibid., p. 194.
[110] Quoted in Maser, *Adolf Hitler*, p. 309.

two days before he and his bride, Eva Braun, jointly committed suicide. He was then 56 years old. And even this marriage might never have taken place, had it not been for his certain knowledge that his death almost immediately thereafter would put an end to it. But the reasons which he gave at various times for not wanting to get married were fairly plausible, at least for a man like Hitler:

> It is fortunate for many a leading personality that they never got married. It would have been a catastrophe.
> There is a point at which the wife will never understand her husband. . . . The husband . . . is the slave of his thoughts: his tasks and duties dominate him, and there may be times when he must really say: What do I care about wife, what do I care about child! . . .
> I don't believe that a man like *me* will still get married. In his mind, such a man has assembled an idealized picture [of a woman], taking the body of the one, the hair of another, the mind of a third one, the eyes of a fourth. And it is with this test instrument that he approaches every new female. But no such woman exists.[111]

To Speer, he once said: "In my free time, I want to have peace. I could never get married. If I had children, what problems!"[112] And as a matter of practical politics, Hitler and some of his advisers always felt that as long as he was unmarried, his political attraction to the female population was greatly enhanced. Thus, Speer quotes him as saying: "Many women are attached to me because I am unmarried. That was particularly important during the early period of my struggle [*Kampfzeit*]. It is the same with a film actor: when he gets married, he loses a certain something in the eyes of the adoring women; he will be less of an idol."[113]

The possible existence of latent homosexual tendencies in Hitler is negated further, and perhaps more convincingly, by heterosexual activities on his part, no matter how abnormal they may have been. These will be discussed below, but it might be added here that the nature of these activities was probably such they would have been

[111] *Hitler's Table Talks*, p. 164.
[112] Speer, op. cit., p. 106.
[113] Ibid., p. 106.

much less satisfying to him had he carried them on with a wife rather than a mistress.

As to the question whether Hitler was a chronic *masturbator*, the evidence is scarce. August Kubizek, with whom Hitler shared a room as a young man in Vienna, says simply that Hitler "refrained from masturbation."[114] But masturbation is nothing that a person of Hitler's cautious reticence would have permitted to come to the knowledge of a male roommate. Others, at any rate, though much less intimately acquainted with Hitler, have taken a different view. Hanfstaengl was "convinced in his own mind that Hitler is a confirmed masturbator" but he "could not or would not give any evidence for this belief."[115] Elsewhere he said that Hitler was "the type of ego-centric and masturbic Narcissus. . . ."[116] The above-mentioned *Source Book* quotes Axel Heyst as having written that "some observers . . . suspect that Hitler is an addict to the vice of masturbation. . . ."[117] Presumably on the basis of these conjectural statements, Dr. Langer himself says merely that "some believe that he is a chronic masturbator."[118]

More important, perhaps, is an allegedly observed incident of masturbation by Hitler in the course of a heterosexual relationship with the actress Rene (Renate?) Mueller. She reported it to her director, A. Zeissler, who, in turn, told the OSS interviewer about it. Apparently she said that, after some other abnormal acts, Hitler, "as a final climax, masturbated before her."[119] If this actually took place, it would indeed seem to suggest that Hitler was a habitual masturbator, because it does not seem likely that any other man would masturbate before a woman. Chronic masturbation might also be in line with Hitler's general character structure of a reserved, inward-turned, joyless, ascetic person. The incident with Rene Mueller, moreover, may raise doubt as to Hitler's sexual potency.

This finally brings us to Hitler's *heterosexual* relations. Apart from the sexual aspects, Hitler's attitude toward women was one of

---

[114]Kubizek, op. cit., p. 237.
[115]OSS interview, *Source Book*, p. 912, to Langer, op. cit.
[116]Hanfstaengl (anonymous), *Adolf Hitler*, p. 30.
[117]Ibid., p. 601.
[118]Langer, op. cit., p. 137.
[119]*Source Book*, p. 922, to Langer, op. cit.

complete male superiority. "A woman's world is the man." "The intellect of a woman doesn't matter at all." "In politics, a woman cannot separate reason and emotion." ". . . a woman loves a hero . . . . She wants the heroic man." "A man must be able to put his brand [*Stempel*] on every girl. A woman doesn't really want anything else." "There is nothing more beautiful than to form a young thing for one's own purposes: a girl of 18 or 20 is as flexible as wax."[120] But this entire attitude of superiority or even contempt for women was really only a brave front. It probably vanished in any actual heterosexual encounter.

There is, first, the matter of Hitler's possible impotence, which, indeed, might have been caused, among other things, by chronic masturbation. But nobody really knows much about it.[121] Hanfstaengl wrote that "during almost fifteen years of association with Hitler, the whip with which Hitler loves to gesticulate figures as a kind of substitute or auxiliary symbol for his missing sexual potency. All this wielding of the whip seems to be connected with a hidden desire . . . for some state of erection which would overcome his fundamental sexual inferiority complex."[122] It seems to be Hanfstaengl's conclusion from this that "The truth is that Hitler is in all probability still [in 1942] in the stage of puberty . . . ," which is in line with our earlier discussion of Hitler's eternal adolescence.

Dr. Langer says, "It is probably true that he is impotent. . . ."[123] Dr. Murray states flatly that "Hitler himself is impotent," giving as sole and rather inadquate reasons that he is unmarried and "his old acquaintances say that he is incapable of consummating the sexual act in a normal fashion."[124] (The "old acquaintances" are not identified.) Dr. Murray then draws this important conclusion:

This infirmity we must recognize as an instigation to exhorbitant cravings for superiority. Unable to demonstrate male power

---

[120] *Hitler's Table Talks*, pp. 194, 212, 193, 164.

[121] Maser, *Adolf Hitler*, pp. 319–320, seems convinced that Hitler was not impotent and that, in fact, his sex life was normal, but his sources seem of questionable value to this author.

[122] Hanfstaengl (anonymous), op. cit., p. 33; see also the OSS interview with Hanfstaengl in *Source Book*, p. 903, to Langer, op. cit.

[123] Langer, op. cit., p. 138. See also p. 182.

[124] Murray, op. cit., p. 6.

before a woman, he is impelled to compensate by exhibiting unsurpassed power before men in the world at large.

Quite in line with this, Hitler once said in a reminiscing speech in 1935, after his seizure of power:

> While our enemies believed they had destroyed us, the real truth was that the semen of our Movement, with one stroke, had been hurled across the whole of Germany.[125]

Erich Fromm has pointed out generally that

> in a psychological sense, the lust for power is not rooted in strength but in weakness . . . . It is the desperate attempt to gain secondary strength where genuine strength is lacking . . . . Impotence . . . results in the sadistic striving for domination.[126]

In Hitler's case, however, this possible impotence seems to have resulted in sadism only in the political sphere, and as we shall see, in masochistic drives in the sexual sphere.

There is another result which Hitler's possible impotence may have had. Psychologically he replaced woman, with whom he may have been sexually unable to deal, by the "mass of the people," whom he repeatedly declared to be feminine in character *(feminin veranlagt)*[127] and whom, as it were, he could rape by "brutal fighting speeches."[128] Dr. Vernon says that "From the analytic point of view . . . [the need to speak] may well be interpreted as a compensation for sexual difficulties."[129] There is little doubt that Hitler did more speaking and talking in his life than any other public figure in history.

It is even possible that psychologically the adoption of the official greeting with raised out-stretched arm (colloquially, the "Nazi salute") was a result of Hitler's sexual impotence. This might well

---

[125] Speech of Nov. 8, 1935, Domarus, op. cit., p. 552.

[126] Fromm, *Escape*, p. 162.

[127] *Hitler's Table Talks*, p. 345; see also *Mein Kampf*, p. 201.

[128] Bracher, *Die deutsche Diktatur*, p. 140. Walter Görlitz, *Adolf Hitler*, p. 23, claims that Hitler's discussion of the treatment of the masses in *Mein Kampf* plagiarized the French writer Gustave Le Bon. The present author has not investigated this.

[129] Vernon, op. cit., p. 302.

seem a naïve and simplistic thought, but it is, in fact, suggested by an incident which the aforementioned actress Rene Mueller appears to have reported to her director A. Zeissler. According to the OSS interviewer of Zeissler, she told the latter that

> On one occasion Hitler seemed to become [sexually] quite excited and she thought the moment had arrived when he would actually do something, but instead he jumped up on his feet and raised his arm in the Nazi salute and said in a very bragging tone of voice that he could hold his arm that way for an hour and a half at a time without tiring while even Goering [sic] could not hold his up for even twenty minutes.[130]

It is, thus, conceivable that Hitler substituted the raised arm for an erect penis.

But the fact of Hitler's potency or impotence may ordinarily not even have entered into the peculiar heterosexual relations which he chose, although it is possible that impotence encouraged this very choice. At any rate, potency was presumably not required in these relations. The probabilities are that sexually Hitler was a confirmed masochist. We shall discuss the available evidence, but we should emphasize that it is almost exclusively hearsay and that the reliability of it may be questionable.

We know of three women with whom Hitler had intimate sexual relations (and these three possibly were the only ones): Rene (Renate?) Mueller, Angela (Geli) Raubal, and Eva Braun.[131] The actress Rene Mueller was mentioned earlier in connection with Hitler's masturbation and the possible significance of the "Nazi salute." A more complete report, as told by her to her theater director A. Zeissler and retold by him to an OSS interviewer, follows:

> ... she did her utmost to seduce Hitler but in this she never succeeded. ... When Zeissler asked her what was troubling her she told him that the evening before she had been with Hitler and that she had been sure he was going to have intercourse

[130] *Source Book,* p. 922 to Langer, op. cit.

[131] Maser, *Adolf Hitler,* pp. 311–313, mentions a good many other women, but says that physical relations between them and Hitler cannot be established beyond doubt.

with her; that they had both undressed and were apparently getting ready for bed when Hitler fell on the floor and begged her to kick him. She demurred but he pleaded with her and condemned himself as unworthy, heaped all kinds of accusations on his own head and just groveled around in an agonizing manner. The scene became intolerable to her and she finally acceded to his wishes and kicked him. This excited him greatly and he begged for more and more, always saying that it was even better than he deserved and that he was not worthy to be in the same room with her. As she continued to kick him he became more and more excited and as a final climax, masturbated before her. He then suggested that they get dressed and thanked her warmly for a pleasant evening. [132]

The story may well be essentially true. It rings true, and if it is true, it reveals solid masochism.

A different but even more intense form of masochistic behavior by Hitler was reported by Geli Raubal, his niece, nineteen years younger than he was. For about six years she was his frequent companion, and for a while she lived in his Munich apartment. He once told his secretary that Geli was the personification of his ideal of a woman;[133] and if he ever loved a woman, it was Geli.

Her report about Hitler's sexual relations with her comes to us partly secondhand, partly thirdhand, through Otto Strasser, a former political associate of Hitler who fell out of his favor. In 1948 Strasser published a book which was highly critical of Hitler. His reputation and reliability seem, therefore, quite doubtful, but Dr. Langer saw "no reason to question his sincerity."[134] In his book, Strasser, with much delicacy, speaks only of "eccentric practices," "perverted methods," and "a story scarcely credible to a healthy-minded man," which Geli (and, allegedly, another woman) had told him.[135] Later, however, when interviewed by the OSS, he went into detail:

[132]Interview with A. Zeissler of June 24, 1943, in *Source Book*, p. 922, to Langer, op. cit.

[133]A. Zoller, *Hitler privat*, pp. 87–91. We shall have frequent occasion to cite that book, which can be regarded as a valuable, reliable source. The secretary, Christa Schröder, told her story to an American interrogation officer, A. Zoller, after the war.

[134]Langer, op. cit., p. 138.

[135]Strasser, *Hitler and I*, pp. 72–73 (English translation, Boston, 1940).

. . . one morning he [Strasser] claims Geli appeared at his apartment in Munich in a very upset state of mind. Strasser . . . tried to quiet her down but for some time all he could get out of her was that she did not know what she would do with her uncle. . . . Strasser tried to make light of the matter and said to Geli: "Well, why don't you sleep with him? What difference does it make if he is your uncle?" Geli responded that she would be very glad to sleep with him if that was all he wanted but she just couldn't go through with the other performance again. After much urging concerning the nature of this performance, she finally told Strasser that Hitler made her undress and that he would lie down on the floor. Then she would have to squat down over his face where he could examine her at close range and this would make him very excited. When the excitement reached its peak he demanded that she urinate on him and that gave him his sexual pleasure. [136]

Apparently, nothing else happened. Geli committed suicide in 1931.

Eva Braun would have been the one who could have given us the most reliable information. She was Hitler's mistress for fourteen years (and his wife for two days and two nights). But she was as discreet as Hitler himself. She did leave a handwritten diary of 22 pages, covering, however, no more than the period from February 6, 1935, to May 28, 1935 (when she made one of several unsuccessful suicide attempts). [137] On the whole, the diary consists of the lament of an immature young woman about being neglected by the man she loves. But the diary does contain one brief statement which might possibly have some significance here. After complaining bitterly about Hitler's inattention, she says: "He uses me only for certain purposes" *(zu bestimmten Zwecken).* [138] While this might conceivably mean that Hitler used her generally for sexual purposes, [139] it is more likely to

[136] Interview with O. Strasser on May 13, 1943, in *Source Book*, p. 919, to Langer, op. cit. Vague confirmation of Strasser's story was given to the OSS by the French psychiatrist Dr. Raymond de Saussure, *Source Book*, p. 932. Konrad Heiden, *Der Fuehrer—Hitler's Rise to Power*, (English translation), pp. 384–385, seems to report merely a wild rumor.

[137] The original diary has been retained by the U.S. government as a "prize of war" (*The New York Times*, Nov. 17, 1968). Xerox copies of it and of an inaccurate and incomplete English translation can be obtained from the National Archives.

[138] Braun, Eva Braun's *Diary*, p. 12, entry of Mar. 11, 1935.

[139] This is Maser's interpretation (*Adolf Hitler*, p. 320).

mean that the purposes were of an unusual kind. In other words, her statement has some limited speculative value as corroborating Rene Mueller and Geli Raubal.

Otherwise, we know only that Hitler's relations with Eva Braun were quite intimate. Her bedroom in Berlin adjoined his,[140] and at the Berghof there was a connecting door between his bedroom and hers.[141] Her underwear was reported to have been found in his bedroom.[142] Both he and she, however, "avoided anything that indicated an intimate friendship—and yet late at night they went to the bedrooms upstairs."[143] But sometimes Hitler did hold her hand,[144] a surprisingly normal human gesture. We shall have more to say about Eva Braun later.

There is a fourth woman with whom Hitler had "intimate" (but hardly "sexual") relations of sorts. She was Leni Riefenstahl, an actress with much sex appeal, the official director of documentary films, and a well-known skier.[145] We have a fourthhand report through Otto Strasser that

> Leni was dying to sleep with Hitler but that Hitler was always evading the issue. The [theater] director said that not long before Leni had told him that Hitler had invited her into his bedroom and that she thought that the time had finally arrived, but much to her dismay he asked her to undress. When she had done so and was ready to get into bed he ordered her to begin masturbating herself while he sat on the other side of the room and watched her.[146]

Evidently, that was all. The story sounds inherently unlikely, but if it is true, its meaning seems obscure, except that it might support the hypothesis of impotence and would indicate voyeurism.

[140]Speer, op. cit., p. 144.

[141]Krause, *Zehn Jahre Kammerdiener*, p. 45.

[142]Langer, op. cit., p. 83, but this is probably no more than a dubious rumor.

[143]Speer, op. cit., p. 59.

[144]Ibid., p. 104.

[145]With pornographic humor, some Germans called her "Reich-glacier-crevasse" *(Reichsgletscherspalte)*.

[146]OSS interview, *Source Book*, p. 919, to Langer, op. cit. In an interview with Maser in 1970, Leni said nothing (*Adolf Hitler*, p. 479, fn. 65). See also *The New York Times*, Aug. 23, 1972, p. 31.

On the basis of some of the foregoing facts or conjectures, the opinions of the psychiatrists are substantially in agreement. Dr. Langer regards Hitler as "an extreme masochist who derives sexual pleasure from having a woman squat over him while she urinates or defecates [?] on his face."[147] Dr. Murray says that "sexually . . . [Hitler] is a full-fledged *masochist*"; that in his mind there is an "association . . . of sexuality and excretion."[148] Going into more detail, Dr. Murray gives this analysis:

> . . . the sexual pattern has resulted from the fusion of (i) *a primitive excretory soiling tendency*, and (ii) *a passive masochistic tendency* (hypertrophy of the feminine component in his make-up). The second element (masochism) derives much of its strength from an *unconscious need for punishment*, a tendency which may be expected in one who has assiduously repressed, out of swollen pride, the submissive reactions (compliance, cooperation, payment of debts, expression of gratitude, acknowledgment of errors, apology, confession, atonement) which are required of everybody who would adaptively participate in social life. While Hitler consciously overstrives to assert his infinite superiority, *nature instinctively corrects the balance* by imposing an erotic pattern that calls for *infinite self-abasement.*[149]

Hanfstaengl called Hitler a "sado-masochistic type," but nothing indicating sadism in the *sexual* pattern seems to have come to light, though Hitler's sadism revealed itself elsewhere in abundance. But Hanfstaengl probably concluded quite correctly that Hitler's "sexual situation is untenable and even desperate. There seem to be psychic if not also physical obstacles which make real and complete sexual fulfillment ever impossible."[150] The failure of sexual fulfillment drove him on to fulfill himself in other spheres.

We shall omit here other, purely speculative views concerning Hitler's sex life which have been expressed.

The journalist Nerin E. Gun claims to have evidence concerning

---

[147] Langer, op. cit., p. 138. The evidence, however, seems to be silent as to defecation, as distinguished from urination.

[148] Murray, op. cit., p. 5, 6.

[149] Ibid., p. 18 (italics quoted).

[150] Hanfstaengl (anonymous), op. cit., pp. 30–31.

Hitler's sex life very different from that discussed above. He asserts, with an air of mystery, that he "received from a person who *alone* is qualified to give evidence in this delicate domain a written testimony that enables me to give *irrefutable* information on the subject" and "According to this intimate source, sexual relations between Hitler and Eva Braun were perfectly normal," even though "not of Latin intensity."[151] But Gun neither quotes the "written testimony" nor even gives the name of the "intimate source," and the reliability of his book, at any rate, is generally doubtful because of various errors, etc. (But, in other respects, he does provide some documentation not published elsewhere.)

Another (undocumented) assertion which Gun makes is that "Eva's mother confirmed to me that her daughter's vagina was 'narrowly built'"—a condition for which allegedly she was first medically treated and then operated on with success.[152] It is inherently unlikely that Mrs. Braun, a respectable middle-class woman, would have given a journalist this report about her dead daughter. If, however, the story was really true, it might indicate that there actually was an effort at vaginal penetration by Hitler, that this was unsuccessful, and that Eva sought to facilitate future efforts. But it is all purely conjectural.

It was actually as early as in *Mein Kampf* that Hitler, without the remotest intention of doing so, revealed an abnormal type of sexuality. The probabilities are strong that up to that time (1924 or so) Hitler had not as yet had any heterosexual relations, even though he was about 35 years old.[153] *Mein Kampf*, however, devotes thirteen passionate pages (pp. 269-282) to a diatribe against syphilis and prostitution, and this at a time when the average German gave little thought to syphilis and more or less approved of prostitution. Hitler calls syphilis a "horrible poisoning of the body of the people," "this dreadful epidemic," "this pestilence," and he sees the main cause of it in "our prostitution of love" which, at the same time, is a "Jewification of our spiritual life," a "pestilence of our sexual life," a "mockery of nature," and a "disgrace of humanity." "Fight against syphilis requires fight against prostitution."

[151] Gun, *Eva Braun: Hitler's Mistress*, p. 196 (italics added).
[152] Ibid., p. 197.
[153] This view was taken also by Langer, op. cit., p. 182.

But going beyond that, he says that "our entire public life today is like a hothouse of sexual images and enticements," and there is a "slow process of prostituting our future." What must be done, then, is to "clean away the excrements of our moral pestilence of a cosmopolitan 'culture'," to cleanse life of "the symptoms of a decaying world," and "to free public life from the suffocating perfume of modern sex." Moreover, it all becomes "a test of the value of a race."

And somehow the Jews were behind prostitution. In Vienna, Hitler says, he was able to study "the relationship of Jewry to prostitution and, even more, to the traffic in young girls" and he ". . . recognized, for the first time, the Jews as . . . the shamelessly efficient managers of this shocking business of the vice of big city scum."[154] Quite illogically in his fury, he said that "the Jews are able to educate [the European nations] to become sexless bastards,"[155] whatever that may be. And finally, to round things out in this connection, his "eyes were opened upon discovering the Jews as the leaders of socialism."[156] Bolshevism became "this Jewish disease."[157]

Clearly, in Hitler's psychology, there existed a whole pestilential syndrome of syphilis, prostitution, vice, moral decay, impure blood, filth, Jewry, and Communism. It was all interconnected, and by and large this syndrome continued to dominate Hitler's mind and emotions to the end of his life. Between the lines of *Mein Kampf*, it becomes quite apparent that even before he had had sexual experiences he conceived of sexual intercourse as something filthy, which indeed was what his own later sex life was apparently to be. Unconsciously, by his usual method of projection, he seemed to condemn not merely prostitution but *all* heterosexual intercourse in a kind of monkish hatred of sex. It is interesting, in this connection, that much later, in the *Table Talks*, in speaking of the biblical fall of man, he said that "we became humans by the mortal sin,"[158] when he probably meant "the original sin." Again unconsciously he projected his own sexual

[154]*Mein Kampf*, pp. 63–64.

[155]Ibid., p. 723.

[156]Ibid., p. 64. Even earlier, Hitler had described Moses as "the first leader of bolshevism." See Maser, *Adolf Hitler*, p. 190. See also Gertrud M. Kurth, "The Jews and Adolf Hitler," in *Psychoanalytic Quarterly*, Vol. 16, 1947, pp. 11–42.

[157]*Mein Kampf*, p. 277.

[158]*Hitler's Table Talks*, p. 185.

desires to the Jews. This is underlined by the much-quoted statement in *Mein Kampf:* "The black-haired Jew-boy lies in wait for hours — satanic joy in his face — for the unsuspecting [German] girl whom he soils with his blood. . . ."[159] The murder of the Jews, twenty years later, may have been an act of attempted sexual purification of Hitler himself.

At the root of Hitler's deeply troubled attitude toward heterosexual intercourse may have been, in part, the trauma of his observation of intercourse between his parents as a child (if this really happened), and also his intensely religious Catholic upbringing — at times in the celibate atmosphere of a monastery. As we shall see in the section on Hitler's religiousness, it was, in fact, his ideal as a child to become the abbot of a monastery.[160] We may note, in this connection, that *Mein Kampf* is silent as to homosexuality. Masturbation was not likely to be mentioned in such a book in any case.

In psychiatric terms, Dr. Murray says that Hitler "seems to have developed a *syphilophobia* with a diffuse *fear of contamination* of the blood through contact with a woman. It is almost certain that this irrational dread was partly due to the association in his mind of sexuality and excretion. He thought of sexual relations as something exceedingly *filthy*."[161] Dr. Langer believes that Hitler "uses the horrors of syphilis as a justification for his unconscious fear that genital sexuality is dangerous for him. . . ."[162]

One thing is sure, at any rate: Hitler had no capacity to love anyone deeply. He would not have exactly admitted this, but it was implied when he once said: "A woman can love much more deeply than a man."[163] He meant himself.

f. ERICH FROMM'S TWO THEORIES

Erich Fromm is one psychiatrist who has developed fairly methodical and complete theories concerning Hitler's psychology, and who has made an effort to present a comprehensible picture, to summarize, and to give meaning to this very complex personality. Fromm's first

[159] *Mein Kampf*, p. 357; see also p. 630.
[160] Ibid., p. 4.
[161] Murray, op. cit., p. 6 (italics quoted).
[162] Langer, op. cit., p. 182.
[163] *Hitler's Table Talks*, p. 194.

theory—presented as far back as 1941 in *Escape from Freedom*—
has stood the test of time surprisingly well, although the only sources
then available to him were *Mein Kampf* and press reports of Hitler's
speeches and actions. The second theory came much later—in 1964—
in *The Heart of Man*. Both theories will be discussed here. In connection with this discussion, we shall present facts concerning Hitler's
personality which were probably unknown to Fromm, but which will
either support or negate his theories and which, at any rate, may
be of use to other psychiatrists in future analyses of Hitler.

We have heretofore made many references to Fromm's first
theory—at some length, for example, in the chapter on Militarism—
and we shall not repeat them at great length here. The upshot of them
is that "Hitler's personality, his teachings, and the Nazi system express an extreme form" of the "authoritarian character structure,"
and "by this very fact he made a powerful appeal to those parts of
the population which were—more or less—of the same character
structure." The "essence" of this character is "the simultaneous
presence of sadistic and masochistic drives," sadism "aiming at unrestricted power over another person more or less mixed with destructiveness," and masochism "aiming at dissolving oneself in an
overwhelmingly strong power and participating in its strength and
glory."[164]

The presence of *sadism* with *destructive tendencies* in Hitler's
character is too obvious to require much discussion. There is no question that it had profound effect on European history from 1933 to
1945. Fromm says that "The love for the powerful and the hatred
for the powerless which is so typical for the sado-masochistic character explains a great deal of Hitler's and his followers' political
actions."[165] This character, he points out, "feels the more aroused
[to attack], the more helpless his object has become."[166] Giving an
example, Fromm continues:

As long as . . . [Hitler] felt Britain to be powerful, he loved and
admired her. His book [*Mein Kampf*] gives expression to this
love. . . .
    When he recognized the weakness of the British position

[164]Fromm, *Escape*, p. 221.
[165]Ibid., p. 231.
[166]Ibid., p. 168.

before and after Munich his love changed into hatred and the wish to destroy it. From this viewpoint "appeasement" was a policy which for a personality like Hitler was bound to arouse hatred, not friendship. [167]

This is borne out, at least in part, by statements by Hitler that have since become known. In a confidential address to his generals and admirals on August 22, 1939, shortly before he started World War II, he said, "Our enemies are tiny little worms. I saw them in Munich." [168] And later, in the *Table Talks*, he declared that the Englishmen "with whom we dealt officially, were no men." [169] Presumably he had in mind Neville Chamberlain and Lord Halifax. (In the same conversation, however, he mentioned that he had met many other English men and women whom he regarded highly.)

One Englishman, at any rate, whom Hitler viewed as no mere worm was Winston Churchill. For Churchill, he had nothing but intensely emotional hatred, and this brings us to the *hate component* of Hitler's sadism. Hatred, in fact, was probably Hitler's dominant emotion, and often it seemed to be a source of immense strength to him. Against Churchill his hatred was so violent that he became vulgar and almost completely irrational, at least in the company of his dinner-table companions. He spoke of Churchill as a "spineless pig that is drunk 30 percent of the day," a "drunkard," a "bought helper of the Jews," a "jackal." [170] He gave a sort of summary of his feelings toward Churchill in the following statement:

> . . . an objective judgment of Chruchill is that he is nothing but an utter big-mouth [*ausgemachte Quadratschnauze*], unscrupulous, immovable in his self-assurance by anything, no gentleman even privately but a liar who can be bought, and a man who is not ashamed in his speeches to dish up the same old bullshit [*Bockmist*] of a booze drinker. . . . One can only feel sorry for Britain that she cannot find a better man than Churchill to lead her in this decisive fight. [171]

[167] Ibid., p. 232.
[168] Quoted in Gisevius, *Adolf Hitler,* p. 357.
[169] *Hitler's Table Talks*, p. 136.
[170] Ibid., pp. 218, 268, 479, 487 (indirect speech transposed).
[171] Ibid., pp. 361–362 (indirect speech transposed).

The cause of this limitless hatred undoubtedly was that in Churchill Hitler had finally encountered a man of real strength whom he could not deal with by mere words. In fact, he once recognized this himself when he said that "such people as Churchill—that is clear—cannot be dealt with by words but only with the clear language of inescapable facts."[172]

His hatred for Roosevelt seemed somewhat less intense, though intense enough by normal standards. He called him "mentally sick," a "criminal," an "insane fool," "acting like a Jew."[173] He described the Roosevelt regime as a "clearly Jewish organization."[174] Mrs. Eleanor Roosevelt, curiously, was branded as half Negro.[175] All reason left him when his really furious hatred broke through.

But it was, of course, the Jews who were the most durable object of Hitler's most intense hatred and, ultimately, the victims of an entirely unrestrained sadism (and we might here mention his secretary's statement that she could "say with absolute certainty that Himmler kept Hitler completely informed about what went on in the concentration camps"[176]). Some have said that anti-Semitism was his only genuine emotion, but this seems very doubtful. His anti-Semitism was really his favored rationalization on which his sadism focused. At any rate, it was an emotion which lasted, undiminished, from his early years in Vienna to the final day of his life in the Berlin bunker when he still cursed International Jewry in his Political Testament. It was for the Jews that he reserved the nastiest, most cruel epithets—uncounted numbers of them, used day after day. The Jews were not only subhumans and vermin, but also a "tumor," a "maggot in a rotting body," the "pestilence . . . , worse than the black death of yesteryear," the "spider [that] began slowly to suck the blood out of the pores of the people," a "pack of rats," a "parasite within the body of other peoples," the "eternal leech," the "vampire," "that accursed race which, as a veritable scourge of God, has flogged . . . the nations for thousands of years."[177] Many of these descriptions

[172]Ibid., p. 426.
[173]Ibid., pp. 201, 268, 337, 425.
[174]Ibid., p. 492.
[175]Ibid., p. 425.
[176]Zoller, *Hitler privat*, p. 194.
[177]*Mein Kampf*, pp. 61, 62, 212, 331, 334, 339, 358, and Speech of Mar. 21, 1943, Domarus, *Hitlers Reden* p. 2001.

suggested in themselves that nothing but physical extermination of the Jews could give relief to the tormented non-Jews.

Hitler's hatred of his foreign enemies (and even his allies) becomes very visible also in the *Situation Conferences (Lagebesprechungen)*, throughout which he interrupted the sober reports of his generals by such exclamations as "those pigs!" and the like.

The limitless nature of Hitler's hatred in general was described quite well in the memoirs of a high national socialist official, Hans Frank: "He was a hater without limit. Whoever had once incurred his disfavor was finished or lost, and it was never possible to return to a forgiving Hitler. That was true for individuals as well as for groups. It was true for whole races and nations."[178] Similarly, his private secretary writes: ". . . to forgive was something he did not know."[179]

Someone who hated as much as Hitler necessarily could not really love even his own people, and this in spite of his countless solemn affirmations of love to the Germans. Thus when he found that he could no longer stop the invasion of Germany by the armies of his enemies, he began to hate even the Germans and did not hesitate to issue his "scorched earth order"[180] for the destruction of all German industrial plants, public utilities, post offices, railroads, telephone plants, radio installations, food supplies, farms, cattle, works of art, castles, churches, theaters, and many other things. He had no interest in further German life; the Germans were to go down with him. It was to be the final orgy of destructiveness, but he no longer had the political and military power to carry it through.

There were also smaller, but significant manifestations of Hitler's sadism. For eleven years, from 1923 to 1934, he carried a riding whip at all times.[181] He actually used it probably on only one occasion — during the so-called *Röhm-Aktion* on June 30, 1934 — but presumably it was a symbol to him of humiliating and subduing other men. Psychologically it may have been a fetish. Earlier we discussed the sexual significance which the whip may have had.

[178]Frank, *Im Angesicht des Galgens*, p. 363.
[179]Zoller, op. cit., p. 131.
[180]*TMWC*, Vol. 41, pp. 430–431; see also Speer, *Erinnerungen*, pp. 411–413, 456. The order was never executed.
[181]See Treher, *Hitler, Steiner, Schreber*, p. 126.

And then there was Hitler's story of the cat and the mouse, which he told to his dinner companions, apparently with some relish:

I once watched a cat as it made preparations to eat a mouse it had caught. The cat, far from immediately putting the mouse in its mouth, first played with it and again and again gave it an apparent chance to escape. It was only after the mouse, because of all this back and forth, had become completely drenched in a cold sweat of terror, that the cat gave it a final blow with its claws and ate it up. Obviously, the mouse in this condition seemed tastiest and most digestible to the cat. [182]

Mice, incidentally, like other small mammals, do not sweat; but the story was a little reminiscent of the treatment administered to Czechoslovakian and Austrian politicians and to the Jews.

Another small incident which may indicate sadism or perhaps some other abnormal character trait was reported by his secretary. During a meal with her and other persons, and referring to his strict vegetarianism and to the fact that his physician had relieved him of some blood to reduce his blood pressure, he said: "I will have them make blood sausages for you from my excess blood, for a supplemental diet, since you are so fond of meat." He added that his blood was very appetizing. [183]

One result of Hitler's sadism was, as Golo Mann has pointed out, [184] that he was always deadly serious when the matter of the use of power was involved; and this [to an extent] accounted for his superiority. He was, indeed, always engaged in war, even in peacetime; and in war it was proper to take advantage of everything. His early opponents, on the other hand, were under the impression that there was peace and that there were laws.

In fact, as we have said before, from Hitler's point of view, World War I had never ended. "It was [as he said] . . . only the beginning, the first piece of this drama; the second piece and the ending are now being written. . . . [185]

[182] *Hitler's Table Talks*, p. 450.
[183] Zoller, op. cit., p. 232.
[184] Mann, *Deutsche Geschichte*, p. 842.
[185] Speech of Nov. 8, 1941, Domarus, op. cit., p. 1781.

It is a strange fact, at any rate, that Hitler derived his enormous strength and willpower almost exclusively from his sadistic, destructive drives, and that these drives seemed to generate even whatever elements of greatness he possessed.

Ultimately, although not without the compulsion of circumstances, Hitler's destructiveness turned upon himself. Quite prophetically, and with much early insight, the psychiatrist W. H. D. Vernon said three years before Hitler's suicide:

> It is . . . quite possible that Hitler will do away with himself at whatever moment German defeat becomes sufficient enough to destroy the fiction of Fate which has shielded him from the violence of his own guilt. Hitler may then turn upon himself the destructiveness which so long has been chanelled toward his own people and their neighbors. [186]

As far as the masochistic side of Hitler's sadomasochistic character structure is concerned, the earlier chapter on Hitler's sex life discussed the available evidence of his possible intensely masochistic acts in the heterosexual sphere. Fromm had as yet no information concerning this manifestation of Hitler's masochism when he developed his theory in 1941. But Fromm found strong evidence of more sublimated masochism. The essence of masochism, according to Fromm, is that the individual tries to dissolve himself in an overwhelmingly strong power. He aims "to feel utterly small and helpless" himself. [187] Except in his sex life, Hitler was a very big man, and he actually regarded himself as even greater than he was. It is clear that, outside of the sexual sphere, any power to which he could submit had to be the very strongest in the world. He chose nature, race, Providence, fate, history, the laws of history, the Eternal Creator, the Almighty, Heaven, and other similar concepts. Of some of these terms, Fromm says quite aptly that they had "about the same meaning to him, that of symbols of an overwhelmingly strong power." [188] Quite often Hitler used them interchangeably.

---

[186] Vernon, *Hitler, the Man*, p. 308. Langer, op. cit., pp. 247-248, made a similar prediction in 1943.
[187] Fromm, *Escape*, p. 152.
[188] Ibid., p. 235.

The pages of *Mein Kampf,* of *Hitlers Zweites Buch,* and of the *Table Talks* are virtually studded with these terms, and they occur also in hundreds of his speeches. Hitler continued to use them practically unchanged over a period of twenty years. Characteristically, he frequently indicated the overwhelming and cruel power or force of these concepts by such descriptions as "hammer blows" or "whip-lashes" of fate which he had to endure and which helped him. "Nature . . . is cruel and pitiless. . . . Whoever thinks . . . that he can rebel against that law will not eliminate the law but only himself."[189] ". . . I have to obey the orders of fate" (speaking of his impending suicide).[190] Some of this was rationalization of masochism by way of social Darwinism. Fromm thinks that Hitler, at the same time, projected his own sadism upon nature.[191]

All in all, Hitler represented a well-rounded, extreme sado-masochistic personality with intense destructive drives—a highly malignant character structure. The malignancy manifested itself particularly in his ability and eagerness to stimulate similar destructive drives in those millions of Germans who fundamentally, in varying degrees, had the same character structure, and perhaps even in other Germans. To them, *he* became the higher power in which *they* could masochistically dissolve, and he merely had to name to them the victims on whom their own sadism could feed.

Fromm's *second theory* is very different and was developed much later (*The Heart of Man,* 1964). Fromm says that he was led to it by "a deeper understanding of . . . various kinds of aggression and destructiveness."[192] Yet his new theory does not really seem to explain as much of Hitler's psychology as his old one, and it may be overly dramatic. But this theory, too, offers valuable insights into Hitler's character structure; and here, again, we shall discuss the facts which may support or negate the theory and which, at any rate, may be of interest to future analysts of Hitler.

Fromm sees in people generally three tendencies or "orientations" which are "directed *against* life, which form the nucleus of

[189]Speech of May 30, 1942, in appendix to *Hitler's Table Talks,* p. 493.
[190]*Lagebesprechung* of Apr. 27, 1945.
[191]Fromm, *Escape,* p. 227.
[192]Fromm, *Heart,* p. 11.

severe mental illness, and which can be said to be the essence of true evil."[193] These three orientations are necrophilia, narcissism, and symbiotic fixation to mother (or incestuous symbiosis). In their gravest forms, the three orientations converge and eventually form what Fromm calls the "syndrome of decay." "This syndrome represents the quintessence of evil; it is at the same time the most severe pathology and the root of the most vicious destructiveness and inhumanity." In Hitler, all three orientations converged. He was, Fromm says, "an almost totally necrophilous, narcissistic and incestuous person."[194] The three orientations will require individual discussion here, particularly in their relation to Hitler.

Necrophilia literally means "love of the dead." Necrophiles, Fromm says,

> . . . are those people who love to talk about sickness, about burials, about death. They come to life precisely when they can talk about death. A clear example of the pure necrophilous type is Hitler. He was fascinated by destruction, and the smell of death was sweet to him. While in the years of his success it may have appeared that he wanted to destroy only those whom he considered his enemies, the days of the *Götterdammerung* at the end showed that his deepest satisfaction lay in witnessing total and absolute *destruction:* that of the German people, of those around him, and of himself.[195]

It may well be that Hitler was a necrophile, but some of the facts which Fromm states are not the true facts. Hitler was, of course, a highly destructive person, but it goes too far to say that his "deepest satisfaction" lay in witnessing the total destruction of the German people, of those around him, and of himself. In fact, for a long time, he tried frantically to prevent the total destruction of the German people. Moreover, most of "those around him" in the Berlin bunker were given permission or ordered to leave before it was too late. His own suicide, furthermore, was something that he approached with

[193]Ibid., p. 37.
[194]Ibid., p. 108.
[195]Ibid., p. 39.

great hesitation and that seemed far from giving him "deepest satisfaction."[196] It is true that the smell of death of the Jews and probably of the Poles and Russians was figuratively sweet to him, but it is also true that this sweet smell was not his final goal and that he would have derived his "deepest satisfaction" from winning the war and presiding over a German empire of a vast Lebensraum. This was his real dream and purpose, although it is quite likely that after achieving it he would have gone on to even greater ventures which again would have involved destruction.

Also, Hitler did not very often speak of sickness, burial, and death. It is true that in *Mein Kampf*, for special reasons, he still talked a great deal about the dangers of syphilis, but his *Table Talks* contained no more about sickness, burial, and death than the conversations of average persons (and he was highly reticent about his own serious illness). On the other hand, it is a fact that one of his physicians noted Hitler's "constant thoughts of an early death" and "his frequent taking of his own pulse."[197] Also, in April 1945, shortly before his suicide, he declared that he should have made the decision to kill himself ("the most important decision of my life") as far back as November 1944,[198] but this was really quite a rational thought.

Fromm says further that "The highly necrophilous person . . . often has an expression on his face as though he were smelling a bad odor. . . . This expression could be clearly seen on Hitler's face. . . ."[199] Opinions about facial expressions can easily differ, but one may well find it hard to detect such an expression on Hitler's face.

Hitler did make various statements concerning the need to die for Germany's goals. Thus, in a speech on September 1, 1939, at the outbreak of World War II, he said, "It is totally unimportant whether we shall live, but it is necessary that our nation, that Germany shall live!"[200] Similarly, in a Proclamation of January 30, 1943, he called upon the Germans ". . . to spare no lives . . . in order to preserve

---

[196] See Trevor-Roper, *The Last Days of Adolf Hitler, passim.*
[197] Quoted in Maser, *Adolf Hitler,* p. 387.
[198] Ibid., p. 430.
[199] Fromm, *Heart,* p. 42.
[200] Domarus, op. cit., p. 1317.

our nation's life for the future. . . ."[201] Many additional statements of this general kind could probably be found. But are they really anything very abnormal, coming as they did from the leader of a nation in time of war?

It is a fact, of course, that most of Hitler's important goals could be reached only by the death of others. Fromm says that

> The influence of men like Hitler and Stalin lies precisely in their unlimited capacity and willingness to kill. For this they were loved by the necrophiles. Of the rest, many were afraid of them and preferred to admire, rather than to be aware of their fear; many others did not sense the necrophilous quality of these leaders, and saw in them the builders, saviors, good fathers.[202]

Fromm points out further that "The necrophilous person is attracted to darkness and night."[203] This was definitely one of Hitler's characteristics (and apparently also one of Stalin's). Even in regard to a fairly early period, Albert Speer reports that Hitler never left the daily after-supper party before 2 A.M. and that in the morning he got up about 11 A.M.[204] These habits became increasingly worse. Toward the end, he still held conferences after midnight, and they sometimes could last until daybreak. He might still call for a secretary at 6 A.M.[205] One secretary reports that "he always saved his important dictation for the night" and that "during the final period, . . . he usually went to bed at 8 A.M.[206] His insomnia was severe, and he hated to go to bed. His secretary says that "sunshine caused him nausea" and that "like a reptile which shuns the light of day, he crawled away, more and more often, into the cold, dreary rooms of his bunker."[207] Erik H. Erikson may have the underlying emotional condition in mind when he says, "That extreme form of identity diffusion which leads to significant arrest and regression is characterized most of all by

---

[201] Ibid., p. 1979.

[202] Fromm, *Heart*, pp. 40–41.

[203] Ibid., p. 41.

[204] Speer, op. cit., pp. 105, 102.

[205] Zoller, op. cit., pp. 15, 21, 44, 75, 149; see also Johann Recktenwald, *Woran hat Adolf Hitler gelitten?* pp. 20–24, and Bullock, *Hitler*, p. 785.

[206] Zoller, op. cit., pp. 15, 151.

[207] Ibid., pp. 70, 25.

a mistrustful difficulty with mere living in time. Time is made to stand still by the device of ignoring the usual alternation of day and night. . . ."[208]

The second orientation which, in Fromm's view, is part of the syndrome of decay is *narcissism*. In relation to Hitler's narcissism, he says:

> A particular instance of narcissism which lies on the borderline between sanity and insanity can be found in some men who have reached an extraordinary degree of power . . . , Hitler, Stalin. . . . They try to pretend that there is no limit to their lust and to their power, so they . . . kill numberless men, . . . they "want the moon" . . . . This is madness, even though it is an attempt to solve the problem of existence by pretending that one is not human. It is a madness which tends to grow in the lifetime of the afflicted person. . . . This Caesarian madness would be nothing but plain insanity were it not for one factor: by his power Caesar has bent reality to his narcissistic fantasies. He has forced everybody to agree that he is god, the most powerful and the wisest of men — hence his own megalomania seems to be a reasonable feeling.[209]

Fromm says that the open outbreak of the potential psychosis of such men is prevented by gaining the acclaim and consensus of millions of people:

> The best-known example . . . is Hitler. Here was an extremely narcissistic person who probably could have suffered a manifest psychosis had he not succeeded in making millions believe in his own self-image. . . .[210]

Dr. Murray, incidentally, made an almost identical diagnosis as far back as 1943:

> . . . he [Hitler] has gained a large measure of control over his hysterical and paranoid trends by using them consciously and successfully in the achievement of his aims; . . . he has been

[208] Erikson, *Young Man Luther*, p. 100.
[209] Fromm, *Heart*, p. 66.
[210] Ibid., p. 76.

supremely successful in imposing his visions and delusions (conforming, as they did, with existent trends) upon the German people, and so convincing them of his unparalleled superiority. Thus his irreal world has become real, insanity is sanity. [211]

The narcissistic person, Fromm continues, "ends up with an enormous distortion. He and his are over-evaluated. Everything outside is under-evaluated." [212] In Hitler's case, his consistent underevaluation of other nations and their leaders initially led to some brilliant political and military successes as a result of daring surprise action which no one whose objectivity had been preserved would have undertaken. Later his underevaluation of, and complete contempt for, the Soviet Union and the United States led to disaster. His absolute conviction that he and the Germans were stronger than their enemies and that in nature the stronger always wins was responsible for vast miscalculations. One is tempted to say that never before in history have so many lost their lives because of the narcissistically distorted judgment of one man.

Even in quite small things Hitler demonstrated the enormous distortion of judgment which his narcissism had induced. Thus, speaking in his *Table Talks* of the Vienna Academy of Arts refusing (twice) to accept him as an art student for lack of talent, he seemed to suggest that the Academy, as in the case of another painter, had been unable to recognize genius. ". . . Apparently, only a genius can totally understand a genius." [213] Indeed the very fact that Hitler permitted a record of his *Table Talks* to be made indicated in itself an appalling overestimation of the value of his own views and ideas, many of which were banal and commonplace. Obviously, however, he and some of his equally narcissistic associates (particularly, Martin Bormann) believed that his remarks at the dinner table represented pure wisdom which had to be preserved for posterity. (Of course, for purposes of historiography and psychoanalysis, that record is now invaluable.)

Not only was Hitler himself a man of extreme personal narcissism, but he also "stimulated the group narcissism of millions of Germans." [214]

[211] Murray, *Analysis*, pp. 27–28. To the same effect, Langer, op. cit., p. 134.
[212] Fromm, *Heart*, p. 74.
[213] *Hitler's Table Talks*, pp. 323–324 (indirect speech transposed).
[214] Fromm, *Heart*, p. 85.

For those who are economically and culturally poor, narcissistic pride in belonging to the group is the only . . . source of satisfaction. Precisely because life is not "interesting" to them, . . . they may develop an extreme form of narcissism. Good examples of this phenomenon in recent years are the racial narcissism which existed in Hitler's Germany, and which is found in the American South today. In both instances the core of the racial superiority feeling was, and still is, the lower middle class; this backward class . . . has only one satisfaction: the inflated image of itself as the most admirable group in the world, and of being superior to another racial group that is singled out as inferior . . .—"I am white"; or, "I am an Aryan."[215]

The process of stimulating group narcissism seems to involve symbiosis and identification between leader and group. "In the very act of submission to the powerful leader . . . , the narcissism of the individual is transferred onto the leader. The greater the leader, the greater the follower."[216]

But the group requires "a certain degree of confirmation in reality" for the satisfaction of its narcissistic self-image. In the case of the national socialist group, the radical persecution of the Jews (among others) had to serve as proof of the superiority of the Aryans.[217] Political and military conquests presumably accomplished the same purpose.

The third orientation which, according to Fromm, makes up the "syndrome of decay" is what he calls *"incestuous symbiosis,"* the failure of an individual to cut the umbilical cord. Sometimes he calls it "mother fixation." In our discussion of Erikson's views of Hitler's psychology, we have already spoken of his attachment to his mother. This mother fixation is, indeed, the point at which Erikson's and Fromm's analyses converge, at least superficially. Not unlike Erikson, Fromm says[218] that, as the child grows up, the mother is often replaced by larger units (or by impersonal concepts), such as clan, nation, race, religion, nature. All these and others can become a "common mother" of a group, and they will unite all minds. Fromm points to the cult of the Virgin and of nationalism. "Empirically the

215 Ibid., p. 79.
216 Ibid., p. 87.
217 Ibid., p. 86.
218 Ibid., pp. 98–99.

fact can easily be established that there is a close correlation between persons with a strong fixation to their mothers and those with exceptionally strong ties to nation and race, soil and blood."[219] Depending on the degree of fixation, Fromm speaks of the "pathology of incestuous fixation," and Erikson of "pathological attachment."[220] (R. G. L. Waite, however, is hardly correct in saying that "the word incest was often on [Hitler's] mind."[221] The confusion is caused by the fact that Hitler sometimes misused the German word for incest, *Blutschande*, to mean something like a violation of nature's laws of racial purity by intermarrying with other races, as for instance in one of the two examples given by Waite, namely *Mein Kampf*, p. 135 of the German text.)

The incestuous orientation, Fromm continues, conflicts with reason and objectivity, as narcissism does. The mother idol becomes sacred. The impairment of judgment is much less obvious when the "mother" is impersonal, such as nation or race. In fact, fixations on the latter two are regarded as virtues by the group which looks upon strangers as "barbarian" and is unable to experience humanity. Even the capacity to love may be destroyed. (We have previously mentioned that Hitler had little, if any, capacity to love.) The substitution of an impersonal mother is accomplished by many rationalizations. When the nation becomes mother, for example, the reasoning may be that one owes everything to it, that it is extraordinary and quite wonderful.

In summing up his entire theory, Fromm says that

. . . Hitler was an almost totally necrophilous, narcissistic and incestuous person. . . . The more malignant the three orientations are, the more they converge. . . . There is close affinity between incestuous fixation and narcissism. . . . [The individual] and his mother (as one) are the object of his narcissism. . . . [In the case of group narcissism] we find very clearly incestuous fixation blended with narcissism. It is this particular blend which explains the power and the irrationality of all national, racial, religious and political fanaticism.[222]

[219]Ibid., p. 99.

[220]Fromm, *Heart*, p. 106; Erikson, *Childhood*, p. 106.

[221]R. G. L. Waite, "Adolf Hitler's Guilt Feelings: A Problem in History and Psychology," in *Journal of Interdisciplinary History*, Vol. I, No. 2, 1971, p. 234.

[222]Fromm, *Heart*, p. 108.

In the most extreme cases, necrophilia joins the other two orientations, forming Fromm's rather dramatic syndrome of decay:

> The person suffering from this syndrome is indeed evil, since he betrays life and growth and is a devotee of death and crippledness. The best-documented example . . . is Hitler. He was . . . deeply attached to death and destruction; he was an extremely narcissistic person for whom the only reality was *his own* wishes and thoughts. Finally, he was an extremely incestuous person. . . . Hitler's incestuousness was mainly expressed in his fanatical devotion to the race. . . . Narcissism, death, and incest made a man like Hitler one of the enemies of mankind and life.[223]

Undoubtedly few Germans were afflicted with the three orientations to the same malignant extent as Hitler, but there were enough who were sufficiently afflicted to permit him to evoke all kinds of echoes in their psychology and, above all, to stimulate the already existing group narcissism to malignant extremes. If the German people had not been an effective resonating surface, if there had not been that continuing echo and re-echo between Hitler and them, he might, after World War I, have reverted to being no more than an obscure, lonely, highly neurotic painter of watercolor postcards in Munich or Vienna who would have vented his resentment on fellow residents of cheap rooming houses or during occasional visits to local cafés.

C. Hitler's Religiousness

Earlier in this study, we called attention at various times to the religious coloration of statements by Hitler. There is no question that he was a deeply religious man, and he said so himself: "I may not be a sanctimonious churchgoer; that is not what I am. But still deep down I am a religious person. . . ."[224] "I, too, am religious, that is, religious

---

[223]Ibid., pp. 108–109.

[224]Speech of June 26, 1944, quoted in Speer, op. cit., p. 570. The whole subject of the pseudoreligious character of the national socialist ideology is treated thoroughly and well in an article by Hans Müller, "Der pseudoreligiöse Charakter der national-sozialistischen Weltanschauung," in *Geschichte in Wissenschaft und Unterricht*, Vol. 12, 1961, pp. 337–352. See also Waite, op. cit., pp. 244–248; and Domarus, op. cit., pp. 16–19.

deeply within myself. . . ."[225] Speer, in fact, calls Hitler "the proto-type of a believer",[226] and Friedrich Heer speaks of him, perhaps with a little exaggeration, as a "religious fanatic" and a "religious-political preacher."[227]

The origins of Hitler's religiousness naturally lie in his childhood. He grew up in an intensely Catholic milieu. His mother, particularly, was a devout Catholic. He went to the boys' school of a Benedictine monastery from 1896 to 1898.[228] In *Mein Kampf* he reports that he received singing lessons in the monastery and "there I had the best opportunity, again and again [*oft und oft*], to become intoxicated with the solemn magnificence of the extremely splendid festivals of the Church."[229] No doubt this was a profound childhood experience, and his description of it makes clear the extraordinary impression which he still retained of it as an adult. He goes on to say that he then de-cided—"what was more natural?" he asks—that becoming the abbot of a monastery "was the highest ideal worth striving for," as his father before him had once wanted to become the village priest. Even so, his father was opposed to Adolf's taking the cloth, which is re-grettable. History might have taken a very different turn. At any rate, the intensity of the Catholic milieu is suggested by the fact that at least three of Adolf's schoolmates ultimately became priests.[230]

Not only did little Adolf take singing lessons in the monastery, but, according to other reports, he actually sang in the church choir and served as an altar boy.[231] No doubt he attended hundreds or thousands of church services during his childhood and adolescent years, with or without his mother. His boyhood friend August Kubizek

[225]Speech of Nov. 8, 1943, Domarus, op. cit., p. 2057. See also *Hitler's Table Talks*, p. 149.

[226]Speer, op. cit., p. 368.

[227]Heer, *Der Glaube des Adolf Hitler*, pp. 441, 350, 462. It is not generally pro-posed here to cite Heer as an authority on Hitler. His book—752 pages dealing with Hitler's Austrian Catholicism—is a turbulent, chaotic work. He seems to be deeply troubled by his own Catholicism and by the effect of the Catholic faith on a person like Hitler. Yet Heer has assembled useful information, even if his references (108 pages) can be a researcher's nightmare.

[228]Maser, *Adolf Hitler*, p. 56.

[229]*Mein Kampf*, p. 4.

[230]Maser, op. cit., p. 56.

[231]Franz Jetzinger, *Hitlers Jugend—Phantasien, Lügen und die Wahrheit*, p. 89; Recktenwald, op. cit., p. 74; *Hitler's Table Talks* (Introduction), p. 49; Maser, op. cit., p. 56.

says: "As long as little Adolf remained close to his mother, he was completely influenced by her devout behavior and receptive to all the grandeur and beauty of the church. The pale little choir boy was absorbed by his faith."[232] (The common religious experience of mother and son was undoubtedly a significant factor in the creation of Hitler's mother fixation, discussed before.) He was confirmed in the great Cathedral at Linz, and this magnificent event presumably also left an unforgettable impression with him. Many years later, in his *Table Talks*, he still commented on the gorgeous clothes of the Papal Nuncius and a bishop at a reception and compared them with the "unclean collars and filthy coats" of the Protestant ministers.[233]

He still took a favorable view of the Catholic Church—and, indeed, also of the Protestant Church—at the time he wrote *Mein Kampf* when he was about thirty-five years old. In it, he said that the National Socialist Movement "regards both creeds as equally valuable pillars for the existence of our nation."[234] But thereafter he changed his opinion, and this was one of the very rare instances in his life in which he ever changed a view adopted in his formative years. He became, in fact, strongly hostile to all churches and especially so to the Catholic Church. In the *Table Talks* he declared that " . . . all these teachings of the [Catholic] Church are a single big piece of nonsense" and that even "an educated man of the Church cannot possibly believe in the nonsense the Church is dishing up."[235] Some of these teachings he called "satanical superstition."[236] His hostility to the Church developed to such an extent that, as was his custom in such cases, he became quite irrational: "Christ was an Aryan," he said, but St. Paul (whom the National Socialists generally regarded as a Jewish rabbi) "used Christ's teachings to mobilize the underworld and to organize a pre-Bolshevism."[237] Hitler boasted that he had "six SS divisions who are totally outside of any Church and yet they die with complete peace of mind."[238]

[232] Kubizek, *The Young Hitler I Knew*, p. 80.
[233] *Hitler's Table Talks*, p. 260.
[234] *Mein Kampf*, p. 379.
[235] *Hitler's Table Talks*, pp. 266–267 (indirect speech transposed).
[236] Ibid., p. 185.
[237] Ibid., p. 154.
[238] Ibid., p. 154.

Perhaps Hitler's strongest antichurch statement—coming from a once devout Catholic—was:

"When they bury me, I want no cleric around within a radius of 10 kilometers. [For "cleric" he used the contemptuous German word *Pfaffe*.] If one of those could help me, I would despair of Providence. [239]

"I don't go to a church for a religious service," he said, "I merely want to look at the beauty of the building." [240]

(According to Speer's recollections, however, Hitler considered the Church "absolutely necessary in the life of the state," but this was conditioned on his cynical assumption that "in the course of a long period of time, the Church will undoubtedly learn to adapt itself to the political goals of National Socialism, as God knows it has always done in history." [241] Still, there remains a residue of contradiction between Speer's usually reliable recollections and Hitler's own quite clear and definite statements in his *Table Talks*.)

It seems that Hitler never explained in explicit terms the reasons for becoming intensely hostile to an institution to which he had once been deeply devoted. And, of course, an admission of a change of mind—any change of mind—would have been distasteful to him. But it is likely that much of his hatred and contempt for both Churches resulted from the fact that they had, for a time, opposed some of his policies. In the *Table Talks*, in 1941, he said, speaking of his original seizure of power, that he "had conquered the state over the curse *(Fluch)* of both Churches." [242] Evidently, he felt rejected by the Churches, and he never ceased hating anyone who had once rejected him. Reconciliation, as mentioned before, did not exist for him. Moreover, he undoubtedly realized that no Church in the world could possibly be expected to approve the mass murder of Jews and other people which he secretly undertook in his later years. His hostility to the Churches may thus, in part, have been one element in his syndrome of rationalizations.

[239] Ibid., p. 186.

[240] Ibid., p. 186. A very lengthy statement of contempt and hostility against the Church, etc., is at pp. 436–439. See also pp. 26–27.

[241] Speer, op. cit., p. 109 (indirect speech transposed).

[242] *Hitler's Table Talks*, p. 155.

In any case, his abandonment of the Catholic Church does not seem to have been an easy matter for him, but rather appears to have caused him a good deal of emotional difficulty. In a speech in 1937, he said that "after grave inner conflicts I have liberated myself from religious images that still remained from my childhood" and "I now feel fresh like a foal in the pasture."[243] In the *Table Talks*, he stated in more general terms, but no doubt with himself in mind, that "it is difficult to free a person from all the tormenting images which the Catholic Church hammered into him in his youth."[244] It is doubtful whether he himself ever succeeded completely.

All this does not mean that he did not retain great admiration for the organization, structure, and power of the Catholic Church. He called its organization "very great" and even "grandiose" and wanted to model the future election of a German Führer on the papal election system.[245] ("The election should not take place before the eyes of the people but behind locked doors."[246]) At any rate, Hitler's abandonment of the Church was far from meaning that he abandoned also religion or, specifically, the Christian religion. On the contrary, as we have seen, he remained deeply religious. In fact, he once spoke of Christianity as "this wonderful thing," even though he contended that it had been "murdered" by the Jews of the Ancient World,[247] meaning presumably that it had been robbed of its original significance. The last-mentioned statement may conceivably also indicate his resentment of the crucifixion by the Jews.

The extent of Hitler's references in his writings, speeches, proclamations, *Table Talks*, etc., to God, to the Almighty, the Great Creator, Providence, Christianity, and the like is indeed enormous. In the course of the years, there must have been thousands of such references. The sheer volume of them is a measure of the extent to which religion was at all times on Hitler's mind. Here are some quotations: In *Mein Kampf*, he wrote (in italics) of

. . . the holy duty . . . to see to it that God's will is not only talked

[243] Domarus, op. cit., p. 745
[244] *Hitler's Table Talks*, p. 266.
[245] Ibid., pp. 228, 235, 236, 411.
[246] Ibid., p. 236.
[247] Ibid., p. 178.

about superficially, but that God's will is also, in fact, done and that God's work is not desecrated. [248]

Again in *Mein Kampf* (projecting his own fanaticism back to the early Christians):

The greatness of every powerful organization in personifying an idea in this world lies in its religious fanaticism. . . . The greatness of Christianity lay, not in attempted negotiations for a compromise with possibly similar ideologies of the Ancient World, but rather in the relentless, fanatical proclamation and representation of its own doctrine. [249]

Later, he became more specific:

[The Party program] is like the dogma of the church! [250]

The final Party Congress in Nuremberg must be organized exactly as solemnly and ceremoniously as an act of the Catholic Church. [251]

From a speech on May 1, 1933, soon after the seizure of power:

We are not asking the Almighty: "Lord, make us free!" We want to be active, to work, to conduct ourselves like brothers, to struggle together, so that the hour may come when we may go before the Lord and may ask him: "Lord, you see we have changed our ways. The German people is no longer a people without honor, . . . of little courage and little faith. No, Lord, the German people is again strong in its will. . . . Lord, we shall not give you peace! Bless our fight for our freedom . . . !" [252]

Frequently, as in the following excerpt from an address to Party leaders in 1936, Hitler's speeches, without expressly mentioning the Lord or the like, took on a biblical flavor:

[248] *Mein Kampf,* p. 630.
[249] Ibid., p. 385.
[250] Quoted in Heer, op. cit., p. 300.
[251] Zoller, *Hitler privat,* p. 193.
[252] Domarus, op. cit., p. 264.

In this hour, don't we again sense the miracle that brought us together! Once you heard the voice of a man, and it touched your hearts, it awakened you, and you followed that voice. For years, you went after the voice without even knowing its owner; you merely heard a voice and you followed it.

Now that we meet here, we are filled with the miracle of this coming together. Not everyone of you sees me, and I do not see everyone of you. But I feel you, and you feel me! It is the faith in our people that has made us small men great; that has made us poor men rich; that has made brave and courageous men of us faltering, discouraged, anxious men; that has let us errant men see and that has led us together!

. . . Now we are with each other, are with him, and he is with us, and now we are Germany! . . . It is something magnificent for me to be able to be your Führer. [253]

The Almighty is still, and increasingly, cited in the days of waning German power during the war. In a Proclamation of January 30, 1943, Hitler said:

The Almighty will be the impartial judge. But it is our task so to do our duty that—before him, the Creator of the universe, and according to his laws—we shall prove ourselves in the fight for life and that we, without losing courage, shall spare no life and no effort to maintain the existence of our people for the future. . . ." [254]

He referred to Providence even in a purely personal letter to Eva Braun after the attempt to assassinate him on July 20, 1944. He sent her his torn, tattered uniform and said: "I have sent you the uniform I was wearing that ill-fated day. It is a proof that Providence protects me and that we need no longer fear our enemies." [255] And finally, even in his "Private Testament" of April 29, 1945, the day before he killed

[253] Ibid., p. 641.
[254] Ibid., p. 1979.
[255] The whole letter is quoted in English translation in Gun, *Eva Braun*, p. 207. A very similar statement is reported by Hitler's secretary in relation to the earlier unsuccessful assassination attempt in the Munich Bürgerbräu (Zoller, op. cit., p. 181). See also Maser, *Adolf Hitler*, p. 268, and Langer, "A Psychological Analysis of Adolph Hitler," pp. 175-176.

himself, he still referred to the "termination of this earthly life [*irdische Laufbahn*],"[256] like a believing Christian who expects another life in the beyond.

Yet, on some occasions, he could take a sober view of Christian doctrine and could even make fun of it: "God created man. We became humans by the mortal sin [original sin?]. It was God who made this possible for man. For 500,000 years, he looked on as man slid into this. Then it occurred to him to send down his only begotten son. A frightful detour—enormously tedious, that whole procedure."[257]

Certain national socialist symbols also may have had their origin in Christianity or Catholicism. The brown shirts of the SA, which Hitler, too, wore in the early years of the Movement, are reminiscent of the habit of the monks with whom Hitler had much contact in his youth.[258] The black color of Himmler's SS uniforms may have been adopted because it recalled to Himmler's unconscious the color of the clothes normally worn by the Catholic clergy. He, too, had been a devout Catholic. There was also Speer's "cathedral of light" at the mass rallies. The most important symbol, the swastika, the hooked cross, may have been adopted because Hitler became very familiar with it as a child and adolescent. It was part of a coat of arms on the portal of Lambach Monastery where Hitler went to school[259] and where it was also carved into the pulpit.[260] Little Adolf, in fact, drew the hooked cross in his notebooks in school.[261] Hitler, the adult, said very vaguely that "in the hooked cross [we see] the mission of the fight for the victory of Aryan man and, at the same time, the victory of the idea of creative work which itself was eternally anti-Semitic and will be anti-Semitic."[262] Unconsciously, he may have been inspired by the Christian cross when he officially adopted the hooked

---

[256]*TMWC*, Vol. 41, p. 553. For other religious statements, see Müller, op. cit., *passim*, and Waite, op. cit., pp. 244-248.

[257]*Hitler's Table Talks*, p. 185.

[258]But Bracher, *Die deutsche Diktatur*, p. 150, assumes that their adoption was due to the Party's having an opportunity of purchasing left-over brown shirts. This, however, would not necessarily exclude our interpretation.

[259]Heer, op. cit., p. 21; but Peter G. J. Pulzer, *The Rise of Political Anti-semitism in Germany and Austria*, p. 244, and William L. Shirer, *The Rise and Fall of the Third Reich*, pp. 43-44, suggest different origins.

[260]Maser, *Adolf Hitler*, p. 56.

[261]Ibid., p. 193.

[262]*Mein Kampf*, p. 557.

cross. If so, it was an ugly distortion, even though it is true that far more wars and cruelties have taken place in 1900 years under the Christian cross than in the twelve Hitler years.

It was probably inevitable, in all the circumstances, that Hitler should have begun to see himself as a divine figure. His extreme narcissism, his quick, almost unbelievable rise from the Vienna men's home to the German Chancellery, his total conviction that he was the savior of the German people, his unshakable belief that he knew "the truth," the intoxicating adulation and adoration he received from millions of Germans, the complete lack of any sober criticism of his thoughts and actions by friends, the exuberance created by his early miraculous successes, his seeming invincibility, the apparent blessing of all his acts by his god—all these seemed to combine to create a total distortion of his judgment and to suggest the role of god's emissary to him. In fact, he vaguely began to identify with Jesus long before he accomplished his greatest political successes. Thus, in a very early speech—April 12, 1922,—he said: "I would be no Christian . . . if, like our Lord 2,000 years ago, I were not to wage a battle against those who today plunder and exploit this poor nation."[263] A few years later, discussing his anti-Semitism in *Mein Kampf*, he spoke of Jesus' own anti-Jewish views and said that Jesus ". . . if necessary used the whip to drive from the temple of the Lord this enemy of all humanity. . . ."[264] This corresponds to statements made by Hitler to Ernst Hanfstaengl. The latter told the OSS interviewer that on one occasion, Hitler

> . . . worked himself into a state of great excitement and finally shouted: "When I came to Berlin a few weeks ago and looked at . . . the luxury, the perversion, the iniquity, the wanton display, . . . the Jewish materialism disgusted me so thoroughly that I was almost beside myself. I nearly imagined myself to be Jesus Christ when he came to his father's temple and found it taken by the money-changers. I can well imagine how he felt when he seized the whip and scourged them out." Hanfstaengl says that Hitler accompanied this speech with violent agitations with his whip as though to drive out the Jews. . . . [265]

[263] Quoted in Eva G. Reichmann, *Die Flucht in den Hass—Die Ursachen der deutschen Judenkatastrophe*, p. 235.
[264] *Mein Kampf*, p. 336.
[265] *Source Book*, p. 903, to Langer, op. cit.

It was not a loving gentle Christ, but Christ furious.

Later, Hitler was more careful not to draw explicit parallels between himself and Christ, but his meaning was, nevertheless, reasonably clear in various statements:

In a speech on August 26, 1934, referring to traitors among the Germans: "Among the twelve apostles there was a Judas."[266]

In a speech on March 20, 1936: "From the people I have come, within the people I have remained, to the people I shall return. . . . I have taught you to have faith, now you shall give me your faith!"[267]

In a speech on September 14, 1936: "Woe to him who has no faith. He sins against the meaning of all life."[268]

In a speech in Vienna on April 9, 1938: "I believe it was God's will to send a boy from here to the Reich, to let him grow up, to elevate him to be the Führer of the nation. . . ."[269]

In the *Table Talks* in 1942: "If I am needed for anything, I am here because of a higher power."[270]

In a speech on November 3, 1943: ". . . the national socialist rebirth . . . a miraculous victory of faith . . . over the . . . possible. . . ."[271]

Hitler's associates, indeed, went much farther than he himself in proclaiming him to be a Godlike figure or even in identifying him with Christ:

Hermann Göring: ". . . God gave the savior to the German people. . . . we have faith, deep and unshakable faith, that he was sent to us by God to save Germany."[272]

Robert Ley: "We believe that National Socialism is the only true faith granting salvation to our people. . . . We believe that . . . God has sent us Adolf Hitler. . . ."[273]

Joseph Goebbels: Hitler spoke "almost like the gospel." . . . "The hour may come when the mob . . . will cry 'Crucify him!' We shall then stubbornly stand and call and sing 'Hosanna!' "[274]

[266] Domarus, op. cit., p. 446.
[267] Ibid., p. 609.
[268] Ibid., p. 647.
[269] Ibid., p. 849.
[270] *Hitler's Table Talks*, p. 186.
[271] Domarus, op. cit., p. 2050.
[272] Quoted in Müller, op. cit., p. 339.
[273] Quoted in Grebing, *Der Nationalsozialismus*, p. 71.
[274] Quoted in Fest, *Das Gesicht des Dritten Reiches*, p. 121.

Sometimes, Hitler was demoted to be merely the equal of the Pope:

> If the Catholic Christians are convinced that the Pope is infallible in all religious and moral matters, then we National Socialists proclaim with equally strong inner conviction that for us, too, the Führer is completely infallible in all political and other matters which concern the national and social interests of the people. [275]

This was quite in line with Hitler's own ideas as to his infallibility and with his general maxim that a real leader of a nation must never change his basic ideology. [276]

It is even possible that Hitler's decision to forgo marriage (until two days before his death) was unconsciously influenced by the priestly celibacy of the Catholic Church, but no statements from him or others to this effect exist.

It is understood that Hitler's religion was not a religion of love, as indeed even the Christian religion often has not been in practice. His was a fighting religion which acknowledged only believers or enemies. But every fight against an enemy was ipso facto blessed by God. In fact, it was done *for* God. Hitler's statement "In fighting against the Jew, I am fighting for the work of the Lord" [277] is an example. The psychiatrist W. H. D. Vernon says about Hitler that "The feeling of being directed by great forces outside one, of doing the Lord's work, is the essence of the feeling of the religious mystic." [278]

Incidentally, neither Hitler nor the members of his hierarchy seem to fall exactly within the types of "fascist" religious or irreligious persons discussed by T. W. Adorno, [279] even though he is undoubtedly correct in saying broadly that "Psychologically, fascist hierarchies may function largely as secularizations and substitutes of ecclesiastical ones." [280]

As a practical matter, Hitler's religiousness had far-raching

[275] Hermann Göring, quoted in Müller, op. cit., p. 344.
[276] See *Mein Kampf*, pp. 71-73.
[277] Ibid., p. 70.
[278] Vernon, "Hitler, the Man—Notes for a Case History," p. 299.
[279] T. W. Adorno and others, *The Authoritarian Personality*, pp. 730-732.
[280] Ibid., p. 734.

consequences. His strong sense of a divine mission filled him with a confidence that was altogether unjustified by reality and seemed to exclude the corrective action which an objective view of the facts normally produces. He accepted only such information from the outside as fitted into his preconceived scheme of things. "With the sureness of a sleepwalker I go along the path where Providence tells me to go," he said.[281] Essentially, he lived in a dream world and he contributed to the creation of the general German dream world of which we have spoken before. Religiousness helped to distort further a judgment that was already being greatly distorted by narcissism and other factors. Speer says that Hitler even "transferred military realities . . . into the sphere of his religious faith and, indeed, could see in a defeat a constellation for coming success that Providence was secretly creating." Speer quotes from Hitler's speech of June 26, 1944 (after three military catastrophies): "Often it seems to me as if we must pass through all trials by the devil and satan and hell before we can win final victory after all. . . ."[282]

Hitler, in fact, was quite able to have faith in his own lies, and so, incredibly enough, was the cynical, highly intelligent propaganda chief Joseph Goebbels (another once devout Catholic), whose personal diary makes strangely clear that he himself actually believed that Hitler was a divine figure. At any rate, it is obvious that such a divine figure as head of government represented a considerable propaganda asset.

D. Miscellaneous Character Traits

Altogether Hitler represented a strange, puzzling, complex personality. In all the hundreds of pages of his *Table Talks*, in which he was at his most relaxed, open and truthful, his real personality is still hard to grasp. To the outside, his very strong self-control and self-discipline prevailed at most times, even through interminable torrents of words, and were pushed aside only occasionally by seemingly uncontrollable flashes of hatred, contempt, and similar emotions.

A search for possible psychiatrically significant details brings

[281] Speech of Mar. 14, 1936, Domarus, op. cit., p. 606.
[282] Speer, *Erinnerungen*, pp. 367, 570.

to light some peculiar habits and characteristics which we shall now discuss, mostly with the idea that they may be of some help to future psychoanalysts of Hitler. One of these was his habit of frequently washing his hands, taking several baths a day (if possible), rinsing his mouth after meals, frequent changes of underwear, etc.[283]

His talents as an actor were remarkable. His secretary says that he was a "master in play-acting" and " an excellent mimic" of other people.[284] Speer reports that Hitler deliberately employed his acting talents in negotiations with foreign statesmen.[285]

One of Hitler's definite characteristics was that he was always determined not to go halfway, but all the way; not to compromise, but to fight on to definite victory; not merely to wound, but to kill. A mere defensive strategy of any kind, whether politically or militarily, ran counter to all his thinking and feeling; the offensive was all he wanted or could really imagine, and for this the German army had to pay a high price in the days of its waning power. One of his principles was never to concede anything good about an enemy. If he did undertake negotiations, threats of force usually lurked behind. If he seemed to compromise, it was frequently for purposes of deception only. If his opponents were willing to compromise, he could see them only as cowards whose weakness aroused an even stronger wish in him to beat them to the floor. And he was always willing to face the two alternatives which, in his view, a real fight implied. As to his whole career, he told Speer, "I have only two possibilities: Either I succeed with my plans completely or I founder. If I succeed, then I shall be one of the greatest in history. If I fail, then I shall be found guilty, be detested and damned."[286] To that extent at least, he faced the realities.

A seemingly abnormal characteristic was Hitler's passionate craving for hot chocolate, cake, and pastry. To be sure, Austrians, generally, eat more cake and pastry than other people, but in Hitler this seems to have reached quite extraordinary proportions. In his late years, this kind of meal appears to have taken place in the early morning hours, between 6 and 8 A.M., before Hitler went to bed. His secretary says that he then

[283] *Hitler's Table Talks* (Introduction), p. 30; Krause, op. cit., p. 31.
[284] Zoller, op. cit., pp. 124, 23.
[285] Speer, op. cit., p. 111.
[286] Ibid., p. 115.

. . . was filled only with the thought that now the most beautiful meal of the day was to come: hot chocolate and cake. His ravenous hunger for cake had really become pathological. While he formerly ate three pieces of cake at most, he now consumed three platefuls, filled to overflowing. I could not understand how a man, who constantly urged ascetic living on us, could gorge himself on these excessive quantities of cake and sweets. He explained that he intentionally ate less for dinner in order to be able to eat all the more cake. While he greedily abandoned himself to this delight, he fell almost completely silent. Somehow as an excuse, he would say that he could not understand people who did not love sweets. . . . This excessive cake eating at an hour when Berlin was being transformed into a rubble heap was a repulsive sight. It seemed like a bad dream to me every time. I looked at that human wreck devouring cake. [287]

All this grim cake eating was going on while the bombed-out city was under heavy attack by the Red Army. Even the remaining pitiful skeleton of the city was afire. One is tempted to say that, whereas Nero fiddled while Rome burned, Hitler ate cake while Berlin burned. The ravenous hunger for hot chocolate and cake may support E. H. Erikson's theory that Hitler remained an unbroken adolescent to the end.

In general, Hitler's self-control, even in the face of severe adversity, appears to have been impressive, at least on most occasions. The tales of a frustrated Hitler lying on the floor and biting into the carpet seem to have been a myth. His secretary knows of no such thing. [288] On the contrary, she says that

Even though, little by little, he lost control over his nervous system [as a result of his illness], he remained master of his emotions to the end. When news of a disaster was received in the course of a private conversation, Hitler would remain entirely calm. His emotional agitation would be indicated only by

[287] Zoller, op. cit., p. 201. See also Langer, op. cit., p. 87 (two pounds of chocolate a day). For his earlier craving for sweet things, see, f.i., the interview with Friedlinde Wagner (seven spoonfuls of sugar in a cup of tea), *Source Book*, p. 935, to Langer, op. cit.

[288] Zoller, op. cit., p. 150; see also Langer, op. cit., pp. 61-62, and O. Dietrich, *12 Jahre mit Hitler*, pp. 222-225.

the tensing of his cheek muscles. But he would calmly continue the conversation as before.[289]

Speer admired Hitler for his self-control and composure. "Generally, it was his very self-control that was one of Hitler's most remarkable characteristics; in my presence he lost his composure just a few times." And:

The persons around him admired the composure which he preserved at critical times. This surely contributed greatly to the confidence which his decisions inspired. Quite obviously, he was always conscious of the many people who were watching him and of the discouragement which even brief moments of loss of composure on his part would have caused. This self-control represented an extraordinary accomplishment of his willpower to the last day. He wrested it from himself in spite of aging, in spite of illness, in spite of Dr. Morell's experiments on him, and of relentlessly increasing pressures on him. Often, his will seemed to me unrestrained and rude, like that of a six-year-old child whom nothing will discourage, not to mention tire; but ridiculous as it was in part, it also demanded respect.[290]

Yet it seems that all restraint left him when he felt antagonized or betrayed by some person, and when his hatred broke through. Hitler's secretary describes these occasions:

Toward the end, his well-known outbreaks of rages grew increasingly violent and numerous. On such occasions, he became fierce. He screamed at the top of his voice, his clenched fists hammered on his desk or on the walls, and his face became distorted by hatred and agitation. He yelled at the accused person, using the worst drill sergeant's language, no matter whether he was dealing with a general or an officer.[291]

[289]Zoller, op. cit., pp. 33–34.
[290]Speer, op. cit., pp. 111, 367.
[291]Zoller, op. cit., p. 200; see also Langer, op. cit., p. 62.

E. Some Human Traits

We have spoken much of Hitler's evil character traits, and we should now mention also a few good ones—some normal human traits.

He had considerable intelligence and was genuinely interested in a thousand subjects. In social situations, he had a good deal of charm, particularly with women. He was considerate with employees and generally perceptive of the feelings of people he liked. He did have a sense of *humor*, even at times of trial. To be sure, Speer said that "Hitler had no humor," but he qualified this by adding: "He left the telling of jokes to others, laughed loudly and without inhibition, and could literally be bent over with laughter. Sometimes he wiped tears of laughter from his eyes after such outbreaks of gaiety. He liked to laugh, but essentially always at the expense of others."[292]

If humor is not only a comic quality causing amusement but also the ability to perceive what is amusing, then Hitler certainly had the latter kind of humor. He did need stimulation, but when he received it, he could apparently laugh more heartily than the average person. E. H. Erikson was thus only half right (and was presumably guessing) when he said that Hitler "probably never laughed from his heart and never made anyone else laugh heartily in his life."[293] His secretary reports that at least before the war, "Hitler still knew how to appreciate gaiety and humor."[294] Hanfstaengl says that Hitler "likes comedies and will laugh heartily at a Jewish comedian."[295] The reporter of the *Table Talks* tells of at least two occasions when Hitler laughed very much (not merely at the expense of others), and it was apparently his habit then to hide his face behind his hand.[296] This gesture may indicate reluctance to show a relaxed human emotion. Still, it was there.[297]

Another human character trait was Hitler's enormous *loyalty*

[292]Speer, op. cit., p. 138. See also p. 158. For a different impression, see Zoller, op. cit., p. 84. His boyhood friend August Kubizek, *The Young Hitler I Knew*, pp. 25–26, reported that Hitler had no sense of humor and that this earnestness was extraordinary.

[293]Erikson, *Identity*, p. 192.

[294]Zoller, op. cit., p. 24.

[295]Hanfstaengl (anonymous), *Adolf Hitler*, p. 26.

[296]*Hitler's Table Talks*, pp. 227, 243.

[297]Percy Ernst Schramm, p. 30 of the Introduction to *Hitler's Table Talks*, believes that the gesture was intended to hide bad teeth.

to his old associates and, generally, to people whom he had known long. One example was Max Amann, who was Hitler's company sergeant in World War I and whom he ultimately raised to the position of business manager of the Party's newspapers and publishing house.[298] Another example was Captain Fritz Wiedemann, Hitler's superior officer in World War I, whom he made his personal adjutant and later Consul General in San Francisco.[299] But the outstanding examples were at least three early companions who later became very high officials: Alfred Rosenberg, Julius Streicher, and Hermann Göring, to all of whom Hitler remained loyal to the end or almost to the end, even though he was quite aware that they had become serious political liabilities or an embarrassment to him. On the other hand, if he saw or believed to see disloyalty on the part of any old companion, his own loyalty would immediately change to cold hatred (as in the case of Göring in the last few days of his life).[300]

Another quite human attitude was his unquestionably deep devotion to the arts, the theater, opera, music, painting, architecture, and so forth (no matter how bad his tastes were in various aspects).[301] Hitler felt that singers and actors should not be drafted for military service, but in small matters of this sort his own power was sometimes curiously limited. He therefore hit upon the simple solution of having his adjutant request the official draft files of these persons from the draft offices, in order to tear them up and throw them away.[302] In the *Table Talks*, Hitler mentioned that he had called back artists into civilian life after one or two years of army service.[303]

Finally, Hitler's most human gesture was probably his marrying Eva Braun, in the knowledge that he would kill himself a day or two later. She had been his loyal friend, companion, and mistress for fourteen years, and it could have made no difference at all to him or to the world whether he finally married her. (The German people, at that time, did not even know of her existence.) But the marriage to the man she loved did mean a great deal to *her*, though she knew

[298] See Bullock, *Hitler*, p. 51.

[299] See Speer, op. cit., p. 135.

[300] See, in this connection, Zoller, op. cit., p. 132.

[301] See, for example, *Hitler's Table Talks*, pp. 285, 302-303, 310-311, 329, 378-379, 421-423, 480.

[302] See Speer, op. cit., p. 182.

[303] *Hitler's Table Talks*, p. 421.

that she would die with him shortly thereafter. It is strange that Hitler—ill and utterly exhausted, conscious of his own total failure, of the collapse of Germany around him, and of his impending suicide—should have been able or willing to give a thought to so futile a step as this marriage and to go through a fairly elaborate ceremony in his beleaguered underground bunker. He did it solely for Eva Braun, and that was a genuine human gesture. He did not really love her because he hardly knew how to love, but we can only assume that he was grateful to her for her love.

These were some human touches—all too few—in an ocean of inhumanness.

F. Conclusion, and a Postscript about Eva Braun

Hitler's tremendous willpower continued unbroken to the end, in a body wasted away by disease, with almost no sleep and in complete exhaustion. In the last week or two in his Berlin underground bunker, using every ounce of his remaining strength, he still dragged himself 60 feet or so from his modest bedroom to the conference room, holding on to the wall or to people, dragging one half-paralyzed leg behind, his back bent low, his left side and hand shaking, his face muscles twitching, saliva dripping from the corners of his mouth. By that time his empire, the Lebensraum over which he still ruled, had shrunk to no more than the rubble heap which the encircled city was; and it soon shrank further to a few destroyed streets of it. Yet, even then, with his burning willpower alive, he still held "situation conferences" with his generals and gave orders for the movement of troops which no longer existed. He still ordered the execution of traiterous associates and replaced them by others. He dictated long Private and Political Testaments. And there were still strong men who obeyed his will.

Yet, though a drama unfolded in the bunker, it was not the epic of a hero. Hitler did not have the moral courage to go out into the streets of the besieged city to die by a Russian bullet. Instead he died by his own hand in his underground bedroom comforted by a loving woman (whose own death with him represented a far more heroic deed). The best he could say in his Political Testament about the kind of death he planned to die was that he did not want "to fall into the hands of enemies who need a new spectacle, arranged by Jews, for the entertainment of their incited masses." It was still his tiresome propaganda language. Apparently, however, he himself felt that this death would be quite heroic because he likened it in his Testament to that of the navy captain who goes down with his ship: "As is already true in our Navy, it should be part of the honor concept of a German [Army] officer . . . that the leaders [*Führer*], as shining examples, must show the way into death in the truest performance of their duty."[304] Perhaps he actually thought that this was what he was doing, even though it seemed rather inconsistent with his further exhortation in the same document that "the fight be continued, no matter where."

Generally, the Testament lacks all greatness. It repeats some of the tired phrases of hundreds of his speeches, and much of it consists of his customary diatribes against international Jewry. It ends in the exhortation: "Above all, I impose the duty on the nation's leadership and their followers carefully to observe the racial laws and to resist mercilessly the poisoner of all peoples, international Jewry."[305] Clearly, he had learned nothing, in spite of his tremendous trials, his sickness, and his utter failure. Essentially, he merely restated, for the thousandth time, the views he had acquired as an immature young man. To the end, he remained the unbroken adolescent.

Actually, the life in his diseased body had, for a long time, been no more than a weak flickering flame, sustained perhaps more by his willpower than by his doctor's injections. His secretary spoke of him as "nothing but a physical and mental wreck toward the end of his life."[306] And apparently, he had at least moments, long before his actual suicide, when he doubted whether his life was worth living. His secretary reports him as saying: "When a person is a mere living wreck, why then continue to live. The destruction of his physical powers cannot be stopped."[307] He had been slowly dying for a long time, and his actual death should have been a deliverance to him (as it was to the German people and the world). If Nerin E. Gun can be

---

[304] Testament, *TMWC*, Vol. 41, p. 550. (He had mentioned the captain going down with his ship also in the *Lagebesprechung* of Apr. 27, 1945.)

[305] Ibid., p. 552.

[306] Zoller, op. cit., p. 61, also p. 26.

[307] Ibid., p. 229.

believed—and this is doubtful—Hitler told someone as far back as at the time of the assassination attempt of July 20, 1944 (nine months before his suicide): "I'm no longer afraid of death; it will be a deliverance for me." [308]

The legacy which he left to the German people, in any positive sense, is nearly nothing. To his credit were a few technical advances, such as the building of a network of good highways and of an inexpensive small automobile, as well as perhaps some innovations in the techniques of warfare. Possibly, the changes made by National Socialism in the social structure, particularly the elevation of the lower middle class, accelerated Germany's entry into our age of the common man; and quite unintentionally the psychological basis for future authoritarian governments may have been greatly weakened. But unlike Napoleon I, to whom Hitler can in some respects be compared, he did not participate in the inspiring ideas of his age; nor did he leave a *Code Napoléon*, or an efficient administrative system, or a lasting redefinition of the intra-European borders. He, more than anyone else, had desperately wanted to leave a vast legacy: a huge German empire with enough Lebensraum for all Germanic people, which was to last a thousand years. But the events failed to take place according to the laws which Hitler believed to be controlling: the racial laws, the inevitable victory of the stronger Germanic man. Events moved, rather, according to quite different laws which we are as yet hardly able to understand. The real legacy he left to the Germans was one of death and destruction, a divided country much reduced in size, which is no longer a big world power and now lives in fear of a neighbor grown overwhelmingly powerful in the East. And, above all, as we have said before, he left the Germans with a vast embarrassment at what they did.

The foregoing thoughts about Hitler's personality are not intended to represent anything even remotely approaching a complete or systematic study of his character structure. They do not much more than scratch the surface. As we said at the outset, what is missing and is urgently needed is a thorough analysis of Hitler's personality by a qualified psychiatrist. The material which would now be available to him is enormous and probably far greater than has ever

[308] Gun, *Eva Braun*, p. 222.

been available about the leader of any nation. There are Hitler's own books, speeches, and proclamations; his *Table Talks* and *Situation Conferences;* the diaries of close associates and his mistress; memoirs of his secretary, valets, photographer, interpreter, and boyhood friend, and of numerous politicians, generals, and others.

While Hitler was still alive, President Roosevelt and the U.S. Office of Strategic Services did make great efforts to obtain information on Hitler's psychology; and their psychiatrists, Doctors Murray, Langer, and Vernon did produce valuable analyses which we have discussed here at length. But it hardly seems as if, at the time, anyone paid much attention to them. The analyses were "secret" or "classified" and were left unpublished. (In fact, one study was not declassified until this author requested declassification in October 1971.) Had they all been given publicity in Hitler's lifetime, they might have done much practical good. Reports of Hitler's abnormal sex life, for example, would have been a sensation if broadcast to Germany and could have done much to undermine his position.

In fact, even the then available published literature, above all *Mein Kampf,* seems to have been widely disregarded. That book, except for excerpts, was apparently not translated into English, in Britain, until 1938, and even then (or later) few people read it and fewer still realized that it represented a surprisingly frank and open statement of Hitler's basic ideology and of his plans for action. It is, indeed, a tiresome book to read, and it was so radical and extreme that it was not easy to take seriously. But there his program was, neatly laid out, and almost no one wanted to read or believe it. No one, moreover, wanted to know that Hitler was a man of considerable intelligence, vast willpower, and determination. Instead, nearly everyone thought that Hitler was a fool with a silly moustache and was laughable. Charlie Chaplin made the film *The Great Dictator* which depicted Hitler and Mussolini as total fools and clowns. The film did untold damage to the already weak capacity of the world to understand its enemy. Hitler himself was wise enough to say in *Mein Kampf* (of an earlier time) that "it was . . . fundamentally wrong to ridicule the enemy,"[309] but he, too, actually violated this principle on many occasions. At any rate, the whole Hitler period is characterized by an astonishing degree of mutual underestimation and contempt.

[309]*Mein Kampf,* p. 198.

Even today, with all the vast information about Hitler that is now at our disposal, there still remain blind spots in our comprehension of his personality and psychology. If we bear in mind that both his father and mother came from peasant stock, that his mother in her youth was still a farm worker and, later, a domestic servant, that his father, a man of limited education, was no more than a small cutoms official, then it is hard to understand, for example, the origins of Hitler's intelligence, his extraordinary gifts as an orator, his self-assurance, his conviction, throughout his life, that he was a unique personality and vastly superior to everyone else. Above all, there seems to be nothing in his background and psychology that can explain his enormous willpower and determination, which enabled him to withstand a long series of formidable obstacles, such as his two failures at the Academcy of Arts, his homeless life as a young man before and after the first World War, the failure of his *Putsch* in 1923, his imprisonment, a string of political defeats in the Weimar Republic, the disaster of the initial winter warfare in Russia, Stalingrad, and many other military reverses, and, more than anything else, years of severe illness. It took the combined power of the Soviet Union, the United States, and Great Britain to beat him down.

At any rate, it was this strange, uncouth, almost barbaric personality that entranced the great majority of the Germans of that period. They understood it even less than we understand it today. It is an awesome fact that he was loved by his people far more deeply and widely than any monarch in a thousand years of German history. For a few years, he gave to most of the people, and particularly to the young, a sense of happiness and well-being, of unity and purpose, as had probably never been experienced before in all their long history. This may be an explanation of Hitler's acceptance by the German people, but at the same time it may imply the deepest reproach.

Now a brief postscript about the personality of Eva Braun, although this may be of mere peripheral interest in our study.

Albert Speer is supposed to have said that historians will be disappointed by Eva Braun. This would be true only of those historians who expected to find that she took an active part in shaping political history. She had no interest in politics, knew little of what was going on in the world outside the house, but was a passive, not overly intelligent, shy person who—merely as a woman—dedicated herself to Hitler. As a human being, however, she was not a disappointment but commands a good deal of respect.

Hitler was about twenty-three years older than she was. It was the same age difference, incidentally, as between Hitler's father and mother. Eva was about twenty when she first met Hitler, and she may still have been a virgin, having been brought up as a devout Catholic, partly in a convent school.[310] There is little doubt that Hitler never loved her even to the minimal extent to which he might have been able to love anyone. His secretary says that "Hitler confessed to me one day that he felt no great love for Eva Braun but that he had simply become used to her. On one occasion he said 'I am very fond of Eva but I really loved only Geli [Raubal]. I would never marry Eva'."[311] (His love for Geli is also questionable.) It is significant that even in his Private Testament, which he dictated a day before his suicide, he still spoke merely of "friendship" with Eva but not of love. He said that he had decided "to take for my wife that girl who, after long years of loyal friendship, entered this almost surrounded city of her own free will to share my fate."[312] This expression of friendship contrasts with his profession of "love . . . for my people" in his Political Testament of the same date.[313]

Eva, however, was deeply in love with him. Even her early diary of 1935 is nothing but a confession of this passionate love. Once, after he had come to see her she wrote: "I am so immensely happy he is so fond of me, and I pray this will never change. I never want it to be my fault, should he ever stop being fond of me."[314] Her love continued undiminished through the years, in spite of long periods of neglect by him, in spite of being relegated to the upstairs whenever he had guests of importance, and in spite of an interest he occasionally showed in other women. Shortly after the assassination attempt of July 20, 1944, she wrote him: "I am beside myself. Desperate, miserable. . . . You know, I've always said so, that I shan't go on living if

[310]Gun, op. cit., pp. 35–36.
[311]Zoller, op. cit., p. 92.
[312]*TMWC*, Vol. 41, p. 553.
[313]Ibid., p. 548.
[314]*Eva Braun's Diary*, p. 7, entry of Feb. 18, 1935.

anything happens to you. From the time of our first meetings, I promised myself to follow you everywhere, even in death. You know that my whole life is loving you."[315]

On April 19, 1945, eleven days before the end, she wrote to her friend Herta from the Berlin bunker: ". . . I'm so happy, especially at this moment, at being near HIM. Not a day passes without my being ordered [by him] to take refuge at the Berghof [in Bavaria], but so far I've always won."[316] Four days later, on April 23, 1945, she wrote a long, calm letter to her sister, making final dispositions concerning her jewelry, cigarettes, chocolate, and canned coffee. The day before, in a last letter to her friend Herta, she had said: "I shall die as I lived. It's no burden."[317] She was then thirty-three years old.

[315]Gun, op. cit., p. 208. The translations of all of Eva's letters quoted here are by Gun.

[316]Ibid., p. 236.

[317]Ibid., pp. 241–243.

Chapter 13

Economic and Political Conditions after World War I

Even a man of Hitler's ability, determination, and ideological convictions would not have been able to establish himself in Germany as a dictator of unprecedented power, had he not encountered a constellation of political, economic, and sociopsychological conditions and developments during the period from 1919 to 1933, which were singularly favorable to the impact of his personality and to the assertion of the ideology which he could present. What he found when the army discharged him in 1919 was a historical catastrophe: a defeated nation being deeply humiliated by the victors; domestic political turbulence, if not chaos; disunity; economic disorder or disaster; and a people in despair. It was precisely the soil in which demagoguery, lust for power, and a sadistic destructive personality could prosper. It was also the condition in which the defeated but still proud nation was apt eagerly to respond to an ideology that told it of its fundamental greatness, its superiority over all others; explained away the causes of the defeat or the defeat itself; and described with apparent certainty a program by which the nation could emerge from disaster into health and into a glory greater, in fact, than anything the country had known before in history. It is reasonably certain that Hitler would never have accomplished his breakthrough without at least two external factors (if not more): the desperate economic conditions and the continuing humiliations of Germany by the Allied Powers even after the conclusion of the Peace of Versailles. In fact, the very terms of the peace treaty furnished Hitler with some of his most effective ammunition. Abnormal times seemed to call for an abnormal man and his abnormal solutions. This was the moment in history for him and for the ideology of National Socialism.

A. The Economic Situation

The date of birth of the Weimar Republic might be said to be February 6, 1919, when its National Assembly opened in that city. This coincided roughly with what Hitler called "my first more or less purely political activity."[1] The five or six years which followed were probably the most turbulent period in modern German history— politically as well as economically. Hitler himself contributed relatively little to that turbulence. He was still a comparatively unknown agitator who received more attention from the Munich police and the courts than from the general public. Most people still did not take him seriously.

Politically the first few years of the Weimar Republic were characterized by violent domestic struggles, bloodshed in many cities, a succession of weak central and local governments, widespread refusal to accept their authority, crime, and general disorder. Economically the blockade of Germany by the Allied Powers was continuing, and with it the general starvation or undernourishment which had begun during the war. Business stagnated and unemployment was severe. The discharged soldiers, some still armed, were roaming the streets in tattered uniforms, unable to find anything to do and to fit themselves into an orderly civilian society. But it was also a time when a small number of clever business operators succeeded in making large profits out of the general chaos.

The economy of this early period after World War I was dominated by the problem of the so-called reparation payments which the Treaty of Versailles required Germany to make to the victorious powers. The impoverished economy of the country found it difficult or impossible to meet these very large payments, for the transfer of which, at any rate, it was unable to earn enough foreign currency by exports. Government after government fell over the issue of these payments. The crisis deepened when, in January 1923, the French and Belgian governments decided to have their troops occupy the German Ruhr district to obtain payment by force from the profitable heavy industry of that area, and from German customs duties. But the population of the district adopted an attitude of passive resistance and became a financial charge on the already overburdened central

[1] *Mein Kampf,* p. 227.

government, which, incompetent as it seemed to be, saw no remedy other than to print new money. The result was the wildest, most uncontrolled inflation in the history of any country. By June, 1923, the mark was quoted at 150,000 to the dollar; on July 30, at 1 million; on November 20, at 4.2 *billion.* In other words, the mark was really no longer worth anything, and there was monetary chaos. In the wild days of November, 1923, a worker's pay check which, at the beginning of the week, might still have paid for rent and food, would, at the end of the week, do no more than buy a postage stamp. Manufacturing was near a standstill, and farmers failed to ship their products to the cities.

At long range, the situation was severely aggravated by an unfortunate decision of the German Supreme Court which held that "a mark equals a mark," in other words, that, for example, 100,000 of the completely devalued mark of 1923 was good tender in payment of a debt in that amount which dated back to the days of the gold mark before 1918. Thus a mortgage of 100,000 or 1,000,000 marks could be paid off with a postage stamp. Savings accounts were wiped out. Later a revaluation law restored a small percentage of the losses in some situations, but the financial damage that had been done to large population groups, especially the middle classes, remained severe and frequently irreparable.

There followed a difficult period of deflation. The currency was finally stabilized, but business conditions remained uncertain with much unemployment and general poverty. Moreover, the extensive political unrest, which bordered on civil war, was not conducive to an improvement in the economy. Slowly, however, the situation eased. The reparation terms were lightened, the Ruhr mines and the customs duty collections were returned to German hands, and in January, 1926, the last French troops were withdrawn. The economy was far from prospering, but it was at least functioning; and by 1928 unemployment amounted to no more than 1,624,000.[2]

Not long thereafter, however, the worldwide Great Depression struck; and it came as a particularly heavy blow to a country which had hardly recovered from inflation and deflation and was still con-

[2]This and the following unemployment figures were taken from Fritz Stern (ed.), *The Path to Dictatorship* 1918–1933, p. 210.

valescing. It had few, if any, reserves. Unemployment climbed to 3,217,608 in January, 1930; to 4,886,925 in January, 1931; to 6,041,010 in January, 1932; and it stood at 6,013,612 in January, 1933, two months before Hitler came to power. This was a very considerable number of unemployed in a country whose total population was only about 60 million with an estimated total labor force of about 20 million. In an industrial city like Berlin, only about 40 percent of the possible jobs were available, but unemployment insurance for a worker with a wife and two children amounted to about $4.25 per week. [3]

Hitler took full political advantage of the general misery. Beginning in the early days of his political career to the day of his seizure of power (and even thereafter) he never ceased hammering away at the theme that "the system"—meaning democracy and the Jews—was responsible for all the economic disasters, and that determined leadership, such as he was able to give, would quickly guide the country into stability and prosperity. And in this respect, he did not really have to do much persuading. If there was any tipping of a scale, it was the Great Depression that tipped it in Hitler's favor. By and large, the people and even many politicians, party leaders, writers, and others were quite ready to identify the economic disasters with their new democratic form of government. The two, after all, had coincided in point of time, and no one had had previous experience with democracy. At any rate, in times of desperate economic crises, unemployment, and even starvation, a great many affected people cannot be reached by rational argument; and in a state of exhaustion or helplessness, they will not be very particular in their choice of means of relief. It was a fertile field for Hitler.

The groups which had been most severely affected by the inflation and the subsequent economic crises were the lower middle class and the middle class. They had lost most or all of their savings and much of their social prestige. Many small businesses had gone bankrupt. Some members of these groups had been forced to move down into the proletariat, and others were in imminent danger of having to do so. To all, their new poverty looked like a profound disgrace. There was, in fact, an atmosphere of social panic in these groups. It was not surprising, then, that these were the groups which,

[3]See Helga Grebing, *Der Nationalsozialismus — Ursprung und Wesen*, p. 48.

as we have seen, were to become the backbone of the National Socialist Movement. It seems, in any case, that in times of economic crises the middle classes incline toward the radicals of the right, whereas the proletariat inclines toward Communism. The greater the social and economic disorganization, the more numerous are the persons who are attracted to the total condemnation of democracy which totalitarianism expresses, and to its total all-encompassing leadership.

It is noteworthy in this connection that even the degree of ethnic intolerance, such as anti-Semitism, which at all times was one of Hitler's central themes, stands in direct proportion to downward social mobility and apprehension of, or actual, unemployment. Bettelheim, in his studies in the United States, found that

> The highest degrees of association established in this study were those between intolerance on the one hand and feelings of deprivation and downward social mobility on the other. . . . Even a shift from low to moderate apprehension about unemployment (let alone actual unemployment) may considerably increase the frequency and intensity of ethnic intolerance.[4]

When Hitler came to power in March 1933, more than 6 million were unemployed. By October of that year, the number was reduced to 3,744,860. By 1936, unemployment had been eliminated. The small businesses of the lower middle class, moreover, had been rehabilitated. In part, this highly significant success was due to the rearmament policy and other measures of the regime; in part, it was due to the worldwide lifting of the Great Depression. But no matter what the causes were, those millions of Germans who had finally been rescued from misery and had been given security were inclined to see Hitler as their savior; and from then on, not surprisingly, they were willing to put their trust in him.

B. The Political Situation

Culturally, the Weimar Republic was magnificent while it lasted.[5] It represented a splendid late flowering of a true civilization, as Ger-

---

[4]Bruno Bettelheim and Morris Janowitz, *Dynamics of Prejudice*, p. 174.

[5]See the good study *Weimar Culture* by Peter Gay; also Peter Gay, "Germany 1919-1932. The Weimar Culture," in *Social Research*, Vol. 39, No. 2, Summer 1972, pp. 207-364.

many may never see again. The "Golden Twenties" were perhaps more golden in the Weimar Republic than anywhere else. There were Gropius and the Bauhaus, which changed the face of the world; there was *The Magic Mountain* of Thomas Mann and much other outstanding literature; there were painters like Klee, Kandinsky, Grosz, and the whole expressionist school; there were the theater of Max Reinhardt and the plays of Bertold Brecht; German films were opening up a new world of art; Einstein changed the world of physics. But it was a kind of feverish life of the mind. Peter Gay calls it "a dance on the edge of a volcano."[6] It coexisted closely with extreme turbulence in politics and economics, with misery, deprivation, injustice, and many political murders. It almost seemed that the creative restless culture of Weimar, while self-absorbed and introspective, fed in some mysterious way on the decay of its surroundings. And when it all ended with Hitler's seizure of power, "the exiles [Gay says] were the greatest collection of transplanted intellect, talent and scholarship the world has ever seen."

Politically, the life and death of the Weimar Republic was deeply affected by two untruths or lies. One was the dogma of the *Kriegsschuldlüge*, that is, the doctrine that Germany carried no guilt at all for the outbreak of World War I, but that the war was forced upon the Germans by their enemies. The other lie was the legend of the traitorous "stab in the back" (considered here before) by which the unbeaten German army was deprived of victory in 1918.

It was surprising to what extent the war-guilt-lie became unshakable dogma and remained so, in fact, until quite recently.[7] The dogma was official policy of all successive Weimar governments, just as it represented the privately held opinion of 99 percent of the people. Dinning it into the head of every school child was an important function of the teaching profession, and the whole effort was thoroughly successful. Virtually no one questioned the dogma. Hitler's tirades merely repeated what everyone was convinced was the truth.

Had this not been German dogma, which for about forty years was not even subject to examination, the political views and emotions of a good many Germans would have been very different. If the Ger-

---

[6]Gay, *Weimar Culture*, p. xiv.

[7]Except for minor attacks, the dogma was not seriously shaken until the recent publication of two books (1961 and 1969) by the historian Fritz Fischer, heretofore cited.

man cause in World War I was not just but unjust, then the defeat in the war would not have seemed to be an undeserved blow of fate; and even the alleged traitors—Hitler's "November criminals"—who executed the legendary stab in the back might not have seemed quite so wicked. The loss of the war might not have been felt as quite so monstrous an injustice of fate, so that' less resentment and hatred would have resulted. Above all, the very harsh terms of the Treaty of Versailles (while still far too harsh to be compatible with the generosity of a truly wise victor) might not seem wholly unjustified. And if there had been any kind of moral justification for the Versailles terms in German eyes, then much of the ideological underpinnings of aggressive German nationalism and later of National Socialism would have been knocked away. Strange to say, in retrospect it looks as if the dogma of the war-guilt-lie, which the Weimar Republic itself so ardently propagated, carried in it some of the seeds of Weimar's destruction. In thousands of speeches and proclamations, and in his writings, Hitler never ceased to hammer away at the infamy, disgrace, dishonor, and shame of Versailles. With him this was an entirely basic tenet and a most useful propaganda tool. At any rate, to millions of Germans the Treaty of Versailles looked like ample, new justification for all the traditional deep-seated aversion against the West.

Even more important was the second lie with which the Weimar Republic had to live: the legend that Germany was never militarily defeated in World War I and that the war was lost merely because of a stab in the back by traitors. (The legend indicates the wisdom of the Allied Powers in World War II insisting on unconditional military surrender and occupation. Had Hindenburg been forced to sign an instrument of surrender after World War I, the legend might never have been born.) The legend was, however, never as widely believed as the dogma of the war-guilt-lie. The Left denied it; in the Center, some did and some did not believe it; and the Right took it for its gospel. But, at any rate, none of the various Weimar governments ever made a determined effort to disprove it. The legend thus created a serious permanent split down the middle of the nation. Large parts of the population were unwilling to acquiesce in the defeat and regarded it as the fruit of national disloyalty. To them, acquiescence, like the stab in the back itself, remained un-German, and the legend did not let them rest. All kinds of groups, large and small, crackpots and respectable, continued to agitate for action to undo the defeat. Hitler's Movement was one of them, and ultimately all others merged or were forced to merge into it.

One of the worst results of the legend was that somehow the Weimar Republic and with it democracy in general were identified with the loss of the war and thus became objects of hatred and contempt. Large parts of the nation were never willing to recognize Weimar as a legitimate political entity, any more than they were willing to acknowledge the military defeat. Hitler and National Socialism grew out of this hatred, out of this emotionally conceived lack of a legitimate government, and in a sense they were thus a product of World War I.

The two lies poisoned the body of the nation; no nation could have been healthy with them long. It was not until long after the end of the Second World War, if then, that the Germans learned to face the true facts of World War I or lost interest in them. Had they faced them in 1918, the Weimar Republic might have been saved; there might have been no Hitler. He and others in the Germany of that period promoted a permanent attitude of resentment and hatred of the victors and, equally so, of any German who was inclined to forget the past. Loyalty to Weimar was treason.

It is not proposed here to discuss all the other infirmities of the Weimar Republic at any length. It suffered from a considerable array of them. There is little doubt that, quite generally, it lacked statesmen who had a true ability to lead. The Weimar constitution, good as it was in many ways, lacked safeguards against too easy parliamentary overthrows of Chancellors and Cabinets by eternally hostile parties who might fight about mere trifles. As a result, government followed government, and the cabinet crisis became a way of life. There hardly ever was a genuine majority. Even few of those who governed had real faith in the Weimar system. The democracy for which the constitution provided had few genuine believers among the governors and the governed. Fundamentally no one knew much about what a democracy should be like. Its uncertainties, its demands for reasonableness and compromises, seemed repulsive. The old desire for the domestic political certainty of the former monarchy survived, consciously among some, unconsciously among others.

Power, then, was assumed mostly by those unenviable men who had been solely in the opposition before 1918 and had no leadership training at all. Unlike the nobility that had previously governed, the new governors lacked all self-assurance; and, above all, none of them had really been prepared for the suddenness of their assumption of power after the unexpected Revolution of November 1918. They faced a population that was, at best, suspicious and, at worst, thoroughly hostile. At long range, this nation was hardly governable by the men then called upon to govern it.

It was characteristic of the whole distressing situation that, in 1925, seven years after the Revolution, the aged General Paul von Hindenburg, a member of the nobility and a veritable relic of the monarchy, was elected President by 48 percent of the voters. (So large a number of Germans had rarely agreed on one man.) He was then 81 years old and had little enthusiasm for the job. He was, in fact, soon to become senile; but, at any rate, he was enough of a symbol of a more stable and authoritarian age to appeal to the electorate. This did not mean that the nobility, as a group, had come back to furnish the leadership which it had provided until 1918. The nobility, in fact, seemed to have largely lost the will to power which had marked it for centuries. Perhaps it was the defeat of the monarchy that had shattered this will. Financially, too, the nobility was half bankrupt. To be sure, in 1932, in the dying days of the Weimar Republic, Hindenburg did appoint two successive chancellors who were members of the nobility; but they were petty politicians and failures. One of them, Franz von Papen, was foolish and unprincipled enough to persuade the reluctant old President to appoint Hitler as Chancellor. Papen thought that he could "make use" of Hitler for his own purposes—one of the major historic miscalculations.

Papen's foolishness and Hindenburg's senility were useful stepping-stones to ease Hitler's climb to power, but sooner or later he would have seized power even without them. By 1933, there was only one force in Germany that could still have stopped him: the Army. But the Army was not all inclined to do so. In fact, at least the young officers strongly favored Hitler. It has sometimes been said that Hitler stepped into a power vacuum. The nobility, as we have said, no longer had the will to power. The middle class, for over ten years had furnished a long series of more or less incompetent half-hearted governments of which nearly everyone was thoroughly tired. The Socialists, who had taken over after the Revolution, had, in effect, not long thereafter handed the job back to the parties of the middle class, apparently lacking all will to creative power and all leadership material. Unlike the National Socalists and the Communists (of whom we shall speak later), the Socialists (in Walter Laqueur's words) "had no ideas, no faith or promise to offer to the young generation, only the sober, reasonable, unemotional, and tired explanation that democracy was probably the least oppressive of all political systems." This, as Laqueur says, "was not very satisfactory for a young generation in search of the Holy Grail."[8] Altogether, the politics of the Weimar Republic had been an embarrassment.

C. The Sociopsychological Situation

The weakness, decline, and death of the Weimar Republic was, of course, a psychological problem as much as it was an economic and political one,[9] all three aspects interacting with each other. Erich Fromm says that "psychologically speaking, the petty bourgeois had built his existence . . . on the monarchy and the state," and "their failure and defeat shattered the basis of his own life."[10] His economic position and social prestige declined so far in the postwar years that "there was nobody to look down upon any more."[11] Middle class security was shattered by the loss of the father's authority in the postwar developments. "The increasing social frustration led to a projection which became an important source for National Socialism. . . . The national defeat and the Treaty of Versailles became the symbols to which the actual frustration—the social one—was shifted."[12] (We might interpolate here that the political frustration seemed hardly less actual than the social one.)

The old middle class's feeling of powerlessness, anxiety and isolation from the social whole and the destructiveness springing from this situation was not the only psychological source of

---

[8]Laqueur, "A Look Back at the Weimar Republic," *New York Times Magazine*, Aug. 16, 1970, p. 25.

[9]The psychological side is discussed, with some misunderstandings of the political and economic situation, by Erich Fromm, *Escape from Freedom*, pp. 214-221.

[10]Ibid., p. 214.

[11]Ibid., p. 215.

[12]Ibid., p. 216.

Nazism. The peasants felt resentful against the urban creditors . . . , while the workers felt deeply disappointed and discouraged by the constant political retreat after their first victories in 1918 under a leadership which had lost all strategic initiative. The vast majority of the population was seized with the feeling of individual insignificance and powerlessness. . . .

Those psychological conditions . . . constituted . . . [National Socialism's] human basis without which it could not have developed. . . .[13]

National Socialism, Fromm says, "resurrected the lower middle class psychologically,"[14] and there is little doubt that this was, in fact, one of the most important factors in the whole emergence of this Movement. The lower middle class was given back the security and glory of a powerful state organization; it was given objects to whom it could feel superior, as well as outlets for the discharge of its accumulated hostility and destructiveness.

Erik H. Erikson puts it a little differently when he says that ". . . Germany's defeat and the Treaty of Versailles resulted in a widespread traumatic identity loss, especially in German youth, and, thus in a historical identity confusion conducive to a state of national delinquency under the leadership of a gang of overgrown adolescents of criminal make-up."[15]

And the nation followed Hitler with ardor and devotion—first the lower middle class, which had been given the biggest psychological lift, and then, in an ever-widening circle, many other classes and groups, a motley assemblage of the malcontent, the frustrated, the dispossessed, the meek and the adventurers, students and professors, romanticists and cultists, nationalists and patriots, sadists and masochists, and those, particularly the young, who did not really know what they wanted. But they all had one thing in common: they desperately wanted things to change, and a good many did not care much about the direction of the change. They all saw hope for change in the National Socialist Movement. In demanding a national dictator, some

[13]Ibid., p. 217–218.
[14]Ibid., p. 221.
[15]Erikson, *Identity, Youth and Crisis*, p. 192. The analysis by a third psychiatrist, Bruno Bettelheim, in *Dynamics of Prejudice*, p. 170–171, fn. 6, seems faulty in part.

of these politically inexperienced people wanted, in effect, no more than to restore something resembling the vanished monarchy; but they thought it would be a decent dictator who, after resurrecting a strong Germany, would govern like a benevolent king. They had the urge to venerate someone, to be given shelter and law and order. Others supported National Socialism, not because they were really in sympathy with its ideas, but for the purely negative reason that they saw in it an instrument to destroy the hated Weimar Republic.

There was much destructiveness, particularly among the young who committed various political murders. The murderers were proud of their deeds, and millions of Germans approved and admired them. Karl Dietrich Bracher says that the "political motives of such deeds manifested a progressive demagogic stupidity, particularly of the young generation for whom—quite simply—Bolshevism, democracy and the international Jewish conspiracy were all one, and who, therefore, regarded loyalty to the Weimar Republic as treason, but every action against it as true patriotism."[16]

The Weimar Republic was born in the German defeat of World War I, it lived a sickly life of thirteen years in postwar turmoil, and it died a silent death when Hitler's moment in history had come. He did not even bother to abolish the Weimar Constitution. It simply faded away.

[16]Bracher, *Die deutsche Diktatur*, p. 111.

V

THE HELPERS

In speaking of "helpers," we do not mean all the countless millions of Germans and persons of other nationalities who were members of the Movement or were its followers. We mean, rather, certain special groups, inside and outside of Germany, who by words and acts of commission or omission did much to help National Socialism to come to power or to retain it. In earlier chapters we already spoke of some of these groups, particularly the generals, the historians, and the Germanistics scholars. But there are additional groups which gave Hitler a good deal of help.

Chapter 14

1. The German Communists; Moscow

On the face of things, it may seem grotesque to include the German Communists and Moscow in the groups which helped Hitler, but there can be no doubt that they must be included.[1] Indeed, they contributed no little to Hitler's rise to power. In considering the role which the German Communists played, we must recognize first that their actions were dictated from Moscow; and Moscow, on its part, as on various other occasions, operated on the basis of fallacies and miscalculations induced by its own ideological and dogmatic preconceptions. In Moscow's view, *all* German political parties to the right of the Socialists, including the National Socialists, were "bourgeois parties," and the Socialists themselves had been corrupted by the bourgeoisie. In other words, the bourgeoisie was already in power, and there could be no revolution by the Hitler Movement because it could not revolt against itself.[2] Moscow, according to George F. Kennan, did not much care whether a moderate Weimar government or Hitler was in power.

The political line which was adopted at the Sixth Comintern Congress in Moscow in 1928 was that the political activity of the German Communists was to be directed squarely against the Socialists, who were, in fact, to be identified as "Social-Fascists." Kennan says the following about Stalin:

> He feared and disliked the moderate Socialists in Germany. He regarded them as pro-Western. . . . He feared particularly their

[1]The Soviet role is described well, even if in somewhat contradictory terms, in George F. Kennan, *Russia and the West under Lenin and Stalin*, Boston, 1960, 1961, pp. 285-292. As to the German Communists, see Ossip K. Flechtheim, *Die KPD in der Weimarer Republik*, 1969.

[2]Kennan, op. cit., pp. 287-288.

influence on political trends within the Russian Communist Party. . . . He was content . . . to exploit [the German Communists] as a weapon with which to weaken the Social-Democrats [Socialists], to damage Germany's relationship with the West, and in general *to disrupt the strength of the Weimar Republic*, and to restore Germany's waning dependence on Moscow.[3]

This policy line was not changed in the years thereafter, in fact not until 1941, in spite of the onset of the Great Depression, enormous unemployment, and the rising strength of the Hitler Movement. The German Communists, faithful to party discipline, remained thoroughly hostile to Hitler's opponents. In fact, wherever they could, in various elections, the Communists voted with the National Socialists against the Socialists and other moderate Weimar parties. In some crucial elections, they tipped the scale in favor of the parties of the Right, and they did this consciously and deliberately.

It was all the result of a grotesque failure on Moscow's part to understand the true nature of National Socialism and its relative position in the German political spectrum. In the Russian view, National Socialism represented merely the final stage in the crisis of monopoly capitalism; and after it, the road to a dictatorship of the German proletariat would be open. Kennan reports that "less than a fortnight before Hitler's assumption of the chancellorship, the blunt answer was given by a secretary of the Soviet embassy [in Berlin]: 'Moscow was convinced the road to a Soviet Germany lay through Hitler'."[4] (By the circuitous route of an unwanted war, which cost about 20 million Russian lives, the answer has turned out to be correct to the extent of *East* Germany.) Clearly Stalin and Hitler could both be equally doctrinaire; and in this particular situation, their doctrines interacted in a strange superimposition of the dream world of the one on the dream world of the other, all to the detriment of their nations and the world.

There is no doubt that Moscow and the German Communists contributed materially to the destruction of the Weimar Republic. It was significant that in election campaigns the Communists themselves

[3]Ibid., p. 287 (italics added). See also Peter Gay, "Germany 1919–1932. The Weimar Culture" in *Social Research*, Vol. 39, No. 2, p. 335.
[4]Kennan, op. cit., p. 289.

propagated the slogan that the German people faced nothing other than a choice between Communism and National Socialism. The great majority of those Germans who believed this would certainly have been in favor of National Socialism, the true nature of which was then still unknown to them, whereas they knew for sure that a German Communist regime would mean rule by Moscow. It was logical, then, that a great many people, even political moderates, could be impressed with Hitler's promises, repeated over and over, that National Socialism — and nothing else — would save Germany from Communism. The protagonists of the Left and Right appeared to frame a neat issue, and the Center seemed to have little of significance to say.

It might be added that Soviet help to the national socialist regime continued into World War II, until the German armies actually invaded the Soviet Union. Moscow furnished the Germans with strategic raw materials; and after the partition of Poland between Germany and the Soviet Union, Moscow permitted German submarines to use one of its naval bases. Moreover, Moscow gave orders to Communists in the Western countries to carry on antiwar activities, which at that stage of the war could be interpreted only as a pro-German effort.

Chapter 15

2. The Western Powers

Again it may seem grotesque, on the face of things, to include the Western Powers in the groups which helped Hitler. Yet they must be included, even though the difference between them, on the one hand, and Moscow and the German Communists, on the other, was that the latter two were quite deliberate in helping Hitler, whereas the Western Powers did so unwittingly and indirectly. Their mistakes lay, in fact, largely in their preventing a healthy development of the fragile Weimar Republic and sometimes in their outright hostile acts against it, as well as in their failing to oppose Hitler long before the outbreak of World War II.

The first mistake was the *Treaty of Versailles* itself.[1] There is no question that the Treaty was harsh and vindictive and that it demonstrated the very opposite of that leniency and generosity which an intelligent, far-seeing victor will show his defeated enemy.

Even the making of the Treaty, the treatment of the German delegation (widely publicized in Germany), was "one long calculated insult."[2] The terms were largely dictated, not negotiated, and they showed little resemblance to the famous "Fourteen Points" of President Woodrow Wilson which the Germans had thought would be the basis of the peace. The principle of self-determination was readily abandoned in transferring large sections of Germany to Poland and Czechoslovakia; a union of Germany and Austria was prohibited; reparation payments were assessed at 132 billion gold marks, a wholly unrealistic assessment which naïvely disregarded Germany's inability to earn the necessary foreign currency.

[1]The existing literature on the Treaty is naturally vast. For present purposes, the matter is perhaps best summarized in Geoffrey Barraclough, *The Origins of Modern Germany*, pp. 444–446. See also Peter Gay, *Weimar Culture*, pp. 14–16.

[2]Gay, op. cit., p. 14.

Moreover, a psychologically highly important provision of the Treaty was that Germany was to be excluded from the League of Nations; in other words, she was to be an outcast from the family of nations. This contrasts sharply with the treatment of West Germany after World War II when (while still excluded from the United Nations for technical reasons) she was welcomed into the European Economic Community (EEC) and into NATO—in other words, was taken into the family of Western nations. In fact, instead of having to pay reparations, Germany was given a great deal of financial help under the Marshall Plan of Secretary of State George C. Marshall and President Harry S. Truman.

While after World War II, the Germans could thus orient themselves toward the West, Versailles and other actions of the Western Powers after World War I practically forced them to turn inward, to feel outcast, adding fuel to that old characteristic awareness of a German uniqueness *(Sonderbewusstsein)* which has always led to excessive nationalism and compensatory feelings of racial superiority. Moreover, as Barraclough says, "The treatment of the new German republic as a weak and defeated power equated the republic and weakness and thereby strengthened immeasurably the hand of all reactionary forces within Germany opposed to the republican regime. . . . The outcome . . . has been the Germany of Hitler that we know. . . ."[3] The last sentence may be exaggerated, but there is a measure of truth in it.

Of course, it might well be argued that Versailles had been preceded by the even harsher Treaty of Brest Litovsk of 1918, which the Imperial German Government had imposed upon the defeated Soviet Russians. But this was something to which the Germans closed their eyes; and at any rate the Weimar government did not equate itself with that of Wilhelm II.

Versailles was by no means the end of the unwise, insensate postwar treatment of the Germans by the Allies, especially the French. There followed, for example, years of harassment because of the German inability to pay reparations. This finally culminated in the occupation of the Ruhr district by French and Belgian troops in 1923 to extract money by force. It was, apart from Versailles itself, the most humiliating event in the life of the Weimar Republic, and it did in-

[3]Barraclough, op. cit., p. 446.

calculable harm to the cause of democracy in Germany. At the same time it furnished a greater lift than anything else to the reawakening of intense nationalism, patriotism, and militarism. Characteristic for that period, for example, was that in the Berlin film theaters the audience would spontaneously rise before the start of the performance and sing the national anthem. In retrospect, it was as if the French were deliberately creating a climate in which National Socialism could thrive. Clearly the Ruhr occupation was a severe blow to the future of the Weimar Republic.

The tender flower of German democracy in the interwar years needed all the care it could possibly get, if it was to survive. But instead of care, it received harsh treatment at best. For years it was under constant harassment from the Western Powers, especially France; from Moscow and the German Communists; from the National Socialists; from other nationalists; and even, as we saw earlier, from the Jewish intellectuals. In the face of all these attacks, it seemed extraordinarily difficult to convince the impoverished, struggling nation that it was on the right road or that its experiment in democracy was at all successful or might ever lead to success. The consolidation of moderate government forces was made difficult beyond any tolerable levels, and it is perhaps surprising, in these circumstances, that Weimar lasted as long as it did. George F. Kennan, who lived in Germany at that time, says, "I know of no more pathetic and tragic episode in the history of this past half-century than this first relatively brief and ill-fated German experiment in democratic government— an experiment which was the object of so much misunderstanding and indifference abroad, and which rested on so fragile a basis at home."[4] With some substantial help from the Western powers, rather than indifference and harassment, the developments might have been different, and the nation would very likely have become more Western-oriented, less German-centered, less accessible to Hitler.

The sociopsychologists have assessed the events in corresponding terms. Erik H. Erikson, in discussing the defeat, the Treaty of Versailles, and the resulting "widespread traumatic identity loss, especially in German youth," speaks of "the constructive potentialities which, in a given nation, can be perverted largely by the de-

[4]Kennan, *Russia and the West under Lenin and Stalin*, p. 284.

fault of other nations."[5] Elsewhere, he says that the Western Powers

> . . . failed in their responsibility to "re-educate" Germany in the only way in which one can re-educate peoples—namely, by presenting them with the incorruptible fact of a new identity within a more universal political framework. Instead, they exploited German masochism and increased her universal hopelessness.[6]

A "new identity within a more universal framework" is precisely what more far-sighted statesmen gave to the Germans after World War II by making them members of NATO and of the EEC and, generally, by helping to make them more secure and affluent within the family of Western nations. It is interesting, in this connection, that according to Bruno Bettelheim, clinical experience demonstrates that great and permanently effective modifications of personality structure can be produced "by those modifications of the environment which make it reassuring, secure, comprehensible, and thus manageable for the young individual." Such environments reduce frustrations, restrain and contain hostility, and decrease intolerance.[7]

A very strange phenomenon in the relationship between Germany, the Western Powers, and the Soviet Union was that as much as the West and the East had harassed Weimar, they cooperated with Hitler after Weimar's death. It all might be regarded as a lesson that in international politics it is far more profitable to act like a wolf than like a lamb. The Western Powers made no real objection to Hitler's rearmament, his reoccupation of the Rhineland, his annexation of Austria and parts of Czechoslovakia, and other actions—all in violation of the Treaty of Versailles, on the strict observance of which by Weimar they had insisted for so many years. Hitler looked to them like a wild man who had to be appeased by every possible concession. If the West and the East had assisted Weimar as much as they later were to assist Hitler, Weimar might have flourished and Hitler might have remained an obscure political agitator in Munich. (And yet, if the West had objected at the time of the Rhineland, Austrian and

---

[5]Erikson, *Identity, Youth and Crisis,* p. 193.
[6]Erikson, *Childhood and Society,* pp. 350–351.
[7]Bruno Bettelheim and Morris Janowitz, *Dynamics of Prejudice,* p. 173.

Sudeten affairs, and if the objection had been successful, this might well have been denounced later as "imperialist action to prevent German self-determination.")

Clearly the majority of Hitler's great initial successes in international politics could not have been achieved if it had not been for the indecisive attitude of the Western Powers. We know now, for example, that when German troops reoccupied the Rhineland in 1936, German rearmament was still so incomplete that the French Army alone, without British help, could easily have forced Hitler into an embarrassing retreat. This would have gravely impaired his standing within Germany—perhaps irreparably so. Munich, of course, was worse. The whole appeasement policy, in the eyes of the German people, gave support to the national socialist doctrine that the Western nations were racially weak, decadent, and ripe for destruction by the racially strong Germanic people who had finally shaken off the yoke of the Jewish-dominated Weimar regime. Munich greatly strengthened Hitler's position within Germany and choked off resistance even to his most adventurous policies. Moreover, as we have seen, Hitler's discovery of the weakness of his opponents at Munich psychologically aroused his personal sadism and destructiveness to an even higher level than usual.

But, of course, much of the West's failure to offer early resistance to Hitler and its eagerness to appease him was understandable. Apart from being motivated by the desire to avoid war, the Western Powers had finally come to the realization that the political positions which they had taken against Weimar were not permanently tenable. German reoccupation of the Rhineland seventeen years after the war could not really be branded as wholly unreasonable. The union of Germany and Austria seemed a natural development, as long as the Austrian people were willing, which they were. And even the reincorporation of the Sudetenland, with its predominantly German population, appeared justifiable. Certainly, none of these things seemed so bad as to justify war, perhaps another world war. Again it was Hitler who profited from the mistakes of Versailles. Moreover, at the time these events were taking place, nobody knew, and nobody other than a watchful psychiatrist could perhaps be expected to know, what cumulative psychological effect Hitler's early successes would have on him and that letting him get away with them would ultimately lead to real disaster, even though he had stated his aims quite clearly in *Mein Kampf*.

Also, it should not be forgotten how difficult it was for normal non-Germans (and for Germans) to negotiate with Hitler or sometimes even to develop a minimum of understanding of the operations of his mind and emotions. Normally, even in hostile international relations, as in domestic political life, politicians retain an insoluble small residue of human decency and respect for conditions in which human beings can coexist with each other with a minimum measure of confidence and dignity. In private life we expect even a hardened criminal—for instance, a kidnapper—to live up to the terms of a bargain he made and to release the victim upon payment of the ransom. But in Hitler (as also in Himmler) no such residue of human decency seems to have been left, at least when matters of major political concern to him were in question. To him, any deception, any lie, any breach of a solemn agreement, any cruelty was an acceptable weapon against an enemy or potential enemy. The dignity of others meant nothing to him. There was really no one in the international community who knew how to deal with such a man—not even Stalin or Molotov. They were deceived and abused by him no less than Neville Chamberlain and Halifax.

Versailles, the Ruhr occupation, Munich, and the Moscow Non-Aggression Treaty—these were helpful stepping-stones in the development of an international aggressive policy by National Socialism. All were supplied by the Western Powers or the Soviet Union.

Chapter 16

3. The Nobility. Big Business

The national socialist revolution differed from the communist revolution in Russia in an important respect: National Socialism, unlike Communism, as a rule, was always willing or eager to accept, or enter into alliances with, groups which had in the past been the "elite" or had exercised some measure of power. This so-called revolution, on the whole, was initially to be "within the law." There were only a few exceptions to this rule: no one Jewish, for example, and no one in leading positions in the former governments of the Left could be accepted. But the National Socialists, unlike the Russian Communists, never murdered the old aristocracy or business leaders, or forced them into emigration. However, the condition for an alliance with former elite groups was, of course, that they cooperate and ideologically coalign themselves with the national socialist regime.

This attitude of National Socialism was naturally fully in line with its general ideology, which, far from representing a break with the German past (except the immediate past), had fundamentally sprung from much of the cultural heritage of the nation.

The attitude of large parts of the German *aristocracy or nobility* toward Hitler and National Socialism represents one of the sordid chapters of modern German history. It is evident that in part the nobility was quite unable to comprehend the true nature of National Socialism, and, probably for a much greater part, did not really care. What they actually *could* see—and liked—was the resurrection of extreme nationalism, patriotism, and militarism. The nobility, as we have seen before, had always been devoted to the army and had for many centuries furnished the army with its officer corps. The reduction of the army by the Treaty of Versailles to 100,000 men with only a few thousand officers had been a severe blow to the nobility. A great many of them had been deprived of their normal traditional occupation and had been forced into commercial work. For this they had few qualifications and, moreover, it was not considered *standesgemäss*, that is, not up to the standards of their rank or caste. It was at any rate a distasteful kind of work to them. Many older members of the nobility thus lived uprooted lives of quiet desperation, and even the younger ones had difficulty in finding their place in the Weimar Republic.

Thus all the military activity engendered by National Socialism looked like salvation to large numbers of the nobility. They had, it is true, considerable distaste for the low-class, petty-bourgeois characteristics of Hitler and most other leaders of his regime; and the nobility did not willingly undertake social intercourse with the national socialist group, not to speak of intermarriage. In fact, as before, many members of the nobility found the cultivated Jews of Berlin and Frankfurt socially more acceptable, at least until the anti-Jewish laws put an end to such relationships. Yet all these distastes and doubts about the regime seem to have been outweighed by the conviction that the new rulers were initiating a patriotic national revival and were recreating a powerful army in which the nobility could assume its accustomed place, even the leadership, at least initially. The prospect of war, too, was acceptable, if not welcome, to the nobility. War, after all, had essentially been part of its way of life, if not its raison d'être, for many centuries.

But the really appalling development was that the nobility soon let itself be carried away by its enthusiasm to join not only the army but also Himmler's SS. In fact, in the officer corps of the SS, the nobility assumed a large number of high positions. By 1938 it furnished 18.7 percent of the full generals *(Obergruppenführer)*, 9.8 percent of the lieutenant generals *(Gruppenführer)*, 14.3 percent of the major generals *(Brigadeführer)*, 8.8 percent of the brigadier generals *(Oberführer)*, and 8.4 percent of the colonels *(Standartenführer)*. [1] We do not know the percentage among the lower officers, but it was probably quite large. Without question, all these men had full or nearly full knowledge, and some were even the leaders, of the systematic killing

---

[1] Heinz Höhne, *Der Orden unter dem Totenkopf; die Geschichte der SS*, Hamburg, 1966, p. 127. For the rank identifications, see Gerald Reitlinger, *The SS—Alibi of a Nation 1922–1945*, p. xi.

operations of the SS against the Jews, the Polish intelligentsia, the Soviet Commissars, etc. Also, it was the SS that ran the concentration and extermination camps.

Apart from knowledge of, and participation in, the mass killings and torturing, an additional element in the situation was that the extensive membership of the nobility in the SS was apt to invest that organization with some amount of respectability in the eyes of the German people, and thus to stifle opposition. It is true that the Germans by and large had gradually lost faith in the leadership qualities of the nobility, particularly after the end of World War I; but they still did believe that these descendants of the great old German families were at least conservative, honorable men of high integrity who would not become partners of murderers and torturers.

The air of conservative respectability of the SS could only be enhanced further by the fact that even princes of former ruling houses became connected with that organization: for example, the Hereditary Prince Josias zu Waldeck-Pyrmont, Prince Philipp of Hesse,[2] Prince Friedrich Theodor zu Sayn und Wittgenstein,[3] and others.

On the other hand, we should not fail to say that members of the nobility played a leading part in the resistance movement. To mention only the main example, it was Count Claus Schenk von Stauffenberg who, in the assassination attempt of July 20, 1944, placed the bomb in Hitler's conference room. He and his coconspirators showed a degree of heroism and ethical certainty which few men possess or can be expected to possess. For this, they died a slow and most painful death after long torture. But compared with the numbers of the nobility who worked *for* the regime, the number who worked *against* it was extremely small; and, in fact, the smallness of their number was the very element that prevented success. Moreover, even these few conspirators seem to have intended to propose to the British a most naïve program for truce or peace negotiations. It included, among other things, continued German occupation of the territories occupied in Poland and Russia, restoration of the Eastern German frontier as

[2]Both listed among the "Dramatis Personae" in Reitlinger, op. cit., pp. 461 et seq.
[3]As to the last mentioned, see the sad petition to him by the Jews of Kamenka, Poland, in Raul Hilberg, *The Destruction of the European Jews*, pp. 206-207.

it existed before the *First* World War, autonomy for Alsace-Lorraine, accession of South Tyrol to Germany. [4]

Big business, too, was among the helpers. Companies like Thyssen and I. G. Farbenindustrie contributed money to Hitler quite early in his career and facilitated his rise to power although perhaps to a lesser extent than frequently assumed. [5] Later, various large manufacturers took advantage of the slave labor of Jews, Poles, Russians, and German concentration camp prisoners, who had to work under wretched conditions. Big Business did, indeed, play a miserable role. In recent years, East German historians have consistently taken the dogmatic position that Hitler never was more than a servant or stooge or puppet of German monopoly capitalism, and, in fact, that historians need not look elsewhere for the origins of National Socialism. [6] This is grotesque nonhistory.

[4] The entire program is set forth in a Gestapo report of Aug. 2, 1944, quoted in Walther Hofer, *Der Nationalsozialismus:Dokumente 1933-1945*, pp. 345-346.

[5] See Henry A. Turner, "Big Business and the Rise of Hitler," in *American Historical Review*, Vol. 75, Oct. 1969, pp. 56-70.

[6] For instance, D. Eichholtz and W. Schumann (eds.), *Anatomie des Krieges. Neue Dokumente über die Rolle des deutschen Monopolkapitalismus bei der Vorbereitung und Durchführung des Zweiten Weltkrieges*, East Berlin, 1969.

Chapter 17

4. The Educators. The Students

In the final analysis, it was from the German educators that National Socialism received its greatest help, and this by no means only after Hitler's seizure of power in 1933 but even more so for decades before.[1] The educators were the *Wegbereiter*, the ones who laid the groundwork, paved the way. Among them were a good many of the men who conceived or propagated the ideas which ultimately were to become the components of national socialist ideology. For decades long before Hitler they worked hard to instill these ideas into the minds of the young. After Hitler came to power, the educators made a decisive contribution to the widespread acceptance of his ideology and to general German acceptance of the practical policies of his regime.

Earlier we discussed two groups of scholars, the historians and the Germanistics professors who had for many decades acted less as objective scientists than as self-appointed purveyors of intense, even pseudoreligious nationalism, as custodians of the sacraments of the Germanic cult, and generally as dedicated preachers of many future national socialist ideas. In fact, they saw themselves not as mere researchers and teachers, but also as shapers of the German future.

---

[1] In connection with this chapter see particularly Frederic Lilge, *The Abuse of Learning — The Failure of the German University;* Hans Peter Bleuel, *Deutschlands Bekenner — Professoren zwischen Kaiserreich und Diktatur;* Karl Dietrich Bracher, *Die deutsche Diktatur,* pp. 284-298 and *passim;* Joachim C. Fest, *Das Gesicht des Dritten Reiches,* pp. 338-355; Hans Kohn, *The Mind of Germany, passim;* George L. Mosse, *The Crisis of German Ideology, passim;* Klaus Schwabe, "Zur politischen Haltung der deutschen Professoren im Ersten Weltkrieg," in *Historische Zeitschrift,* Vol. 193, 1961, pp. 601-634; William Setchel Learned, *The Oberlehrer — A Study of the Social and Professional Evolution of the German Schoolmaster;* Max Weinreich, *Hitler's Professors,* the last mentioned containing many faulty translations.

But the thoughts and attitudes of the historians and Germanistics scholars were by no means confined to them alone. They were common also among many other disciplines, though it is true that history and Germanistics offer their most natural forums. Other disciplines tried their best. Political scientists, economists, sociologists, philosophers, law professors, and others all contributed their share to the progressive decline of the German intellect.

The process started in the second half of the nineteenth century, particularly after Bismarck's spectacular political successes, when the teaching profession shared the general intoxicating admiration for successful power politics and closed its eyes to the potential conflict between these politics and the profession's own humanistic traditions. The feeling that the Germans had to make up for "missed history" became overpowering, even to the teachers. They took an active intellectual leadership in the assertion of the position that Germany—now finally a world power—had a manifest right to reap the benefits to which history and destiny entitled a great nation. In their view, anything like scholarly detachment and objectivity would have been "anemic," would have lacked bone marrow (as they put it) in the great German struggle for political power. In the hands of many teachers, history and various other disciplines became vehicles for narrow political prejudices and nationalistic propaganda. The teaching of ethical principles to the young took a back seat, if indeed it was not abandoned altogether. At the very least, morality was—expressly or impliedly—declared to be inapplicable wherever it conflicted with the German view of power politics.

All this was hardly less true in the Wilhelmian era than it was later in the war and interwar years. And it was true equally of many teachers in the secondary schools as in the universities. Of course, changes in the political situation, the ups and downs of German power, necessitated considerable variations in the kind and emphasis of the political doctrines which the teachers might feel called upon to preach. Thus in the Wilhelmian era they promoted loyalty to the Kaiser and the principles of a monarchy, and they backed the saber rattling of that period. During the Weimar Republic, the teachers kept alive the memory of a proud German past, condemned the traitors who had wrecked it, and anchored the faith of their students in a better future. In the Hitler years, the majority of the teachers showed devotion to the Führer and his aims. The slogans intoned by all at the end of school assemblies varied in the course of time from *Seine Majestät der Kaiser, hip, hip, hurrah!* to *Sieg Heil!* and *Heil Hitler!* But the teaching profession, at *all* times, taught the same fundamentals: the Germanic cult, hero worship, faith in a superior Germany and its destiny, political aggressiveness, the right of the stronger, faith in the German soldier, the supremacy of the state over the individual, and—more or less furtively—anti-Semitism and contempt for democracy.

On the other hand, little or nothing was taught, either in secondary schools or in universities, about freedom of the individual, civil liberties, liberal government, friendship and help for the weak, humaneness even toward an opponent, honesty and honorableness even in international relations. And if men are not impressed with the desirability of these postulates in childhood, adolescence, and early adulthood, they will find it very difficult to accept them in later life.[2] It is here that numerous German educators failed and made one of their greatest contributions to National Socialism. A conglomerate of ideas which represented much of the later national socialist ideology became, in effect, "institutionalized where it matters most: in the education of young and receptive minds."[3]

One little fact which was characteristic of the situation was that, in the years immediately after World War I, swastika buttons and pins became popular among children and, in fact, among students of all ages, although the National Socialist Movement was then still in its infancy. The matter reached such proportions that, by an Order of November 8, 1920, the Prussian Ministry of Education (a rather liberal department) had to prohibit the wearing of the swastika in the schools.[4] Another small fact of significance was that after the war General Ludendorff of World War I fame was given an honorary doctor's degree with a citation which spoke of "his undefeated sword" and of "a future savior and avenger of our people."[5] Also, a theologian at Berlin University in 1919 began a memorial service for students who had died in the War with the words *Invictis victi victuri* (To the

[2]See, in this connection, Eva G. Reichmann, *Flucht in den Hass—Die Ursachen der deutschen Judenkatastrophe*, pp. 221-222.
[3]Mosse, *Crisis*, p. 152.
[4]Ibid., p. 267.
[5]Kohn, op. cit., p. 309.

undefeated, the defeated ones who will be the future victors).[6] More important, even during the Weimar Republic some textbooks which were used in secondary schools remained antidemocratic and nationalistic and promoted a romantic idyllic view of the Germanic past as opposed to the "empty" civilization of modern life. One guiding historical image, impressed on the minds of the young, was Emperor Frederick Barbarossa holding eternal vigil in Kyffhäuser Mountain, surrounded by his sleeping warriors, waiting for the day of re-union of all Germanic peoples in a great empire. Another guiding image was that of the Teutonic Orders fighting off the onslaught of the Slavs. Essentially, in these respects, there had been little change in the textbooks of the secondary schools from the early nineteenth century to the Weimar Republic.

In the secondary schools, no less than in the universities, the teachers, some of whom were invalided war veterans, gave vent in the classrooms to their unrealized dreams of German glory, proclaimed the doom of democracy and their hopes for a strong man who would lead Germany into a better future. These and other politically radical teachers of the Weimar period may have been at least as effective in aiding the rise of National Socialism as the propaganda apparatus of the Movement itself.

After Hitler came to power, there was, of course, no limit to the political radicalism which the teachers could purvey in the secondary schools, and many of them seemed glad to fall in behind the official ideology. Anti-Semitism could, in effect, be taught even in the schools of a city like Berlin, which had a considerable percentage of Jewish children (until all Jews were forced out). These educators impressed upon their young charges a picture of Germany in which every great German (except some who were left unmentioned) was something of a spiritual father of National Socialism. And the schools, in conjunction with the Hitler Youth organization, did succeed in shaping an obedient, enthusiastic, and highly useful human instrument that was ready to serve, and die for, the regime.

What the secondary schools began, the universities continued, and this was essentially true from the early nineteenth century to the Hitler period, though with some interruptions. But in the univer-

[6]Ibid., p. 309.

sities there was considerable independence of action on the part of the student body, all directed as we shall see, not toward liberalism and Western civilization, but rather toward much the same aims for which National Socialism was to struggle. One difference between the educators at the secondary schools and those at the universities was that the latter proclaimed their political views even outside the lecture hall and with much more noise than the school teachers whose sole forum on the whole was the classroom (Oswald Spengler being a notable exception).

The role of the German university professor as a political lecturer dates back many decades. A remarkable, fairly early example was Heinrich von Treitschke (1834–1896), the prototype of the patriotic historian, the fighting professor, who considered himself not only a scholar but also a passionate agent of history. He was a panegyrist of the Hohenzollern dynasty, a promoter of the cult of the heroic, and during most of his life was engaged in violent attacks on anyone who might stand in the way of Germany's rising power. This meant the Socialists, Catholics, Poles, the British, and, to an extent, the Jews. His influence on the minds of his students was profound. But he was only one of a long line of fighting professors representing all kinds of disciplines, who put their minds and great prestige at the service of German power politics and to whom their lecture halls became political forums. The very large number of such professors became apparent particularly during World War I. In October, 1914, no fewer than 3,016 of them signed a "Declaration of University Teachers of the German Reich" which contained this statement: "It is our belief that the welfare of all Europe's culture depends on the victory which will be gained by German 'militarism,' by the manly discipline, the loyalty, the readiness for sacrifices, of the united, free German people."[7] As H. P. Bleuel says, in the view of the professors "the German nation . . . personified the whole cultural expectation of humanity."[8] The eminent Prof. Werner Sombart proclaimed that it was a war "by shopkeepers against heroes."[9]

Another declaration by eager professors in World War I was issued in 1915. In it, 1,341 professors demanded that Germany's bor-

[7]Bleuel, op. cit., p. 76.
[8]Ibid., p. 76.
[9]Sombart, *Händler und Helden*, 1915.

der in the West be established on a line from Boulogne to Belfort, and in the East on a line from Lake Peipus (south of Leningrad) to the mouth of the Dnieper.[10] They demanded also unrestricted submarine warfare. The areas which they wanted Germany to annex were huge and paralleled rather closely the expanded Lebensraum which Hitler proposed confidentially twenty-five years later. But Hitler had at least sense enough not to say so in public. To a considerable extent, these ideas of the professors grew out of the German "missed-history" and "need-to-catch-up" theories previously discussed.

Nor did the professors seem in any way prepared to accept the defeat of 1918 as a verdict of history and to help the German people to reach a realistic understanding of what had happened (as the philosopher Karl Jaspers did after World War II). On the contrary, countless professors stood in the forefront of those who established the two lies with which the Weimar Republic had to live: that Germany carried no guilt in the causation of World War I and that the German armies, undefeated, were stabbed in the back by traitors. The professors were thus an important element in weaving that web of German self-deception which was to become an element of national socialist ideology.

In the interwar years, in fact, the professors constituted a powerful force against the Weimar Republic and democracy. Many of them were not only against Weimar but for a strong man and an "awakened" aggressive Germany. The prominent historian Eduard Meyer, in taking over the presidency of Berlin University in November, 1919 (one year after the end of the monarchy), declared that rule by majority meant dividing the people into parties which merely pursued their special interests, and that only a government with a monarch at its head was truly independent.[11] Going beyond that, various professors tried earnestly and scientifically to furnish proof that the singular character as well as the history of the German people were incompatible with a republican form of government and that nothing but an authoritarian caste system was suitable and innate or natural for this nation.[12] In countless lectures and special addresses, the pro-

[10]Bleuel, op. cit., p. 90. (Schwabe, op. cit., p. 615, apparently refers to the same Declaration but mentions only 352 signers.)

[11]Bleuel, op. cit., p. 110.

[12]Ibid., p. 111.

fessors preached the virtues of aggressive German nationalism, of military power, the heroic way of life, and the German world mission. It was the traditional German romantic and irrational view of history and politics. The lectures, incidentally, were often like political assemblies with frequent loud applause by the students. In 1923, the rector of Munich University, a Catholic theologian, made an inflammatory speech:

> Our people sinned against its God-ordained destiny when it threw down its arms. Away with the suicidal phantasy of an international fraternization of the masses! Away with the specter of world-wide pacifism! Away with the disgrace of the League of Nations! What we need is a great Siegfried but he must not tarry too long. [13]

Presumably it was natural that out of all this the professors would develop a hope for, and expectation of, a coming messiah, a mythical hero figure, who would lead Germany out of its misery and into a glorious future. Such ideas were indeed put forward quite early in the Weimar era. In 1924 the theologian Otto Proksch told the faculty and students of Greifswald University in his inaugural address:

> Today, the name Versailles makes the blood run cold in our veins. . . . We are without army, without defense, without honor. . . . [The German words *heerlos, wehrlos, ehrlos* are more poetic.] If the German race and the Christian faith will join together, then we shall be saved, then we want to . . . *wait for the day when the German hero comes, be he prophet or king.* [14]

And the historian Adolf Schulten wrote:

> The hero is something miraculous which we shall never understand—something divine. We want to venerate the hero all the more, want to be uplifted by him, and *we want to hope for a new hero.* [15]

[13] Ibid., p. 181.
[14] Quoted in M. Rainer Lepsius, *Extremer Nationalismus*, p. 13 (italics added).
[15] Bleuel, op. cit., p. 187 (italics added).

The prominent educator Eduard Spranger summed it all up by saying that "everywhere in Germany there is a veritable expectation of a messiah." [16]

Clearly the professors, without knowing it, were preparing the students and others for the advent of Hitler. They were, moreover, as Bleuel says, "issuing academic legitimation for the Führer principle." [17] Altogether, this highly respected group was a kind of intellectual midwife for the Third Reich.

In the light of this history of the professors before Hitler came to power, it is perhaps not surprising that when the day finally came, thousands of them eagerly and hastily expressed their approval and loyalty. No one had forced them to do so. Of course, many of them had no clear understanding of Hitler's ultimate aims, and there was also some plain opportunism. But by and large the professors were truly and sincerely enthusiastic about this new-found long-awaited heroic figure whose ideas of the German future seemed to correspond closely to their own and who, above all, promised decisive action. The deep professorial enthusiasm was well expressed by Ordinarius Julius Petersen of Berlin University:

Tomorrow has now become today; the mood of the end of the world has changed to that of a new beginning; the final goal becomes visible in our time. . . . Deep down in our nation all forces of a past longing have come alive, and the dream images in which the past indulged have been drawn into the light of day. . . . The new Reich has been created. The Führer, longed for and prophetically predicted, is now here. [18]

The practice of public mass declarations, issued by professors during World War I, was resumed under Hitler. As early as March 3, 1933, three hundred professors of all disciplines declared themselves for him. [19] A few months later, almost a thousand issued a "Profession of Faith by the Professors at the German Universities and Technical

[16]Ibid., p. 186.
[17]Ibid., p. 187.
[18]Ibid., pp. 213–214.
[19]Fest, *Das Gesicht des Dritten Reiches*, p. 342.

Institutes in Adolf Hitler and the National Socialist State."[20] Many world-famous professors were among the signers, including the philosopher Martin Heidegger.

It will be interesting, in fact, to examine Heidegger's reaction to National Socialism more closely, not only because he was a philosopher of world renown, but also because in this reaction he can be regarded as an early prototype of the German professor in general. Moreover, his case is better documented than most others.[21] Here was a seemingly outstanding creative mind who in 1933 embraced National Socialism *in toto*. He became for a while one of its active intellectual leaders. His importance as a philosopher was still attested to in 1971 by Hannah Arendt. She said that "his thinking has shared so decisively in determining the spiritual physiognomy of this century" and that

> . . . the wind that blows through Heidegger's thinking—like that which still sweeps toward us after thousands of years from the work of Plato—does not spring from the century he happens to live in. It comes from the primeval, and what it leaves behind is something perfect. . . .[22]

Higher praise is hardly possible. Yet, upon sober consideration of what Heidegger *said* and *did* in the early years of the Hitler era—thinking or not thinking—his legacy seems far from "perfect." He was the head (rector) of Freiburg University. In May, 1933, soon after Hitler's seizure of power, Heidegger became a member of the Party, and this act—not without justification—was taken by the Freiburg student journal to mean that he had "declared himself for the world of the mind of National Socialism."[23] In his formal inaugural speech as rector, he undertook a full coalignment of the university with the ideas of the regime (even before the regime had laid down

[20]Bleuel, op. cit., p. 222; Lilge, *The Abuse of Learning*, p. 166–167.

[21]As to Heidegger, see particularly Guido Schneeberger, *Nachlese zu Heidegger*; Paul Hühnerfeld, *In Sachen Heidegger—Versuch über ein deutsches Genie*; Hannah Arendt, "Martin Heidegger at Eighty," in *The New York Review of Books*, Oct. 21, 1971, pp. 50–54; Alistair Hamilton, *The Appeal of Fascism—A Study of Intellectuals and Fascism 1919–1945*, 1971, pp. 146–149.

[22]Arendt, "Martin Heidegger at Eighty," pp. 51, 54.

[23]Schneeberger, op. cit., p. 41.

its official coalignment policy), and, in fact, he seemingly made an effort to supply the young regime with some philosophical understructure:

> The much praised academic freedom is being cast out of the German universities; it was not genuine because it was solely negative, and it signified licentiousness in acting and failing to act. The concept of freedom of the German student is now being led back to its truth. From this truth, there will unfold three kinds of commitments and service of the German student body. . . . The first commitment is to the folk community . . . through the labor service. The second commitment is to the honor and the destiny of the nation in the midst of the other nations. It demands . . . disciplined readiness for service *(Einsatz* [24]*)* to the last. This commitment embraces the entire existence of the student as a military service. The third commitment is to the spiritual trust of the German people . . . [through] knowledge service. The three commitments . . . are equally original to the German character. The three services which spring therefrom— labor service, military service, and knowledge service—are equally necessary and have equal rank. [25]

Labor service and military service had been known, but "knowledge service" was a useful addition to the vocabulary of National Socialism. It was a concept, moreover, that fitted well into the entire totalitarian structure of the regime, as, indeed, did Heidegger's "casting out" of academic freedom. No freedom of this sort was compatible with totalitarianism. New also, from the viewpoint of a university, was giving "equal rank" to all three "services." Previously the professors had regarded themselves as a great deal higher in rank than the others, but the change fitted vaguely into the socialist aspect of early National Socialism to which the Movement normally paid little or no attention. Heidegger, thus, clearly went all out in coaligning the university with the ideology of the regime; and he did this long before official coercion to do so was applied. He may have stimulated the

---

[24] The use of the German word *Einsatz* in this context seems distasteful in retrospect because later the *Einsatzgruppen* (mobile killing units), led by many former students, were to kill about 900,000 Jews and others, but Heidegger did not, of course, have anything of the sort in mind.

[25] Hühnerfeld, op. cit., pp. 96–98; Schneeberger, op. cit., pp. 91–93.

proposals of one of the official leaders for political education who, a few months later, demanded that every "future scholar be only a soldier in science" and that there be "science camps."[26]

It was under the rectorship of Heidegger that eleven Jewish professors were denied the right to continue lecturing at the university.[27] Among them was Heidegger's immediate colleague, the philosopher Jonas Cohn. No word of protest seems to have been heard from Heidegger or, for that matter, from other non-Jewish professors. He personally decreed that Jewish, half-Jewish, and Marxist students were no longer entitled to scholarships, stipends, etc.; and he said expressly that this rule was to apply even if the fathers of the students had been German frontline soldiers in World War I.[28] Again he personally ordered that at the beginning of every lecture the students and the professor were to greet each other by raising their right arm (the *Hitler-Gruss*).[29] It was under his rectorship that the Freiburg students could stage the burning of the books of Jewish and Marxist authors.[30] He seems to have uttered no word of protest. And it was Heidegger who, in a symbolic gesture at a gathering of students and faculty, pledged one student by a handshake, on behalf of all others, to loyalty to "the work of Adolf Hitler, to the new state, and to the university."[31]

Heidegger attended countless festivities, torchlight parades, and ceremonies in honor of Hitler and National Socialism; and his own speeches and proclamations, appropriate to such occasions, were numerous.[32] He pledged "unconditional loyalty . . . to the savior of our nation from its suffering, disunity, and forlornness, toward unity, determination, and honor, and to the teacher of, and inspiring fighter for, a new spirit."[33] At a summer solstice celebration, in front of a burning pyre, he called for "the flame to tell us, light us, show us the way from which there is no return!"[34] He declared that "truthful re-

[26]Schneeberger, op. cit., p. 112.
[27]Ibid., pp. 118, 130.
[28]Ibid., p. 137.
[29]Ibid., p. 136.
[30]Ibid., pp. 29–30.
[31]Ibid., pp. 159, 155–157.
[32]Ibid., *passim*.
[33]Ibid., p. 144.
[34]Ibid., p. 71.

search [has] . . . its roots in the people, and its commitment is to the state. . . . We fight with the strength of the new Reich to which the people's Chancellor Hitler will give reality." [35] He praised the fact that "the educational work of the entire school system has turned into the path prescribed by the national socialist state." [36]

It is not surprising, then, that the student body, which had agitated in large numbers for Hitler long before he seized power, looked upon Heidegger with enthusiasm. Naturally there was no generation gap. The student newspaper said that "Freiburg University can be regarded as an example in this new constructive work [of educating the coming elite] where the new program has been started with great energy as a result of trusting cooperation between rector and student body with full assistance of Baden's state government." [37] The local Party newspaper wrote that the citizens of Freiburg "may be proud of the outstanding position which our university occupies among the new German student bodies" and that "the Freiburg student has put on the brown shirt and is marching for Germany under the swastika flag." [38]

In the light of all this, it is impossible to agree with Hannah Arendt's assessment that this "episode" in Heidegger's career reflected merely an "error," a "misunderstanding of what it was all about," and that, indeed, this misunderstanding was "inconsiderable" [39] (even if she may be right in saying that in the case of thinkers like Heidegger "it does not finally matter where the storms of their century may have driven them"). She cannot have read Guido Schneeberger's documentation. Benedetto Croce, in 1933, took a different view. He said that "Germany is becoming imbecilic with Heidegger" and that "he dishonors philosophy." [40]

Actually the strong enthusiasm of Heidegger and many other German professors for National Socialism should really not be too surprising. It was not an "error," but rather almost something logical or even necessary because the philosophies or ideologies of these

[35] Ibid., p. 75.
[36] Ibid., p. 171.
[37] Ibid., p. 85.
[38] Ibid., pp. 90, 104.
[39] Arendt, "Martin Heidegger at Eighty," p. 53.
[40] In letters quoted in Schneeberger, op. cit., pp. 111-112.

professors grew from the same century-old roots as those of National Socialism: German Romanticism with its strong *schwärmerisch* irrational tendencies; intense, almost obsessive love of nature (as in Heidegger's case) and equally strong hatred of the spirit of the cities and Western modernity, coupled with smug contentment in a narrow milieu of the petty bourgeois; and superimposed on all this an excessive all-pervasive nationalism with an accompanying intolerance for the views of strangers. Even the kind of language which Heidegger and many other professors spoke and wrote—pompous, pretentious, seemingly deep, imprecise, and often absurdly obscure—fitted well into the theory and practice of National Socialism.

Other professors were less subtle than Heidegger, but no less passionate in their allegiance to Hitler. Some, of course, were purely opportunistic and were anxious to hold on to their positions. Others were merely eager to ingratiate themselves with their radical students, no matter what their own real views may have been. But most were genuine believers. The results, at any rate, were often sordid. The professors were quick to teach their subjects "on a racial basis," to tie them somehow to the Führer principle, to link them to the spirit of the venerable Germanic past, to extract something heroic from them, to have them serve the reawakening of the German nation. And it did not matter whether the subject was history, law, medicine, theology, anthropology, or linguistics. New courses on racial science and military science were introduced. Professors were called "SA men of the mind."[41] Of course, none of these professors knew or suspected that the road they were taking would ultimately lead millions of others to the extermination camps. Professor Eugen Fischer, speaking in Berlin a few months after Hitler's seizure of power, declared naïvely that the national socialist revolution had been "a revolution in decency, a revolution in peace and order without hostages against a wall, without the flowing of blood, without barricades and civil war. There is no other nation in the world that could have done anything like it."[42]

The regime did not really have to use coercion to bring the professors into line, except in relatively few cases of professors who had

[41]Fest, op. cit., p. 348.
[42]Lilge, op. cit., p. 165.

the mind, the humanity, and the courage to speak out. The majority fell all over themselves to pay homage, allegiance, and admiration to Hitler. If anything, the regime had to ward them off. Immediately upon Hitler's seizing of power, the Stuttgart Institute of Technology offered him an honorary doctor's degree, but he declined. [43] The professors presided enthusiastically over the burning of the books by the students. Professor Alfred Baeumler of Berlin University marched to the pyre at the head of the columns of students wearing brown shirts and carrying torches. [44] They burned more than 20,000 books on that occasion.

Among these books were many whose Jewish or liberal authors had been colleagues of the same professors. No voice of protest against the dismissal of old colleagues could be heard. The persecuted minority was silently abandoned. Heidegger, for one, quietly removed the dedication from a new edition of his book *Sein und Zeit* to his non-Aryan old teacher Edmund Husserl. Evidently the dedication had been an "error." The University of Bonn "found itself obliged" in 1936 to withdraw the honorary doctor's degree which it had conferred on Thomas Mann. [45] He was then in exile. The fact that someone of the fundamental importance of Albert Einstein was Jewish was, of course, an embarrassment, but efforts were made to overcome this by founding "German mathematics" and "Aryan physics." [46] The professors of Munich University submitted to a speech by the *Kultusminister* (an aborted elementary schoolteacher), who told them that "From now on, it will not be important for you to determine whether something is true, but rather whether it is in accord with the principles of the national socialist revolution." [47]

The last-quoted statement indeed suggests that the regime proposed anti-intellectualism to the professors. And the strangest phenomenon of all, in this whole chapter, is that some of these intellectuals, these custodians of intellectualism, obediently developed anti-intellectualism. Thus the historian Ulrich Kahrstedt of Göttingen said in a speech in 1934: "We repudiate international science, we re-

[43] Ibid., p. 164.
[44] Schneeberger, op. cit., p. 34.
[45] Lilge, op. cit., p. 164.
[46] Bracher, *Die deutsche Diktatur*, p. 292.
[47] Ibid., p. 293.

pudiate the international community of scholars, we repudiate research for the sake of research. *Sieg Heil!*"[48]

The book burnings, the "Aryan physics," the veneration of power and violence, the abandonment of scientific objectivity in favor of a daydream of Germany's destiny of greatness—all these were symptoms of this anti-intellectualism. They were, in a way, treason against the mind. Hitler could find himself fully confirmed in his deep contempt for the intellectuals. Already in *Mein Kampf* he had spoken of "the pitiful cowardice of our so-called intelligentsia" which, he said, lacked "the necessary willpower."[49] Fundamentally this anti-intellectualism of the professors can be understood, not as the result of short-range propaganda, manipulation, or coercion by National Socialism, but rather as a final spasmodic manifestation of about a hundred years of erosion and corruption of German ethical and political values, which had slowly given way to the ideas that were ultimately to constitute the ideology of National Socialism. The professors themselves promoted the dehumanization of German higher education, its moral default. Under the emotional suction of the intense nationalism and the romantic, irrational political aims of the regime, the professors no longer appeared able to recognize the threat to all genuine civilization, nor, if they vaguely understood it, to develop the strength to resist, not even, it seems, in the privacy of their studies. Some could even rationalize the whole development as a kind of mental recovery process, a revolt of instinctual drives in modern man against the former intellectual sublimation, against the exaggerated intellectualism of earlier generations.[50] It was in line with Hitler's thinking that "professorial science . . . leads away from instinct."[51]

Thus, the group whose very purpose it should have been to guard the freedom of the mind—the group that had the forum, the qualifications, and the prestige to oppose tyranny, failed utterly to do so; and, on the contrary, many members of this group aided the dictator's rise to power and later helped him to consolidate his position. One might well ask whether the average German could be expected to resist National Socialism when he saw so many of the intellectual leadership of the country support it with enthusiasm.

[48]Ibid., p. 297.
[49]*Mein Kampf*, pp. 288, 480.
[50]See Fest, op. cit., p. 342.
[51]*Hitler's Table Talks*, p. 179.

(Incidentally, the technological experts seemed to be in a class by themselves. Without any noise and seemingly undisturbed by moral or political considerations pro or con, they did their work for the war machine at Peenemunde; and later, after 1945, they transferred just as quietly to Huntsville, Alabama, or to the corresponding research center in Soviet Russia. They seemed to be tied mainly to their technology.)

After the war, one professor, Julius Ebbinghaus, who had not collaborated with National Socialism, assessed the conduct of the universities during the Hitler years in a long rectoral address at the reopening of the University of Marburg, from which the following may be quoted:

> One fact remains unfortunately all too true. The German universities failed, while there was still time, to oppose publicly with all their power the destruction of *Wissenschaft* and of the democratic state. They failed to keep the beacon of right and freedom burning during the night of tyranny so that it could be seen by the entire world. However, one must remember that even then few scholars of international reputation remained whom the new tyrant would have hesitated to suppress. The many others, whose effectiveness lay only in their unity, lacked leaders. In many cases, too, they lacked political insight and manly resolution. . . .
>
> We stand before a youth in despair who accuse us of not having told them clearly and plainly why the political teaching, for which they now suffer, was false and perverse. Whether we so warned, or whether we must reproach ourselves for insufficient insight and courage to speak, are questions which each must answer before his own conscience. . . .[52]

What are today's reactions of surviving professors who were national socialist collaborators, when confronted with their published statements of those days? Rolf Seeliger, in four volumes published in 1965 under the title *Braune Universität* [Brown University], has attempted to answer this question by a documentation. He sent to the professors copies of their old statements, asked for their comments, and then published both, substantially without anything fur-

[52]Speech of Sept. 25, 1945, quoted in Lilge, op. cit., pp. 169–171.

ther. Some professors refused comments. The reactions of those who answered vary widely. They range from contrition to different interpretations to pugnacious attacks. Here are some brief and necessarily quite incomplete excerpts:

The demonic traits of the system were then still hidden from me, or they retreated behind the other traits which even a non-National Socialist could welcome, simply as a German man. The real spirit of the Third Reich manifested itself to us only gradually.[53]

The events very soon refuted the statements then made, and I have felt depressed for a long time about having expressed myself in this manner. I now severely condemn the contents as well as the tone. . . .[54]

. . . correctly quoted . . . statements but removed from their historical context. . . .[55]

We who . . . taught at German universities, apart from a few praiseworthy exceptions, all carry some of the responsibility and, in varying degree, are implicated in the disaster which that regime caused for the German people and the world, and above all our Jewish fellow citizens. . . .[56]

. . . it is . . . beyond atonement, and it silences any attempt to make one's own involvement appear harmless. . . .[57]

My failure at that time can only be understood, not excused: I feared men more than God.[58]

The Yid hits—and yells "violence." (A Yiddish proverb) [followed by strong anti-Semitic statements].[59]

---

[53]Seeliger, *Braune Universität—Deutsche Hochschullehrer gestern und heute,* Vol. III, p. 13.
[54]Ibid., p. 31.
[55]Ibid., p. 35.
[56]Ibid., p. 39.
[57]Ibid., p. 49.
[58]Ibid., p. 61.
[59]Ibid., p. 66. (The editor of the book, R. Seeliger, may be Jewish.)

Anyone who quotes anything in the academic sphere should know that quotations may be used only *in*, not *against*, the context.[60]

. . . individual sentences torn from their context offer no basis for serious discussion. . . .[61]

Now, a word about the *students*. We have already said a good deal about them in this and in earlier chapters, and little more will be said here. The students were among the vanguard of the National Socialist Movement and, in fact, of some of the related movements preceding it. Often they were, in a sense, Hitler's stormtroops, at least in fact and sometimes in name. They had indeed had an early start. Their nationalism and anti-Semitism had been intense and open for decades. As far back as 1894, Jews had been effectively excluded from fraternities.[62] In 1907 when a professor of law mentioned in class that a Jewish legal textbook author had been murdered, the students broke into thunderous applause.[63] In 1922 Berlin students forced the university to cancel a memorial service for the assassinated liberal Jew Walther Rathenau. At that time Hitler was still relatively unknown. These are just a few examples.[64]

It was logical, then, that the students joined the budding National Socialist Movement with all their heart and soul. They had at all times been strongly against the Weimar Republic. Deeply frustrated by Germany's political disasters, economic chaos, etc., the students found in National Socialism an ideal guise of political discontent under which their pent-up hostility could be discharged. It should be borne in mind, in this connection, that (as of 1930) more than 60 percent of the student body came from the impoverished lower middle class which was at all times the backbone of the Hitler Movement, and that about 32 percent came from the upper middle class, which was strongly nationalistic, hostile to Weimar, and in part

[60]Ibid., p. 76.
[61]Ibid., p. 94.
[62]Mosse, *Crisis*, p. 196.
[63]Ibid., p. 197.
[64]For some useful information, see Wolfgang Zorn, "Student Politics in the Weimar Republic," in *Journal of Contemporary History*, Vol. 5, No. 1, 1970, pp. 128–143.

friendly toward National Socialism.[65] It was not surprising, then, that the "earliest breakthrough" of National Socialism (the description is K. D. Bracher's) took place in the student body. In the student elections of 1931, the national socialist candidates received an absolute majority, at a time when in the whole country the Party obtained only about half that number.[66]

These results were accomplished over several years with enormous noise, physical violence, sabotage, disruption of the academic life, wearing of the brown shirt, etc. This continued until complete victory had been achieved with Hitler's seizure of power in 1933. In 1932, for example, anticipating Hitler, the Student Convention demanded that the autonomous academic administration be abolished in favor of the Führer principle.[67] A year later, Berlin students wanted the rector to "extirpate the un-German spirit" at the university. Among other things, Jewish professors were to be permitted to publish in Hebrew only.[68] The well-known book burnings by the students followed throughout Germany. It was their cultural low point. A hundred years earlier, Heinrich Heine had said prophetically that where books are burned, men will in the end be burned, too.

One might ask: who were the leaders and who were the led—the professors or the students? Most likely the responsibility cannot be clearly attributed to either group, although there were times, in the course of the decades, when the one group stood more definitely in the forefront than the other. For seventy years or more, the professors had preached aggressive nationalism, the German destiny of power, hero worship, irrational political Romanticism, and so forth, and had increasingly deemphasized, if not eliminated, the teaching of ethical and humanistic principles. In that sense, the professors were the leaders. But some of these professors' students became professors themselves, and, while they had a mind of their own, they intensified the same teachings further. Essentially neither group wanted to have anything to do with democracy. In the Weimar Republic, after the disaster had struck in 1918, both groups, on the

---

[65] For these figures, see Lilge, op. cit., p. 146.

[66] Peter G. J. Pulzer, *The Rise of Political Anti-semitism in Germany and Austria*, p. 308; Bracher, op. cit., pp. 181–182.

[67] Bracher, op. cit., p. 295.

[68] Ibid., p. 295.

whole, seemed equally determined to tear down that Republic. The professors did their part by fiery lectures, speeches, and writings; the students did theirs in noisy demonstrations, torch-light parades, vandalism, and physical violence. By about 1930 the students, being more impatient than the professors, finally ran away with the action and, as we have seen, voted for National Socialism in their own sphere. They put on the brown shirt. When Hitler came to power, both, professors and students, fell all over themselves to demonstrate their allegiance.

All this does not, of course, apply to each and every professor and student, but only to the majority. There were thousands in both groups who were rational, Western-oriented, and appalled at the general dehumanization process. Most of them were silent; a few spoke out, to little effect. A good many of these died later in the concentration camps.

Finally the question might be raised: How good was the quality of German education in general, and particularly in the humanities, and how good was it during the two or three decades preceding Hitler's seizure of power? Traditionally, German education seemed to have a high reputation throughout the world, but was this reputation justified and was it justified especially in the humanities?

The true quality of education hardly lends itself to exact measurement, but a few facts of some significance are fairly clear. The quality of the teachers in German elementary and secondary *boys'* schools during World War I and the postwar years was low. In those schools, the teachers had traditionally been almost exclusively male. Most of them were drafted into the armed services, many were killed or disabled, and often they had to be replaced by very old men, or men with meager qualifications. Some were men whose main qualification seemed to be that they were war invalids. A good many ill-humored cranks, misfits, and neurotics were among the whole group. Few seemed to have any real scholarly knowledge or to be even inclined to give the boys a good education. Fewer, still, were inspiring as teachers. All elementary and secondary school teachers, moreover, suffered from the fact that traditionally they were held in low social esteem. Their pay, too, was meager. And the children, on their part, often had little respect, and indeed had contempt, for the teachers. Discipline was very low, and conditions in the classrooms were sometimes chaotic. Absenteeism and cheating were widespread. There was hardly a child, at any rate, who did not have a strong dislike for school. The drop-out rate in the secondary schools was very high; and it is, in fact, still very high in West Germany today, amounting to about 60 percent. [69]

`All this was rarely conducive to learning. The over-aged teachers, moreover, were apt to dispense a disgruntled philosophy which compared the advantages of the good old days (the monarchy), or of a "strong man," with the undisciplined liberal practices of the Weimar democracy. The war-veteran teachers were likely to extoll the front-fighter spirit, heroism, nationalism, and the like. [70] All teachers were united in a firm belief in the stab-in-the-back theory, and, to an extent, this colored much of the teaching. Few of them took any interest in the teaching of ethical principles in politics, of democracy, freedom, or justice. And, indeed, the treatment which the Weimar Republic was then receiving from the victorious Western powers would have furnished poor illustrations for such principles.

There was, in those days, little coeducation in Germany. The secondary school for *girls* was mainly the *Lyzeum* which was staffed, to about 50 percent, by women teachers. Generally at that time girls were not believed to need as much education as boys, and this was reflected in the scholastic level of their schools. On the other hand, in the years of World War I and the interwar years, the girls had the advantage that at least their women teachers had not been affected by military service.

Another significant fact is that Germany had no colleges in the American or British sense. Every boy—and a few girls—of any social standing or ambition went to the *Gymnasium* for nine years, from age 9 to 18, and from there he could directly enter a university or technical institute for the specialized study of medicine, law, theology, philosophy, economics, chemistry, and so forth. In other words, in the universities he was not normally exposed to the humanities (unless

[69] Ralf Dahrendorf, "The Crisis in German Education," in *Journal of Contemporary History*, Vol. 2, No. 3, 1967, p. 144.

[70] In this, they were supported by the textbooks. See John F. Cramer and George S. Browne, *Contemporary Education—A Comparative Study of National Systems*, p. 19.

he enrolled as a student of philosophy, theology, etc.). Of course, the preceding nine-year course at the *Gymnasium* amounted to much more than, for example, an American high school, and theoretically it should have been the equivalent of about two years of college. This, however, could be true only if the teachers at the *Gymnasium* were able men, and in those days, at least, most of them were not. [71]

Of course, there is no doubt that the student, once he had entered a university, could receive a good or excellent education, under able professors, in the *specialized* discipline he had chosen; and it seems to have been this fact which maintained the international reputation of the entire German educational system. But what the world did not realize, in the face of all the splendid German achievements in the specialized disciplines and the elite of remarkable individual thinkers, was that the ideals of an education in the humanities had dwindled or withered away. The humanities were often still present as no more than a kind of silent assumption, a "national endowment" which one took for granted, [72] but much of their essential meaning had been lost. The most basic preparation for civic responsibility was lacking. All this was a void which contributed greatly to the nation's vulnerability to the temptations of National Socialism.

At least one German philosopher, Max Scheler, realized long ago the damage which the lack of a systematic teaching of the humanities was doing to the German people. He proposed that all university students, after completion of their specialized studies, should have to attend various basic courses in the humanities; in other words, they were to be given a kind of postgraduate college education. But nothing came of this idea.

In any case, it is a dismaying and alarming event in Western civilization that the political, social, and spiritual history of a highly developed country can lead its intellectuals—professors and students—to identify so completely with so primitive and intolerant an ideology as that of National Socialism. It is true that when the longed-for hero and strong man had been in power for some years and had

---

[71]Learned, *The Oberlehrer—A Study of the Social and Professional Evolution of the German Schoolmaster,* takes a very favorable view of the German schoolmaster, but it was published in 1914 and can at best apply only to the years before World War I.

[72]Lilge, op. cit., p. 76.

ceased to be a mere apparition seen in a vision, the intellectuals—
including even some of the students—began to perceive that they had
sold their soul to a brutal, destructive man of no distinction. But then
it was too late, and all they could do, or were willing to do, was to
turn away from him in silence.

VI

CONCLUSION.
SOME THOUGHTS
ABOUT
THE PRESENT
AND FUTURE

We began this study with the question "How was it possible — how could it happen?" But now in retrospect — looking at those events in the light of the German ideology, in the light of the state of mind and the emotions of the German people, of the economic and political conditions of those days, and particularly of the seemingly overwhelming impact of Hitler's personality — one is perhaps more inclined to say "How could it *not* have happened?" There was some sense in the seemingly senseless — in fact, to the average German there was a certain compelling interior logic in all of the causative factors, in their aggregation and interaction — something that under Hitler's leadership could drive with nearly irresistible force toward a disaster such as did, in fact, occur.

Of course, one may well differ as to the weight or pressure which the one or the other of the individual factors may have exerted in the causation of the disaster. Clearly, a few of them might have been dispensed with completely, without seriously affecting the totality of the national socialist thrust. Anti-Semitism, for example — in spite of all the noisy never-ceasing aggressive emphasis on it, in spite of its seemingly central ideological position — was really an element that in theory might have been omitted from the ideological arsenal without doing much more than deprive the Movement of a hateful out-group whose existence was tactically convenient and psychologically advantageous. (But, of course, useful outgroups of this type are not easy to find.) On the other hand, there were factors without which National Socialism could probably never have been born or have prospered or without which, at least, the Movement would have taken a very different turn. Among such factors were, for example, the belief in German racial superiority; the mistreatment of the Weimar Republic by the Western powers; and the cooperation by the German generals with Hitler, instead of resistance to him. Going back much farther in time, an indispensable antecedent probably was the invasion of the German states by Napoleon, with the resultant turning away from the West by the Germans and the conscious development of a German uniqueness. Adapting the old lawyers' saying that bad facts make bad law, one might say that bad facts can also make bad history.

Altogether, the twelve years of the Third Reich represent a sad and largely useless period in German history and civilization — quite empty in spite of bombast without parallel, feverish activity, and very hard labor. These years were an almost exclusively destructive time, reflecting in large measure the destructive personality which dominated it. No doubt, also, Geoffrey Barraclough is generally correct in saying that the Germany of National Socialism was "too much of an aberration, too much *sui generis*, to provide general lessons which we can readily transpose to other times and places."[1] Whatever lessons might be drawn are trite at best. One is that no country should let the young and immature dominate its crucial decisions. In retrospect, some of the conduct of the German people in those years seems to parallel the tantrums of a willful child or the actions of an adolescent who relishes alienation and refuses to adapt to human society. Another trite lesson is that the theories of the natural sciences, such as that of the survival of the fittest, do not furnish safe bases for political decisions, if only because our knowledge appears never to be complete. Had Hitler lived into the age of ethology, he might not have carried his Lebensraum doctrines to extremes, because he might have heard of what Robert Ardrey calls "the universal ethological observation that [in territorial controversies] it is the territorial proprietor that almost always wins. . . ."[2]

At any rate, recent efforts to draw an analogy between Weimar Germany and the United States today seem contrived and sometimes absurd.[3] They appear to have been made in part by those who evidently "fear that the seizure of power by American fascism is just around the corner."[4] Or else these efforts were undertaken by those who seem forever engaged in a search for lessons from history, no matter how deceptive.

But one thing that is made clear by a study of the history of that period, more than of any other, is that historiography cannot be left to historians alone. They need help from psychologists or psychiatrists and from other disciplines. It would be still better if psychiatrists could work alongside our statesmen as history is being created, but this is a mere daydream at best.

---

[1]Geoffrey Barraclough in *New York Review of Literature,* Jan. 7, 1971, p. 14.

[2]Robert Ardrey, "Four-Dimensional Man," in *Encounter,* February 1972, p. 19.

[3]Peter Gay, "Germany 1919–1932: The Weimar Culture," in *Social Research,* Vol. 39, No. 2, Summer 1972.

[4]Walter Laqueur, "America & the Weimar Analogy," in *Encounter,* May 1972. p. 24.

Empty and useless as that historical period was, National Socialism did accomplish one thing of fundamental importance, even if much against its will. In a violent catharsis of evil and hatred, it carried much of the dominant German ideology *ad absurdum* and to its death. The catastrophe into which National Socialism and Hitler had led the German people under the banner of this ideology was in itself a silent but definite and total ideological refutation; and Hitler's suicide was the ultimate symbol of the obliteration of an ideology. The extent of the final defeat was so stunning, so traumatic in its impact on the German psychology, that the essential parts of the ideology were swept away like water through a broken dam. In the defeat, the German or Germanic race was shown to be no better than others. The results of anti-Semitism proved to be a cruel horror. Militarism had been thoroughly discredited, if not destroyed, by Hitler himself. Venerable traditions of many kinds had to be revised with a speed and thoroughness as perhaps never before in history. E. H. Erikson said that German "ideals are like monuments: they are hard to shake, but once they totter, they fall fast,"[5] but they really tottered and fell by the force of most extraordinary circumstances. And the Germans could not help being aware that it was not their own strength or initiative which freed them from tyranny but that the job had to be done for them by outside powers.

By and large, the average German today would find it foolish and embarassing to proclaim that he is racially superior or anti-Semitic or militaristic or that he needs more Lebensraum. Remnants of the Germanic cult seem to have survived, but, lacking the interaction with the other ideological components, they amount to little more than purposeless romantic phantasies. There is, of course, still a good deal of nationalism—and this, indeed, seems essential to national life in our age—but it is no longer the extreme, aggressive kind and it is not really different from the French or British variety. It is, in fact, probably less intense than American nationalism.

Thus, the great catharsis essentially destroyed all political and various other continuities in Germany. The year 1945 became as important a turning point in German history as 1806 had been. That year was the beginning of Germany's turning away from the West, of the

---

[5] Erikson, "Hitler's Imagery and German Youth," in *Psychiatry*, 1942, p. 492.

developing consciousness of a German uniqueness. The year 1945 represented the start of a nearly complete about-face, a turning back toward the West—an about-face as drastic and thoroughgoing as may ever have occurred in history in twenty-five years or less. Strangely enough, the division of the country into East and West may have facilitated this process. The Western sections of the country had always been a little more "European" than the East.

As in earlier periods of German history, developments in the German language are symptomatic of the change and they indicate the extent of the turn toward the West. German is now studded with English terms, especially in magazines, newspapers, and advertising.[6] English words are used even when perfectly good German equivalents are available. And it is almost pitiful to discover that the specialized vocabulary of the young German "drug culture" is 80 or 90 percent English. The extremes of the trend are suggested by the development of new, merely English-*sounding* words, nonexistent in English, such as *twen* (corresponding to "teen") meaning a person in his twenties. Some, but by no means all, of this is due, of course, simply to the presently guiding American image in Western civilization. But to an extent, today's German inclination toward English parallels the far-going domination by the French language in eighteenth century Germany. It was then that the Germans were last oriented toward the West.

Another startling about-face is the turning away from militarism, indeed the revulsion against it. Today the army is held in low regard in Germany, and it was, in fact, brought back to life with reluctance, largely upon American urging. Certainly today's army is far from dominating any aspect of civilian life, and the vast majority of the civilians no longer identify with the military. It is a rather sloppy army. "On duty, the soldiers rather give an impression of being unstable and tired, almost apathetic." . . . "It happens again and again that on Mondays some soldiers fail to report for duty."[7]

Naturally, the turn to the West has been greatly facilitated or even made possible by far-sighted Western statesmen who (as we have said before) after World War II welcomed Germany into the

[6]See in this connection, Timothy Buck, "Merkwürdiges Anglodeutsch," in *Die Zeit,* Apr. 20, 1971.

[7]See the report on the Army in *Die Zeit,* Apr. 4, 1972.

family of Western nations, instead of rejecting and punishing her as did their predecessors after the first World War. At any rate the Germans are now quite definitely moving with the mainstream of European history and are anxious not to be unique.

For twenty years or more, there has been much reproachful talk in Germany to the effect that the Germans have so far failed to "master their past." The exact meaning of "mastering one's past" seems unclear. The present generation of German historians, sociologists, etc., have left no doubt that most of them thoroughly understand the background of the disaster. In any case, the best practical way of mastering the immediate German past might well be what the Germans are now doing—that is, to live the life of a useful, cooperative, and peaceable member of the Western family of nations. Ultimately, any possible problems of a redevelopment of a German uniqueness may be resolved in the formation of a United States of Europe, which for many years was regrettably retarded by an intense nationalist, Charles de Gaulle.

All this does not necessarily mean that all is well in German society today. What is perhaps regrettable above all is that the reduction in status from big to medium power seems to be accompanied by a shrinking of the German cultural contribution. In some ways the Germans of today appear to have become smaller in mind (and they stand in strange contrast to the culturally highly fertile generation of the Weimar Republic). The old intelligence, it is true, is still there and is very noticeable, for example, in the daily press. But little seems left of the former intellectual daring and boldness of thinking, even in such fields as science, medicine, and philosophy, in which the Germans once excelled. They now seem to be waiting for inspiration from abroad and to be satisfied to limp behind. The philosopher Karl Jaspers asked in 1966 "whether education, teaching, research, intellectual life generally, are weakening today, and whether initiative is flagging." He deplored the "lack of creative power" and "lameness and absence of buoyancy of life."[8] One might say that, with its political respectability, stable society, and reduction in power, Germany has become an intellectually uninteresting country, not unlike Holland or Sweden. It is possible that the lack of brilliant minds can be ac-

---

[8]Jaspers, *Wohin treibt die Bundesrepublik?* Munich, 1966, p. 153.

counted for, in part, by the loss of millions of the best young people in the war. There is little question, moreover, that the loss of the Jewish group has heavily contributed to the decline of German cultural productivity. But it may be too early to reach definite conclusions.

The old militaristic society has been replaced by a consumer society—a very radical change indeed. There is naturally much pride in the German postwar "economic miracle," even though this received a severe jolt when it was discovered that the Japanese economy had overtaken the German—an event which, more forcefully than anything else, illuminated to the Germans the shrinkage of their own power. But at any rate, as in other consumer societies, there is a great sense of economic well-being and a desire to participate fully in the enjoyment of the good things in life. It is a society whose values are measured more and more by the size of the bank account. The Spartan leanness of the old days has given way to much wallowing in luxury and opulence. And, as a good many see it, if this is what democracy signifies, then it certainly deserves full support. But a great many others have begun to understand quite well what a genuine democracy means. Some residue that was left from the Weimar experiment in democracy was, in fact, helpful. And there had, of course, always been fairly large groups of democratic- and European-minded Germans.

Strangely, too, the traditional German yearning for an all-encompassing ideology, a *Weltanschauung* which can explain everything, appears much diminished and may have given way to the prevalent placid sense of physical well-being. The search for identity, once so much misguided by Hitler, may have found at least a partial, even if less than admirable, goal in the achievement of affluence and security.

The present behavior of large numbers of German university students may be a source of alarm. No one will find fault with the fact that the students are now strongly antiauthoritarian, deeply sceptical of traditional values, and even distrustful of any new middle-class or bourgeois teachings. But what is alarming is that in all these attitudes the students have become violently destructive and seem determined to destroy even the university itself. The details of their conduct are astonishing. Physical assaults on the professors are a frequent occurrence. The students throw tomatoes and *Farbeier* at them (plastic paint-filled bags), conduct other so-called *Schweinejagden* (pig hunts) against them (one professor was held by the neck outside of a window), imprison them, scream insults at them in class, paint insults on classroom walls, and so forth. Some Women's Lib students stripteased in front of the aged Professor T. W. Adorno, forcing him to end his lecture. Throughout Germany many universities are in chaos; and compared with today's revolutionary students, the brown-shirted students during the Weimar Republic and the Hitler years conducted themselves with relative decorum.

There are a variety of guiding images for various German student groups today. These groups can be Maoists, Trotzkyites, old-fashioned Anarchists, or simply orthodox Communists who maintain Red Cells and proclaim their solidarity with the Soviet Union. There is a Marxist revolutionary movement which calls itself *Spartakus*, after the German revolutionary movement led by Karl Liebknecht in 1919. These groups carry on warfare not only against society but also against each other.

It is difficult to say what all this means in psychological terms, and perhaps it is much too soon to try to interpret it. But an assumption which easily—probably much too easily—suggests itself is that German youth, having nothing but contempt for their own fathers, have set out to find substitute father figures, and see them in Mao or Trotzky or the monolithic Communist state. If so, these students differ, to some extent, from the young of the earlier generation, because the latter, it will be recalled, saw Hitler not as a father but as an older brother, a tough adolescent leader of the gang. It is significant, also, and probably natural after the collapse of the Third Reich, that German youth today, unlike their fathers, derive their guiding images from other countries.

In 1960 the philosopher Karl Jaspers wrote hopefully that when the new youth "matures, it might—without encumbrances but from the base of the great traditions and in creative originality—fill the state with that ethos which gives it sense."[9] It was a beautiful hope, but youth, whether inside or outside of the universities, has done nothing to fulfill Jaspers' hope. Instead youth has been able to do no better than to seize upon the old ideas of Hitler's own ideological adversaries: the Russian Communists, Trotzky, Liebknecht, Mao.[10] With these father figures, the young are presumably, to an extent, still

[9]Jaspers, *Freiheit und Wiedervereinigung*, Munich, 1960, p. 123.
[10]Even Mao, born in 1893, was only four years younger than Hitler.

fighting Hitler and, through him, their personal fathers. It is significant, in this connection, that the New Left in Germany has spoken of the United States as a fascist country and of Chicago as Auschwitz.

In another sense, the young have again fallen into the old German habit of carrying an idea, once seized, to extremes, without giving thought to the practical consequences. It is still the reckless German urge toward *das Masslose, das Uferlose*, the measureless, the boundless, the unrestrained, as it was in National Socialism. And, at the same time, it is again the old drive to escape from reality into the abstract. But this time, while some of the professors go along with the young, the adult world in general and particularly the political parties and the government have little sympathy for the young revolutionaries and are likely to keep them under control. In fact, these revolutionaries seem to be living in a little political world of their own within the universities, with limited contact with, or effect on, the world outside. (And as usual, and as the young everywhere, the young Germans are unaware of youth's built-in obsolescence.)

One question often asked is, "Could it happen again? Could there be another disaster like the one under Hitler?" The answer, it seems, must be that the same disaster could never happen again, if only because the world has changed too much. Most of the factors that caused that disaster or made it possible are no longer present. More important than anything else, perhaps, is the fact that the vast majority of the Germans today definitely want no bloodshed and no war and are not likely to change their minds. Quite generally, Germany now gives the impression of a "burned-out crater of big power politics," as the historian Friedrich Meinecke called it. [11] He likened Germany to Holland and Sweden, which also once were big powers. And even if the Germans should once again dream of power, there now is the entirely dominant fact that the Soviet Union, the United States, and even Britain and France possess overwhelming nuclear missile power which within an hour or so could transform a country of Germany's size into a radioactive rubble heap with few survivors. And this would be true even if Germany had now secretly built nuclear weapons of its own (which is possible) or were to do so in the future. The nuclear deterrent is so enormous that aggressive German action seems incon-

[11]Meinecke, *Die deutsche Katastrophe*, p. 162.

ceivable in the present situation. Stalin was right in saying in 1945[12] that the "hundred-year war" between the Slavs and the Teutons had ended with an irreversible victory of the Slavs.

And as far as German anti-Semitism is concerned—assuming it were revived—it could never create another comparable holocaust, if only for the sad reason that most European Jews perished in the first one.

It is true, of course, that the partition of the country, with a wall through Berlin, represents a monstrous historical wrong and thus a potential source of future trouble. In fact, it enables former National Socialists and others to argue that important parts of Hitler's ideology have thus received posthumous vindication. Did he not always insist that Germany was the last and decisive bulwark against the steady advance of militant Communism? (And those arguing along these lines find further support in the continuing American obsession with the dangers of Communism.) The partition of Germany is indeed one of those bad facts which can make bad history. Erik H. Erikson, who has furnished much insight into the psychology of National Socialism, has taken a very gloomy view of the possible consequences of the partition:

> . . . again Germany has been divided against herself; the forma-
> tion of a German political identity has again been delayed.
> . . . total defeat, too, breeds a sense of total uniqueness, ready
> to be exploited once more by those who may seem to offer a sense
> of total power together with permanent unity, and a new sense
> of identity which redeems the now senseless past. [13]

But Erikson wrote this in 1950, only about one year after the establishment of East Germany as a state. Today much of the potential danger inherent in the partition seems mitigated by various facts. West Germany has become well established as a respected member of the Western family of nations, some of which indeed maintain joint armed forces within West Germany. The economy of the country is the most successful in Europe, stands very much on its own solid feet,

[12]According to Golo Mann, *Deutsche Geschichte des 19. und 20. Jahrhunderts*, p. 968.

[13]Erikson, *Childhood and Society*, p. 357.

and is a source of much German pride. Contrary to Erikson's expectation in 1950, a *West* German political identity has actually emerged and is generally acknowledged. The partition of the country, at any rate, is not really comparable to the disunity of the numerous German states before 1871, as Erikson seems to believe. It is a forced division, not the result of German disunity; and West Germany's Western friends deplore it hardly much less than she herself. President John F. Kennedy expressed his solidarity and sympathy in the statement *Ich bin ein Berliner*. Most Germans would agree with Chancellor Willy Brandt's pronouncement that what has been lost was gambled away by Hitler long ago.

The Germans today, psychologically and otherwise, face a situation wholly different from that of their fathers after World War I. Today they are willing to understand and do understand, by and large, what their position in the world is. The two lies which clouded the life of the Weimar Republic have not been repeated: Germany is aware that it caused the war and there is no legend that the war was lost by a traitorous stab in the back. People no longer live in a dream world of future greatness and power. The feeling, so prevalent in Germany's past, that the country's prestige in the world was not what it ought to be, no longer really exists. The people realize that their present prestige is largely what it can be and that it is, in fact, infinitely higher than anyone could have hoped for in the dark days of 1945. This fact in itself is apt to be a depressant on any strong revival of aggressive nationalism which feeds on a sense of unjustly diminished prestige.

Moreover, the Germans are aware—or ought to be—that other nations after this war lost as much as they did, if not more. Both Britain and France have lost the essential parts of their colonial empires. Britain has had to abandon uncounted colonial riches, and its once strong economic position is now weaker than that of the Germans. Even Poland, which gained territorially, has been reduced to a Soviet dependency. None of the European nations is still a big power. German frustration and disappointment at the defeat in World War II should thus be much less than it was after World War I, and there should be no deep-seated resentment and hatred of the West. All this, however, may not apply to the German-Russian relationship, but even here German antagonism may be reduced by the realization that in the war the Germans, without provocation, inflicted on the Russians far greater losses in men and property than they suffered themselves. At any rate, Soviet power is now overwhelmingly strong and beyond the reach of any potentialities of German power. The sadomasochistic character (assuming it continues to prevail in Germany) feeds on aggression against the weaker, not the stronger.

But, in any case, the German personality structure may now have been considerably modified by several decades of a secure, prosperous, reassuring existence within the shelter of a benevolent family of Western nations. We may once more cite Bruno Bettelheim:

> Clinical experience . . . demonstrates that considerably greater and more permanently effective in producing modifications of personality structure than the extreme methods of National Socialism are those modifications of the environment which make it reassuring, secure, comprehensible, and thus manageable for the young individual. Such environments and their gentle but powerful challenge to identify with persons offering gratification, and, therefore, to restrain hostility, produce changes in personality which are far-reaching indeed. This they do by partly reducing frustrations which derive from the environment, and partly by providing amply for all needs which can be satisfied. Under such conditions, little additional hostility is created, and existing or developing controls and powers of integration prove sufficient to contain it. As one of many indications, it suggests that environmental changes may well be able to produce changes in personality structure and hence in tolerance.[14]

West Germany, in fact, on its part has lately been granting considerable development aid to underdeveloped countries—an action which, in itself, has probably contributed a good deal to the present German feeling of security and abundance. Today the old authoritarianism seems greatly reduced in Germany (and thoroughly discredited among the middle-class young). Sadomasochistic drives should have diminished correspondingly.

In all this, however, we should not forget that so far the new Germany has not been tested in any real crisis situation. Since World

[14]Bruno Bettelheim and Morris Janowitz, *Dynamics of Prejudice*, p. 173.

War II, West Germany has not been involved in a severe political crisis or economic depression. (A possible exception to this was the Berlin Blockade by the Soviet Union in 1948–1949, but this was handled mostly by the Western powers on behalf of West Germany.) A severe, prolonged crisis might still recreate or reawaken attitudes and drives which now seem largely dead. Even today there still are a few small, intensely nationalistic publications, such as the *Klüter-Blätter*, and organizations such as the *Deutschland-Stiftung*, and a neo-national socialist party which, however, is extremely small and steadily declining. The practical significance of all these seems no larger than, for example, that of the John Birch Society in the United States.

West Germany's fundamental difficulty may be that democracy there is nothing homegrown and that, unlike the United States, Britain, and France, it cannot reach back into a reservoir of long democratic traditions. It cannot take strength from the guiding images of a history in democracy, which could help the nation to withstand the pressures of severe crises and disasters without a collapse of rational political thinking. Such a collapse occurred in the interwar years, and it might conceivably occur again, even though it now seems quite improbable. With the accelerated pace of history today, democratic traditions might be effectively developed in a few decades. Moreover, in the West today the idea of democracy does seem to have attained a measure of a transnational status. At this point, at any rate, the democratic process, with its normal infirmities, is functioning well in Germany. But if, by any chance, democracy should once more collapse there, then a new totalitarianism is more likely to arrive from the Left than from the Right.

In a larger sense, the lack of an acceptable German political (as distinguished from social and cultural) tradition may in the long run carry in it more dangers (or possibly benefits) than anything else. The violent catharsis by which much of the old ideology was expelled and the far-reaching destruction of political and other continuities in 1945 left the Germans with a nearly unprecedented vacuum in political traditions, indeed with a wish to divorce themselves from their own recent political history. Such a situation seems without parallel in the past of Western nations, and its ultimate results cannot be gauged at this time. Of all the present German problems, the question of political continuity and discontinuity is perhaps the most difficult and obscure.

Paradoxically it is the absence of a liberal Jewish intelligentsia which may contribute to the stability of the German democracy today, in contrast to the Weimar Republic. There no longer is that large, articulate group of Jewish intellectuals who kept the struggling young Weimar Republic under a ceaseless drumfire of merciless criticism. The "Tucholsky syndrome," of which we spoke at some length, has not been revived, even though it is true that a few Jews, strangely enough, again stand in the forefront of radical causes, presumably unaware of some of the origins of the former German anti-Semitism.

On the other hand, the Germans themselves often manifest an abnormally high degree of dissatisfaction with their political leadership and administration, no matter of what party. The willingness to grant some measure of cooperation even to a political enemy still is small. Numerous letters to editors show a viciousness and nastiness which is perhaps unparalleled elsewhere, although many of these letters indicate a very high level of abstract intelligence.

Looking back at their national socialist disaster, looking at their present and toward their future, the Germans need what they often lacked in the past but now seem increasingly to be acquiring: clarity of sober, unromantic thought; intellectual and emotional self-restraint in dealing with ideas, old and new; a sense of reality; an ability to see not only their many admirable qualities but also their faults; a genuine effort to shed their contempt for other nations and to see the good points that others may have. They need to develop or maintain a calm sense of self-assurance based on a realistic, unemotional appraisal of their own merits in relation to those of others.

A Selected Bibliography

Adorno, T. W. (and others), *The Authoritarian Personality*, New York, 1950, 1969.

Arendt, Hannah, *The Origins of Totalitarianism*, New York, 1966.

——, *Eichmann in Jerusalem*, New York, 1965.

Barraclough, Geoffrey, *The Origins of Modern Germany*, 2d ed., New York, 1947, 1963.

Barzun, Jacques, "History: The Muse and Her Doctors," in *American Historical Review*, Vol. 77, No. 1, February 1972, pp. 36-64.

Baumont, Maurice (ed.), *The Third Reich*, New York, 1955.

Berning, Cornelia, *Vom "Abstammungsnachweis" zum "Zuchtwart,"* Berlin, 1964.

Bettelheim, Bruno, "Individual and Mass Behavior in Extreme Situations," in *Journal of Abnormal and Social Psychology*, Vol. 38, 1943, pp. 417-452.

—— and Morris Janowitz, *Dynamics of Prejudice*, New York, 1950.

Bleuel, Hans Peter, *Deutschlands Bekenner—Professoren zwischen Kaiserreich und Diktatur*, Berne, 1968.

Bley, Helmut, *Kolonialherrschaft und Sozialstruktur in Deutsch-Südwestafrika 1894-1914*, Hamburg, 1968.

Bracher, Karl Dietrich, *Adolf Hitler*, Munich, 1964.

——, *Die deutsche Diktatur*, Cologne, Berlin, 1969.

Braun, Eva, *Eva Braun's Diary* (in German), handwritten original, National Archives, Washington, D.C.

Bromberg, N., "Totalitarian Ideology as a Defense Technique" in *Psychoanalytic Study of Society*, Vol. I, 1960, pp. 26-38.

Broszat, Martin, *Nationalsozialistische Polenpolitik*, 2d ed., Frankfurt, 1965.

Buchheim, Hans, *Aktuelle Krisenpunkte des deutschen Nationalbewusstseins*, Mainz, 1967.

————, Martin Broszat, Hans-Adolf Jacobsen, and Helmut Krausnick, *Anatomie des SS-Staates*, 2 vols., Munich and Freiburg, 1965, 1967.

Buchheit, Gert (ed.), *Der Führer ins Nichts*, Rastatt, 1960.

Bullock, Alan, *Hitler, a Study in Tyranny*, rev. ed, New York, 1964.

Butler, Rohan D'O., *The Roots of National Socialism 1783-1933*, London, 1941.

Cecil, Robert, *The Myth of the Master Race: Alfred Rosenberg and Nazi Ideology*, New York, 1972.

Chamberlain, Houston Stewart, *Die Grundlagen des 19. Jahrhunderts*, Munich, 1899.

————, *Houston Stewart Chamberlain der Seher des Dritten Reiches. Das Vermächtnis Houston Stewart Chamberlains an das Deutsche Volk in einer Auslese aus seinen Werken*, edited by Georg Schott, 4th ed., Munich, 1934, 1941.

Craig, Gordon A., *The Politics of the Prussian Army 1640-1945*, Oxford, 1955.

Cramer, John F., and George S. Browne, *Contemporary Education—A Comparative Study of National Systems*, 2d ed., New York, 1956, 1965.

Dahle, Wendula, *Der Einsatz einer Wissenschaft*, Bonn, 1969.

Dahrendorf, Ralf, *Gesellschaft und Demokratie in Deutschland*, Munich, 1965.

Daim, Wilfried, *Der Mann, der Hitler die Ideen gab*, Munich, 1958.

Dallin, Alexander, *German Rule in Russia 1941-1945*, London, 1957.

Deak, Istvan, *Weimar Germany's Left-Wing Intellectuals*, Berkeley, 1968.

Deutscher, Isaac, *The Non-Jewish Jew and Other Essays*, Oxford, 1968.

Dodds, E. R., *Minds in the Making*, London, 1941.

Domarus, Max, *Hitlers Reden und Proklamationen 1932-1945*, 4 vols., Munich, 1962-1963, 1965.

Erikson, Erik H., *Young Man Luther*, New York, 1958, 1962.

————, *Childhood and Society*, 2d ed., New York, 1963.

————, *Identity, Youth, and Crisis*, New York, 1968.

Fest, Joachim C., *Das Gesicht des Dritten Reiches*, Munich, 1963.

Fick, Heinz-Erich, *Der deutsche Militarismus der Vorkriegszeit*, Ohlau, 1930.

Fischer, Fritz, *Griff nach der Weltmacht*, Düsseldorf, 1967.

————, *Krieg der Illusionen*, Düsseldorf, 1969.

Freud, Sigmund, *Der Mann Moses und die monotheistische Religion*, in *Gesammelte Werke*, Vol. 16, London, 1950.

Fromm, Erich, *Escape from Freedom*, New York, 1941.

————, *The Heart of Man*, New York, 1964.

Gasman, Daniel, *The Scientific Origins of National Socialism: Social Darwinism in Ernst Haeckel and the German Monist League*, London and New York, 1971.

Gatzke, Hans W., *Germany's Drive to the West*, Baltimore, 1950, 1966.

Gay, Peter, *Weimar Culture*, New York, 1968.

———, "Germany 1919-1932: The Weimar Culture," in *Social Research*, Vol. 39, No. 2, Summer 1972, pp. 207-364.

Gilbert, G. M., *Nuremberg Diary*, New York, 1947.

Gisevius, Hans Bernd, *Adolf Hitler*, Munich, 1967.

Goebbels, Joseph, *The Goebbels Diaries, 1942-1943*, edited by Louis P. Lochner, New York, 1948.

Görlitz, Walter, *Adolf Hitler*, Göttingen, 1960.

Grebing, Helga, *Der Nationalsozialismus—Ursprung und Wesen*, 17th ed., Munich, 1964.

Grunberger, Richard, *The 12-Year Reich*, New York, 1971.

Gun, Nerin E., *Eva Braun: Hitler's Mistress*, London, 1969.

Haffner, Sebastian, *Die Sieben Todsünden des Deutschen Reiches*, Hamburg, 1965.

Hamilton, Alistair, *The Appeal of Fascism—A Study of Intellectuals and Fascism 1919-1945*, London, 1971.

Hanfstaengl, Ernst (anonymous), *Adolf Hitler*, unpublished typescript, dated Dec. 3, 1942, in President's [Roosevelt] Personal File 5780, Franklin D. Roosevelt Library, Hyde Park, N.Y.

Hayes, Carlton J. H., *The Historical Evolution of Modern Nationalism*, New York, 1931, 1950.

Heer, Friedrich, *Der Glaube des Adolf Hitler*, Munich, 1968.

Heiden, Konrad, *Der Fuehrer—Hitler's Rise to Power* (1944), English translation by Ralph Manheim, Boston, 1969.

Henkys, Reinhard, *Die nationalsozialistischen Gewaltverbrechen*, 2d ed., Stuttgart, 1965.

Hertz, Frederik, *Nationality in History and Politics*, London, 1944.

Hilberg, Raul, *The Destruction of the European Jews*, Chicago, 1961, 1967.

Hildebrand, Klaus, *Vom Reich zum Weltreich—Hitler, NSDAP und koloniale Frage 1919-1945*, Munich, 1969.

Hillgruber, Andreas, *Deutschlands Rolle in der Vorgeschichte der beiden Weltkriege*, Göttingen, 1967.

———, "Die 'Endlösung' und das deutsche Ostimperium als Kernstück des rassenideologischen Programms des Nationalsozialismus," in *Vierteljahrshefte für Zeitgeschichte*, Vol. XX, Heft 2, April 1972, pp. 133-155.

Hitler, Adolf, *Mein Kampf*, 1925, 1927 (1938, 1 vol. ed. by Eher).

———, *Hitlers Zweites Buch* (1928), Stuttgart, 1961.

————, *Hitlers Tischgespräche im Führerhauptquartier 1941-1942* (Dr. Henry Picker), new edition by Percy Ernst Schramm, Stuttgart-Degerloch, 1965.

———— (H. Heiber, ed.), *Hitlers Lagebesprechungen 1942-1945*, Stuttgart, 1962.

Höhne, Heinz, *Der Orden unter dem Totenkopf; die Geschichte der SS*, Gütersloh, 1967.

Hofer, Walther, *Der Nationalsozialismus: Dokumente 1933-1945*, Frankfurt, 1957.

Horkheimer, Max, and Theodor W. Adorno, "Elemente des Antisemitismus," in *Dialektik der Aufklärung*, Frankfurt, 1969.

Hühnerfeld, Paul, *In Sachen Heidegger—Versuch über ein deutsches Genie*, Hamburg, 1959.

Huss, Hermann, and Andreas Schröder (eds.), *Antisemitismus—Zur Pathologie der bürgerlichen Gesellschaft*, Frankfurt, 1965.

Jäckel, Eberhard, *Hitlers Weltanschauung—Entwurf einer Herrschaft*, Tübingen, 1969.

Jetzinger, Franz, *Hitlers Jugend—Phantasien, Lügen und die Wahrheit*, Vienna, 1956.

Kahler, Erich, *The Jews among the Nations*, New York, 1967.

Kahn, Fritz, *Die Juden als Rasse und Kulturvolk*, Berlin, 1922.

Kampmann, Wanda, *Deutsche und Juden*, Heidelberg, 1963.

Kaznelson, Siegmund (ed.), *Juden im deutschen Kulturbereich*, 3d ed., Berlin, 1962.

Kelley, Douglas M., *22 Cells in Nuremberg*, New York, 1947.

Klesse, Max, *Vom alten zum neuen Israel*, Frankfurt, 1965.

Kogon, Eugen, *Der SS-Staat—Das System der deutschen Konzentrationslager*, Frankfurt, 1946, 1965.

Kohn, Hans, *Prophets and Peoples—Studies in Nineteenth Century Nationalism*, New York, 1946.

————, *The Mind of Germany*, New York, 1960, 1965.

————, *The Age of Nationalism*, New York, 1962.

Krause, Karl Wilhelm, *Zehn Jahre Kammerdiener bei Hitler*, Hamburg, 1949.

Krieger, Leonard, *The German Idea of Freedom*, Boston, 1957.

Krummacher, F. A. (ed.), *Die Kontroverse—Hannah Arendt, Eichmann und die Juden*, Munich, 1964.

Kubizek, August, *The Young Hitler I knew* (translated by E. V. Anderson), Cambridge, Mass., 1955.

Kurth, Gertrud M., "The Jew and Adolf Hitler," in *Psychoanalytic Quarterly*, Vol. 16, 1947, pp. 11-32.

Langbein, Hermann, *Der Auschwitz-Prozess—Eine Dokumentation*, 2 vols., Vienna, 1965.

Langer, Walter C., *A Psychological Analysis of Adolph [sic] Hitler: His Life and Legend*, with the collaboration of Henry A. Murray, Ernst Kris, and Bertram D. Lewin. With *Source Book*. Typescript prepared (1943) for M.O. Branch of U.S. Office of Strategic Services. National Archives, Washington, D.C. (In connection with this typescript, see Walter C. Langer, *The Mind of Adolf Hitler*, New York, 1972, which professes to be a publication, in book form, of the typescript "as an historical document"—without the *Source Book*—but contains, nevertheless, various additions to, and modifications of, that typescript. It also omits some portions. All page references in the present study are, therefore, to the original typescript.)

Laqueur, Walter Z., *Young Germany—A History of the German Youth Movement*, London, 1962.

——, *Out of the Ruins of Europe*, New York, 1971.

Lasswell, Harold D., "The Psychology of Hitlerism," in *Political Quarterly*, Vol. IV, 1933, pp. 374ff.

Learned, William Setchel, *The Oberlehrer—A Study of the Social and Professional Evolution of the German Schoolmaster*, Cambridge, 1914.

Lepsius, M. Rainer, *Extremer Nationalismus*, Stuttgart, 1966.

Lerner, Daniel, *The Nazi Elite*, Stanford, 1951.

Leschnitzer, Adolf, *The Magic Background of Modern Anti-semitism*, New York, 1956.

Lessing, Theodor, *Deutschland und seine Juden*, Prague-Karlin, 1933.

Liddell Hart, Sir B. H., *History of the Second World War*, New York, 1970.

Lilge, Frederic, *The Abuse of Learning—The Failure of the German University*, New York, 1948.

Lipset, Seymour Martin, "Der 'Faschismus'—Die Linke, die Rechte und die Mitte" in *Kölner Zeitschrift für Soziologie und Sozialpsychologie*, 1959, pp. 401–444.

Lowenberg, Peter, "The Psychohistorical Origins of the Nazi Youth Cohort," in *American Historical Review*, Vol. 76, No. 5, December 1971, pp. 1457–1502.

Mann, Golo, *Deutsche Geschichte des 19. und 20. Jahrhunderts*, Frankfurt, 1958, 1966.

——, *Der Antisemitismus*, Frankfurt, 1962.

Maser, Werner, *Hitlers Mein Kampf*, 2d ed., Munich, 1966.

——, *Adolf Hitler—Legende, Mythos, Wirklichkeit*, Munich, 1971.

Massing, Paul W., *Rehearsal for Destruction*, New York, 1949.

Mau, Hermann, and Helmut Krausnick, *Deutsche Geschichte der jüngsten Vergangenheit 1933-1945*, Tübingen, 1960.

Meinecke, Friedrich, *Die deutsche Katastrophe*, Wiesbaden, 1946.

Messerschmidt, Manfred, *Die Wehrmacht im NS-Staat—Zeit der Indoktrination*, Hamburg, 1969.

Minogue, Kenneth R., *Nationalism*, London, 1967.

Mosse, George L., *The Crisis of German Ideology*, New York, 1964.

——, *Germans and Jews*, New York, 1970.

Müller, Hans, "Der pseudoreligiöse Charakter der nationalsozialistischen Weltanschauung," in *Geschichte in Wissenschaft und Unterricht*, Vol. 12, 1961, pp. 337–352.

Müller, Josef, *Die Entwicklung des Rassenantisemitismus in den letzten Jahrzehnten des 19. Jahrhunderts* (1940), Vaduz, 1965.

Müller, Klaus-Jürgen, *Das Heer und Hitler—Armee und nationalsozialistisches Regime 1933-1940*, Stuttgart, 1969.

Murray, Henry A., *Analysis of the Personality of Adolf Hitler*, President's [Roosevelt] Secretary's File, unpublished typescript, prepared (1943) for U.S. Office of Strategic Services, Franklin D. Roosevelt Library, Hyde Park, New York.

Neumann, Franz, *Behemoth: The Structure and Practice of National Socialism, 1933-1944*, New York, 1942, 1966.

Olden, Rudolf, *Hitler*, Amsterdam, 1935.

Peterson, Edward N., *The Limits of Hitler's Power*, Princeton, 1969.

Philippi, Alfred, and Ferdinand Heim, *Der Feldzug gegen Sowjetrussland 1941 bis 1945*, Stuttgart, 1962.

Pinson, Koppel S. (ed.), *Essays on Antisemitism*, New York, 1946.

Plessner, Helmut, *Die verspätete Nation*, 4th ed., Stuttgart, 1959.

Poliakov, Leon, *The History of Anti-Semitism*, New York, 1965.

——, and Josef Wulf (eds.), *Das Dritte Reich und die Juden*, Berlin, 1955.

Poor, Harold L., *Kurt Tucholsky and the Ordeal of Germany, 1914-1935*, New York, 1968.

Pulzer, Peter G. J., *The Rise of Political Anti-semitism in Germany and Austria*, New York, 1964.

Rauschning, Hermann, *Gespräche mit Hitler*, New York, 1940.

Recktenwald, Johann, *Woran hat Adolf Hitler gelitten?* Munich, 1963.

Reichmann, Eva G., *Die Flucht in den Hass—Die Ursachen der deutschen Judenkatastrophe*, Frankfurt (1956?).

Reitlinger, Gerald, *The SS—Alibi of a Nation 1922-1945*, New York, 1957, 1968.

——, *Die Endlösung*, 4th ed., Berlin, 1961.

Ritter, Gerhard, "Das Problem des Militarismus in Deutschland," in *Historische Zeitschrift*, Vol. 177, 1954, pp. 21-48.

————, *Staatskunst und Kriegshandwerk*, Vols. I and IV, Munich, 1954 and 1968.

Scheffler, Wolfgang, *Judenverfolgung im Dritten Reich*, Berlin, 1964.

Schneeberger, Guido, *Nachlese zu Heidegger*, Berne, 1962.

Schoenbaum, David, *Hitler's Social Revolution*, New York, 1966.

Schramm, Percy Ernst, *Hitler als militärischer Führer*, 2d ed., Frankfurt, 1965.

Schwabe, Klaus, "Zur politischen Haltung der deutschen Professoren im ersten Weltkrieg," in *Historische Zeitschrift*, Vol. 193, 1961, pp. 601-634.

Seeliger, Rolf, *Braune Universität—Deutsche Hochschullehrer gestern und heute*, Vol. III, Munich, 1965.

Shirer, William L., *The Rise and Fall of the Third Reich*, New York, 1960.

Silberner, Edmund, *Sozialisten zur Judenfrage*, Berlin, 1962.

Snyder, Louis L., *The New Nationalism*, Ithaca, N.Y., 1968.

Speer, Albert, *Erinnerungen*, Berlin, 1969.

Stein, George H. (ed.), *Hitler*, Englewood Cliffs, N.J., 1968.

Stern, Fritz, *The Politics of Cultural Despair*, New York, 1961, 1965.

———— (ed.), *The Path to Dictatorship 1918-1933*, New York, 1966.

Sternberger-Storz-Süsskind, *Aus dem Wörterbuch des Unmenschen*, Hamburg, 1968.

Strasser, Otto, *Hitler and I* (English translation), Boston, 1940.

Thieme, Karl (ed.), *Judenfeindschaft*, Frankfurt, 1963.

Treher, Wolfgang, *Hitler, Steiner, Schreber*, Emmendingen, 1966.

Trevor-Roper, H. R., *The Last Days of Hitler*, London, 1950.

————, "Hitlers Kriegsziele," in *Vierteljahrshefte für Zeitgeschichte*, Heft 2, 1960, pp. 121-133.

Trunk, Isaiah, *Judenrat: The Jewish Councils in Eastern Europe under Nazi Occupation*, New York, 1972.

Tucholsky, Kurt, *Deutschland, Deutschland uber Alles*, Berlin, 1929.

————, *Deutschland, Deutschland unter Anderen*, Berlin, 1957.

————, *Gesammelte Werke*, Hamburg, 1960.

Turner, Henry Ashby, Jr., "Big Business and the Rise of Hitler," in *American Historical Review*, Vol. 75, Oct. 1969, pp. 56-78.

————, "Fascism and Modernization," in *World Politics*, Vol. 24, July, 1972, pp. 547-564.

Vagts, Alfred, *A History of Militarism*, New York, 1937.

Vernon, W. H. D., "Hitler, the Man—Notes for a Case History," in *Journal of Abnormal and Social Psychology*, Vol. 37, 1942, pp. 295-308.

Waite, R. G. L., "Adolf Hitler's Guilt Feelings: A Problem in History and Psychology," in *Journal of Interdisciplinary History*, Vol. I, No. 2, 1971, pp. 229-249.

Wangh, Martin, "National Socialism and the Genocide of the Jews: A Psycho-Analytic Study of a Historical Event," in *International Journal of Psycho-Analysis*, Vol. 45, 1964, pp. 386-395.

Ward, Barbara (Lady Jackson), *Nationalism and Ideology*, New York, 1966.

Wawrzinek, Kurt, *Die Entstehung der deutschen Antisemitenparteien (1873-1890)*, Berlin, 1927, 1965.

Weinreich, Max, *Hitler's Professors*, New York, 1946.

Weltsch, Robert (ed.), *Deutsches Judentum—Aufstieg und Krise*, Stuttgart, 1963.

Werner, Karl Ferdinand, *Das NS-Geschichtsbild und die deutsche Geschichtswissenschaft*, Stuttgart, 1967.

Weymar, Ernst, "Geschichte und politische Bildung," in *Schriftenreihe der Niedersächsischen Landeszentrale für politische Bildung*, 1967.

Wheeler-Bennett, John W., *The Nemesis of Power*, New York, 1964, 1967.

Winkler, Heinrich August, "Extremismus der Mitte," in *Vierteljahrshefte für Zeitgeschichte*, Vol. XX, Heft 2, April 1972, pp. 175-191.

Zmarzlik, Hans Günter, "Der Sozialdarwinismus in Deutschland als geschichtliches Problem," in *Vierteljahrshefte für Zeitgeschichte*, Vol. XI, Heft 3, 1963, pp. 246-273.

Zoller, A., *Hitler privat*, Düsseldorf, 1949.

Zorn, Wolfgang, "Student Politics in the Weimar Republic," in *Journal of Contemporary History*, Vol. 5, No. 1, 1970, pp. 128-143.

Index

(Headings of chapters and subchapters are not generally repeated in this index. The reader is referred to the table of contents.)